SUCCESSFUL HOUSES
AND HOW TO BUILD THEM

SUCCESSFUL HOUSES

AND HOW TO BUILD THEM

BY

CHARLES E. WHITE, JR., M.A.I.A.

AUTHOR OF "SOME WESTERN HOUSES," "SATISFACTORY TYPES
OF GARAGES," "WHEN YOU BUILD A LITTLE HOUSE,"
"HOW TO BUILD A FIREPROOF HOUSE"

DRAWINGS BY THE AUTHOR

Fredonia Books
Amsterdam, The Netherlands

Successful Houses and How to Build Them

by
Charles E. White, Jr.

ISBN: 1-4101-0244-0

Copyright © 2003 by Fredonia Books

Reprinted from the 1916 edition

Fredonia Books
Amsterdam, The Netherlands
http://www.fredoniabooks.com

All rights reserved, including the right to reproduce this book, or portions thereof, in any form.

In order to make original editions of historical works available to scholars at an economical price, this facsimile of the original edition of 1916 is reproduced from the best available copy and has been digitally enhanced to improve legibility, but the text remains unaltered to retain historical authenticity.

CONTENTS

CHAPTER		PAGE
I.	WHY BUILD A HOME	1
II.	CHOOSING THE SITE	9
III.	HOW TO KNOW THE ARCHITECTURAL STYLES	25
IV.	THE LITTLE DETAILS THAT ATTRACT	45
V.	OWNER, ARCHITECT, AND CONTRACTOR	67
VI.	PLANNING THE ROOMS	91
VII.	SPECIFICATIONS EXPLAINED	131
VIII.	A CHAPTER ON LEGAL DOCUMENTS	145
IX.	EXCAVATION AND FOUNDATIONS	161
X.	ADVANTAGES OF A FRAME HOUSE	179
XI.	EXTERIOR FINISH	197
XII.	HOUSES OF MASONRY	213
XIII.	HOW TO BUILD A FIREPROOF HOUSE	237
XIV.	CARPENTRY AND CABINET WORK	259
XV.	THE IMPORTANCE OF A GOOD ROOF	273
XVI.	PLUMBING THAT IS SANITARY; WATER AND SEWER PIPES	285
XVII.	LATEST TYPES OF PLUMBING FIXTURES	307
XVIII.	LITTLE DETAILS OF GOOD PLUMBING	333
XIX.	SEWAGE DISPOSAL IN THE COUNTRY	343
XX.	EFFICIENT HEATING METHODS	351
XXI.	PLASTERING; INSIDE AND OUTSIDE	379
XXII.	FINISHING TOUCHES; PAINTING AND GLAZING	389
XXIII.	USEFUL APPARATUS AND APPLIANCES	401

CHAPTER		PAGE
XXIV.	Gas and Electric Lighting	425
XXV.	Practical Hardware for the House	437
XXVI.	Handy House Devices	455
XXVII.	Remodeling; Making an Old House New	465
XXVIII.	Sensible Types of American Houses	481
XXIX.	Garages and Garage Apparatus	497
Index		509

SUCCESSFUL HOUSES
AND HOW TO BUILD THEM

SUCCESSFUL HOUSES AND HOW TO BUILD THEM

CHAPTER I

WHY BUILD A HOME?

AN inherent desire seems to be born in every one to have a home of one's own, — to possess a little place, however small, — to be one's own lord and master. This desire is natural. It betokens a healthy mind, a worthy ambition, — a lofty ideal.

There are many reasons why it is not to one's best interests to rent. Recall the most responsible men and women of any town and you will find they are the property owners. The man who does not own his home is looked upon by others as an underling or weakling. He is regarded in the eyes of his neighbors as lacking in initiative, in the eyes of his family he is considered unfortunate, in his own mind he realizes that he has never quite achieved success.

Look about and see the men on small salaries who own their homes. They have toiled no harder than others, but rigid economy has made it possible to squeeze out a few dollars a month to apply to their house contract, and in after years they have something to show for the money expended.

Why should we help to support our landlord? If a small amount of capital invested each month by those who have not the ready cash to pay for a house and lot will in the end provide a home, why not use these sums in that way instead of handing them to the landlord, enriching him at our own expense?

To be sure, the houseowner has a load on his shoulders, — one that may keep him toiling, grinding, to provide payments for his house, but this discipline is usually a benefit. Many a dollar which would otherwise go into unnecessary things is swallowed up in the house-building project, and the result is, in later years the houseowner has something substantial to show for his hard work, — not merely a collection of rent receipts.

The houseowner is independent. He is not obliged to move from pillar to post at the will of his landlord, nor is he constrained to adjust his mode of life to the pattern of a rented house. The houseowner has stability which the renter does not have. He occupies a stronger position in the community. His social status is higher. His family is more important. The houseowner can take more interest in life because he has gone through that most important of life's experiences, — the building of a home. He enjoys his rest and recreation because he feels that he has a roof over his head, — a shelter for himself and his family, — one that it has been his glorious privilege to build and remains his to maintain.

Many plan to build their own home but are deterred because they are afraid to make the start. They fear the plunge as they would a cold-water bath, forgetting that contemplation is the cruelest part of cold water, the bath itself being much less terrible. Many live right up to their incomes, when a slight amount of pinching might secure a sum sufficient to build the house. And so, when old age claims them, many are still living the lives of transients, drifting about from block to block, town to town.

Generally speaking, there are two kinds of building investments ; one, building to own, and the other, building to rent or sell. Both are very different, and no prospective houseowner should make the mistake of supposing that a house built for one's home and one built to rent or sell are the same. Optimistic real-estate dealers sometimes work out wonderful results on paper, but in all truth it should be said that investing in a home does not usually yield such profits as investing in a house to be sold or rented.

When a house is built to sell or rent it is not, as a rule, so well built as the house built for one's own home. Construction is lighter throughout, — trim is more simple, — arrangement of rooms less ideal, least costly. On the other hand, the man who starts out to build a house for himself is not satisfied to build along stereotyped, real-estate lines. He has notions of his own, ideas which he is bound to express in the new building; consequently the new home is more expensive than a house built solely for investment. Houseowners should realize this point; — they should not look upon the building of a home in the same way they look upon an investment, for the chances are, the same sum invested in a home will bring less returns than a like amount invested in property for sale or rent. If the increased comfort and pleasure in owning one's home are not taken into consideration, the home as a mere money-maker is not a success. Considering the lifelong advantage of living in one's own house, however, the home becomes an investment, — one that will give returns beyond the utmost expectations of the most sanguine owner.

The man who has amassed sufficient fortune to build a house, paying cash for it, is greatly to be envied. By far the majority of houseowners build on borrowed money, and it frequently takes years before the property passes entirely into their hands, but in the meantime, while they have been paying for their houses, they have been living in them. They have been rearing families in their own homes, and by this example they have planted the seeds of thrift so that their children may reap some of the benefit.

To build on borrowed money is comparatively easy for the business man or salaried employee who has been thrifty enough to save, say, $250 to $500 to start with. On favorable terms building loan associations (or individuals) take this first payment and proceed to erect the building, the prospective owner having signed a contract to pay a certain sum per month until the value of the house, lot, and interest has been paid. For instance, on a small cottage and lot worth $3600 (including interest) the owner starts with a payment varying from $250 to $500, after which he pays $30 a month until the debt is cleared. Thus, in less than ten years his indebtedness is paid off and he owns the property, clear.

On the other hand, see how an owner comes out if he rents his home. Assuming that his rent is $30 per month he will have paid out $3600 in ten years, or nearly enough to have paid for the property. Quite likely at the end of that time he is obliged to move, losing what has been a home for himself and family so long that it seems to them to be actually theirs.

Frequently, instead of entering into a building contract with a loan company the prospective owner purchases a lot outright, after which he borrows money from a bank, the bank securing itself by a mortgage upon the property. The cost per year of a $5000 property when the owner is able to pay $2000 to start with, is about as follows: —

Taxes ($22 on $1000), assessed valuation, $4500	$ 99.
Fire Insurance, 40 cents per hundred, 3 years (80% of valuation per year, on house costing $4000)	4.27
Repairs (approximate)	70.
Interest on Borrowed Money, 6% on $3000	180.
Interest on Capital of $2000 (3%, savings bank rates)	60.
(Water, Gas and Electric Light not included)	
Per Year	$413.27
Per Month	34.44

This is, in effect, paying rent, but the result is different, for in the end the houseowner has the property, clear. In the mean-

WHY BUILD A HOME?

time he has had the use of it; so long as he keeps up payments the property is in effect his own and after the payments are completed it is his very own, to dispose of or retain, as he desires. In fact, even before payments have been entirely completed he can sell the property, subject to the mortgage upon it, frequently getting his money back with profit, besides.

Buying property on installments is a boon for the poor man and often a great convenience for the well-to-do, — the man who dislikes to take capital away from his business to build a house. Buying property in this way teaches every man to save systematically. It inspires him to apply his surplus earnings in a permanent investment instead of wasting it as he goes along, and he has the additional satisfaction that comes with the knowledge that he is doing what is best for his family.

A man who owns his home is usually able to save more money than the man who rents, because he has an incentive to do so; it is a great satisfaction to him and to his family; it is a great convenience, especially when children are considered. Owning one's home is conducive to better health. It increases the stability and dignity of the family, and after the new property advances in value (as most properties do) the owner reaps the benefit — not the landlord.

Owners usually take better care of their own property than renters do of the landlord's. Every one knows that depreciation on property occupied by the owner is much less than when occupied by tenants. Lawns and gardens on a place occupied by the owner are usually kept in better condition, for the owner feels more pride in a place of his own, and he realizes that the work done to improve the property will not be lost to him, later.

The following renting table is of interest, as it shows the value of sums paid to a landlord for rent during a period of years: —

RENT TABLE (PAID TO THE LANDLORD), 6% INTEREST, COMPOUNDED ANNUALLY

Per Month	In 10 Years	In 15 Years	In 20 Years
$ 8	$1265	$2234	$ 3531
10	1581	2793	4414
12	1898	3351	5297
15	2372	4189	6621
20	3163	5586	8828
25	3954	6982	11,035
30	4730	8358	12,251

When placed in a savings bank the rapid increase of even small sums is startling when one realizes it for the first time. For instance, the small sum of $2 saved each week and banked at 4% interest, reaches in ten years the quite respectable sum of $593.52. Beginning with such an amount, gradually saved by laying away a small sum each week, and investing it in one's own home is undoubtedly a very wise thing to do.

The houseowner is a broader-minded individual than the tenant. His credit is better; he has more importance in the eyes of the world. The houseowner makes a better citizen, for he abides more strictly by the law; he is temperate in all things because of his added responsibility. He is more frugal, more thrifty, more likely to seize an opportunity when it comes his way, because he knows from experience the value and power of money. It requires greater exertion to build and maintain a home than to rent one, so the houseowner is not so prodigal or extravagant as the tenant.

The following table shows the amounts resulting from small sums, placed in a bank at 3% interest:—

SAVINGS TABLE, BANK INTEREST 3%, COMPOUNDED SEMI-ANNUALLY

Per Week	In 5 Years	In 10 Years	In 15 Years
$1	$ 278.24	$ 595.09	$ 909.94
2	554.79	1208.38	1968.79
5	1396.87	3019.22	4919.28

HOUSE OF THE ENGLISH TYPE ON A WOODED SITE

CHAPTER II

CHOOSING THE SITE

OF not less importance than building the house is selection of the building site. By careless, immature consideration of location an unfortunately large proportion of house-building projects are spoiled before ever the house is built. Through ignorance or indifference owners frequently omit appreciative consideration of this most important matter, in many cases looking about them and hastily selecting a site in some locality in which they wish to dwell, with but one idea in view, — price and general appearance of the property. Countless times owners have made this mistake, choosing their building site without considering it from every point of view.

Before a lot is bought, one should decide to take as much land as one can afford. Even if the house is made smaller to make up for the added expenditure, it is wise to get as large a lot as possible. Many otherwise beautiful suburban communities have been ruined by building large houses on small lots. Row after row of them, with only a few feet between each house, their appearance is very unattractive. Many houseowners solve the problem of more land by striking farther out into the country where land is cheap. They find it is possible to get 100 to 150 feet at the price of 40 or 50 feet nearer town. Room to breathe is what every houseowner wants; space in which his wife and children may thrive. You cannot get all there is in out-door life when the house covers the entire lot.

Selecting a site requires care, not a little skill, and much patience. It is rarely wise to invest hastily in any piece of property unless one has been familiar with it for some time.

Before deciding to build in a certain town one should walk about from street to street in all districts and make a minute inspection of the character of every neighborhood. It is probable that the choice will be largely determined by proximity of friends or relatives, or at least acquaintances, and it will be well to get from them facts relating to the different sections of the town, with advice as to the advisability of living in any particular district.

Information concerning the town itself is extremely desirable if the prospective buyer is not already familiar with it, — information concerning the character of its government, as judged by the laws passed. Sound, stable, just laws usually lead to a healthy, constructive, progressive growth of the town, but unjust, destructive ordinances, or local laws favoring vicious or unscrupulous elements, bring about the reverse.

Of course price will play its part in the selection of the desired location. Property in the choicest parts of town may be beyond one's means, and it may be necessary to choose a less desirable site for that reason, but in the majority of cases good building lots can be purchased somewhere in any town for the price one desires to pay. If cost of land near the center of town is too high, it is always possible to go to the outskirts where property has not been so extensively developed, and a lot can be purchased at a less price than in more settled districts.

Buying building property on the edge of town, however, is sometimes more or less of a lottery, as it is impossible to determine in advance just what the future development of such a property will be. This uncertainty is somewhat of a problem, and the judgment of even the most expert is often at fault. It sometimes happens that a section which has every indication of desirability, and which every one expects will be built up with houses of the best class occupied by people of standing, sometimes goes very much the other way. Thus it seems impossible to form a very accurate opinion in advance of the actual growth of such property. However, common sense is more often right than wrong, and slow, calm, unbiased consideration of the problem will usually lead to a correct estimate.

All things being equal, the character of the first houses built on a new property stamp it for all time to come, and nothing means more to its future development than tasteful houses of

EXTENSIVE PLACE A FEW MILES FROM TOWN WHERE PROPERTY IS COMPARATIVELY CHEAP.

good design. On the other hand, cheap-looking houses or houses in poor taste will do more to curtail healthy development than anything else. Frequently after purchasing a lot in a new section one's own is the first house built. This gives an opportunity to start the growth of the place in the right way, and it will probably insure the upbuilding of a high-grade residence district if the first house is properly designed.

After general consideration of the section of town in which you desire to live, next examine its natural advantages, such as location of schools and churches and distance from railway or trolley lines. Any or all of these conditions should have their influence when there is under consideration an investment which represents so much capital tied up, possibly for a lifetime. Such an ordinary circumstance as unpleasant neighbors might make the difference between happiness and discomfort. Pleasant neighbors are above all else desirable, and one should find out as carefully as possible just who one's neighbors are and how they stand in town.

Good roads are necessary to the proper growth of any section, and the wise owner always considers this point. If the street on which your lot is situated presents a bad appearance find out when it is to be put in condition. Will the new owner be called upon to pay an assessment for this work? The owner should find out these points, as it may make ccnsiderable difference to him if he is to be called upon at some future time to pay for street improvements. If this is part of his contract — to pay such assessments — the purchase price of the building lot should be correspondingly less.

When a well-improved street does not already exist in front of the property it should be the aim of an owner to have street improvements made as soon as possible, for poorly built streets are a great detriment to any locality. Streets in outlying districts near the new property should also be examined to see if the general trend of that section is healthy.

In many cities and towns of the middle west it is a custom to improve streets before the property is placed on the market, putting in sewer, water and gas pipes and building sidewalks and curbs. Of course a proportionate share of such improvements is charged to each lot and included in the purchase price. The general effect of this method is good, and almost any owner is glad to pay the increased price for his lot in order to have all the improvements, rather than bother with them, himself. If gas pipes, water and sewer pipes are not already laid in the street the owner should know it on the start. Before he can definitely decide upon the desirability of that site, he must know whether or not he will be called upon to make these improvements.

Examine also into the matter of fire and police protection. Is the district well policed? Is the fire department efficient? Insurance rates are directly affected by the latter, and the one fact of a poorly organized fire department might well cause a prospective owner to hesitate before he makes an investment in such a town. Building restrictions will, of course, be looked up before the owner pays down his money. In a residence district there should be a restriction against flat buildings, otherwise his property might be depreciated by the erection of an apartment building next door. Restrictions should also exist regarding distance of building line from the street — (such and such a number of feet from sidewalk to the front wall of the house). All property owners being under the same restrictions, one man is prevented from shutting off his neighbor's view by building his house closer to the street than another.

In a residence district, it is customary to have restrictions regarding stores and other business blocks not ordinarily considered desirable there. Often, there are also restrictions regarding the locating of barns and garages, placing fences, and not infrequently districts are restricted as to the cost of houses, none being allowed which cost less than a certain amount. All these restrictions, though they may seem arbitrary to the prospective owner, will in the long run work out to his benefit, for they insure the future development of property along the lines he most desires. Of course, some of the restrictions may not work out with his own plans, in which case it will be necessary for the buyer to purchase his building site elsewhere. Restrictions are sometimes inserted in the contract made between the owner of the property and the buyer, and often they are noted directly in the deed. They remain binding upon the buyer and his successors, whoever they may be.

14 *SUCCESSFUL HOUSES AND HOW TO BUILD THEM*

In considering schoolhouses and churches do not allow their location to influence you too strongly. For instance, one might prefer to locate near a school for the convenience of the children, or it might seem practical to buy a lot near a church where the walking distance is not too great. You should remember, how-

Showing Lack of Trees, a new House which will be greatly Improved when Trees are Planted.

ever, that a few blocks more or less do not greatly influence the time it takes to go to school or church, and so many other considerations are more important it is not well to allow lesser ones to interfere.

In judging the appearance of surrounding property the prospective owner should consider the condition of the lawns, grounds, and buildings of his neighbors, for this will inform him without further inquiry whether it is a progressive neighborhood or not. Well-kept lawns, carefully preserved trees, tastefully displayed flowers and shrubs of neighboring places do much toward keeping up the valuation of the property. Houses ill kept and in bad repair are a detriment to any neighborhood, undoubtedly tending to depreciate real estate in the entire district. Looking "run down at the heels," such a section is bound to have a downward trend, new owners preferring to invest in some other locality where conditions are better.

Trees along the street undoubtedly help the general effect of property, while lack of trees may be considered as lowering its tone. Well-matured trees increase the purchase price of the building lot, but this is more than worth while to the buyer, not only to enhance the beauty of his house and grounds, but as a guarantee of the future desirability of his property, which almost always follows when the streets surrounding it are shady and attractive.

The future development of the district and consequent increase or decrease in the value of his property should not be overlooked by the prospective buyer. Though he may not be building for an investment, the wise man considers carefully the financial end of the problem. No one wishes to load upon his family after he is gone the burden of an undesirable piece of property. On the contrary, it should be the aim of every owner to buy property that will grow in value so that, upon emergency, it may be sold at a good profit.

Cost of the prospective house should also figure in the building-site transaction, for it will not do to build an expensive house on a cheap lot, nor, on the other hand, is it well to build an inexpensive house on a costly lot. Every owner should realize that something may happen to him in course of time, business reverses, sickness, or disability, which may make it necessary for him to sell his place and move elsewhere. It is very difficult to dispose of a cheap lot when there is a somewhat pretentious house upon it, for the reason that a buyer who can afford such a house most certainly desires a better location and larger lot. For the same reason a small, cheap house built upon a large, expensive lot is also difficult to dispose of because the buyer who desires a small house usually requires one at a moderate price; an expensive lot in connection with a small house would prove too expensive for most small house buyers.

By examining houses already built in town the owner can determine what size is generally built on a lot of standard proportions. He is then in a better position to judge the size and price of the building lot most practical for his own house. Such practices may seem unduly conservative to the prospective buyer, but later on in life when conditions have changed he will be glad that his business acumen led him to invest money wisely, even in his own home.

The size of lot chosen by the owner is largely determined by the price he wishes to pay. In good sections of some towns ordinary lots with frontage of 50 feet cost as high as $5000. Of course this means in the residence districts of moderate-sized towns, for land in large cities is more dear, even, than this. The purchaser must carefully consider the price he wishes to pay and invest his money where he will get the most good from it. It would be absurd for the man who wants to buy a lot for $1000 to expect to get it in a location where land is two or three times as high. For him, the most desirable pieces of property are where land is cheaper, away from the center of town. Some owners make the mistake of preferring a small lot in the choicest section of town to a large lot on the outskirts. This is usually unwise, for a lot too small can never be really enjoyed, while, on the other hand, a larger lot in the outskirts gives greater pleasure and may some day prove as desirable a location as any in town.

The 50-foot lot in town or country, though it is a size frequently sold, is too small for most purposes. Property with a frontage of 75 feet is better; a frontage of not less than 150 feet is ideal. Many are just beginning to realize this fact, and new

CHOOSING THE SITE

houses are going up in localities out in the fields where land is cheap. This does not mean that a house on a 50-foot lot cannot be comfortable and attractive, nor do we intend to imply that even 40 feet is too small for a pretty house. We would simply call attention to the fact that a narrow lot greatly adds to the complexity of the problem; a problem already sufficiently encumbered with difficulty to make it desirable to simplify as much as possible.

After you have tentatively selected the section of town in which you wish to live, having viewed the problem from every side, you are in a position to give further consideration to the actual lot best for your house. On this score you must remember that there is not always a great deal of choice between two or more pieces of property, and it may not be easy to make a decision. Points of compass, location of trees, grade (whether the property is high or low, wet or dry), position of neighboring houses, and many other conditions affect the desirability of a building lot. Some decision will have to be made as to whether a corner lot or an inside lot is most desirable. The character of the soil is also quite important.

Many buyers prefer a lot with a west frontage. Others claim an east frontage is best, to catch the morning sun in the front of the house. There is some truth in the latter idea, for if the house faces due east, the morning sun will come in at the front windows during the coolest time of day, while the afternoon sun, entering the front windows of a house facing west, is sometimes disagreeably warm in hot weather. This is straining the point very fine, of course, for on the other hand, the hot afternoon sun is unwelcome shining in the kitchen windows of a house with an east front. It is only a matter of determining which one prefers, sun in front or in back, and the houseowner must settle this point himself. As a matter of fact, many successful houses are located with frontage to the east, and many with frontage to the west. The

18 SUCCESSFUL HOUSES AND HOW TO BUILD THEM

same holds true as to north and south fronts. Either may be successful, if a house is arranged to make the most of it; so the owner need not worry too much about this point, though he should give it some study before buying his lot.

If the house is to be built somewhere near the center of a lot, trees at this point will require thinning out to make room for

VALUE OF TREES NEAR A HOUSE.

the house. For this reason, trees on the edge of a lot and along the sidewalk are best. Not a tree should be cut down until the house is started, however, and then only enough to provide room for the building. After the house is entirely completed and one has lived in it awhile, it is easier to determine what trees should be sacrificed to let sun into dark rooms or make pretty vistas from the windows.

How many houseowners make mistakes when it comes to grading? A large proportion, without doubt; and yet it is easy to use good judgment in considering this important point. A little thought will convince any one that a low lot, not much more than a hole in the ground, will be expensive to level up sufficiently to provide proper drainage. The finished, graded surface of any lot must have enough slope to carry water away from the building and prevent its soaking through into the cellar, and this fact must be borne in mind when the lot is bought. A site requiring too much filling is less desirable than one that is already high and dry. At the same time, a lot on a hillside may require expensive retaining walls to hold the banks, in addition to steps which might be needed to reach one level from another, work which tends to make the finished premises more picturesque and attractive but adds greatly to the expenditure.

The position of neighboring houses should influence your decision in buying a lot, for if they are located too near your line, it might be impossible to arrange the house as you wish, without getting too close to your neighbors. Then, too, the character of neighboring houses may add to or detract from the appearance of your property. Good-looking places near by should help, but ugly houses, or houses in vulgar taste certainly will not improve the appearance of your own property. Even more undesirable than ugly houses are houses in poor repair, which always detract from the appearance of an entire neighborhood.

There are many advantages in an inside lot and others equally as important (or greater) in a corner lot. The inside lot usually costs less than a corner lot, and it costs less to improve the former, as a general rule. In addition to these advantages, inside lots require but one sidewalk, whereas corner lots require two, — one on each street, — another advantage in favor of the inside lot. There is also less lawn to build and keep up, — fewer trees to set out in the parkway and, in most cases, less shrubbery.

On the other hand, a corner lot is usually more sightly than an inside lot, and there will be a better view from the windows of the house. At the same time, more view of house and grounds may be had from the two streets bounding a corner lot.

Some knowledge of soils, — their characteristics and the treatment required for lawns, flowers, trees, and shrubs is useful when hunting for a building lot. You cannot have a good lawn when the soil is imperfectly drained, nor can you have a dry basement under the new house if the foundations stand in a mudhole. It is surprising what little thought some buyers give to many of these little things, frequently ignoring them entirely. They seem to think their duty is done and a successful result assured when they have selected a site within their means, in a desirable location, and they are not inclined to go much into details. Many years of most discouraging work might be avoided by a little careful consideration of drainage, for it is very hard to correct poor natural conditions.

Sand is excellent to build a house upon, providing the excavation is shored up with planks to prevent it from caving in while the wall is being laid. Sand, or sandy loam, consisting of sand interspersed with clay, makes a good foundation, and such lots are usually well drained besides having the natural advantage of a soil ordinarily rich enough to make grass, flowers, and shrubs grow luxuriantly.

Clay soil is less desirable, though it will do very well when well drained. Poorly drained clay soil gets muddy in wet weather. In dry weather, clay under the lawn bakes very hard, making it almost impossible to get a good growth of grass. Sometimes such lawns crack open in hot weather. Of course all these faults can be remedied by laying a good subsoil, but such practices are expensive, and the owner should understand what he is getting into beforehand.

Lots situated on a hillside are very desirable, if too much grading is not required to make them habitable. As a matter of fact, hillside lots or lots on the edge of a bluff invariably have a beautiful effect when the building is completed. Such sizes as these gladden the heart of the architect, who can get a picturesque result with the houses built upon them. Lots of irregular shape are frequently desirable for the same reason. They enable the skillful architect to erect houses somewhat out of the

A Hillside Site with Great Possibilities.

ordinary. Plain, rectangular lots can be treated only in a somewhat conventional way though they are, of course, not undesirable. It is true that the greater proportion of building sites are rectangular and level, or nearly so, and any architect who is really skillful can get good results from them.

The legal side in purchasing a lot should be understood by the buyer before he embarks in his enterprise. In the first place, he should demand evidence of a "clear title,"— that is, the abstract which will be handed to him to examine before the sale is made should contain a complete history of the property from its first owners down to the present. Every transaction in which the property was involved should be therein recorded; every lien that was ever placed on the property should be inscribed and a note made of the manner of disposing of such liens.

There is a difference between a deed and an abstract. The former merely records one transaction in which the seller conveys the property to its new owner. The latter contains a complete history of the lot. To the layman, the abstract is a piece of paper difficult to read understandingly, couched as it is in legal terms. It is an excellent idea to have a lawyer examine this paper, looking up the various legal processes through which the property may have passed with a view to assuring the new owner that the title is clear. Another excellent custom is to secure what is known as a "warranty deed" in which a warrant for the title is given to the new owner, agreeing to refund the price of any liens or claims that might come up in the future. Thus the buyer is guaranteed that his title to the property is perfect, the seller being willing to indemnify him for any loss he might be put to through any imperfection in the title. A percentage on the purchase price is usually charged for a warranty deed, but the additional insurance given the owner that his property will stand is well worth the price of the deed.

In addition to the deed, the warranty deed and an abstract of the lot, another precaution is sometimes well taken by the owner. He should examine the city, town, or county records to see if all taxes have been paid to date. Otherwise, an unscrupulous seller might deed to the buyer property on which taxes are due. It is better to require that the seller shall deliver property free from all incumbrances, though oftentimes the buyer is willing to assume these obligations. There is no reason why the new owner should not take on these liabilities so long as he knows beforehand what the incumbrances are, and what expenditure will be required to clear them off. Most property owners require from a seller his tax and assessment receipts as proof that all liabilities are paid.

THE CHARM OF ROUGH BROWN SIDING AND GRAY PLASTER.
Tallmadge and Watson, Architects.

CHAPTER III

HOW TO KNOW THE ARCHITECTURAL STYLES

"DESIGN" is that subtle quality which makes your house a misdemeanor or an architectural triumph. Correctly speaking, the term "design" includes the practical side of house building — construction, as well as the æsthetic side — for when we say "such a man is a clever house designer," we should mean he is a good constructionist as well as an artist. But the word "design" has come to have a popular meaning well understood by most people. Used in this way, "design" refers merely to the æsthetic side of the problem, and according to this popular interpretation of the word, when we say "that is a good design," we mean merely that it is artistic.

Since primitive cave men first hollowed out their dwellings and then went to the extra labor of embellishing them by smoothing the walls, hanging skins of wild animals here and there, the craving for "design," as indicated by treatment of exterior and interior wall surfaces, has been incorporated in the life of mankind the world over. An innate desire to beautify seems to cling to the entire human race, and most men, not content with mere comfort, require in their dwellings something more. Probably early attempts at decoration were combined with a desire to secure greater comfort. Skins were at first thrown upon the floor to furnish convenient resting places, and the crude lintel over a doorway was molded, primarily, to drip the water off. However this may be, man has always instinctively appreciated pleasing composition in form and color, and his modern habitations are merely more skillful applications of the principles handed down from his primitive ancestors.

Of course, many modern houses fall short in what we term "design." Many attempts to beautify result in chaos, and many buildings, spoiled by the unrestrained efforts of immature designers to get an effect, would be more pleasing, architecturally, if no such attempts had been made. Ugly houses fail, usually, in the very qualities their designers labored so hard to get.

The best way to obtain some knowledge of design is to study houses already built. Select houses known to be in good taste, and analyze them. Try and discover what features in the exterior produced the successful result, and you will be surprised to see how quickly one begins to understand the principles of design.

Man is more imitative than he is imaginative, and for this reason the most satisfactory ideas in house design are the process of years of evolution rather than spontaneous accomplishment. Architects, when they work on a composition, rarely start with an absolutely new idea such as inventing, in fact, an entirely different type of building. They are more or less influenced by houses already built which they, with natural instinct, appreciate and understand. This has brought about a condition in architectural design which practically divides the entire field of house building into schools or styles. Styles or types in house design which have been in vogue at different times, are quite marked. For instance, when we study any period of history and examine the style of architecture then in vogue we find that most houses of that period are similar in design. Of course the individuality of each designer was stamped more or less on every building, but in the main, all houses of the same period are very much alike. Then, gradually, such types began to change. One designer, more clever than his colleagues, may have introduced a new idea, possibly nothing more than a change in the outlines of a cornice; or some new building material may have been introduced into the country, changing conditions so that old forms were no longer practical; or some fad or fancy from a foreign land may have crept into the work, until gradually, the architectural forms changed and a new style was evolved.

Style is not a mere external covering, — a something to be applied outside. Style is vital, — structural, — as well as ornamental. The designer needs to have the style he proposes to use well in mind from the beginning, otherwise he will be apt to produce a disjointed, unrelated result.

But right at the start let it be said that "style" is not necessarily a copy of any fashion that has gone before. You don't have to design your building in English, Dutch, Colonial, or Spanish Renaissance to give it style, unless you wish to. A character or style of your own can be given to it if you choose, "style" in this case being merely the individual characteristics your design has.

The problem in any house is to get up a design that shall be simple enough to come within the appropriation, but individual enough to make the design attractive. These are the almost impossible elements to reconcile, yet this is done successfully every day by skillful designers.

Style is not of chief importance in a design, for a building may be in any style and appear beautiful or ugly according to the efficiency of the designer. Most styles are beautiful when well done. Some buildings of no particular style are artistic successes. There are few designs, however, which do not show some influence of a previous style, most of them reflecting the mannerisms or fashions of some former period. "Nothing is new under the sun" is as true of architecture as any other art or science, and the cleverest designer in the world cannot hope to do more than stamp his own strong individuality upon work which undoubtedly borrows something from the architecture of all ages.

In this chapter we will not attempt to go into architectural

28   SUCCESSFUL HOUSES AND HOW TO BUILD THEM

history, nor will we take up valuable space in discussing the many interesting points showing how one architectural style melted into another, or how sudden reversions from the fashions of one period gave birth to a new style. We will simply note

OLD COLONIAL HOUSE AT SALEM, MASSACHUSETTS

a few of the most beautiful and useful styles in house design, as employed in modern times.

Everybody is interested in the so-called "Colonial" style, brought to America by early colonists from England. Nothing proves man's imitative nature better than this example of architectural ideas from the fatherland, brought to the new world and applied hit-or-miss to new conditions. Considering, first, that period when the colonists had reached a position of afflu-

HOW TO KNOW THE ARCHITECTURAL STYLES 29

ence (beyond the pioneer, log-cabin period) when they could build houses architecturally adorned, the structures were almost identical in style with houses in old England. Indeed, portions of houses were brought bodily in ships; mantelpieces, doors, windows, and sometimes large sections of wall paneling purchased abroad were built into the new houses of the colonists, and American towns resembled modified forms of English towns.

HISTORIC OLD HOUSE IN THE SOUTH.
(Formerly owned by Henry Clay.)

House styles usually grow slowly, modified by changing conditions. Even to-day, Colonial houses strongly resemble their prototypes, though there are now many points of difference. Changed customs of life, with new and more modern methods of construction, have modified the architecture of the colonists, though many little details of design are still adhered to.

Modern architectural design in the Colonial style is a sort of free adaptation of the old houses of New England, New York, Pennsylvania, and the South. Usually these houses are broad, with a hall in the center and rooms on both sides, such as make the best appearance on lots not less than 100 feet wide. Sometimes a narrow, corner lot with 50-foot frontage on one street and more on a side street, is large enough for a good Colonial design, when the house is placed with its long frontage on the side street. Of course, small Colonial cottages are frequently built on very small building sites, but cottages are usually more successful when free and picturesque, not following the more stereotyped forms of the real Colonial style. Care should be taken, however, to keep the design so simple in outline that it will not depart too much from the established lines of old Colonial houses.

MODERN ADAPTATION OF OLD COLONIAL HOUSE.
Lionel Moses, II, Architect.

Modern Colonial work is often handled in a delightfully fresh and original way, but it takes a real artist to do this. Houseowners should insist that their Colonial designs be sensible and quite plain. Quaint and refined as Colonial houses are, they should not be distorted to fit building lots of peculiar shape or take care of unusual requirements of plan. If the site will not permit of a rather long building with central entrance, on a fairly level space, you had better choose for your house some style other than Colonial.

The Colonial style in its strictest form demands more or less set conditions, but there are many adaptations of Colonial that can be used for sites of peculiar shape and grade, or where the con-

House somewhat Colonial in Type.

ditions of the problem require unusual treatment of the design. When using Colonial cornices, Colonial porches, balustrades, and windows (the latter set symmetrically, one over the other) such a design can be made very successful. A house like this may not be "Colonial," in that it may not resemble the staid old house of the colonists, but in modern parlance it is known as "Colonial" and may reasonably be called so. In plan, such a house can be arranged with a hall in the center or in an entirely different way, depending upon the characteristics of the building site and requirements of the owner.

It is instructive to observe how our cousins, the English, inheriting from our common ancestors precisely the same types of houses we inherited, have developed theirs along lines best adapted for England. American conditions of life have evolved the American type of design, and English methods of living have evolved their own modern English type. Nowhere in the wide world will you find more beautiful houses than in England. In no other land will you find houses situated in the midst of such beautiful grounds or designed in greater harmony with their surroundings. English country houses seem to blend into the landscape. They have the appearance of being indigenous to the soil, as all houses should, and in gazing upon them one feels they are entirely successful. Every prospective houseowner should study the characteristics of the quaint English houses nestling down in the midst of trees and flowers, that he may secure some of their charm for his own home.

Starting with English houses in the Elizabethan period, which originated long before the Georgian style (foundation of our "Colonial") it is interesting to note the character of design used to meet the conditions then prevailing in England. Timber, while not extremely plentiful, was nevertheless the cheapest and most adaptable material, so timber was largely employed for the framework of every house. Elizabethan builders used no clapboards or shingles to cover the exterior surfaces of their houses but built brick walls between the skeleton framework of wood, allowing the timbers of the skeleton to appear in the design. This gave rise to the quaint patterns of timberwork so delightful to see, built so well they have endured for centuries. Modern houses in the Elizabethan style are still built in England though they are so changed in plan that they present quite a different appearance.

Modern building laws in England are excellent, requiring

HOW TO KNOW THE ARCHITECTURAL STYLES 33

in most towns structures of solid masonry. Besides this, lumber is now expensive because of its scarcity, and these modern conditions have evolved an architecture of brick and stone quite as attractive as houses of older periods. In modern English work the old timberwork style has been largely superseded by

ENGLISH "TIMBER-WORK" HOUSE AS BUILT IN AMERICA.

brick and stone houses. Most often, houses of brick are covered on the outside with stucco. Sometimes timberwork is used sparingly on porches and gables, but in most modern English work an entirely different type has been evolved.

The English type is entirely practical for American houses, though American conditions, decidedly different from those in England, greatly modify them. English servants work for

D

very much lower wages than Americans, hence the servant problem is much less of a problem in England than it is in America. Lower wages in England make it possible to employ more servants, and houses are not designed along such rigid lines to secure convenience. English houseowners of even moderate incomes usually employ from two to four servants. Thus, it is not necessary to strive particularly to reduce distance from room to room and provide a convenient arrangement based upon the most scientific easy housekeeping requirements.

AMERICANIZED ENGLISH TYPE.
Lawrence Buck, Architect.

All these conditions are changed in America, making it impossible for the American to build his house with more than the barest resemblance to the houses of England. Nor does he wish to, for it is better that American conditions should produce modes of building typically American.

English designs are noted for their picturesque effect. Roofs, usually broken by gables, frequently slope more on one side than another, sometimes quite down to the ground. Very rarely do English houses have a basement under the entire house, as the country is so well drained cellars can be omitted. Storerooms are usually built in little wings on the ground floor, connected with the house by walls and frequently housed under the main roof. All this produces a delightfully rambling, quaint look, decidedly pleasing.

English designs adapted for America can still have much of the charm of houses in England, though they will look quite different, American houses requiring cellars, which makes it necessary to set the buildings higher from the ground. Houses in this country must be conserved in size and arrangement to meet the complex conditions of American housekeeping and, as American materials are different, we have produced a distinct American type founded upon English lines. The Elizabethan style

ENGLISH TYPE OF BRICK HOUSE AS BUILT IN AMERICA.

when modified is entirely practical for American country places, though most American adaptations of the Elizabethan style are ordinary frame houses, covered with lath and plaster and ornamented with imitation timberwork (thin boards nailed to the framework of the house).

Originally imported from Holland, there is a development of the modern Dutch style in America. It is a sort of combination of Old Dutch and new American Colonial and is very practi-

36 SUCCESSFUL HOUSES AND HOW TO BUILD THEM

cal and attractive for suburban houses. Modern Dutch houses are usually quite prim and symmetrical in appearance, frequently placed with a central entrance broadside to the street. Porch columns are large in diameter, with very simple caps and bases. Most houses of this style are of the low cottage type and bedrooms on the second story, cut by the sloping roof lines,

AMERICAN HOUSE ALONG ENGLISH LINES.

are lighted by dormer windows. Latticework is effectively used in modern Dutch houses, and flowers and flowering vines form integral parts of the composition.

California produced the American-Spanish type of building, which has been handed down to us in what is known as the "Mission" style. Here again, methods of building prevalent in Mexico, and later in California, coupled with the architec-

HOW TO KNOW THE ARCHITECTURAL STYLES   37

tural influence of Spain, have evolved a distinct American style showing Spanish influences plainly. The Mission style is austere in character and for that reason is more successful when contrasted with the picturesque mountains and hills of California than it is on the plains of the middle west. It does not reach its maximum attractiveness on a small lot, for the

QUAINT MEXICAN DWELLINGS.

Mission style seems to demand a large amount of land around the building, — preferably rolling land. Mission "flavor" in an ordinary stucco house situated on an ordinary building lot is rarely successful. One should be careful that the building site is adapted to a house of this style. The nearer a lot approaches the character of a California landscape, the more successful will the house be. Cement plaster is the best material to use for the exterior covering, as cement more closely approximates the characteristics of the old adobe buildings. It is a style which seems to demand large, plain wall surfaces such as can be obtained in modern buildings only by using cement. Houses in the Mission style require special treatment as to window grouping. Bright color is needed on the window frames and cornices to enliven what might otherwise be a design severely uninteresting and cold. Quite lavish use of trellises, with flowers and shrubbery greatly relieves the severe monotony of the style.

CEMENT HOUSE SOMEWHAT OF THE MEXICAN TYPE.

In Germany, house designers are evolving from old styles a practical type of house most interesting in character. German designers 'have been very clever in securing effects fitting for their own country, and modified forms of this modern German style are used successfully in America. As a rule, however, German houses are not entirely suitable for our own country, being frequently somewhat complex even in their simplicity. Roofs extend in broken lines. Windows, though well grouped, are not placed in symmetrical fashion the way they are in English and American houses, and the result is an irregularity that seems to be suitable for Germany but is less attractive in America. You need only examine the little toy houses made in Germany for sale in American shops, to understand the principles of German design. Indeed, these toys are quite faithful miniatures of actual German houses.

Medieval houses and castles nestling in valleys or perched on the edge of rugged cliffs have greatly influenced modern German work. German houses reflect in more conservative form the towers and turrets of ancient German buildings, but there are few places in America where such a style can be used unless it be greatly modified, certainly not on the average small American building lot. In a mountainous section, or on an ex-

AMERICAN HOUSE SHOWING GERMAN INFLUENCE.
Perkins and Hamilton, Architects.

tensive country site the German style is perfectly practical, though even under these conditions it should be greatly Americanized.

France has a somewhat indigenous type of house different from other countries, though many French designs are not greatly unlike the English. Here again, different building methods and local building materials have evolved the typical French house for town and country. L'Art Nouveau (the "new art") really started in Germany, but it came quickly into vogue in France a few years ago. It is not to be recommended as a style suitable for American houses. Based on floral forms, it is not ideal for architectural use, as the long, flowing lines of

STONE HOUSE OF MODERN GERMAN TYPE

this style give houses a sort of theatrical appearance. L'Art Nouveau is a rather naïve type of design in which the building is treated in a decorative manner, representing a tree (with roots, trunk, branches, and blossoms). Often in this style the walls start at a base, extending toward the cornice with slightly battered surfaces. Around door and window openings decorative forms are frequently cast in cement or carved out of wood to suggest root, branch, and flower. Cornices are often molded in like fashion.

HOW TO KNOW THE ARCHITECTURAL STYLES 41

There is great difference between the natural growth of a tree (as in nature) and the growth of a building constructed laboriously, unit by unit, by means of hard work and brains. Buildings resemble nature only by suggestion. The actual reproduction of floral forms in the structure of a building is

AMERICAN HOUSE SHOWING JAPANESE TENDENCIES.
Frank Lloyd Wright, Architect.

far-fetched, and the result is rarely pleasing. L'Art Nouveau is not a successful building type for houses, and the houseowner will do well to avoid this style.

Even Japan, strange as its buildings look to our eyes, has contributed to the development of house design in America by influencing American architects, who see much to admire in Japanese houses. Japan is the home of virile religious ideals, and Japanese art is strongly influenced by the hardy, poetic, philosophic life led by the Japanese people. Japanese houses indicate a style developed to the extreme of simplicity, and for that reason they offer many suggestions to the American houseowner.

Of course Japanese houses are not adaptable to American conditions without a great many changes in design and construction. American ideals will not permit one to use more than the barest suggestion of the Japanese, such as low, plain roof lines and other little details practical for American houses.

Clever designers who understand all the intricacies of architectural design frequently get good results without paying attention to any particular style, depending more upon the fundamental principles of their art than on ideas gained from any building already built. In the Middle West a characteristic type of house design has been developed, which, although slightly reflecting the influence of earlier types in America and other countries, is so well defined that it is worthy of a place as a distinct type. Great individuality has been developed in this section of the country, with the result that many of the new ideas are delightfully fresh, being quite free from the influence of precedent. These tendencies have led many to think that America, at last, is to develop a strictly American type, more pronounced than any American styles that have gone before.

EXAMPLE SHOWING MODERN ADAPTATION OF THE ITALIAN STYLE.

AN ENTRANCE WITH FLORAL ADORNMENT
George Maher, Architect.

CHAPTER IV

THE LITTLE DETAILS THAT ATTRACT

NOWHERE is the style (or school) to which a house belongs more in evidence than in the details of exterior and interior trim. Moldings, doors, windows, porch columns or posts, and other accessories of this sort usually stamp the house unmistakably as belonging to this or that style. Of course other characteristics count, such as shape and inclination of the roof and amount of overhang at the eaves, position and character of bay windows and grouping of windows, all of which, intelligently worked out according to any particular style, help to make the building a definite example of it.

Every house contains utilities such as doors, windows, cornices, gutters, water table, and molded casings around doors and windows. These, combined with plain wall surfaces, are all the materials the designer has with which to get his architectural effect. Color, in the shape of paint applied after a building is completed, as well as trees, flowers, and shrubs, are of great assistance in getting the desired effect, but in the main the designer's composition is made up of nothing more than doors, windows, moldings, and wall surfaces. He must skillfully employ them to produce the sensation of beauty.

Ugly designs have the same number of parts as beautiful designs, but doors, windows, moldings, and wall surfaces in this case produce an ugly effect instead of a beautiful one, the line between ugliness and beauty sometimes being very slight. Designing a house is much like mixing a cake; slight variation in the ingredients causes failure. The difference between an ugly house and a beautiful one is caused entirely by the form, arrangement, proportion, and color of the detailed parts of the house. Thus, this design which one considers charming, has refinement in its details; that house which strikes one unpleasantly, is poor in proportion and arrangement of doors, windows, molded work, and wall surfaces.

Choice of style is not so important an element in the house design as character is in each little detail. There are atrocious examples of every style of house (no matter how quaint and charming such a style may be when well carried out) as the result of malpractice by poor designers. On the other hand, there are countless houses not representative of any school or style, which may be considered as marked examples of all that is beautiful in design. They seem to have an indescribable charm which carries them beyond the realm of the commonplace, up to the heights of the noble. After the style of one's house has been determined upon, it will be well to examine some of the characteristics of that style, for it is impossible to make a sensible and satisfactory design without having some knowledge of the details which go to make up its integral parts.

COLONIAL DOORWAY ON AN OLD SALEM HOUSE.

THE LITTLE DETAILS THAT ATTRACT 47

Usually the first part of a house to be noticed by the casual observer is the entrance door, and here is a great opportunity to produce an artistic effect. The entrance door is usually a key to the taste of the houseowner. Without examination of any other part of the building, one may see here at a glance just

VERANDA ON END OF HOUSE.

what to expect inside the house. An entrance way simple and refined speaks for something worth while and true within.

Old Colonial doorways usually have a quaint charm that is irresistible. They seem to invite one to enter, and they make one feel the charm of hospitality upon first glance. In old houses (except old southern houses with their two-story verandas) it was rarely the case that a large veranda encumbered the front, which is one reason why front entrances in old houses are so attractive. As a usual thing, a veranda extending across the front of a house is not the most desirable arrangement. Frequently, it is better to place the veranda at one end so as to leave the view of the front entrance unobstructed. There are other reasons why the veranda should not be on the front, as is explained in another chapter.

SIMPLE DOORWAY FOR A SMALL HOUSE.

Though the principal veranda need not be in the fore part of the house, a small entrance porch is desirable, and the examples of old Colonial houses are excellent to follow in this regard. Frequently, old Colonial entrance ways consisted merely of a flight of steps with a small landing at the top, covered by a roof supported on Greek columns. Sometimes, as in many Salem houses, a bay window on the second story projected above the roof of the entrance porch. In other old houses, particularly in the West, where Colonial architecture is more free in treatment than it is in the East (and less pure, it must be admitted), the entrance occurs in a bay window, covered by a flat roof surmounted by a light balustrade. All these old types are worthy of emulation, and they may be combined with modern

Colonial details to bring about most charming compositions. Some modern adaptations of old entrance ways are quite as beautiful as the originals from which they were taken.

Another practical type of entrance way is one slightly recessed in the front façade of the building. It can be treated in a Colonial way with Greek columns and a Greek entablature above, or it may have details to harmonize with any other style. Cement steps and platforms at the front entrance are frequently used in Colonial work, but red brick set in cement mortar seems particularly suitable, especially if a little red brick walk leads from the sidewalk to the steps. Tile is also practical for the top surface of the platform, — usually red quarry tile, with wide, black joints.

A Colonial entrance way should be kept as close to the ground as possible, indeed, any entrance Colonial or not is prettier without a long flight of steps leading to it. In American houses where the first floor must be several feet above ground to secure good light in the cellar the entrance can be especially arranged, a few outside steps extending up to the doorway and the remainder being placed in the vestibule.

The details of the front entrance door, itself, are capable of very different interpretations, depending upon the ideas of the designer. Remember, your entrance door is a sign of the environment you create for your family; the badge of your taste. Let it, then, be simple in design. A large panel of plain plate glass is attractive in an oak door, and this style is suitable for many houses. The woodwork may be finished light or dark to bring out the beautiful grain of the wood, and it will resist weather successfully if four or five coats of spar varnish are applied, rubbed to a dull gloss. In Colonial work six or eight smaller panes of glass should be substituted for the single large panel. Such a design is especially adapted for pine doors, most attractive when painted white. There is a sweet, neat look to a white door, perhaps impossible to get in any other. Elaborate, over-ornamented entrance doors are, of course, eschewed by people of refined taste.

Nothing can be prettier than the entrance doors of old houses containing six or eight wooden panels with leaded glass sides and transom lights. In olden times the fact that the door itself contained no glass brought about the necessity for side lights to properly light the hall, incidentally making it possible to get a charming effect by the judicious use of leaded glass. In modern adaptations of old entrance ways good effects are obtained by glazing the entrance door itself, using side lights or not.

ENTRANCE PROTECTED BY A SIMPLE ROOF.

An entrance door should be sheltered in some manner, either by a hood extending over, or by recessing the door in the walls of the building to prevent rain from beating in. Green trellises can be used with excellent effect at an entrance way to add a touch of pleasant color to the design, and flowers in flower boxes placed near the entrance add much to its attractiveness. Sometimes a little balcony takes the place of hood or recess, providing shelter from the elements and making a pretty effect from the stair landing above. Considering the problem from all sides, no part of the house is more important that the entrance way. A doorway must be attractive in appearance, not forbidding, and at the same time it should be practical in construction, for there is much wear here.

Next in importance to the entrance door, are windows, singly or in groups, which do much to make or mar the appearance of the house. Whatever its style, a house with poorly proportioned windows, or windows badly grouped, makes a poor appearance. Neither ingenuity in plan nor care in proportioning the parts of the exterior design can overcome the disaster caused by ugly windows. Though primarily intended to illuminate the interior of the house, windows are important elements in the design, giving a touch to the composition that will be good or bad, according to one's taste in using good windows or bad. Plain windows with small lights above and a single large light below are always practical. The upper sash can be divided into six or eight equal lights, with small lights at the side and larger lights in the center. Sometimes, especially in Colonial work, it is desirable to extend the small lights to the lower sash as well.

ORNAMENTAL GLASS OF GEOMETRICAL PATTERN.

Ornamental glass can be used, here and there, with good effect if the designs are simple and the colors harmonious. Ornamental glass in the best taste is designed after simple geometrical patterns. Various arrangements of straight lines and graceful curves are much better than pretentious, elaborate floral or pictorial designs. There should be nothing in the house which is not sensible. Patterns using straight lines are particularly adaptable for designs in metal bar, as the latter material is not so easily bent into curves as the more flexible lead bars. Spots of iridescent glass, or pretty opal bits in just the right places are wonderfully effective. Glass designs employing ridiculous scrolls and brilliant shades of red, green, and yellow glass detract from any house. They look bad from outside as well as inside.

Without doubt it is harder to keep small lights clean than large surfaces of glass. In little panes, crevices up next to the muntins are difficult to wipe out, but in spite of this it is rarely wise to use large sheets of glass, solely. Large lights look like store windows, destroying the charm of the design and making the façade look cold and unattractive. The additional labor of washing small lights is little, and it is more than offset by the increased attractiveness of the design.

In almost all Colonial houses windows are placed one over the other in perfect symmetry. This is a safe way to treat them, as it always produces a dignified effect, and if the rooms are carefully arranged the windows will be quite as useful one way as another. In planning a house the designer, of course, arranges his windows where they will light the rooms best, but in doing so he should always consider their exterior appearance. Frequently, in the kitchen, where an extra amount of light and air is required, it is good practice to have a group of three windows with narrow wood mullions between, thus giving a greater area of light to a room which needs all the light and air it can get. In such an arrangement it is a good idea to center the group under the bedroom window above, so that, even though the windows below do not correspond with those above, they balance with them.

In many modern houses the stairs extend up over the front

entrance way; that is, the front entrance is under the main stair landing. This makes possible an engaging composition on the exterior by permitting the use of a pretty stair window on the landing, over the front door. A little balcony is often incorporated in the arrangement, and the effect is frequently charming.

Bay windows should be used judiciously. They may be effective in the design, or they may greatly mar it, according to the skill of the designer. The interior aspect of bay windows is by no means the only consideration, for by reason of their shape and projection they become chief features in the exterior design. Whether one wishes it or not, bay windows always attract attention. For that reason they must be carefully proportioned and attractively detailed. In many houses otherwise well designed, the effect has been spoiled by injudicious use of bay windows, situated, perhaps, where they are useful, but with an appearance detracting from the general effect. Treated with understanding, bay windows can be made to help out greatly in the design.

BALCONY OVER A MAIN ENTRANCE.

Single-story bay windows are easiest of all to handle satisfactorily. Such a bay can be simply a little projection extending to the window sill line, or it may reach down to the floor. In the former case, the bay requires no foundations, as it is merely hung out from the wall of the building, but in the latter case a foundation is required. The trick to accomplish in a bay window is to make it look properly attached to the building; that

WELL DESIGNED BAY WINDOW.

is, a successful bay looks as if it grew there, while the unsuccessful one has a detached appearance, much as if built at some later period. One of the best ways to make the bay window seem an integral part of the building is to build it of the same material as the façade from which it springs. If the house is covered with clapboards painted white, have your bay window white also; if shingles compose the exterior finish of the house, use a shingled bay; nothing is better for a plaster-covered house than a plaster-covered bay. Of course the clever designer often varies his materials and follows no definite rules in this regard. Frequently white wooden bays look most attractive on a plaster house, but it requires considerable skill to handle them in this way.

Some bays are square and others are three sided. It makes no great difference in the design which kind is selected, though in some styles square bays are more frequently used than three-sided bays. In the English style little square bays, extending down to the window sill height are frequently used with good effect. They seem to be particularly suitable for casement windows, which prevail in English houses. In other styles a bay window the full size of the room projects from the building in the form of a large wing. This is frequently the case in a dining room, where a bay the full width of the room makes an attractive appearance outside as well as in. In such a case the bay usually contains a continuous row of windows.

Two-story bay windows are hard to treat so as to avoid a detached appearance, but it can be done satisfactorily by extending the main roof out over the bay. Thus the horizontal band formed by the cornice seems to dominate the perpendicular bay, attaching it to the building. This perpendicular, towerlike effect of a two-story bay is unattractive as a rule, and that is what makes it difficult to manage. Some two-story bays are successful when covered by gables projecting from the main roof; others are so slight in projection and hug the façade so closely that they do not look detached.

In the Middle West a clever substitute for bay windows has been found in grouping windows at the corner of a room. Thus, the interior of such a room presents somewhat the appearance of a bay, and the exterior effect is good when corner groups are properly designed. For this type of window the actual corner of the building should be made wider and heavier than the mullions between windows, in order to get a good exterior effect; otherwise the corner would look weak, much as though it could not support the weight of wall and roof above.

There is considerable difference between casement windows and ordinary windows (double-hung, as the latter are called). This difference is largely brought about by the practical requirements of each. Ordinary windows can be made as wide as desired. Unless unreasonably wide (and the window does not contain too large glass), an ordinary window operates without great exertion and stays in fairly good repair. This has made it possible to use those broad, low windows now so frequently seen, and which are of such satisfactory proportions. Casement windows, on the other hand, whether they open out or in, must be narrow, so as not to prove too heavy for the hinges by which they are attached. This has given rise to the grouping of casements into three or more, with narrow wooden mullions between; thus where one wide, ordinary window will light a room efficiently, it takes two or three of the narrow casements to do the same work. This is not a detriment, however, for a group of casements is very attractive.

Usually casements are cut up into small lights by wooden muntins, or by leaded glass or metal bars. Most American windows are based somewhat upon those used in England, where casements are universal. Different conditions in America, however, such as the necessity for screens (a condition less annoying in England), have changed the design and construction of American casement windows, as is explained in detail in another chapter.

Inside, windows should be as attractive as outside, and this must be borne in mind when designing them. Broad, low, ordinary windows are always attractive inside or out; they add greatly to the homelike appearance of the rooms, — a quality which most of the unsuccessful houses lack. Casements in pairs, containing small leaded lights with a horizontal transom above are always pretty, viewed from inside. They can be made especially attractive outside if the little leaded bars are painted white, to bring out the design. Groups of long, narrow windows with horizontal transoms are attractive inside as well as out, if they are of good proportions.

In addition to outside doors and windows, designers must pay particular attention to window and door casings, for here is another opportunity to get a pretty effect. As a general thing, casings should be very plain, though they can be molded just enough to catch the light and shade, making a little richer appearance than smooth bands of wood. Modern thought in design is to have everything as plain as possible, but that doesn't

THE LITTLE DETAILS THAT ATTRACT

mean plain until it borders on eccentricity. Casings need not be heavy and clumsy to be plain, nor should exterior cornices be moldless to be simple. Slightly molded surfaces are usually prettier than flat surfaces, and they are just as practical,— equally as cleanly when not too elaborately molded. Fashion has swung back again from the odd, clumsy woodwork of the past few years, for it has been found that, beyond a certain air of unique freshness, heavy, plain bands of wood are not particularly attractive.

Do not, in your effort to reduce the ornamental parts of the house to their lowest terms, eliminate curves entirely. Puritanical lack of ornament is all right for a factory, but it proves distasteful for the house. Cornices on *old* Colonial work are excellent models to follow, and cornices on *new* Colonial work may be very satisfactory. The cornice is a sort of last touch

CORNICES ADAPTED FROM OLD COLONIAL HOUSES.

to the exterior design. It crowns the composition and is, perhaps, of more importance than any other part of the façade. Cornices can be of extreme simplicity, consisting merely of a straight hanging metal gutter, or they may have the more complex details of molded cornices. In every case it is entirely a matter of good taste, a well-designed cornice doing much toward increasing the attractiveness of what might otherwise be a dull design. Besides the ordinary hanging cornice there are cornices formed or built into the roof, some of the most attractive of which are finished with plain boards, simply paneled. Of course the simpler cornices are inexpensive and they may be quite as attractive, though molded cornices are not necessarily expensive. It is the amount of material in a cornice, rather than its shape, which determines its cost, for molded work can be run almost as cheaply through the mill as plain work.

The amount of cornice overhang is quite important. In some styles, like Colonial and English, cornices overhang very little and types of moldings used on such cornices seem to look best that way. On the other hand, plain cornices seem to present the most attractive appearance when they project boldly beyond the wall of the building. Houses with steep roofs should never have unusually wide eaves, as they are too heavy in appearance when a roof is steep. Roofs with slight pitch look well with a boldly projecting overhang, and the edge of such a roof (cornice) should be just the right thickness to look well in the design. Even an inch, too thick or too thin, spoils its proportions, greatly marring the effect of the design.

On houses with cement-plastered exteriors, plaster has proved an excellent material with which to cover the underside of overhanging cornices (eaves). There is something very pleasing in the simplicity of a plaster surface extending right up under the eaves with no change in material. On frame houses covered with clapboards or shingles, eaves are boarded or sheathed underneath with good effect.

When an overhanging cornice is used, the exact amount of projection depends upon the style of the building and its proportions. One must avoid excessive overhangs which cut too much light from bedroom windows. If the underside of the cornice is plastered, or if it is of wood, painted white, reflected light greatly assists in lighting the bedrooms. The maximum overhang to be practical may be set at 4 feet. Most projections are not greater than 3 feet or 3 feet 6 inches.

First-story cornices on porch roofs, bay windows, and single-story wings are usually lighter and more dainty than main roof cornices. As single-story cornices are nearer the level of the eye, they are usually smaller, so as not to appear too coarse. This is a good point to remember, for many houses otherwise refined in detail are hurt by the gross size of cornices used on parts near the ground. First-story cornices should be similar in pattern to the main cornices. Nothing is in poorer taste than a house in which one kind of molding is used for the main roof and another, entirely unrelated, for first-story roofs. In much better taste are houses in which all the cornices are closely related, though of course they need not be identical in pattern; frequently there are more moldings in the main cornice than in first-story cornices, all being of similar pattern.

The water table gives another opportunity to the designer to add to the attractiveness of his design. Whether molded, or a plain board at the level of the first floor, it is capable of treatment which greatly adds to the charm of the design. Porch trimmings are also important, and they should be studied very carefully. Porches and verandas are for comfort, first of all, but that does not prevent them from assisting in the design. They can be of great assistance when used discriminatingly. Rarely is it wise to extend a covered porch entirely across the front of the house, as houses seem to look best with the principal veranda on one end. More about the advantages of end and rear porches is contained in another chapter.

Porch columns can be made a means of making the design attractive. Many types of columns are pretty and many are practical, but none more so than well-designed Greek columns. Formerly it was necessary for architects to carefully design porch columns of Greek style in order to have them well proportioned, for columns carried in stock by mills throughout the country were in very poor taste. Now, however, many mills in different sections make excellent ready-made porch posts patterned along the best Greek lines. Such columns can be ordered with the assurance that they will be correct in proportion, like those used in ancient Greek and Roman buildings.

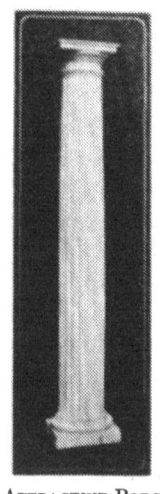

ATTRACTIVE PORCH COLUMN OF STOCK DESIGN.

Greek Doric and Tuscan columns are especially good for houses, as they are the plainest of the Greek styles, and the simple, round capitals may be turned out of the solid wood, whereas in the Ionic and Corinthian styles, more ornate capitals (on posts of moderate cost) must be made of papier-mâché or composition.

Queer posts with little ridges and spool-like turnings are always ugly. They are the product of an unintelligent mind and a revolving lathe. Even posts along Greek lines are ugly when not correctly designed. With ornamental "neckties" around their necks, and thin, flat bases, they pretend to smack of the noble, but are really vulgar.

Entrance porches have already been spoken of. They should be small, and quiet in design. Carriage porches are not so easily disposed of, though they are not usually required on any but the largest houses. A little hood projecting out from a side door is frequently sufficient for the average house. Where a large carriage porch is required care should be taken to avoid a "patched-on" appearance. On English houses carriage porches are frequently made attractive by building the entire porch of wood, harmonizing with the bands of wood in the timberwork. Practical arrangements of porches, on lower and upper story, are explained in another chapter.

Flower boxes are now generally recognized parts of the design for producing pretty effects. Nothing can be more charming in summer than architecturally designed boxes filled with flowers; indeed, some house-owners have the benefit of them the year round by having them filled in winter with low-growing, Japanese evergreens. Flower boxes can be simple little receptacles hung under the window, or they may be built up from the ground. Often, flower boxes built of brick or concrete are located at the sides of the front entrance steps. Frequently little wooden boxes are used with

FLOWER BOX BUILT UNDER A GROUP OF WINDOWS.

THE DECORATIVE VALUE OF AWNINGS.

62 *SUCCESSFUL HOUSES AND HOW TO BUILD THEM*

good effect on second-story balconies or under second-story windows.

Trellises add charm to a house, and they are most frequently attached to the outside wall near the front entrance. All such

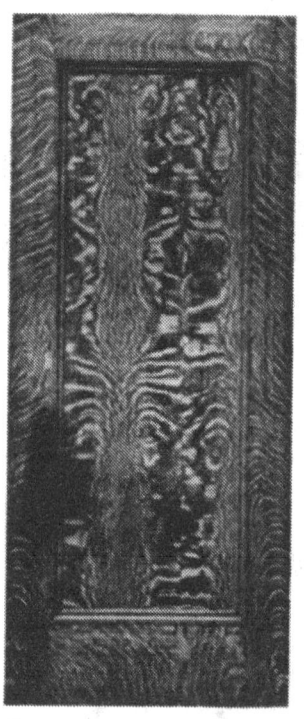

SINGLE-PANEL DOOR OF OAK.

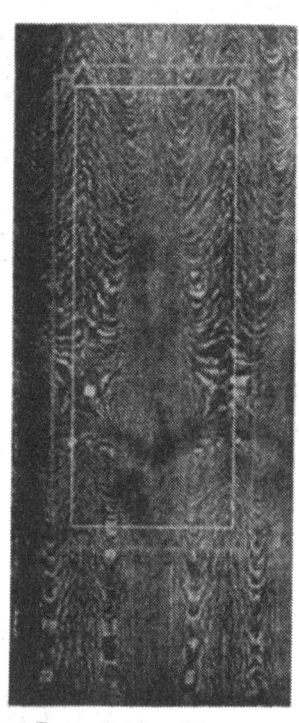

DOOR WITHOUT PANELS.

accessories, simple and inexpensive as they are, add much to the attractiveness of the design, and they should be carefully considered. Even awnings do much to add a pretty touch of color to houses in the summer time. With green and white stripes (or brown and white) they add quite a festive appearance and are, besides, useful in making rooms cooler during hot days.

THE LITTLE DETAILS THAT ATTRACT 63

Inside the house the importance of refined details should be recognised as well as outside. Very plain inside doors do as much as anything toward contributing a feeling of good taste to the interior. Doors were not originally intended to be ornamental. They were first made for the purely utilitarian purpose of shutting up or locking one room from another. It remained for designers of later times to make the inside of the house hideous with ornate, heavy patterns of peculiar paneling and turned, fretted, and molded work. But manufacturers have been quick to appreciate the refined taste of a more enlightened generation,

SMOOTH NON-PANEL DOOR

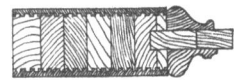
VENEERED PANELLED DOOR

ATTRACTIVE STAIRCASE, RAIL, AND NEWEL.

64 SUCCESSFUL HOUSES AND HOW TO BUILD THEM

and you will have no difficulty in finding excellent ready-made patterns in all kinds of woods. Two-paneled doors of oak, mahogany, and birch are usually attractive, and wear well. There is a feeling of substance about them; a look of fine simplicity. Single-paneled doors are in the best possible taste,

OAK WAINSCOT ON A STAIRCASE.

especially when built of pine or birch, painted dull white. Inside doors with a multiplicity of panels never look so well as doors with fewer panels. Coarse, deeply grooved extraneous moldings and heavily beveled panels are very hard to keep clean. They are also much more expensive than simple designs and very much less attractive.

The staircase newel post is the easiest thing in the world to treat tastily, when properly considered. First of all, its main purpose is to support one end of the hand rail. Thus this humble utility deserves to be treated in a dignified manner. A plain, square post with slightly tapering sides usually looks well. It doesn't seem to thrust itself on one's notice like so many of its ornate brothers and sisters, and plain posts of this sort are especially pretty in oak, mahogany, and all woods finished with stain. For a painted newel post the plain cylinder with dainty cap and base is very attractive. When painted white, with round, white stair balusters and a mahogany hand rail, the result is very engaging. A newel post which is vulgarly ostentatious should never find a place in any house.

All paneling should be of utmost simplicity. It makes no difference whether in the hall, library, or dining room, a modest design of plain panels is best. So many hardwood wainscots are used now it is not necessary to have panels elaborately molded to produce an artistic effect. The grain of the wood is sufficient when left in natural color or when stained some harmonious tone. White paneling, which makes an excellent background for mahogany furniture, should have as little molding as possible; just a simple cap and base are best. Probably more money has been wasted on extravagant paneling than on any other part of the interior finish.

ARCHITECT'S SKETCH AND THE FINISHED HOUSE
Frank Lloyd Wright, Architect.

CHAPTER V

OWNER, ARCHITECT, AND CONTRACTOR

FOR years you have been dreaming about the new house, and at last the time has come when you may hope to have the realization of your dreams. You have, during your many years of observation (it is to be hoped), come in contact with new houses built in your neighborhood. By this time you should be tolerably familiar with the general styles of modern houses; Colonial, English, German, Italian, and the various modifications of each. That is, it is to be expected you can tell at a glance a house with Colonial tendencies, or one which is somewhat along the lines of Italian Renaissance, and so on. It isn't *necessary* to be familiar with the different styles used most frequently in house design, but study of the historic styles is very interesting, — a pastime that requires but little effort on the part of the observer and one which will bring a great deal of enjoyment, proving useful, later, when one's own house is contemplated.

Now you are up to the plan stage, we will say, and your chief concern is what architect to employ. You need not employ an architect, of course, but it is wise to have an architect, if you wish to get the utmost in plan and design, thus avoiding considerable annoyance.

There are builders in every town who are reliable, honest men; contractors who can be depended upon to build a house, using the very best of materials and employing the most skilled workmen. You could, undoubtedly, by dealing with such a builder, get a house as thoroughly built as if it were constructed under the most careful supervision of a conscientious architect. Many builders draw quite a number of plans during the course of a year, and many people wishing to build, simply go to such a builder, have plans drawn (by the builder) to suit themselves, and contract for the building at an agreed upon price. This is a good way to get just what you want, but it is a question if it is the best method of procedure. In the first place, how many know just what they want? How many are sure the ideas they have in mind are practical?

The builder is a very busy man. He has, in most cases, come up through the various grades of apprentice, carpenter, foreman, until finally deciding to go into business. Thus, after working eight or nine hours a day for several years as an employee of some other contractor he finally ends up in business for himself. With the many details of contracting on his hands the average builder finds his time all taken up trying to get work, and endeavoring to execute work after he has got it. It is unreasonable to expect such a man to have any very complete architectural education, for his opportunities to study are, as a rule, extremely limited. Most often the builder is too busy to get much more than a common school education and many have not had so much as that. The architectural knowledge such a builder has is usually limited to experience, common sense, and a few facts he has picked up from observing the work of others. He may have made the most of the time at his command, but his time has been limited.

The architect, on the other hand, devotes many years of his life to his architectural training. Most often an architectural student pursues a university course of four years (sometimes followed by a post graduate course of two years), after which he travels a year or more abroad, making a study of old-world architecture. Then the young architect enters the office of a practicing architect where he works as draftsman from two to three or more years before beginning his independent career. Thus the average architect has been at least six to ten years or more actively employed in the minute study of the different branches of his profession. He is, by reason of the varied amount of learning he has received, acutely prepared to cope with almost any architectural problem which may arise. Even architects who have not had the advantages of university training usually acquire much experience working for years under competent architects, coming in daily contact with actual problems in design and construction.

The architect might be compared to a physician, and the builder to a druggist; the druggist being competent to compound prescriptions which the physician, by his superior training and experience, is qualified to suggest. An architect is trained more particularly to create ideas, while a builder is most proficient in carrying out the ideas created by an architect.

The best houses designed by ordinary builders are usually well-built examples of commonplace design. The peculiar environment in which an ordinary builder lives does not give him very much imagination. His sense of the æsthetic is not, as a rule, so keenly developed as the architect's, and he cannot hope to do more than reproduce a stereotyped design. Indeed, most builders who draw their own plans merely accept the requests of the owner, designing the house as ordered to do with no great thought as to what is best; they do not consider whether such plans are adaptable to the site on which the owner is to build, or whether that particular type of house is best suited for the owner's family or will fit the owner's pocketbook.

The building of a house involves the expenditure of several thousands of dollars. It is, therefore, what might be termed a "vital" proposition. No man wishes to spend money foolishly, nor does any houseowner care to risk the expenditure of such a large sum without feeling sure that it is applied with skill so that he will get the most for his money. No matter how much building experience an owner has had, he is most often a

70 SUCCESSFUL HOUSES AND HOW TO BUILD THEM

business man, whose time is too much taken up with his own business affairs to permit him more than a cursory familiarity with the great art, Architecture. He may have excellent ideas and he may be tolerably sure of just what he wants in a house, but usually, the prospective houseowner is in need of expert services when it comes to making working plans. It

FROM AN ARCHITECT'S SKETCH.

is more sensible to have this expert service rendered by a man trained for the work than by one whose life work is to build, — not to plan.

Many owners have excellent ideas about building, and every architect is glad to acknowledge that he learns much from his clients. Two heads are better than one; three heads are frequently better than two, though sometimes too many ideas ruin the design. However, many of the best ideas in houses have been contributed by owners, but it is doubtful if these ideas could have been successfully worked out without the expert services of an architect.

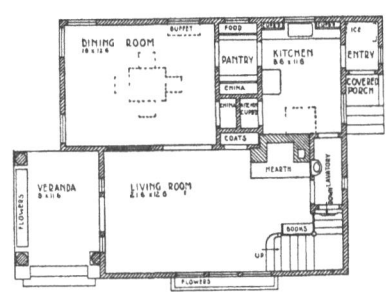

FIRST FLOOR SKETCH OF HOUSE SHOWN ON PAGE 70.

Any one who has given considerable study to plans of houses built throughout the United States, coming in contact with houses planned entirely by builders, — others planned entirely by owners, and many planned by architects, will usually note a difference between these houses. As a rule, houses designed entirely by owners are better than those planned by builders. Many houseowners, their wives and daughters, have very clever ideas about building, and houses designed by owners are frequently charming. Builders' designs, however, are usually somewhat dull in appearance. The average builder is so much more familiar with construction than he is with design that his houses show lack of knowledge of the æsthetic side of the problem.

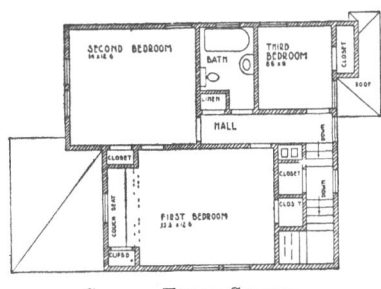

SECOND FLOOR SKETCH.

Houses designed by architects stand out in a class by themselves. It is truly remarkable what some clever experts have done in the way of house design, even in small houses where the expenditure was so slight one wonders how so much could be got with so little. The fact is, a skillful designer can get a pleasing architectural effect by spending very modest sums.

Every house must have a roof, doors, windows, and porches. These can be arranged with skill to produce a pleasing result, or, as is sometimes the case with an unskillful designer, they produce an ugly result. In each case the expenditure is the same. It doesn't cost any more to build an attractive house than an ugly one, and that is the reason highly trained designers are able to get such good results at the same cost. It is all a matter of skill, — and skill can be expected only of the skillful.

The accuracy of a set of working drawings is not the only quality about plans that is desirable. More than the actual draftsmanship of plans (which is mere mechanical work and the easiest part of the architects' profession) are the ideas contained in the plans. An owner who thinks he merely pays for a set of plans to build from is mistaken. He is really paying for years of study on the part of his architect, who has in most instances kept in touch with the best of the architectural work, not only in this country but abroad as well. One will see many sets of working drawings so poorly drawn (as far as neatness of drafting is concerned) that they are positively depressing to look upon. Nevertheless, these plans have that vital spark called "ideas." They contain mature thought, — evidence of genius-like ability to conceive a real masterpiece, and for that reason they are priceless, — far above many drawings mechanically better.

It isn't drawings the owner buys but a *complete house*, and if the working drawings are somewhat indifferently drawn it makes little difference so long as the *completed house* built from these plans is a success. Some of the world's greatest poems were published from manuscript covered with blots and scratches, and some of the most beautiful American houses have been built from plans untidy and ill made.

Most architects, however, are very particular about the draftsmanship of their plans. It is the constant effort of all conscientious designers to have drawings neatly made, with absolute accuracy. Any one who will examine drawings from the offices of architects in every section of the country will be much impressed with the care with which these drawings are made. As a matter of fact, architectural drawings are frequently more complete than need be, and the profession is to be congratulated upon the excellence of the drawings turned out in most architects' offices.

You will, then, probably employ an architect, for it is certainly to your best interests to do so; not merely to get from him a set of plans by which to build the house, but to secure the benefit of many meetings, at which you will discuss the various elements of your problem and get from your architect the unbiased advice that only a wise, conscientious, loyal counsellor can give. This is what the architect really is, — a sensible, experienced, educated advisor who prescribes for your needs much as your family physician or your lawyer.

The architect in his advisory capacity is of greatest benefit. It is so unsatisfactory to merely purchase plans and then attempt to build the house, yourself, for then you take on your own shoulders all the cares of supervision,— the petty annoyance of deciding the thousand and one little points that come up day by day while the house is in process of building. You are loaded down with a large amount of detailed work which can be more sensibly handled by an expert, — usually with more profit to yourself.

"What shall I expect of my architect," is so frequently asked it will be well to explain here the relations of architect and owner. So often, houseowners do not realize just what they should expect from an architect. Sometimes an owner is unreasonable in the demands he puts upon him. At other times he does not secure from his architect the full value of his services.

Regarding duties, the architect is, first of all, to receive your instructions concerning the little details that you wish incorporated in the plans. Most houseowners have more or less definite ideas about the arrangement of rooms and other matters pertaining to the problem, frequently going to their architect with sketch plans of the house as they wish it arranged. All this helps the architect to form an opinion concerning the likes and dislikes of his client, but the owner should be very careful not to insist upon any of his ideas being carried out if they prove impractical. Remember, most architects have had much more experience than their clients, and many of the desires of the owner are not suitable for the house. The client should go to his architect with a determination to consult him upon the points he has in mind, but without insisting that they be carried out. Adopting this method the owner will get from the architect his unbiased opinion — a very valuable acquisition from a reliable house designer. Let the architect, then, be the Court of Last Appeal; let him be your best friend, — the friend who is professionally bound to solve your problem in the best way. Remember, however, he is not the builder, and beyond a reasonable amount of supervision, you cannot expect him to be responsible for everything in the building.

You will usually find that the ideas you have in mind can be incorporated in the plans. Sometimes, however, it is impossible to carry them out, and when the architect has shown this to your satisfaction (as he ought to be able to do) you had better abandon them.

It is very desirable before selecting an architect to look about and examine different houses in your vicinity, bearing in mind that you can never completely judge an architect by his executed work. The reason for this is that sometimes an architect is forced by an unruly client to do a piece of work not quite up to the mark, — a client who, perhaps, demanding a character of plan and design not suitable, bore down so hard on his architect that he wore him out, securing from him a design which the architect's better nature would not have sanctioned. Therefore, when a prospective owner views a house which he thinks not altogether attractive he should ask himself, "how much of the fault was caused by the architect and how much by the client?"

In looking over houses with a view to selecting an architect, you should never be prejudiced by "style," as some owners are who are prone to form an opinion based upon their own preferences. For instance, one man looks over a Colonial house and pronounces it bad because it happens he does not enjoy Colonial designs. Another, who greatly enjoys the modern English style, will not enthuse over the pretty plaster houses of the Middle West, — different from English houses but quite as attractive in their way. In examining a design, make your criticism on the merits of the design itself, no matter what its style and regardless of your particular preferences. Ask yourself, "is the problem well solved? Did this architect give good service to his client? Was he wise in planning and designing, and was the construction skillfully handled?" These, and many other points will help you to form an opinion concerning the ability of the architect in question.

Every building project is more or less of a compromise. Very rarely is it possible for the owner to have all his wants gratified, especially when he must keep within the limits of a definite sum. The useful things must be taken care of first, then the æsthetic part of the problem can be considered. When it comes to supervision, remember that the architect is not merely a critic engaged to examine quality of materials and inspect workmanship. Drawings frequently need interpreting to the builder, who does not always understand the plans correctly, and this is part of the architect's duties, — a very useful part. Drawings, to the architect, are merely symbols or memoranda showing how the house is to be built. The completed structure is clear to his mind, but to convey this picture to the mind of the builder drawings are necessary. These drawings need to be explained to the builder, and the best interpreter, of course, is he who made them. In supervision do not expect your architect to spend all his time at the building, though enough attention should be given by him to properly inspect the job.

Cost is the great reef on which some houseowners are wrecked. It is very hard to determine beforehand the exact cost of the house-to-be, but a little investigation will help greatly to fix it. Of course, prices fluctuate. Materials cost more one year than another, and labor conditions are not at all constant. However, a practical builder can estimate the difference in cost quite accurately, and he usually knows the percentage of increase or decrease one year over another, without going too definitely into the details of building. Consultation with such a builder or with a good architect may save disappointment.

Many houseowners do not understand just how the contractor makes up his estimate. They think he looks over the plans, sizes up the building, and makes a sort of guess what it will cost. The actual facts are that the contractor carefully measures up the plans and finds out just how much lumber is required, how many brick, how much stone and other material. He computes quite accurately just how much labor will be required to build the house and then adds his percentage of profit, varying from 5 to 15 percent. In this way every square inch of house is accounted for. You cannot say, as so many inexperienced houseowners do, " We will make the living room one foot bigger — it will cost no more," for that extra foot adds its quota to the amount of the lumber bill, the plastering bill, painting, labor, and so on.

Those wishing to keep within the limits of a fixed sum will do well to determine beforehand the approximate number of square feet or cubic feet that can be built for the sum desired. This price varies in every town, but it can be readily ascertained by computing the square-foot price of a house of similar quality recently built in the same town. For instance, before you go into the details of building, inquire of some neighbor who has recently built, what his house cost. If the price was $4500 and the house contains 900 square feet of first-floor area, you may know that the cost per square foot was $5, and you may feel fairly safe in assuming that you can build a good house for the same price. Most moderate-cost houses nowadays are trimmed and finished in about the same way, — with oak or wood of equal cost in living room, dining room, and hall, and soft wood, painted, on the second floor, so the square-foot price holding in your town may be usually taken as a safe average, except in large houses, where conditions may be different. If your idea is to include a great deal of built-in furniture, however, and beams or paneling, you must add something to the square-foot price.

As an example of the difference in prices consult the following: —

TABLE OF COMPARATIVE COSTS

Birmingham, Alabama . . . . 12 cents per cu. ft.
Portland, Maine . . . . 15 cents per cu. ft.
Philadelphia . . . . $18\frac{1}{4}$ cents per cu. ft.
Boston . . . . $21\frac{1}{2}$ cents per cu. ft.
Minneapolis . . . . $16\frac{1}{2}$ cents per cu. ft.
New York . . . . $22\frac{1}{2}$ cents per cu. ft.
Colorado Springs . . . . 15 cents per cu. ft.
Chicago . . . . $21\frac{3}{4}$ cents per cu. ft.

After determining the cubic-foot or square-foot price, you know the total size that can be built in your town for a certain sum. Then you can intelligently consider your plans with little fear that the house will overrun your appropriation — that is, if you hold it down tight and keep carefully within limits. In your $4500 house with 900-foot area, allowing $5 per square foot, the first floor may be 45 by 20 feet or $35\frac{1}{2}$ by

25½ feet. The exact shape of the house makes no great difference in cost, so long as the building is rectangular, with not too many projecting wings or bays.

When you have, through observation or acquaintance, selected the architect you wish to do your work, call upon him and lay before him the sketches, drawings, or notes which you may have been collecting for years. Open your heart and tell him everything about the new house and your ideas concerning its planning and design. Naturally, at this first interview you will touch upon the amount of the architect's fee, so it might be well to say a few words here about architects' charges. As most people know, architects' fees are based upon a percentage of the cost of the building. For instance, if a house costs $10,000 the architect's fee would be a certain percentage of that cost, such as 7 or 10 per cent. Years ago charges made by architects were at a much lower rate than they are to-day; sometimes as low as 3 to 5 per cent of the cost of the building. Thus, in those days one could sometimes get plans, specifications, and supervision on a $10,000 house for 3 per cent, or $300. A few years later the majority of reputable architects charged 5 per cent for the same service, — an allowance of $500 for a $10,000 house.

The present increase in architects' fees is owing partly to the increased cost of living, which obliges the architect to pay his employees higher salaries (besides costing him more for his own living expenses), and partly to the increased amount of work now demanded of an architect. He is more highly trained than his predecessors of twenty-five or thirty years ago. Modern methods of building are more complicated, — houses are more scientific, and more time must be spent by the architect in making drawings and in supervising the work.

The present rate charged by most architects varies somewhat according to the section of the country in which they practice, but the American Institute of Architects (the leading organization of architects in the United States), recommends a rate which is accepted by most architects and owners as fair and just. This rate consists of a minimum charge of 6 per cent for complete service on houses costing upwards of $10,000 (which includes sketches, drawings, specifications, and supervision); for houses costing less than $10,000 the charge is usually 10 per cent. This is the minimum rate most often charged by reputable architects. As a matter of fact, many architects in or near large cities charge a minimum of 10 per cent on all houses, regardless of size or cost.

It is more difficult to design small houses costing less than $10,000, than houses costing more, for there is so little money to spend on a small house (and this expenditure must cover so many necessary requirements) it takes a great amount of skill to produce a successful small house. Consequently, architects usually spend more time (proportionate to the amount received) on small house designs than they do on larger houses, and thus a higher rate of commission is charged.

Nothing requires greater skill on the part of an architect than house planning and supervision. Countless details not found in factory work, apartment buildings, stores, and other structures, are required in house building, and for this reason architects' charges on house work are usually more than they are for other buildings.

When you have consulted with your architect, discussing your views with him and arranging satisfactorily the amount you are to pay for his services, it is time for him to begin a set of sketches showing the arrangement of rooms and his suggestions for the exterior. Before proceeding with sketches, you should tell the architect frankly the amount you wish to spend for the house, complete, so that he can consider the cost in the preliminary steps of his design. It is very hard to determine the exact cost of a projected house, but experienced architects who have been in touch with conditions for many years, knowing what houses have cost, can estimate quite accurately. As corroboration of this estimated cost the architect can usually get a builder to make an estimate from sketches, before working drawings are made. In this way, if the preliminary estimate on a house indicates that it will cost more than the owner cares to spend, the owner knows it before the working drawings are made, and he can decide what is best to do, either cutting down the size of the house or increasing his building allowance.

A set of sketches usually consists of first and second-floor plans drawn to scale and an exterior perspective. Sometimes a sketch or two showing portions of the interior are included. It is not usually necessary to work out basement and attic plans on the preliminary sketches. After the owner receives the sketches, he takes them home and looks them over carefully, noting the arrangement of rooms. It is up to him to make a careful study of the plans to determine whether they suit him or not. Then he may have conferences with the architect, discussing certain changes which he believes necessary. If these changes are practical and it is mutually agreed that they are for the best, a revised set of sketches is prepared incorporating the new ideas. One or two more sets of sketches may be necessary before architect and owner are completely satisfied with the arrangement of rooms and the design of façades. Then it is time to get a preliminary estimate from the builder to determine the approximate cost of the house. Some builders will not make up a detailed preliminary estimate unless they are paid for it, which is quite reasonable, after all, as it is considerable of a job, requiring several days' time. You can usually get this service from a builder for from $10 up, and it is well worth any reasonable price, as information of this kind is of utmost value to an owner who wishes to know in advance something about the cost of his house.

When the sketches have been approved by the owner, and the estimate is received from a builder, decision can be made whether to proceed with the working drawings according to the sketches, or to add to or deduct from the size of the house. Then the architect begins his working drawings and specifications, getting them ready for the final bids. During this process of making the working drawings and specifications, numerous conferences will

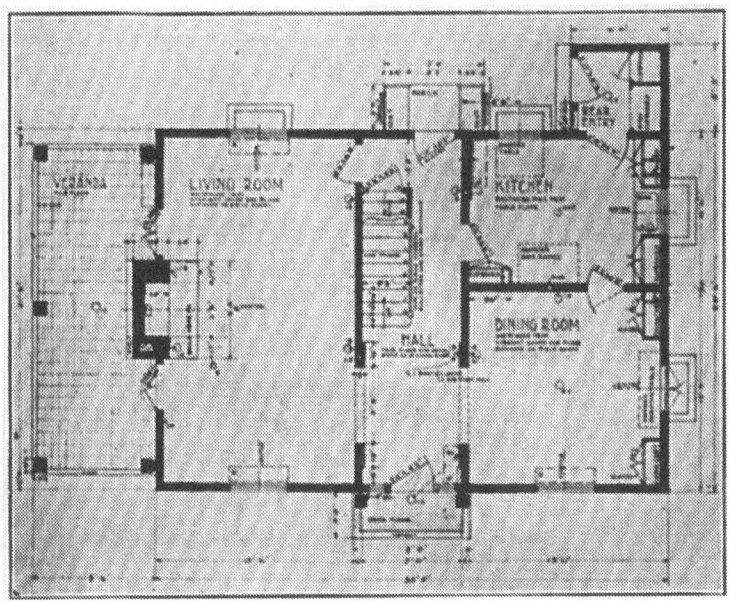

FIRST FLOOR PLAN FROM THE ARCHITECT'S WORKING DRAWINGS.
Charles E. White, Jr., Architect.

be necessary between client and architect to determine the kind of finish wanted in different rooms, details of plumbing and heating, and other matters pertaining to the completed dwelling. The owner should follow the process of plan-making closely enough so that he will understand all the details of his house. Nothing is more disappointing to an architect than to hear the owner exclaim after the house is built, "Why, I don't like that,

82 SUCCESSFUL HOUSES AND HOW TO BUILD THEM

— I thought it was to be different." Usually the architect has a very complete idea about the finished building even before the first shovelful of earth is dug. Good working drawings contain details for every part of the building carried out with great care, and the owner should study drawings carefully before contracts are let, so that he will understand every part of

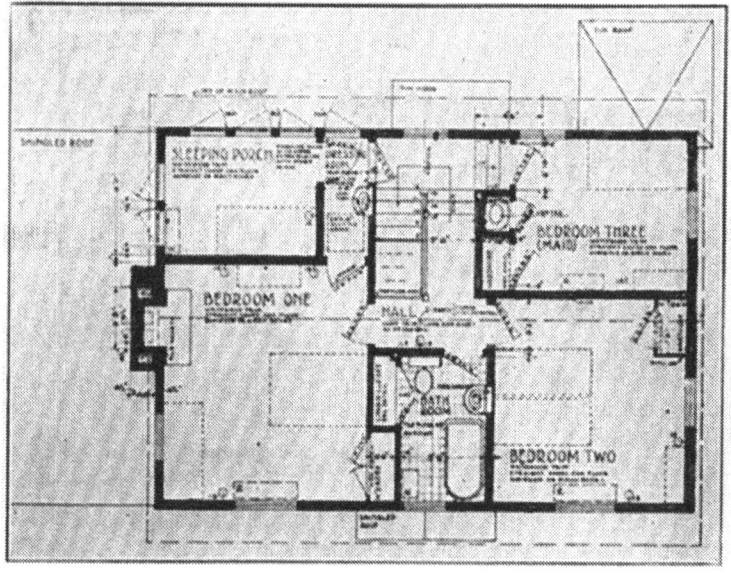

SECOND FLOOR PLAN.

the house and know just as much about it as his architect. This will save disappointment later.

Let all changes be made before the contracts are let, — and then stick to the plans. This is much the more practical way; better than making repeated changes as the work proceeds, at the risk of spoiling the design and causing greater expenditure of money for "extras."

A set of working drawings usually consists of basement plan, first floor plan, second floor plan, attic plan, four elevations, one or two interior sections (showing interior design and construction), and enough details to inform the contractor just how the house is to be built. Sometimes these details are drawn to a large scale (or full size) and sometimes to a small scale, the idea being to give sufficient information to contractors to enable them to make intelligent bids. Incidentally, these details also

help the houseowner to understand just what kind of a house he may expect. He should examine all drawings carefully to make sure they are in accordance with his wishes.

Any reputable architect is competent to design every part of the house without conference with the owner, but if the owner wishes to have the house entirely satisfactory to himself it is up to him to watch the details and see that they are according to his own ideas. Of course, the architect should be the technical advisor.

The details accompanying working drawings usually show pantry cases, dining room paneling, living room beamed ceilings, built-in furniture, main staircase, cupboards, outside cornices, and other parts of the house not easy to describe in the specifications. Usually these details are drawn to a small scale

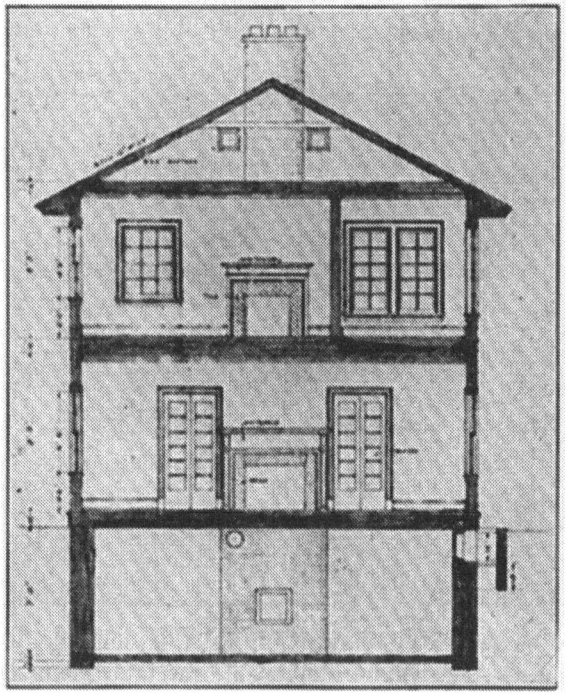

CROSS SECTION SHOWING INTERIOR.

at first, more to show the idea to competing bidders than to provide drawings to build from. Later, after the contracts are let, the details are elaborated into larger drawings for the workmen to follow in building.

The number of these drawings required is usually determined

OWNER, ARCHITECT, AND CONTRACTOR 85

by the architect. If reliable, he will be only too willing to make all the details required for the execution of the work. Most architects dislike impractical or ugly interior and exterior finish, and they take every means to prevent such by making accurate details of every part of the work.

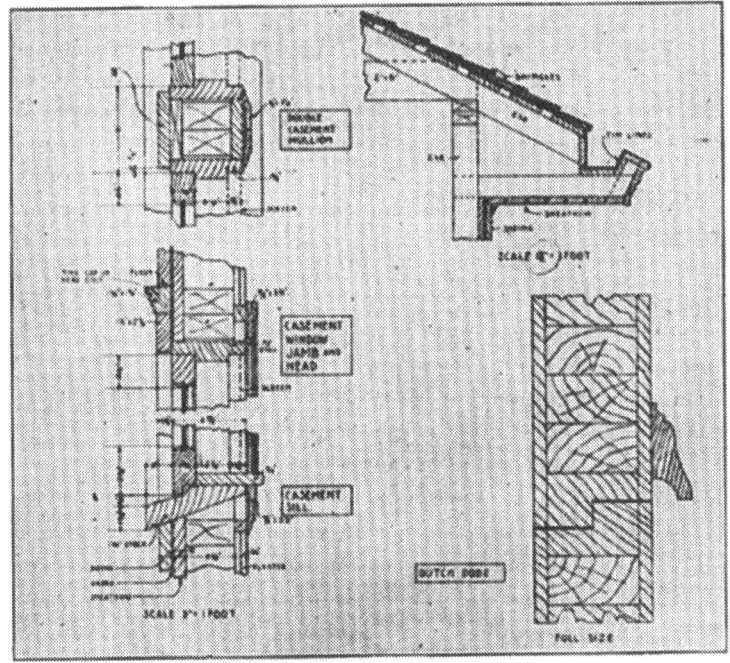

Sheet of Details.

Before he starts sketches, the architect is expected to visit the building site, if it is anywhere within reach of his office. Laying out the floor plan does not consist merely in putting together a certain sequence of rooms according to the ideas of the owner. It consists, rather, in making a complete study of the conditions, designing the building in such a way as to properly fulfill them.

Frequently owners make the mistake of working out the exact arrangement of rooms themselves, then taking these sketches to an architect with the admonition, "This is what we want. Put an exterior on it." That is not the wisest way to proceed if the owner wishes to get the best service out of his architect. Such a procedure is akin to going to a family physician with the statement, "Doctor, I have a little touch of malaria; give me some quinine pills." You expect your physician to diagnose your condition and then prescribe what his judgment and experience lead him to think are best for your particular case. The architect really acts in the same capacity; he studies your problem from all sides and then is able to form some opinion as to the best method of treatment which, in the case of a house, consists of the proper arrangement of rooms and the best design for the exterior. It is part of his problem to make something which you like, of course, but it is very foolish for an owner to demand a certain arrangement of rooms unless the architect, after proper consideration, decides that it is best. His knowledge is usually better than the owner's, so it is wiser to be guided by what he recommends.

When it comes to selecting a builder the same care must be taken that is used in selecting an architect, for one must not expect an architect to get good results with poor tools. No matter how carefully the building may be inspected, an unscrupulous contractor can always slip inferior work through, — somewhere, — sometime, — work that may escape the most vigilant inspection of the owner and architect.

The time to practice wisdom in selecting a builder is at the start, when contractors are invited to submit bids, by inviting only reliable men to bid on the job. If only high-grade builders are invited, the job can be safely let to any one of them, with every assurance that the contract will be properly carried out. The lowest bid is not necessarily the one to accept; but if the lowest bid is from a reliable party, it saves complications to accept that bid. Contractors sometimes take exceptions if an owner lets his contract to a bidder whose tender is not the lowest, and this is not strange when you realize the amount of time used by contractors in good faith. Unless there is a weighty reason why the lowest bidder should not get the job, his bid ought to be accepted.

Whether to let a general contract for the entire building or let separate contracts for each branch of the work is largely a matter of policy to be decided on each job. Taking separate sub-bids frequently lessens the cost of the building to the owner, but on the other hand this method requires more care in keeping track of the job, involving as it does so many separate contracts. Before the contract is let to a builder, the owner should be sure that the contractor is financially able to carry on the work, for in the event of a builder not paying his bills the owner may become liable for the amount of all material and labor used on his house. Liens can be put on the property by creditors of the builder, and the owner would have to settle before he could get a clear title to his property. In order to transfer this responsibility to the shoulders of others it is a good idea for the owner to require the contractor to furnish a bond. Bonds are usually procured by the contractor, himself, from some reliable bonding company. The price paid is approximately $\frac{1}{2}$ of 1 per cent, and the price of the bond is charged to the amount of the building contract, thus eventually being paid by the owner. Bonds are sometimes made at 80 per cent of the value of the building contract, or frequently for the entire value, depending upon the reliability of the contractor and his financial standing. As an example, if the general contract for a house is let at $5000 the contractor would be required to furnish a bond for $4000 (80 per cent) or for the entire amount of $5000. This bond would cost the contractor about $20 to $25, and such amount would be added to the contract price to reimburse the contractor for the price of the bond.

The chief value of a bond is that it transfers responsibility for faithful execution of the contract from the shoulders of the owner to the bonding company. The latter is compelled to look up a contractor's reliability before they issue a bond to him, and this bond guarantees the owner that his agreement with the contractor will be properly carried out to completion, regardless of the financial condition of the builder.

After the house is completed, remember, you cannot expect to move in and feel immediately at home. The new house will seem strange at first, different as it is from the house in which you have been living. You must adjust yourself to these new conditions. You must not expect the new house to adjust itself to you, and entering the new home in this spirit you will doubtless find it a success in every way.

SMALL HOUSE WITH LARGE PORCH ON ONE CORNER.

CHAPTER VI

PLANNING THE ROOMS

NOTWITHSTANDING the homage paid to old-fashioned houses, it is true that skillful planning will produce an arrangement of rooms much superior. Modern housekeeping is on such different lines from housekeeping of even a few years ago that the problem of planning is on an entirely different footing. In a general way, of course, the arrangement of rooms is not dissimilar. For instance, many houses are built with a hall in the center and rooms on both sides, just as they were in olden times, and this arrangement is as practical to-day as it was yesterday, but there are many other arrangements now that would not have been practical years ago. Much has been done in these days of quickened public taste and improved building methods to perfect plan and design, in spite of the fact that houses cost more than formerly.

In planning a house, one of the first considerations is cost — for cost will largely determine size, shape, and style of the building. Cost of houses will be found to vary in every town. For instance, in some places where brick kilns are near at hand, brick is low in cost. Lumber varies in cost several dollars per thousand feet in different sections of the country, and all other materials entering into the construction of a house differ as much. Labor cost varies in each locality, being from $3 per day to $5 or more. All these facts must enter into the calculations of the designer. He must bear in mind cost of the detailed parts of the house before he can attack the problem scientifically.

After the first $3000 set aside for the new house, values increase very fast. In these days of high-priced material and labor $3000 will not build a very large house and build it well. But the next $1000 or $1500 makes quite a difference in the size it is possible to get for the money. An ideal minimum price for a moderate-sized, comfortable house is $4500 to $6000, such prices usually allowing three or four bedrooms. Houses of less cost are frequently as successful, though they must be smaller.

In comparing the higher cost of building to-day with the lower cost of building yesterday, one should remember that present-day houses are more convenient than houses of long ago. Quaint and charming as they were, old-fashioned houses lacked many things to make life comfortable. Planning was not so well understood. Scientific housekeeping had not been developed to such an extent, and the housewife took many unnecessary steps in performing her daily tasks. Consider the typical house of to-day, with its labor-saving devices, — modern methods for heating, vacuum cleaner, and ever ready hot water for the bath, and it will be found to be very much in advance of houses of even fifteen or twenty years ago; improved in kitchen and pantry arrangements and the little conveniences so highly prized by housekeepers.

Modern houses of the best class are marvels of skillful design and clever planning. Every inch costs something to build, so when the houseowner considers his expenditure in advance of building he must be careful to apply his money where it will do the most good. In planning a $3500 house, do not apply to it some of the features you have noticed in a $15,000 house. The former is necessarily of a different type from the latter, though it may easily be as attractive.

"Save space" is the watchword for a successful house plan, large or small. Owners should study the plans over and over again. After the rooms are sketched out, go over them carefully and see if you can eliminate any waste space. Remember, a good arrangement of rooms depends more upon ingenuity than it does on expenditure. Dollars will not take the place of brains, and for that reason the successful small house often contains more features really livable and enjoyable than houses of thrice the cost.

The shape of a house has much to do with its possibilities of plan, rectangular houses permitting a better arrangement of rooms than square houses, though owners have been told for years that "square houses are best." The most economical arrangement is a hall in the center with living rooms on two sides, on the first story, and one bedroom in each corner on the second story. Thus, with the hall in the center, you have a rectangle instead of a square, and this is not only the most economical shape but the most pleasing, as well.

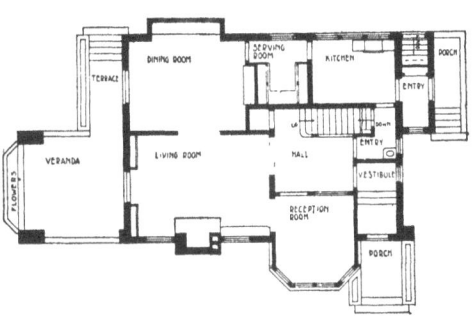

First Floor Plan; Compact Arrangement.

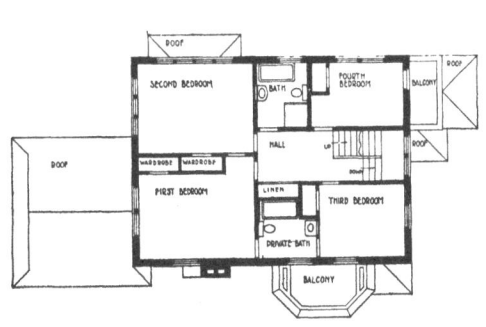

Second Floor Plan.

Floor plans also depend upon the shape of the lot and location of the house upon it. With a frontage of 60 to 75 feet it is an excellent plan to place a house broadside to the street, and by clever planning this can frequently be accomplished, even on the 50-foot lot. Broadside houses look larger and give a greater amount of space exposed toward the front and rear of the lot; usually the desirable thing to do. In a broad-side-to-the-front house a popular plan is to arrange the dining room on one side of the central hall with living room on the other. Such an arrangement is practical and usually attractive, but it is interesting to see that all designers do not treat their houses the same.

Under some conditions it is practical to have the dining room on the front of the house, but in other houses such a plan would be quite impossible. For such as these the dining room can be placed at the rear of the house reached by a broad opening from the living room. Formerly wide openings were closed by sliding doors, until it was found that sliding doors were almost never closed. Then designers began leaving out the doors, and they have been omitted ever since,—a distinct improvement.

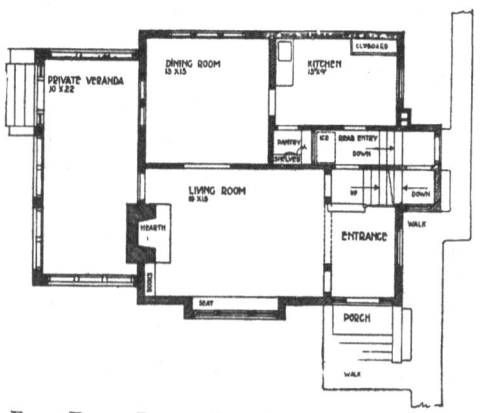

FIRST FLOOR PLAN; GOOD ARRANGEMENT FOR A NARROW LOT.

Many houses are spoiled by having a porch extend entirely across the front, where it is almost certain to darken the living room and rarely ever adds to the attractiveness of the house. A newer and more practical idea is to put the porch at one end, plunging it boldly out from the building to the required distance. Built thus, it makes a pleasing feature outside as well as inside and keeps no light from the living room.

PLANNING THE ROOMS 95

To get the best results, an arrangement of rooms should not be according to any house the owner may have seen. The most practical floor plans are entirely the product of conditions, such as characteristics of building site, amount of money to be spent, size of owner's family, and general type or style of building. Instead of the latter, perhaps it would be more correct to say that the style of the proposed building should be more or less influenced by the floor plans as well as the characteristics of the building site. For

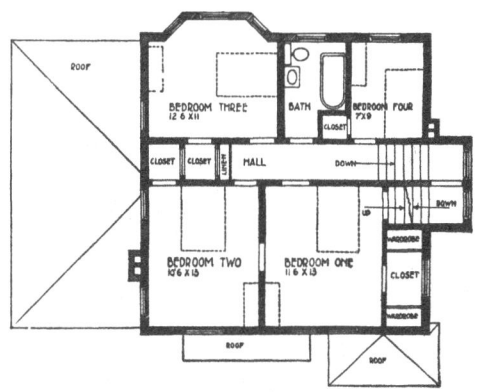

SECOND FLOOR PLAN.

instance, on a wild, irregular site on the edge of a cliff, one might find that a house in the Colonial style would be out of place, not being in harmony with its surroundings. A more picturesque style, such as modern English, might be very much better. That is why plans deliberately copied from a house built on another site are rarely successful. An architect who has built a house on one spot rarely finds that it could be reproduced elsewhere, unless the conditions at the new site are precisely the same as they were on the old; a most unusual condition, surely. Although preconceived notions about the new house on the part of the owner may suggest what style of architecture and arrangement of rooms to use, these facts should be nothing more than a starting point to the designer. Many a houseowner, during the period of dreaming over his house plans, makes the mistake of fixing his ideas about an arrangement of rooms which he has seen in some other

96 SUCCESSFUL HOUSES AND HOW TO BUILD THEM

house, without determining whether it is adaptable to his own lot.

An inside lot requires a very different house from a corner lot. In the first place, if it is not greater than 50 feet wide (and many are not) the inside lot has less light on the sides than a

EXCELLENT TYPE FOR A SMALL LOT.
Claude F. Bragdon, Architect.

corner lot. This means a narrower house with more windows in each room, taking care to provide sufficient space between the new house and its neighbors to give good light and air. Remember that the view from the windows of a house on an inside lot is more restricted. This brings about quite a number of complications not occurring in a corner house where the front and one side (along the two streets) permit an unobstructed view from the windows. For instance, consider the living room of a house on an inside lot. Living room windows should be placed to permit a clear view outside, for it is in the living room that members of the family sit most often. Then the living room will probably be on the front of the house with low front windows looking out on the street. At the side of such a living room high windows can be used, if the house stands close to its neighbors. High windows let in light, but they prevent an unattractive view of some neighboring wall which may well be shut out.

On an inside lot, with the living room placed in this manner, the correct location for the front entrance and porch should be a matter of careful consideration. For a 50-foot inside lot a house with entrance hall in the middle is frequently not desirable. On the other hand, having a living room across the front, one would be obliged to walk right through it to enter the house. Sometimes a more practical arrangement is to put the entrance hall at one corner, conveniently near the staircase. Such a plan gives the maximum of living room on the front, with unobstructed front windows.

First Floor Plan of House illustrated on Page 96.

H

98 SUCCESSFUL HOUSES AND HOW TO BUILD THEM

Some houses are built on lots 40 feet wide, but it is rare that such a narrow site successfully accommodates the average modern house. Much better is a 50-foot lot, and twice that width is greatly to be preferred.

In planning your house for an inside lot, the principal bedroom should be over the living room. With an east or west front, it is well to build the house well toward the north line, so as to have as wide a yard at the south side of the house as possible. Then on this south side lo-

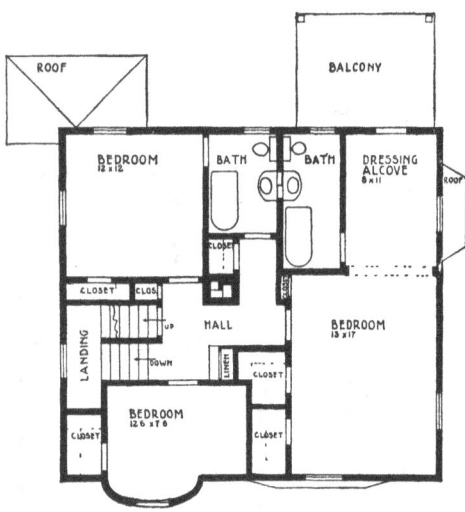

SECOND FLOOR PLAN.

cate the living room and bedrooms you care most about. Inside lots require careful consideration to get the utmost of value from them, and it is quite wonderful what success one may have by skillful planning. Some houses facing east or west are placed as close as 4 feet from the north line. This leaves ample space for a walk to the back entrance. If your neighbor's house is also close up to his north line, a wide strip of open yard at the south of his house will light the north side of your house, so you really get the benefit of his land. Of course if your neighbor puts his house close to his south line, you must locate yours a corresponding distance from your north line to get the correct distance between both houses.

The next step in planning is to consider the size of the family.

How many bedrooms are required? Bedrooms determine the size of a house as much as anything. With only three principal rooms downstairs, — living room, dining room, and kitchen (as is customary now in most houses), a house may be larger or smaller without affecting the downstairs arrangement par-

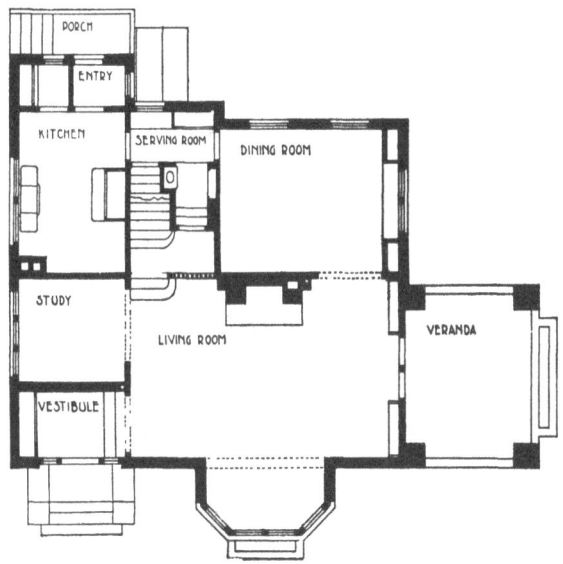

First Floor Plan showing Living Room of Unusual Size.

ticularly. But the second story is not so easily disposed of. A certain number of bedrooms are required, and the house must be large enough to get them in. Five bedrooms require a larger house than three bedrooms, so it is well to consider the number needed even before the first story is planned; then the first story can be made to conform to the required size of the second.

Naturally, in designing a house the exterior should be considered as well as the interior. It will not do to work out floor plans and then try to fit an exterior to them. While the floor plans are developing in your mind, the exterior appearance of the house should be well thought out. Then your house will be a success, æsthetically, as well as scientifically.

The modern living room is usually a large room. In a house costing $4000 or $5000 the living room is seldom less than 14

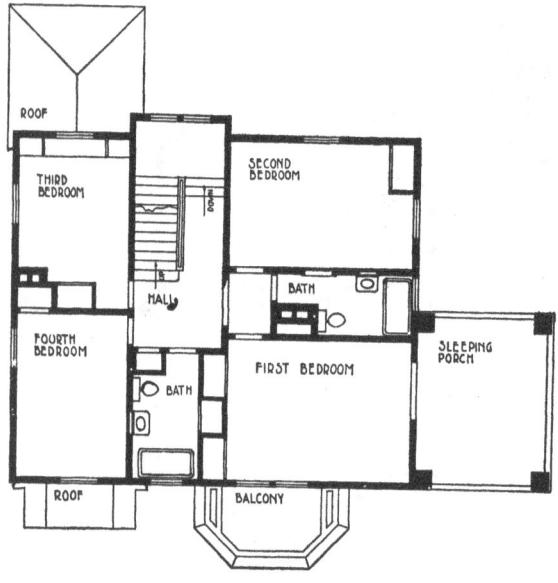

SECOND FLOOR PLAN.

feet by 18 feet, and it is frequently larger. If the house is broadside to the street the living room will naturally be placed on one end of the house, toward the south, perhaps, as the south sun is desirable at all times of the year. There should be plenty of windows in a living room, and when there is no library or reception room it is well to provide an alcove to contain the library table and bookcases. In many of the most successful houses an alcove is also provided for the piano, frequently arranged with glass doors which can be closed while the piano is being used, but may be left open at other times. Another practical idea is to use the alcove as a sort of reception room where one may receive guests who drop in for a little while.

Bay windows are very practical in the living room, and there are many ways to treat them. It is possible to use high windows with bookcases underneath, or the bay may be large enough and windows low enough so one can sit there and get a good view down the street.

Special consideration for the women of the family makes necessary a place somewhere in the living room where they may settle down for little tasks after the morning work is done. Sewing, darning, embroidery, and other handwork may be done in the living room, as well as the clerical work of the house, so the room must be for work as well as play; it should be just the sort of cheerful, cozy, sunny, restful place you will be glad to turn to whenever the occasion arises.

In some cases the living room table is well placed with one end against the wall. Determine its location by the purely utilitarian fact of greatest convenience. Across the corner is the least desirable place. Furniture rectangular in shape, like tables, pianos, settles, or benches, always looks best when placed with one side parallel with the wall of the room. Rugs are better the same way, — not scattered hit or miss over the floor. Chairs may be placed promiscuously, but other pieces should be arranged in an orderly manner. Books neatly stacked upon the table with bindings all the same way and parallel with the table edge look strikingly attractive. Never pile them up crisscross, with edges facing different directions. If you will experiment with your living room and arrange it once in the manner suggested, you will never change back to the old helter-skelter method.

To further carry out the idea of spaciousness, living rooms in modern houses frequently open broadly through wide openings into the hall and dining room. Since omitting sliding doors the tendency in many houses has been to make openings between rooms even larger than usual, frequently eight feet wide or more. In other cases, where it is desired to close off the dining room or hall at times, glass doors are hung in the openings. Ordinarily these stand open, but they can be closed at any time, and closed or open the effect is very pretty.

From the living room a porch or large veranda should be directly accessible, for in these days of outdoor living the veranda is one of the most important parts of the house. It is made large and roomy in houses of best design, — more like an outdoor room than an ordinary veranda.

Dining rooms are similar to those in old-fashioned houses, though modern rooms are more scientifically planned, being frequently smaller than former dining rooms, though equally as efficient. It is the present-day custom of the most skillful architects to build a dining room around the dining table. In other words, the architect in planning the room considers, first, the size of the table, then the necessary number of chairs and amount of space required for them. Added to this, he reckons the amount of space necessary for serving, and the result gives the minimum size of the room. To this net result he adds as much space as he desires for architectural effect, — more in large houses or less in small houses. All modern planning is scientifically done in this way, and for this reason modern houses are much more practical than old-fashioned houses, in which space was not so conservatively utilized.

In planning a dining room one should consider, first, in what part of the house such a room will be most practical, remembering that the dining room is usually considered more of a night room than a day room and need not, therefore, occupy the choicest spot in the house. It is desirable, of course, to place it on the east side of the house, where it will get the morning sun (for nothing is prettier than a cheery morning dining room), but one should not sacrifice the living room in order to bring this about. A north or south dining room can be made very satisfactory. Least desirable of all locations is the west side, where the late afternoon sun in summer always makes a hot room, proving particularly unpleasant for the dinner at night (although this annoyance can sometimes be overcome by using a porch to screen the west windows, or by the judicious use of awnings).

A large dining room is not at all necessary. Some dining rooms are as narrow as 12 feet, — indeed, many fairly good rooms are as narrow as 10 feet at one point where a sideboard projects. Often a narrow dining room can be made more spacious by adding a small bay window at one side. The sideboard can be put in this bay so that it will not project into the room.

The dining room is not considered as important regarding light and view as the living room. As it is really used but a surprisingly short time each day, during meals, the outlook from the room need not be of the best. However, a pleasant view into the garden is always delightful, and this is the ideal to aim for.

If a round table is to be used, the dining room may be made nearly square, though it should be 18 inches to 2 feet longer on the side where the sideboard is to stand. To get the minimum size of the room, measure the table you intend to use, including chairs, placed at the positions they would occupy around the table. Add to this space about two feet behind the

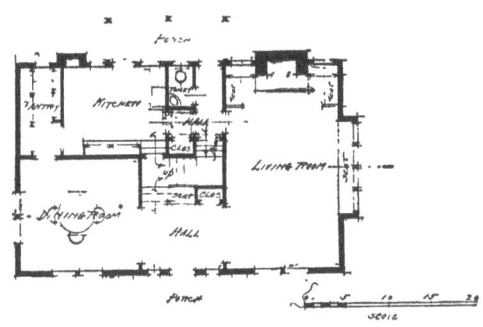

SQUARE DINING ROOM.

chairs for serving, and you will have the net result. In testing the size in this way, you will find that a room 12 feet square is the least size desirable for an ordinary round table 6 feet in diameter, accommodating six people. Of course it is desirable to make the room larger when possible. Dining rooms 12' 6" by 14' are quite satisfactory for small houses. Long dining rooms are particularly effective in houses of large size. A room 17 or 18 feet by 20 or 22 feet is in good proportion.

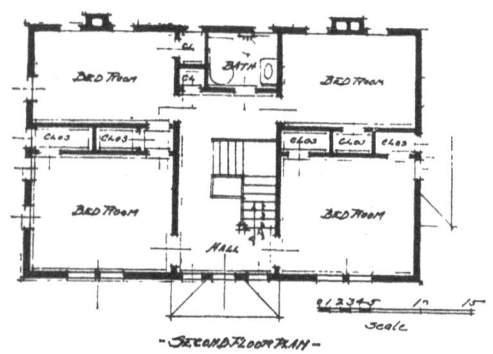

A GOOD FOUR-BEDROOM PLAN.

Fireplaces are practical in the dining room, more for ventilation and architectural effect, we are free to confess, than because they are really useful. Unless a room be quite large, even a small fire in the grate is apt to make the room too warm. If you are planning to build but one fireplace in the house, put it in the living room, by all means, — not in the dining room or hall. A dining room fireplace may sometimes be desirable, but it certainly is not necessary.

If you build a bay window in the dining room, do not put a window seat in it. A little reflection will convince any one that a dining room window seat is used very little, — only, perhaps, while serving refreshments during a reception. The balance of time it uselessly occupies valuable space under the window. As a matter of fact, window seats are rarely comfortable, since it is almost impossible to provide a good back for them, without pushing the windows up so high they are spoiled so far as lighting the room is concerned. Then, cold air blows down one's neck, making window seats uncomfortable in winter. They do look cozy, though even this pretty effect is usually more theatrical than is strictly consistent in a sensible house.

Sometimes a little window seat is built in to cover the radiator, which might otherwise mar the appearance of the paneled wall of the dining room. For this purpose, perhaps, seats are permissible, but it should be remembered that radiators covered in this way are less efficient and must be made much larger. In many successful dining rooms sideboard and china closets are built in. Frequently the sideboard is built into the bay window or alcove. A growing prevalence, however, is for omission of a built-in sideboard, many preferring to buy one ready-made.

Generally speaking, a sideboard looks best when it is at one side of the dining room in the center of the wall. A little careful planning usually makes this possible. If there is a pretty garden visible from the dining room, it is well to have a wide group of three or four windows looking out upon it. Windows like this make the room seem larger.

Two doors are usually placed between kitchen and dining room by means of a little corridor, serving room, or pantry between the two rooms. These two doors are not absolutely necessary, however, notwithstanding popular opinion, for it has been discovered that often the second door (in the kitchen) stands open constantly, and yet odors from cooking are not apparent in other rooms. In houses where a gas range is ventilated by means of a hood connected with the kitchen chimney, one door between kitchen and dining room has been found to be practical. In many cases, much space can be saved by a single door arrangement, and for this reason it is frequently desirable for small houses. Two doors should be employed when possible, however, more particularly on account of noise in the kitchen, which sometimes penetrates the house unpleasantly when only one door is used.

106 SUCCESSFUL HOUSES AND HOW TO BUILD THEM

Modern ideas concerning the hall are very different from old notions. Formerly, even up to within eight or ten years ago, the hall was large, frequently so much space being devoted to it that other rooms were slighted. This tendency has been, happily, corrected, and in many houses halls are now reduced to

DINING ROOM OPENING ON AN INCLOSED PORCH.

the minimum. In a hall-in-the-center house, if the hall is 20 to 25 feet long it can be 8 to 10 feet wide in order to preserve good proportions, but in small houses halls are frequently less in length, in which case they may be narrower. Wide doorways from the living room make a hall look larger, so that, treated in this way, even a small hall can be made to present an attractive appearance.

Many times in a small house it is practical to omit the hall, extending the stairs up directly from the living room. Stairs placed in this way should be conveniently near the front entrance in order that one may pass to the second floor without taking too many steps. Even more important is the distance from kitchen to main staircase. This should be as short as

HALL IN A COLONIAL HOUSE.

possible. Rarely is it practical to have a separate, rear staircase in small houses, as the valuable space such an arrangement calls for cannot be spared; nor is the second staircase necessary or even desirable. In a little house, it is perfectly practical to depend upon a single one. For larger houses, a combination staircase, in which stairs from the kitchen join the main stairs halfway up, is desirable. Large houses should be provided with separate front and rear stairs from first to second stories, one staircase being sufficient, usually, for basement and attic. If there is a billiard room in the attic or basement, however, a separate staircase is frequently desirable, — one more attractive, architecturally, than ordinary "back stairs."

In sketching out his first ideas for a staircase, the owner should bear in mind that just so much space is required for each riser and tread, and sufficient head room must be provided.

In large houses, where the hall is to be treated in an important way, allow plenty of space for chairs and tables, and provide wall space for pictures. Fireplaces add to the attractiveness of halls, though they are not considered necessary. Modern tendencies trend toward reducing the number of fireplaces, too many being found wasteful of space and somewhat of a burden to keep clean. Many practical houses have a large fireplace merely in the living room, with perhaps a smaller one in one bedroom.

A reception room is used chiefly at night, and then rather infrequently. Thus, the reception room should be located on the north side (or least desirable side of the house), in order to preserve more favorable locations for more important rooms. In designing this room, one should remember that a reception room is provided to make a place for casual callers, in order to reserve the living room for the more private family group. Do not make the mistake of placing it far from the entrance door. A reception room misses its function entirely unless it is located where callers can enter without disturbing persons seated in the living room or dining room. To get this result it is often located adjacent to the entrance hall or vestibule, and a clever arrangement is to place the reception room so that it can be opened into the hall or living room when a large reception is given, but closed off at other times. This can be accomplished by hanging glass doors in the broad opening to hall or living room, kept closed ordinarily, but easily opened when the occasion arises.

Another practical way to provide for a reception room is to build a sort of alcove off the hall or living room, partially screened by plaster partitions extending up about 6 feet but left open at the top, or filled with open balusters. Thus, the little reception room is not unpleasantly disconnected from the rest of the house, though it is quite private. In many houses the reception room is combined with a music room containing the piano and music cabinet, in which case the designer must be careful to make it large enough, or music will not sound well.

Where possible it is good practice to have a separate music room, permitting the family to break up into little groups and making it possible to use the piano without annoying others. Any one who has ever tried to read when young people are singing at the piano will appreciate a separate music room. The following table, showing sizes of pianos, can be used in determining space required: —

APPROXIMATE SIZES OF STANDARD PIANOS

	HEIGHT	LENGTH	WIDTH
Upright	about 4 ft. 5 in.	5 ft. 2 in.	2 ft. 4 in.
Small or Baby Grand .	about 3 ft. 1 in.	6 ft. 0 in.	4 ft. 9 in.
Parlor Grand	about 3 ft. 4 in.	7 ft. 8 in.	5 ft. 0 in.

The library is designed for many different purposes. Some libraries are of considerable size, required to hold a thousand volumes, others are small and cozy, more in the nature of a den. Here, again, we may consider the library as chiefly a "night room" and place it in the least desirable location. With the exception of Sunday, at few times in the day is a library occupied, — at least, that is the case in most houses. A library should open from the hall, if possible, to be of convenient access, and it should be well ventilated by having plenty of windows, as it is most frequently used as a smoking room. Fireplaces are excellent ventilators. In several cleverly designed small houses ventilators have been built in to carry away the smoke. Often, the library is placed in a little, single-story wing, and in such cases the ventilator can be placed in the roof, directly above the room. The library should be, above all else, a quiet room. It

LIVING ROOM WITH ALCOVE DEN.

is designed primarily for readers, and for this reason a library should be closed off from other rooms by means of doors. When convenient, it is good practice to have two doors between the library and other parts of the house, an arrangement made possible by having the entrance to the room through a little lobby, with doors hung both sides.

For a den one may have the smallest room imaginable, and

it will be perfectly practical, if well arranged. A good location for the den is under the landing of the main stairs. To get head room you may go down a few steps from the main hall. A little bay window will help to make the room larger, and sufficient light and air will be provided. Especially when there is no library is it extremely desirable to include a den

INCLOSED VERANDA.

or office in the house where the business man may have his desk and shut himself and his work away from the family living room, — a quiet, restful place where any member of the family may go.

Verandas and porches are very important, and the houseowner should consider them carefully. The most useful veranda is situated, not on the front of the house where privacy is difficult to secure, but on one side or at the rear. French windows opening from the living room or hall make an excellent means of entrance from house to veranda. If the latter is to be screened in, it is not a good plan to have steps leading from the veranda to the ground, it being more practical to have a porch entirely private, entered only from the house. Verandas of this sort should be wide enough to admit of a row of chairs and plenty of space for passage in front, — say 10 feet as a minimum extreme width, though 12 feet is much better. Many verandas of this type are screened in summer and glazed in winter, sometimes, even, radiators being installed so that the porch can be used all winter as a "sun room."

Porches other than the main veranda can be much smaller, and they may be roofed or left open like a terrace. Somewhere outside the house it is a good plan to have an open terrace on which one may step from the house, for on fine nights in summer it is delightful to sit out of doors directly under the sky. An additional advantage of the terrace over a covered veranda is that it shuts no light from the living rooms.

MAIN VERANDA BELOW, SLEEPING PORCH ABOVE.

The sleeping porch has become a necessary part of the house. Frequently it is located on top of the principal veranda, thus being, in fact, the second story of a "double-decked" porch. When this is the case, it is best to extend the main roof of the house right out over the sleeping porch wing, otherwise the double-decked porch might look detached. The minimum width of a sleeping porch is 7 feet, but 8 feet is better, its size, of course, being determined by the number of persons who are to sleep there. Cot beds are used mostly, though folding beds are particularly desirable, as they may be closed up out of the way in daytime. Folding beds for this purpose are built into the wall, with ventilators provided at the sides. If windows are to be used in connection with the sleeping porch, casement windows will be found to be best, — in groups, hinged at the sides and opening out. Thus the maximum of air is secured when windows are opened, and the purpose of the sleeping porch is not diverted. In some porches double doors (French windows) open from the principal bedroom, through which an ordinary double bed can be pushed. In this way it is possible to keep the bed in the bedroom during the day, pushing it out on the porch at night.

The sun room may be treated as a sort of glazed-in veranda, or it can be built like any other room, adding plenty of windows opening down to the floor. A sun room is very attractive and will be found quite useful located where one can step directly into it from the living room. It is frequently the custom to open a conservatory off one end of the sun room, and often the sun room floor is a step or two down from the living room floor. Tile floors are excellent for porches and sun rooms, — especially red quarry tile laid with wide black joints. Tile should be oiled after it is laid, to bring out the color.

The most important room in the house is the kitchen, for here the housekeeper finds her work a joy when the kitchen is properly designed. Cross draft, by means of windows and doors on two sides, must be had by all means. Reduce complexities by providing the simplest of kitchen arrangements, with shortest distances between points, — not a cupboard too many, but just enough to exactly accommodate kitchen dishes and kitchen tools. Every unnecessary inch of space in the kitchen makes that much more work. Analyze your needs before the working plans are made, and provide for your actual requirements, adding as much extra provision for the future as your common sense dictates.

Tile walls are excellent for kitchens, sometimes tile floors, though the latter are very hard underfoot. Maple floors are practical, with or without a covering of linoleum. In lieu of tile walls, hard plaster can be used. Modern kitchen design has almost revolutionized housekeeping methods. Old style kitchens were largely space-wasters, — difficult to keep clean, inconveniently planned. Designers apparently paid no attention to the elimination of unnecessary distance between fixtures. Modern kitchens are smaller, even in large houses, as the small kitchen well arranged has been found to accommodate as large a family as a large kitchen poorly planned, and at the same time work is much easier.

In planning the kitchen, when you think it is reduced to the smallest area possible, take off a few feet more, for most often the kitchen is made too large. To make a small kitchen practical, however, you must carefully arrange for every fixture and piece of furniture. The sink should be near the range and both should be where light is good; then, there are cupboards, a table or dresser, and one or two chairs to be provided for. Furniture really requires little room, if the kitchen is thought out

SMALL BUFFET KITCHEN.

scientifically. To do this intelligently, find out the size of furniture and sketch each piece on the plans.

In imagination, the housekeeper should go through the various housekeeping operations to be performed in the kitchen and see if they can be properly and comfortably accomplished in the given space. Is the pantry near? Are closets and cupboards convenient? Will windows and outside doors give cross draft in hot weather? Is the kitchen just the sort of workroom in which one would choose to pass many hours each day? For the house will lack in its most essential spot, if the kitchen is not practical.

In a small house the kitchen may be as small as 10 by 12 feet, or even less, if it be well planned, for gas ranges have made small kitchens practical. When a coal range is used, the kitchen should be larger, so that the room may be as cool as possible. Have plenty of windows, and place the tops high up near the ceiling, so hot air will go out readily. If impossible to get windows on two sides of the room, place the rear entrance door on the side opposite the windows. Thus, when the door is opened, cross draft is provided.

Built-in kitchen cupboards are useful and attractive. Use them plentifully, but with the understanding that it is possible to have too many cupboards, — wasting money uselessly and causing unnecessary work forever after. The most practical way to determine how many cupboards are needed is to consider carefully every article requiring storage space, and make provision for it. One of the new ideas is to omit the pantry and have food cupboards built around the walls of the kitchen, an ice box, built in (with outside icing door), providing storage for perishable food. Other convenient cupboards are at

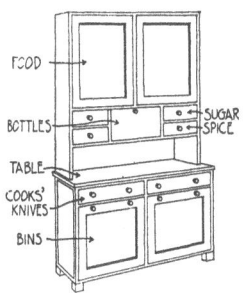

KITCHEN DRESSER.

116 *SUCCESSFUL HOUSES AND HOW TO BUILD THEM*

the side of the sink, frequently a chest of drawers being on one side, with a cupboard at the other, both topped with a flat wood or marble slab, forming a table. For cleanliness the space underneath the sink is left open. One wall cupboard of good size is ample to contain kitchen dishes, and another will hold packages of food supplies, flour, and like materials. With perishable goods in the ice box summer and winter and cupboards for other

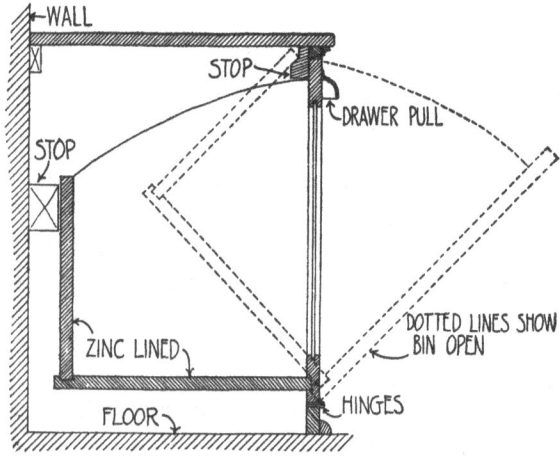

TILTING FLOUR BIN.

supplies, no pantry is necessary, and one more care-requiring accessory is eliminated.

It may be laid down as a fact that most pantries are larger than needs be. The tendency is to devote so much space for this purpose that housekeeping is made harder instead of easier. Large pantries require much labor to keep them spotlessly clean, — floors must be washed and shelves scrubbed, to say nothing of the packages and utensils containing food which require constant inspection. It is much better to consider a food pantry as space for storing supplies for immediate use and not try to keep there the abundance of stores more properly placed in the basement. Canned goods, fruit, and vegetables are better down cellar, in a dark, cool storeroom. Flour in barrels is frequently stored in the pantry, with sugar, salt, breakfast foods, meal, and like supplies.

Many housekeepers prefer to buy flour in paper sacks, in which case one or two flour bins are required in the pantry. The pattern most used consists of zinc-lined boxes swung beneath a broad ledge. If pivots are applied to the sides of the boxes, the bins can be easily lifted out for cleaning. A simpler form of bin is merely hinged on the bottom with ordinary butts, tilted forward when flour is required by taking hold of a drawer pull at the top. Flour bins should always tilt forward in this manner without disturbing the bread board above. The old-fashioned way was to place a barrel of flour under the ledge, lifting up a cover above to get at the flour. This was awkward when a batch of dough was on the bread board.

The best material for the walls and floors of a pantry is tile. Nothing could be cleaner than this dense, moisture-resisting material, but maple will do very well for floors, with southern pine for shelves and cupboards. Where tile is not used the walls should be covered with hard plaster, painted with several coats of good enamel paint. Linoleum is an excellent covering for a pantry floor.

There is one department of the house which has cheated more owners out of hard-earned dollars and vexed more weary housewives than all the others combined. This usually inconvenient and frequently ill-designed part of the house is called the "butler's pantry." As every one knows, most families do not require a butler, nevertheless, perhaps ninety-nine out of a hundred sets of building plans have the words "butler's pantry" indelibly stamped upon them. Now, a room properly arranged for the butler must be large enough for the various functions performed by that dignitary. Such a department,

118 SUCCESSFUL HOUSES AND HOW TO BUILD THEM

necessary as it is for families which do a great deal of entertaining, must be large enough for serving elaborate dinners of many courses, providing space for the cleaning and shelving of the generous supply of china and silver necessary for such an establishment. There can be no economy of space, — everything is on a scale commensurate with the elaborate service required. Here is where the builder of a small house is fleeced, and the housekeeper adds furrows to her brow. Most every houseowner has seen one or two of these elaborately arranged rooms, and with his mind filled with the picture he forgets his more simple problem and schemes for a similar department in his own house, thinking his home will not be complete unless it has some such luxurious arrangement. As a result, money is spent for the "butler's pantry," frequently causing restricted expenditure in some other place in the house, and another housekeeping difficulty has been added to the everyday life of the mistress.

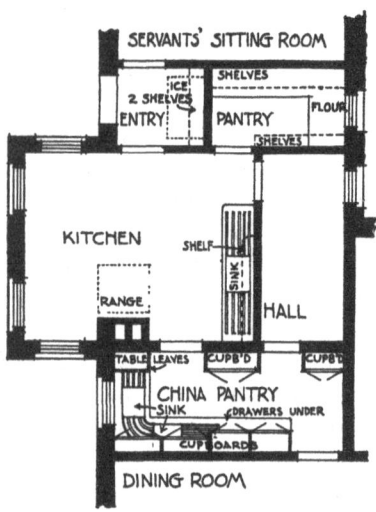

KITCHEN, PANTRY, AND CHINA PANTRY.

The right way to approach the serving pantry (butler's pantry) problem is to estimate the amount of shelf room actually needed. Add to this somewhat for future requirements, including the few conveniences needed; allow an aisle for passage and you will have a serving pantry sufficient for all but the largest families. This serving pantry is usually the connecting passageway between kitchen and dining room. China cases are set up about 16 inches above the drawers and lockers below, allowing the broad ledge to be used as a serving table. It is a good idea to install a plate warmer in one of the lockers.

Of course, there are houses where the simplified form of serving pantry could not be used; large houses in which owners frequently entertain and where a staff of servants is constantly maintained should have serving facilities more extensive. But even in these instances, one should not fail to carefully study

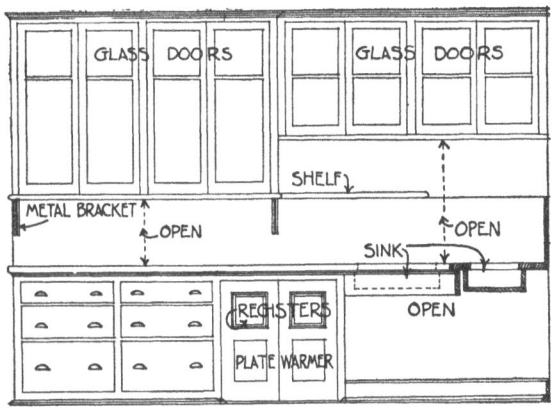

PRACTICABLE SERVING ROOM CASES.

the problem, and proportion the space scientifically for the work to be done there. In a serving pantry of liberal size "tandem" pantry sinks are often provided. Two sinks are very convenient for washing dishes, one being filled with water for washing and the other with rinsing water, — quite as convenient as having a battery of two or three wash tubs in the laundry, — and such an arrangement greatly facilitates dish washing. A cupboard for table leaves, consisting of a grooved rack to hold the leaves (with a door in front) will be found very convenient in a serving pantry.

A billiard room, to be of utmost utility, should be located on the first story off the hall or dining room. In most houses it is placed in the basement or the attic, and it has been found in practice that when a billiard room is up or down a flight or two of stairs it is rarely used. In other words, people do not like to climb up and down stairs to visit a billiard room and the result is, after the novelty has worn off, most basement and attic billiard rooms are deserted. Of the two places, basement or attic, undoubtedly the former is the better place for the billiard room; under the living room is the best location, and a toilet room should be adjacent to it containing a wash bowl and watercloset. Good light must be provided; if ordinary cellar windows will not do, area windows should be used, opening well down to the floor. A fireplace is also very desirable. Billiard rooms should be of sizes indicated in the following table: —

CORRECT SIZES FOR BILLIARD ROOMS

(Add 9 feet to total size of table, for small tables; add 10 feet to total size of table, for large tables.)

Table 3'6" × 7'	Room 12'6" × 16'
Table 4' × 8'	Room 13' × 17'
Table 4'6" × 9'	Room 14' × 18'6"
Table 5' × 10'	Room 15' × 20'
Table 5'6" × 11'	Room 15'6" × 21'
Table 6' × 12'	Room 16' × 22'

Bedrooms need not be so large as one would expect when they are properly arranged, with windows and doors placed so as to leave wall space and floor space for furniture. In fact, bedrooms as small as 9'6" by 11' 6" are frequently perfectly practical. Beds, dressers, and other pieces of furniture should be sketched on the plans, selecting the best locations and allowing proper space around each. A dressing case placed with its back to the wall should have ample space in front; otherwise one may not be able to look in the mirror.

Bedrooms should be carefully planned to have windows on two sides of each room, if possible. This makes them much cooler in summer, and if awnings are added over the south windows the rooms will be quite comfortable even in hottest weather. Many modern houses have overhanging eaves which do practically what the awnings do, — that is, they keep out

BEDROOM WITH WINDOWS ON TWO SIDES.

the direct rays of the hot noon sun, and such rooms are not deprived of too much light if the surface under the eaves is finished white, as light colors reflect daylight into the rooms.

Don't reserve the best bedroom in the house for occasional guests; take it for your own. This room, usually called "owner's room," should be larger than any of the others. In fact, all other rooms might be made a bit smaller to contribute to the size of the owner's room, which is customarily used as an upstairs sitting room.

Off the principal bedroom a dressing room will be found very useful. In many houses a private bathroom is also installed, opening from the dressing room or bedroom. In a well arranged dressing room you will find several wardrobes built in against the walls with generous floor space left between. There is a window (usually at one end), and a dresser (built-in, or not) stands against one wall. On one of the wardrobe doors it is a good plan to have a full-length mirror. For houses of moderate size a dressing room 7 by 8 feet is usually sufficient.

The ideal bathroom is neither too large nor too small. A minimum size for small bath rooms is, 5'6" wide by 7'0" long. An excessively large bathroom is much more difficult to keep clean than a smaller one, if the latter is well arranged. That is the key to first-class bathroom design — let it be "well arranged." Each fixture should be carefully drawn out to a scale on the floor plan, allowing just space enough about each fixture for the proper accommodation of the user, and no more.

It is safe to say that one bathroom will not comfortably care for more than four grown people. A much better apportionment would be one bathroom for three grown people, as it is better to err on the side of providing too many than too few. Bathroom facilities are greatly increased when separate lavatories are provided in each bedroom, or say, one lavatory in each dressing room. Lavatories need not be visible as they can be inclosed with doors.

Of the many house-building maxims that have been handed down by word of mouth, none is more antiquated than the one "always build the bathroom over the kitchen." Years ago, before modern, scientific building laws had been enacted, it was customary to have one stack of soil pipe extend from basement to roof, as an outlet and vent pipe for laundry tubs, kitchen sink, and bathroom fixtures. With such conditions it is not strange that the bathroom was placed directly over the kitchen. Plumbing laws now require in most cases a separate stack from kitchen sink and laundry tubs, extending from the basement nearly to the roof, so it is no longer of any particular advantage to place the bathroom directly over the kitchen. As a general proposition, of course, it may be said that the shorter the distance from bathroom to kitchen, the more economical a plumbing system is, but it certainly is not wise to disarrange one's floor plan to get such a result.

The bathroom window should be higher from the floor than ordinary windows. If you wish to secure good ventilation, make the bathroom window larger than usual. Two windows in each bathroom, especially if on opposite sides, are a great improvement.

The best material in the world for a bathroom floor is tile, either of glass or the more ordinary white tile. White tile should be unglazed for floors, to prevent slipping. On walls, white tiles are glazed. A new enameled metal wall covering which looks like tile is in the market, and it will be found a good material for bathroom walls, at a somewhat less cost than tile. Above the tile dado, walls should be of hard plaster, finished smooth. This can be painted three or four coats of enamel paint.

Scientifically arranged cupboards do as much toward lightening the load of housekeeping as any other house fixtures. Impractical closets are failures, for you cannot keep a house tidy if there is not space of just the right size in which to store every article brought into it. Large closets are sometimes worse than small ones, since they make just so much more space to clean and take up room needed for other things. This is especially true in small houses, which are like ships, — material of a certain amount has to be stored in a limited number of places, — space must be utilized without waste.

If your house is well planned, there will be no left-over spots. Every square inch of floor and wall space should be accounted for in the working plans. Locate carefully every closet, wardrobe, chest, or cupboard. Leave nothing to chance. Plan for the scientific storage of all supplies before beginning building, and your house will be comfortable and serviceable.

In considering closets and cupboards the most practicable way is to take an inventory of everything to be stored. Next to size, the exact location of every cupboard is the most important thing to consider. Place each where it will be nearest to the articles to be stored. Have your dining room china either directly in the dining room or conveniently near. Place the cupboard for kitchen dishware near the sink, and have the cupboard for pots and pans as close to the range as it is possible to get it. Directions like these seem almost trite, and yet it is surprising how easy it is to forget the practical side of closet planning. One should never depend upon left-over spaces for closets. Closets and cupboards should always be incorporated in the house plans from the beginning.

SCIENTIFIC BUILT-IN WARDROBE.

Large, old-fashioned closets are wasteful because garments cannot be hung in the standing place, — the space is extravagant compared with the number of garments accommodated. Wardrobe closets are storage places on a new principle, — to put away the most garments in the least space is the idea. Such closets are only two feet deep and from three to four feet long. You need not stand in a wardrobe closet, for double doors reveal the entire space to your view, and you can readily reach in and remove garments hung on forms without disturbing others. In a wardrobe closet of ordinary size, 35 garments can be hung without effort. A shelf for hat boxes can be built above, with a drawer or shelf below for shoes and rubbers. An ingenious hanger for utilizing waste space in the upper part of an ordinary closet can be fashioned from a handle about three feet long with an ordinary wire coat hanger screwed to the top. In the upper part of such a closet, place a curtain pole on which to hang the garments. By this method you will be able to reach up and hang suits in the high space usually wasted.

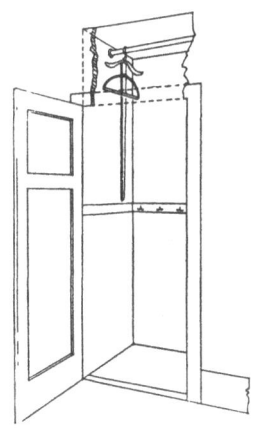

UTILIZING THE UPPER SPACE IN AN ORDINARY CLOSET.

Large hats for women require much clever planning. Where will you put them? One good way is to have a tight, cedar box under the bed. The box is on casters so it may be easily trundled out when needed, and the cover shuts down tight to keep out dust. If your closet is deep enough, you may keep hats in ordinary pasteboard boxes on the upper shelf.

Some women, blessed with a number of hats, have a closet made expressly for them. Such a closet is built with double doors like a wardrobe closet, but the space is filled with shelves. If the doors are tight, hats may lie on the shelves, otherwise, each should be inclosed in a separate box. Wardrobe cabinets, useful for men and women, can be built into any bedroom. They are handy, practical, little space savers, and do not cost overmuch. In cabinets for men, garments should be supported on hangers, and there are trays for shirts and lockers for collars, cuffs, and ties. Cabinets for women have trays for skirts. which can be laid full length without folding.

A medicine cupboard built into the bathroom wall is a practical necessity. It is used for soap, tooth brushes, bottles, and towels, and one of the best patterns is of enameled metal.

Shelves should be adjustable, and a toilet mirror is usually secured to the door. In this case, place the cabinet over the wash bowl.

The ideal linen closet has no drawers to bind or rattle. Drawers are inconvenient for the storage of linen as the depth necessary to hold linen satisfactorily makes them very heavy. In addition, is the annoyance of pulling a drawer forward and taking out all the linen on top to get at that below. Use open shelves in your linen closet and hang double doors like a wardrobe closet. Have the shelves adjustable, so you may lift them up or down at will. For a house on a dusty street have outer and inner doors on the linen closet. A good storeroom for linen usually has an aisle in the middle, with cupboards on both sides. No drawers, — always shelves. Bookcases (which are really cupboards) can be provided of just the right size to hold your library, with generous provision for its future enlargement.

BATHROOM CUPBOARD.

In large houses a coat room should be provided, on the first story near the front entrance, and it is an excellent idea to build the coat room large enough to contain a toilet room as well, with washbowl and water-closet. A coat room about 6 by 8 feet, with a toilet room off, about 4 by 5 feet, is large enough for most houses, and the convenience of such an arrangement is at once apparent. Tile floors and walls are very practical for both coat room and toilet room. For those who do not care to have a separate coat room, a coat closet arranged like an ordinary wardrobe can be built in off the entrance hall. On the door place a full-length mirror and you will have a very convenient outfit.

In the basement several departments must be provided for. The laundry is, of course, the most important room, and it is ordinarily placed under the kitchen, in one corner, with windows on two sides to insure cool, cross ventilation. Latest practice is to place laundry tubs out on the floor instead of against a wall. They are very convenient thus, for then the washing machine and clothes basket can be placed adjacent to the tubs on any side. Where center tubs are desired, one should order tubs without backs and have the water-supply pipes drop down to each from the ceiling, or extend up from the floor. The faucets are secured to the pipe risers. A small wooden grating placed on the concrete floor in front of the tubs will be appreciated by most washwomen, as it is pleasanter to stand upon than the hard concrete. The coolest laundries are those in which a gas stove is used to heat irons and warm the water. Locate the ironing table near a window where light is best, and put a wooden grating here also, for the laundress to stand upon.

Dust-proof coal bins are ideal in every way. Build them with double-boarded partitions, placing good, thick sheathing paper, well lapped, between the layers of boards. Another good way requiring less lumber is to use one thickness of tongued and grooved boards and paint the joints with white lead before they are put together. This makes a tight partition. One should be careful that the carpenter fits partitions closely at floor and ceiling, and a tight door should be hung in front of the ordinary slide boards.

Pay particular attention to the cool cellar for vegetables. Build it on the shady side, in the coolest corner, and provide it with an outside window for ventilation. If you wish to have your vegetables keep the longest possible time, remove them from the crates or barrels and spread them out on racks or bins provided for that purpose. Do not keep your preserves in the ordinary cool cellar. Build a separate closet for them, in a dark, cool corner, without outside light. Use artificial light instead, as strong light from out of doors spoils preserves.

In most houses a toilet is provided in the basement for servants. If the new house is in a poorly drained locality where the sewer is liable to back up into the house, a "back-water valve" must be installed to keep the contents of the sewer from flowing into the cellar by way of the cellar water-closet (as is explained in another chapter). It is best to provide a bathtub and washbowl for servants elsewhere than in the cellar.

A tool room with lock and key is usually a great convenience in the basement. Place it somewhere near the stairs which lead to the yard. If a place is provided for every tool, one can tell at a glance just what is missing and take the steps to find it. It is now quite customary to provide for a basement workshop where father and the boys can putter around with tools. Choose a corner for this, if possible, where windows are on two sides, in order to get the maximum of light and air. Install a workbench of oak or maple. As there is considerable dust around a workbench, the cellar should be plastered overhead, or thick paper can be tacked to the under side of the floor joists in order to prevent dust rising to the floors above.

When there is no attic in a house (and sometimes when there is), the best place to store empty trunks is in the basement. Placed on the cellar floor, trunks soon grow musty, but set upon an open rack where air circulates on all sides, they will keep sweet and clean indefinitely.

COMBINATION BRICK AND CEMENT PLASTER
Dunning and Fife, Architects.

CHAPTER VII

SPECIFICATIONS EXPLAINED

VIEWED by the layman, a set of specifications is a ponderous and often misunderstood legal instrument devised by the architect to instruct a contractor how to build the *greater portion* of the new house. The balance of the house — that part which through some error the architect (so the layman supposes) has forgotten to specify — must be built as an "extra," and the disappointed owner has to pay the bills because there is nothing else to do.

Such, in brief, is the process as it exists in the eyes of the layman, who, in truth, is often right in his opinion. Many houses are built by means of incomplete plans and specifications, involving much trouble for owner, architect, and contractor, causing the owner to pay extra for work which should have been specified in the first place. It is not fair, however, to presume that all house-building projects are carried out in the same way. Countless houses all over the country have been built from plans and specifications so complete that not one dollar has been spent for "extras." In many other houses, every dollar for "extras" was spent, not for work omitted from the original contract through error, but for changes in the original scheme, additions made to it by the owner, — not in any way the fault of architect or contractor.

A set of specifications is really a typewritten or printed letter of instructions from the owner (through his agent, the architect) to the contractor. Just as a business man writes a letter of instructions to his agent in a distant city, so the architect on behalf of the owner writes a letter of instructions to the contractor, informing him just how the house is to be built, what materials are to be employed, and what kind of workmanship is required. The only difference between a set of specifications and a business letter is that the former is couched in legal phrases and is a much more lengthy document than the latter.

The method usually pursued by an architect in writing a set of specifications for a house is to take from his files specifications for a similar house designed at some previous period, following it as a model for the new specifications.

As an illustration: It may be the architect has specifications for a frame house built the year before at a cost of $5000. The new house for which he is about to write specifications is to be a frame house, also, somewhere near the same size. Then the architect takes his former specifications, goes over them carefully, marking each item that is to be different in the new house. If the former house has stone foundations and the new one is to have concrete, he changes this portion of the old specifications to include concrete instead of stone; if different plumbing fixtures are to be used, he makes the necessary changes here, and so on, through the entire set.

It is practical to use an old set of specifications for a model in this way because two houses of similar size and cost are similar as to specifications. Both houses have a certain amount of mason work, carpenter work, plumbing, heating, painting, plastering, and other kinds of work, and though materials may vary in a general way, one set of specifications is very much like another. The task of composing an entirely new set of specifications for each new house would not only be a very difficult one, but it would be almost impossible to do this without forgetting some important clause. Just a slight omission here and there might work great harm. When an old set is used, a model that has been built from many times and found correct, the chance of error is very small.

A complete set of specifications ought to be a very interesting document to the prospective houseowner, for it tells him in detail just how his house is to be built, — with what kind of materials. Some owners are inclined to omit careful consideration of specifications. They devote all their spare time to studying the plans, taking but the merest general interest in specifications. This is a great mistake, for specifications tell as much about the vital things in the construction of the house as the plans do. Much future annoyance and not a little real trouble can be saved by familiarizing yourself with the entire set of specifications from start to finish. They should be gone over carefully, clause by clause. Every word and sentence not clear to you should be explained by the architect, so that in the end you will know as much about your house as he does.

Owners are frequently surprised to find after the new house is begun that it does not come out just as they expected. "Why, I thought the bedrooms were to have oak floors," they say, or, "Doesn't the kitchen have a porcelain sink?" In most cases this is the fault of the owner, not the architect, who is not a mind reader and cannot foresee that his client will not understand what he is getting. If honorable and efficient, honestly looking out for the interests of his client, the architect has specified in detail just how he thinks the house should be built to give best results. If the owner hasn't carefully checked over the specifications to see that they represent what he wants, it is not the architect's fault when they contain methods and materials at odds with his requirements.

When there is trouble during the building of a house, it is often on account of a misunderstanding between owner, architect, and contractor. Nothing contributes more often to this trouble than a misunderstanding on the part of the owner as to the *kind of workmanship* called for in the specifications. As an example, take a prospective houseowner who decides to build, let us say, a $5000 house. The new houses with which he is most familiar are expensive houses, costing from $15,000 to

$20,000. He has examined them carefully, admiring the splendid workmanship, and he is enamored of the beautiful way in which the wood is finished. When his own $5000 house is built, he is surprised to find that it is not as highly finished as the more expensive houses. In his own house the trim is much plainer. It is not so richly finished, and the owner asks the architect why this is so.

"You have one coat of stain and two coats of varnish on your woodwork," replies the architect, "and the other house has a coat of filler, one coat of stain and three coats of varnish, — two coats more than there is in your house."

"But why didn't you specify the same kind of a job you did in the other house?"

"Because your house is less costly," says the architect. "If I had used such expensive finishes throughout your house, it would have cost you considerably more. It seemed to me wiser to spend this money where it would do more good."

Difficulties of this sort can be avoided by reading the specifications carefully, understanding just what kind of work is called for. Although a $5000 house should be just as honestly built as a $15,000 house, it would not be wise to spend so much money in finishing up the former as the latter. A $5000 house, built more elaborately and finished better than the usual $5000 house might cost $6000 or $7000, and very few owners would be satisfied to pay so much more for it. Reading the specifications and fixing in his mind the kind of work called for makes it possible for the owner to control the finishing of his house and have it the way he wants it *before* the contract is let.

In building a house of moderate cost, another frequent disappointment to the owner is the workmanship on interior trim. In an ordinary $5000 house it is not usual to have what is known as "cabinet" work. That is, in putting interior trim in place, every joint is not made in cabinet-work fashion, with doweled and glued joints (like a piece of furniture). Good work and good work only is required, of course, but not necessarily "extra good" work, or "super-extra" work, such as might be expected in an expensive house. Frequently an owner who has noticed the "cabinet finish" in expensive houses is surprised to find that his own little home is on a somewhat cheaper plane. Here again, he is at fault in not being familiar with his specifications. He should have understood, after consultation with his architect, just what the latter intended to specify and then, if "cabinet finish" was what he wanted, the proper description might have been inserted in the specifications.

In writing specifications it is customary in the offices of most architects to write separate specifications for each branch of the work. Thus there are mason's specifications, carpenter's specifications, plumbing specifications, and so on. Even when a general contract is to be let for the entire work, the general contractor usually sublets portions of the work, such as plumbing, heating, and so on, and it is a great convenience for him to have separate specifications for the different branches. Thus he hands the plumbing specifications to the plumber and the painting specifications to the painter, instead of giving them a set of specifications for the entire building.

Although each of the branch specifications is written separately, when one contract for the whole job is let the separate specifications are bound together into one and the contract with the general contractor is made for the complete building.

Many of the separate specifications contain more than one branch of the work. For instance, the specifications for masonry usually include excavation, cement floors, structural steel, and so on. The mason who takes your contract frequently does not do the excavating himself, nor does he erect the structural steel or lay the cement floors, for these branches of his work he sublets to other contractors. He does, however, take the entire contract for masonry, including the work of the sub-contractors, and he is responsible for the entire masonry contract. Subcontracts so closely allied with mason work as excavating and structural steel are included in the mason's contract so as to save the annoyance of making so many separate contracts. The carpenter's specifications usually contain tin work, roofing, mill work, lumber, and the like, — work that is sublet by the carpenter to various subcontractors but is included in the carpenter's specifications to avoid the necessity of making so many separate contracts; the painting specifications contain glazing; and the plumbing specifications include gas fitting.

When the architect uses specifications of a previously built house as a guide for the new specifications, it is excellent practice for the owner to borrow from the architect the specification which it is proposed to follow as a model. Thus, in advance of the actual writing of the new specifications an owner can look over the model and decide whether, in a general way, they embody the kind of work he expects to get in his own house.

Some portions of the work are impractical to specify, by reason of the large amount of detailed description required. This applies particularly to hardware, as it is frequently impossible at the time specifications are made to determine just what kind of hardware the owner desires. Items of this kind can be handled by inserting an allowance in the specifications. Such a clause referring to hardware, would read about as follows: —

Hardware Allowance

Allow and pay the owner the sum of One Hundred and Twenty-Five Dollars ($125) for all finishing hardware used in the building. This sum to be expended by the owner in any way he shall see fit.

When an allowance clause like this is used, the contractor, in making his bid, includes in it the sum of $125. Later, when the owner goes to a dealer to select his hardware he is entitled to enough goods to come up to the value of the allowance, and the contractor is liable for this amount. If the hardware costs less than the amount of the allowance, the owner saves the difference; if it costs more, he must pay the contractor for the increased amount. Tilework (for mantels and hearths) is frequently put into the specification in the form of an allowance (by specifying an allowed price of so much per square foot). Electric light fixtures, furniture, and other things difficult to specifically describe, are also frequently inserted in the form of allowances.

Every set of specifications is preceded by a page or two of General Conditions (considered as part of the specifications). A short list of general conditions such as is frequently used in house·specifications follows:—

REQUIREMENTS. The Contractor shall furnish all
material, labor, transportation, scaffolding, utensils, etc., of every description
required for the full performance of the
work herein specified, except as may be
otherwise specifically mentioned.

He shall lay out his work and be responsible for its correctness, shall keep a competent foreman on the premises, shall obtain
all necessary permits to carry on the work,
paying all lawful fees therefor, shall give
to the proper authorities all requisite no-
tices relating to the work in his charge,
shall afford the Architect or other Inspector every facility for inspection, shall be
responsible for any violation of law or damage to property caused by him or his employees, and shall properly protect his work
during progress.

WORK AND MATERIAL. All materials shall be of
the best of their several kinds in quality,
as herein specified. All labor shall be
performed in the best manner by skilled
workmen and both shall be subject to the
approval of the Architect or other Inspector.

All work and material must conform to the
laws, rules, and regulations in force in the
locality in which the building is to stand,
anything herein specified to the contrary
notwithstanding.

STORED MATERIAL. All materials delivered on
the premises which are to form a part of the
works, are to be considered the property of
the owners, and are not to be removed without their consent, but the Contractor shall
have the right to remove all his surplus
material after completion.

CARTING. The Contractor shall provide and pay
all charges for the delivery of all material
used upon the building, whether furnished
by himself, or furnished to himself by the
Owner.

CUTTING. Such cutting and repairing as is
necessary, in either the masonry or carpentry, for the proper installation of the
heating and plumbing systems (the latter of
which is here understood to include the gas
piping and the rain-water conductors) shall
be done by the general building contractor.

The workmen of the several crafts are to serve each other where necessary for the proper accomplishment of their respective duties.

OBSTRUCTIONS AND REPAIRS. At any time, upon the request of the Architect or Inspector, the Contractor shall clear out all rubbish and surplus material left by him, shall repair any damage to his work, no matter by whom caused (loss or damage by fire excepted), and leave the premises broom clean and in perfect working order so far as his work is concerned.

CARE OF BUILDING. The Contractor shall provide all necessary railings, guards, and night lights while the building is in his care.

WARMING OF BUILDING. The Contractor shall provide such temporary heat in proper apparatus as may be necessary for the continuance of the work in all weather.

INSURANCE. The Owners shall insure the building and the material in and about the premises, covering their own and the Contractor's interests therein against loss or damage by fire, such policies being made payable to the Owners or Contractor as their interests may appear.

DRAWINGS. The drawings referred to in this specification, besides detail drawings, consist of—

No. 1 _____
 " 2 _____

" 3..
" 4..
" 5..
" 6..
" 7..
" 8..
" 9..
" 10...
" 11...
" 12...
" 13...
" 14...
" 15...

The drawings mentioned will be supplemented by detail drawings as the work progresses. All of these drawings are intended to cooperate with and form a part of this specification and the accompanying contract.

Where figures are given, they are to be followed rather than measurement by scale; and actual dimensions of the premises in preference to either, and the accuracy of such figures as are given are to be verified by the Contractor before work shall proceed in order that any errors or apparent discrepancies, should such be found to exist, may be reported to the Architect for his correction, and it shall be the duty of the Contractor to so report them, otherwise he shall make good at his own expense, any errors in the work occasioned thereby.

INTERPRETATION. Anything set forth in either
the drawings or the specifications respec-
tively, and not in both, shall be furnished
or performed the same as if specially set
forth in both; likewise also, such material
or labor as is reasonably implied, though not
set forth in either. When mention is made
in either instrument of a single case of
which duplicates exist, the reference shall
apply equally to all. This refers equally
to work and material of varying amounts and
sizes and to forms performing corresponding
services in various parts of the building,
although not specially indicated in each
particular case.

In order that the Contractor may make suitable provision in his bid for covering the
entire cost of the work proposed, he shall
inform himself on any points which in his
opinion the drawings or specifications do
not set forth with sufficient clearness,
since he shall be held responsible for an
entire and correct understanding of the various instruments thereafter.

Should errors be found to exist in either
instrument they shall be reported to the
Architect for adjustment before the contract
is signed; otherwise, thereafter the Contractor shall take the Architect's decision
as final and perform the work in question in
accordance therewith.

PROPERTY. The drawings and specifications for
this work are to be considered instruments

of service; are to be used for this building only; are the property of the Architect, and are to be returned to him upon the completion of the work set forth therein.

AWARD OF CONTRACT. The owners reserve the right to accept any, or to reject any or all, proposals presented.

WELL-ARRANGED ENTRANCE
Lawrence Buck, Architect.

CHAPTER VIII

A CHAPTER ON LEGAL DOCUMENTS

THE legal side of the building problem is somewhat complicated in the eyes of the inexperienced. Papers couched in legal phraseology appear to be somewhat vague, and the owner does not always quite understand all the documents to which he is asked to affix his signature.

Proposals, contracts, bonds, and all other legal papers ordinarily used in a building project are really very simple. The owner can easily familiarize himself with their uses, for, thanks to the American Institute of Architects, these legal forms have been largely standardized.

In connection with this it should be said that the American Institute, which is the leading body of practicing architects in the United States, has had a committee working for some time on what are known as "Standard Documents," with the idea of improving all legal forms commonly used in building contracts. As a result, an excellent set of documents has been devised, consisting of Bond, Agreement (Contract), Invitation to Submit a Proposal, Form of Proposal, and General Conditions of Contract.

The contract, itself, is about the first legal paper the owner is called upon to sign. After the bids come in and the owner and his architect have decided to whom the job is to be given, the building contract must be signed by owner and contractor, before work can be started.

A contract between two or more parties is nothing more than an agreement between them, in which one party agrees to perform certain work and the other party agrees to pay him such and such sums for that work. Building Contracts might be verbal instead of written, and they would still hold good, if made before reliable witnesses. For instance, Contractor

> **The Standard form of Agreement of the American Institute of Architects**
>
> This form is to be used only with the Standard General Conditions of the Contract. In it Owner, Contractor and Architect are treated as of the singular number and masculine gender.
>
> **This Agreement** made the .... day of .... in the year Nineteen Hundred and ....
>
> by and between ....
>
> ....
>
> hereinafter called the Contractor and ....
>
> ....
>
> .... hereinafter called the Owner
>
> **Witnesseth,** that the Contractor and the Owner for the considerations hereinafter named agree as follows:
>
> **Article 1.** The Contractor agrees to provide all the materials and to perform all the work shown on the Drawings and described in the Specifications entitled
> (Here insert the caption descriptive of the work as used in the Proposal, Specifications, General Conditions and upon the Drawings.)
>
> ....
>
> ....
>
> ....
>
> prepared by ....
>
> ....
>
> .... acting as, and in these Contract Documents entitled the Architect, and to do to the satisfaction of the Architect everything required by the Drawings, Specifications and General Conditions.
>
> **First Standard Edition. Form B.**

EXCELLENT TYPE OF CONTRACT FORM.
(Continued on pages 147, 148 and 149.)

Smith and Owner Jones might meet in the presence of two or three men and orally agree to a building contract. This procedure would be quite legal, and such a contract might hold as well as a written contract. But written contracts are of course the best, as there is less liability of error. Everything being concisely written down, neither party to the contract is liable to misunderstand it.

Article 2. The Contractor agrees to complete the work by and at the following time or times, to wit:

....

....

....

....

and to pay or allow the Owner as liquidated damages, the sum of

....($..................) for each day thereafter, Sundays and legal holidays not included, that the work remains uncompleted.

Article 3. The Owner agrees to pay the Contractor in current funds for the performance of the Contract

....

....($..................) subject to additions and deductions as provided in the General Conditions of the Contract.

Article 4. The Owner agrees to make payments on account of this Contract on the certificate of the Architect, as follows:

....

....

....

....

....

....

In no case, however, shall the Contractor be entitled to a payment which, in the judgment of the Architect, will leave the balance withheld insufficient to complete the work.

Taking the Standard Form of Agreement (which is the form of contract recommended by the American Institute of Architects) and analyzing it, one finds that there are several general provisions which every good form of contract should contain. Such a document usually starts with the date, followed by the names of the contractor and the owner. Next comes a clause stating the extent of the work to be done by the contractor, with mention of the architect whose plans are to be followed and

> **Article 5.** The Contractor and the Owner agree that the Drawings with all notes now thereon, the Specifications and the General Conditions of the Contract are, together with this Agreement, the Documents forming the Contract, and that the said Drawings, Specifications and General Conditions are as fully a part of the Contract as if hereto attached or herein repeated; and that should the Contractor and the Owner fail to sign them the identification of them by the Architect shall be binding on both parties.

under whose supervision the work is to be performed. After this follows a clause stating the date when the work is to be completed, stipulating the damages which the contractor is to pay the owner for every day the work remains uncompleted.

The next clause states the amount the owner is to pay the

contractor for the work, noting the amount of each payment on account and the time when it will fall due (for the owner usually pays for his building from time to time as the work progresses,

The Contractor and the Owner for themselves, their successors, executors, administrators and assigns, hereby agree that they will in all ways be bound by the Documents forming the Contract, and that they will abide by and will promptly and fully carry out all decisions given thereunder, and that they will fully perform all of the convenants and agreements therein contained, in witness whereof they have hereunto set their hands and seals, the day and year first above written.

In Presence of

..............................(Seal)

..............................(Seal)

This Agreement is not intended to diminish the use of the Uniform Contract, the publication of which is continued by the American Institute of Architects and the National Association of Builders. This Agreement is issued in two styles, identical in wording: One, Style A, is intended for carbon duplication, the other, Style B, is intended for reproduction by blue-printing. This is Style B. This form copyrighted 1911 by the American Institute of Architects, The Octagon, Washington, D. C. Sole Licensee for Publication, E. G. Soltmann, Drawing Materials, 134-140 W. 29th St., New York.

— not in one sum after the building is completed). Next follow final clauses binding both parties, "their successors, executors, administrators, and assigns," followed by a space in which the owner and contractor sign their names, witnessed by from two to four witnesses. It is customary to place a seal after the owner's and contractor's signatures.

The Standard Form of Agreement is an excellent type of contract reduced to its simplest form. It should be employed only when a complete set of general conditions is used in connection with the specifications, otherwise, many important clauses covering Insurance, Inspection, Condemned Materials, Delays, and Character of Work, which are not mentioned in the Standard Forms but can be mentioned in the specifications, would not be covered.

Another good form of contract is what is known as the "Uniform Contract," a document prepared by the American Institute of Architects and the National Association of Builders. This is a more lengthy document than the Standard Form, as it contains the general clauses covering Insurance, Inspection, Condemned Materials, etc., just mentioned and which need not, therefore, be included in the specifications.

Many legal interpretations are put upon a contract, some of which are not generally known. Owners and contractors have taken their differences to the courts, and this practice has produced a large number of legal opinions. Though these differ somewhat, in each state, the following will be found to hold in most localities: —

A signature or a mark made by either party is binding, when made properly by a duly authorized party and witnessed.

When a "mark" is made, it must be done by the individual himself; it cannot be made by the other party for him.

One signature binds the party so signing, whether the other party has signed the contract or not.

Ordinarily, every contract must include compensation for services rendered, for if there is no remuneration the contract will not hold. If, however, a seal is affixed to the signature of the owner and the signature of the contractor, the contract holds irrespective of remuneration and no opportunity is left for dispute. Therefore, it is a good custom to affix seals, as it tends to make a contract more binding upon both parties, — less liable to be altered in the courts.

The contract must be signed by the owner himself. If the architect signs for the owner, he, — the architect, — becomes personally liable for the amount of the contract.

One copy of a contract is invalid, — there should always be two copies.

After a contract is signed, amendments can be made by mutual agreement, — becoming as binding as the original contract. If the original signatures were "sealed" (by placing seals after them), the new signatures should be likewise sealed.

The owner should read his contract carefully before signing, noting carefully any insertions of script in the printed document, for written insertions always take preference over printed clauses, and where there is inconsistency, the written portions control. The statement "I did not notice that clause" is never accepted as a valid excuse in a court of law; both parties are bound by the conditions of their signed contract whether the conditions have been read carefully or not.

The courts sometimes hold that certain conditions in a contract are "implied," whether they are specifically stated or not. For this reason the owner should make sure that the general spirit of the contract is faithfully set forth.

The "forfeiture price" (the amount the contractor is to pay per day for every day the building is incompleted beyond the specified time) will not stand in court unless it is a reasonable price.

These are some of the general characteristics of a building contract as interpreted by the courts in many states, and although the law concerning building contracts varies more or less in different sections, general court practice will be found very much alike. Of course, in the eyes of the courts the whole idea of a contract is that it binds both parties impartially. Therefore the courts always try to find out the true intent and meaning of the document.

If, during the erection of a building, extra work is done by the contractor, and the owner has observed this extra work (thereby virtually accepting it), even though the contract specifically states, "the contractor is to have a written order for all extra work," the courts hold that the owner is liable for a reasonable price for the work. It is best practice, however, to give a written order for all extra work, and then there is less chance for dispute.

The clause stating responsibility for safety of workmen and pedestrians is usually put in the name of the contractor. The Employers' Liability Act recently passed in many states makes it desirable for the owner to carry liability insurance, to protect himself from possible suits when workmen are injured on the building. Insurance on the new building is usually carried by the owner in the names of the contractor and himself, so that if there is a fire before the contractor has turned over the building to the owner, the contractor gets his share of the insurance.

When plans and specifications are ready for bids, many architects send an Invitation for Proposal to the various contractors whom it is deemed advisable to invite. Each contractor is given a Standard Proposal Form on which to enter his bid and return to the architect. One should remember that a proposal which is accepted immediately without change, is binding. Thus, if you receive a bid from Contractor Smith to build your house for $5000 and accept it immediately, Smith will have to assume the contract at that price regardless of whether he finds, a day or two later, that he has made a mistake in his figures and is charging a thousand dollars too little. But if you do not accept the bid immediately, or if you make any changes in it, the contractor is released from his proposal if he so wishes.

When a large house is built, it is frequently the custom to put the contractor under bond, requiring him to furnish a bond signed by responsible parties assuring that he will faithfully carry out the agreement. The best forms of bond start out with a clause containing the name of the contractor (Principal) with his address, followed by the name and address of the party or parties who stand back of him (Surety or Sureties). Then

The Standard Form of Bond of the American Institute of Architects

Know all Men by these Presents: That we (Here insert the name and Address of the Contractor)

....hereinafter called the Principal, and

....and

....and

hereinafter called the Surety or Sureties are held and firmly bound unto

hereinafter called the Owner, in the sum of

....($......................)
for the payment whereof the Principal and the Surety or Sureties bind themselves, their heirs, executors, administrators, successors and assigns, jointly and severally, firmly, by these presents.

Whereas, the Principal has, by means of a written Agreement, dated.................................
....entered into a contract with the Owner for

a copy of which Agreement is hereto annexed;

First Standard Edition.

A MODEL FORM OF BOND.
(Continued on page 154.)

follows the amount of the bond (frequently 80% of the contract price) with a notation of the date of the building contract and name of owner. The various conditions of the bond follow, and at the end of the document are the date, with the "sealed" and witnessed signatures of the contractor (Principal) and his Sureties. In effect, the bond states that if the contractor faith-

> Now, Therefore, the Condition of this Obligation is such that if the Principal shall faithfully perform the Contract on his part, and satisfy all claims and demands incurred for the same, and fully indemnify and save harmless the Owner from all cost and damage which he may suffer by reason of failure so to do, and shall fully reimburse and repay the Owner all outlay and expense which the Owner may incur in making good any such default, then this obligation shall be null and void; otherwise it shall remain in full force and effect.
>
> Provided, however, that no suit, action or proceeding by reason of any default shall be brought on this Bond after _____ months from the day on which the final payment under the Contract is made; and that service of writ or process commencing any such suit, action or proceeding shall not be made after such date.
>
> And Provided, that any alterations which may be made in the terms of the Contract, or in the work to be done under it, or the giving by the Owner of any extension of time for the performance of the Contract, or any other forbearance on the part of either the Owner or the Principal to the other shall not in any way release the Principal and the Surety or Sureties, or either or any of them, their heirs, executors, administrators, successors or assigns from their liability hereunder, notice to the Surety or Sureties of any such alteration, extension or forbearance being hereby waived.
>
> Signed and Sealed this _____ day of _____ 19____
>
> In Presence of
>
> _____ Seal
>
> _____ Seal
>
> _____ Seal
>
> _____ Seal
>
> This form copyrighted 1911 by the American Institute of Architects, The Octagon, Washington, D. C. Sole Licensee for Publication, G. G. Soltmann, Drawing Materials, 134-140 W. 29th St., New York.

fully carries out his agreement with the owner, then the bond becomes null and void. If, however, the contractor does not carry out his agreement, then he and his sureties are liable for the amount of bond or such proportion as is necessary to make good the incompleted part of the work.

A CHAPTER ON LEGAL DOCUMENTS 155

After the contract for the new house is let and the contractor is ready to proceed with the work, it is necessary to take out a Building Permit. If the contract is let to a general contractor it is his duty to take out this permit, otherwise the mason contractor usually pays for and obtains it from the proper town or city officials. The permit states in a general way the character of the work and cost of the building, the fee required for the document being, usually, a certain percentage of the cost of the house. Special permits for remodeling an old house must also be obtained in most towns. Other permits frequently required are the plumbing permit and electric permit. In large cities many more are required, such as permits for light and ventilation, obstructions of street and sidewalk, opening street for pipes, tapping sewer and water pipes, and many others.

In asking for a general building permit the contractor is usually required to file a set of plans and specifications with the Building Department and these are carefully examined by one of the officials before a permit is granted. The entire system of permits is intended to be a check upon bad building methods and the fees required for such permits are to pay for the service of clerks and experts in the various departments.

In many places the mere issuing of a permit does not constitute the entire supervision given the new house by town officials. Frequently a Building Inspection Department is maintained, and inspectors visit all new buildings several times during erection, to examine plumbing, sewerage, gas and electric wiring, and see if these phases of the work are properly executed. After such work is completed according to the standards required by the Building Department, certificates are usually issued to the contractor or owner, stating that all conditions have been complied with.

When payments are made to a contractor from time to time as the work goes on, it is usually required that he give the owner a "waiver of lien" from himself and all other firms who have been furnishing material to him. This document states that the undersigned waives all right to put a "lien" on the building. Without such a waiver of lien the owner would be liable for the amount owed any parties by the contractor for work and

WAIVER OF LIEN.

materials furnished on the new building. Thus if the contractor has taken his payments from the owner but has not paid his lumber bill, let us say, the lumber company to protect itself might put a lien on the house, thus preventing the owner from entering into complete ownership until the lumber company's bill is paid. Now, if the contractor hasn't money enough to pay off the amount of this lien, the owner will have to pay it out of his

A CHAPTER ON LEGAL DOCUMENTS 157

own pocket if he wants to own the building, clear. A "waiver of lien" from a contractor (received by the owner before he issues a check) protects the owner from the annoyance of any liens.

When a contractor has performed enough work to entitle him to a payment (according to the terms of the contract) he is not usually paid by the owner, direct. Instead, the architect

```
CERTIFICATE OF PAYMENT
W R B WILLCOX Architect, Burlington, Vermont

Certificate No _____                    Amount of Payment
Payment No _____                        $_____
                                  Burlington, Vt ,_____ 19___
     To_____
This is to certify that according to agreement bearing date of_____ 19___
_____ entitled to receive _____ % of
_____ Dollars,
which is the value incorporated, since the last payment, in the_____

Amount of contract                       $_____
Amount of payment         $_____
Amount previously paid    _____
Total amount paid to date _____
Balance due                              $_____

                                              _____
                                                  Architect
$_____                            _____ 19

     Received from_____
the amount of payment above certified_____

                                              _____
                                                 Signature
```

ARCHITECT'S CERTIFICATE OF PAYMENT DUE CONTRACTOR.

makes out a certificate stating that the contractor is entitled to such a sum, and when this certificate is presented to the owner he issues a check to the contractor for the required amount. Thus, the certificate issued by the architect is really a requisition upon the owner for the required amount, and the document. remaining in the hands of the owner, is a receipt for the money expended, with a detailed statement of what the money was paid for.

158   SUCCESSFUL HOUSES AND HOW TO BUILD THEM

Some architects make a private contract with the owner before they enter into an arrangement to make plans and specifications for a building. This is signed by both parties and the document sets forth the compensation the architect is to receive, stating the work he is to perform and the amount of vari-

DWELLING HOUSE FORM

$ _____ On _____

and Additions adjoining and communicating, including Foundations, Plumbing and stationary Heating Apparatus, Plate, Stained and Ornamental Glass, Fresco Work, Wall Decorations, Gas and Electric Light Fixtures and Wiring, Electric Bell Apparatus, fixed Mirrors, Book Cases, Sideboards, and all furniture set or built in walls; Porches, Verandas, Window, and Door Screens, Shades, Awnings, Storm Doors and Windows, and all other permanent fixtures attached thereto and a part of said premises, or contained therein, including fences and sidewalks, situate

Permission to complete.   This policy covers all materials used in the construction of said building contained therein or adjacent thereto.

Permission for other insurance, and to make additions, alterations and repairs, same being covered under this policy.
Permission given to use kerosene, gas and electricity for fuel and lighting purposes, and to remain vacant and unoccupied pending rental and tenancy changes and during absence of assured or tenants

Permission is hereby given for the use of GASOLINE OR VAPOR STOVES in the building described in this policy, but only under the following restrictions and conditions, to be observed by the assured, viz   That at no time shall there be to exceed one gallon of NAPHTHA, GASOLINE OR BENZINE for each occupant (except that in the stove reservoir within said building or additions), and that kept in an approved metal safety can, free from leak and away from artificial light or heat The stove reservoir to be filled and the Gasoline (or fluid under whatever name) handled by daylight only, and not in the same room or room adjoining (having open communication) where, or while any fire, blaze or artificial light or flame of any kind is burning.

Permission is hereby given for the use of Kerosene Oil and for the keeping of not to exceed one barrel of Kerosene Oil on the premises

This policy shall cover any direct loss or damage caused by Lightning (meaning thereby the commonly accepted use of the term Lightning, and in no case to include loss or damage by cyclone, tornado or windstorm), and not exceeding the sum insured, nor the interest of the insured in the property, and subject in all other respects to the te, is and conditions of this policy.   *Provided,* however, if there shall be any other fire insurance on said property this Company shall be liable only pro rata with such other insurance for any direct loss by Lightning, whether such other insurance be against direct loss by Lightning or not

It is understood that the word noon in the commencement and expiration of this policy means the noon of "Central Standard Time"

Attached to and forming part of Policy No _____

MARSH & McLENNAN,
    INSURANCE, _____ AGENTS.
        CHICAGO.

INSURANCE FORM FOR DWELLING HOUSE.

ous payments due him (as most architects collect portions of their fee from time to time as the work progresses). The chief value of a contract between architect and owner is that it avoids any possible misunderstandings and for that reason it is to be recommended.

During the erection of the building the owner usually takes care of insurance, the ordinary " builders' risk " being the most used form of policy.

CEMENT HOUSE WITH AN OPEN TERRACE
Lionel Moses, II, Architect.

CHAPTER IX

EXCAVATION AND FOUNDATIONS

YOUR contract is let, we will say, and the contractor has ordered his materials delivered at the building site. In the meantime the owner and his architect must consider the exact location of the building on the lot, so that the contractor can proceed with the excavation. As has been noted in a previous chapter, the location of the building should be largely determined before the plans are made. The mistake, so common, of designing floor plans first and considering the location of the building afterwards, will surely bring complications later, when it will most likely be found that the house does not fit well, not allowing use of the ground to the best advantage. Have a complete scheme in your mind before plans are made, and make the house plans fit the building site. Then, when you get to the point of locating the house on the lot, you will find, if you have chosen wisely, that the result will be successful.

When you go with architect and builder to stake out the house, roughly mark out its size and shape by measuring the outside walls as they are drawn on the floor plans, setting little stakes in the ground at the four corners. Then stand off a short distance and view the proposed location to see if it meets with your approval. Your architect should discuss with you the various phases of grade and drainage which enter prominently into the problem, facts which must be considered carefully. Locate the building high enough above the lowest grade of the lot so that water will drain away from it, then your basement will be dry when cellars of less carefully located houses are wet.

162 SUCCESSFUL HOUSES AND HOW TO BUILD THEM

Batter boards (used as guides during building operations) are placed by the contractor under the direction of the architect. They should be located carefully, measurements being checked up afterwards to make sure they are correct, as it is very easy at this stage of proceedings to make an error in reading dimensions from the drawings or in measuring along the ground with a tapeline.

Batter boards are really the means of transferring dimensions from the plans to the ground. They usually consist of horizontal boards 4 to 6 feet long, set at the corners outside the area of excavation. When lines are stretched across from mark to mark on the batter boards, the exact outline of the building is shown, so that the contractor has a guide in building the foundation walls. After locating the building temporarily by means of small stakes set in the ground at the four corners (the owner being satisfied with the result), these permanent batter boards are erected a few feet outside the area of excavation, so that in excavating the corner stakes will not be dug away. For batter boards, stout stakes are driven deep into the ground about 4 feet apart, and to these a horizontal board is nailed, on which to notch the lines. Cord is stretched tightly from notch to notch, forming an accurate outline of the building. Masons plumb down from these lines in laying foundations and, as the batter boards remain as long as needed, it is always possible to check up the measurements. Batter boards should be placed far enough back from the excavation so that horses used to drag scrapers will not strike and knock them down.

EXCAVATION STAKED OUT

After locating the building accurately and checking up the dimensions by measuring from notch to notch on the batter boards, it is a good idea to measure the diagonals to see if the building is square. If square, the diagonals will be equal in length.

EXCAVATION AND FOUNDATIONS

Contractors usually ask the owner or his architect where dirt taken from the excavation is to be dumped, and it is well to give careful consideration to this point, stacking dirt where it will be handy to use in finished grading. Finished grading is not customarily in the contract, in most cases it being taken care of by the owner after the building is completed. This is why contractors are frequently indifferent to the careful stacking of dirt from the excavation. They are in a hurry to complete the job and are apt to dump it as near the building as possible, to save a long haul. Loam or black dirt (the top layer about 8 or 9 inches thick) should be scraped off carefully and stacked some distance from the excavation, where it is less liable to be tramped upon by the workmen. Have the piles of dirt put where they will not be disturbed later in digging trenches for plumbing pipes. To grow grass and flowers, this black dirt must be replaced around the building after building operations are finished, so it is too precious to waste by allowing it to fall carelessly into trenches and get mixed with the common clay or undersoil. Any sod fit to be saved should be cut, then rolled up and stored in a safe place; all trees requiring protection should be fenced off.

In staking out the building, a grade stake is usually driven into the ground near the excavation, to show the level of the top of the foundation wall. This stake should be carefully preserved to use as data at any time. The depth of the cellar or depth of excavation will be largely determined by the depth of the sewer to which the property drains, and amount of head room required in the cellar. In most cases it is desirable to have the finished basement floors at least 18 inches or 2 feet above the sewer in the street so that the basement water-closet and laundry tubs may drain with a good slope to the sewer. At the same time, foundations should extend deep enough below ground to prevent frost from penetrating to the bottom of the footings and heaving the walls out of position (which will certainly happen if frost gets under the footings). In most localities, 4 feet below ground is considered sufficient for foundation walls, though it is sometimes necessary in exceptionally cold climates to extend them deeper. In determining the depth of basement after first settling the grade for the cellar floor (by locating the cellar bottom 18 inches or 2 feet above the sewer level), one must understand that it is not necessary to dig any particular distance below the *present grade* of the lot, but all computations should be made from the *finished grade*. In other words, the present grade of the lot can be raised to any point desired by filling in around the walls in the form of a bank or terrace, after the building is completed. Thus, when a lot is low and damp it is advisable to *raise the grade*, having the finished grade much higher than the original grade. If this finished grade is settled at 2 feet above the original grade, it will be necessary to dig only 2 feet into the ground, which would bring the footings 4 feet below the new grade.

In determining the location of the cellar bottom one must also be governed by the character of the subsoil. If it is soft, not sufficiently dense to carry the weight of the building (as is frequently the case), the excavation must be carried deeper to strike hardpan.

The different kinds of soil upon which the foundations of the house may rest, determine the width of footings necessary to support the weight of the building. The following table, showing the bearing power of soils, will be found useful: —

BEARING POWER OF SOILS

Rock, 15 to 300 tons per square foot
Clay, dry, 4 tons per square foot.
Clay, soft or wet, 1 ton per square foot
Gravel and Coarse Sand, confined, 8 tons per square foot.
Sand, compact and well confined, 4 tons per square foot.
Quicksand, ½ ton per square foot.

It will be seen by reference to this table that rock is perfectly safe to rest a building upon. When the foundations rest on rock, however, care should be taken to level off a shelf on which to build. Otherwise, if foundations are started on a sloping surface of rock, the weight of the building might cause them to slip. Rock is not considered so ideal for footings as clay, sand, or gravel, for surface water following down to the level of the rock is apt to penetrate into the cellar through the joint between foundation and bedrock, — a place very difficult to make tight.

Gravel and sand are excellent for supporting the weight of a house, when compact and firm. Quicksand, of course, is particularly undesirable. Sand and gravel should be well tamped around the finished foundation walls, in order to prevent washouts by water. Dry clay makes a firm foundation, but one must be careful that it does not soften when wet; care must be taken to drain all water away from the building.

Some building sites which have been filled with rubbish or soft soil are very undesirable for building purposes. On such a piece of property it is usually necessary to dig down through the filling until hardpan is reached, though in some cases filling can be "puddled" by soaking it with water until it becomes firm.

The footings of a building make it possible to build upon soils of different bearing power. Thus, footings act as a sort of raft, supporting the weight of the house. Naturally, a raft supporting a given weight on hard, firm clay could be smaller in area than a raft supporting the same weight on soft clay, and it is on this principle that house footings are designed.

Footings are usually composed of concrete, large flat stones, or stepped-up brick. The following table shows sizes of various footings suitable for good, firm soil: —

SIZES OF FOOTINGS

(Required on firm soil)

16-inch brick foundation wall requires concrete footings, 24 inches wide, 8 to 12 inches thick.

Or 16-inch brick foundation wall requires stepped brick footings, 7 courses high, $1\frac{1}{2}$ inches per course.

Or 16-inch brick foundation wall requires 3 stepped courses of wide, thick, flat stones.

20-inch stone foundation wall requires 1 course of flat, thick stones, 24 to 30 inches wide.

Or 20-inch stone foundation wall requires concrete footing, 24 to 30 inches wide, 8 to 12 inches thick.

This table is only approximate and cannot be considered as applying in all cases. Under ordinary circumstances, however, it conforms to best practice.

When concrete is used for footings, a trench should be dug just the right width for the concrete and in this the material is tamped in layers 6 to 8 inches thick. In place of tamping, it is sometimes more convenient to mix the concrete quite wet, pouring it in place. If the soil is wet, concrete can be laid for footings by lining the trenches with oiled cotton, which keeps moisture out until the cement is set. When building on loose sand trenches should be shored up with heavy planks to prevent caving in.

Flat stones used for footings should never be less than 8 inches thick and they must be as large in area as possible, laid with broken joints and thoroughly bedded in plenty of cement mortar. Never allow part of the footings to rest on stone and part on gravel and sand. When one corner of a building rests on solid stone, the balance resting on gravel, concrete footings should be used on the gravel to approximate the conditions of the stone, and equalize the settlement. The idea should be to equalize loads on all parts of the bearing soil, and footings should be carefully designed to carry out this purpose. On sloping ground, footings should be stepped in level sections, thoroughly bonded at the stepping intersections.

Such portions of the house as are to be built without a cellar can stand on posts or piers of stone, brick, or concrete. A wing of the main house, however, even though there is to be no cellar underneath, is always better on solid foundation walls like the balance of the house. Piers should rest on wide, square footings of stone or concrete.

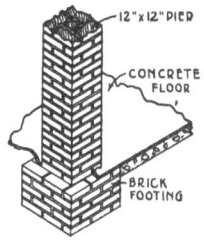

BRICK PIER.

Foundation walls for an ordinary two-story house are usually from 16 to 20 inches thick when of concrete. On some cheap jobs foundation walls are built of brick, 8 inches thick, and brick piers for strengthening the wall are inserted every 15 or 20 feet. This is not the best practice, however, for you should remember that foundation walls not only support the weight of the building, but act as retaining walls as well, to keep the surrounding ground from caving into the cellar. For this reason foundation walls are rarely less than 12 inches thick.

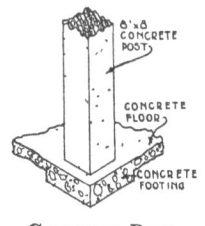

CONCRETE BASEMENT POST.

Girders employed in the floor construction of the first floor can be supported on solid walls in the basement, or they may be carried by brick, stone, or concrete piers, iron columns, or wooden posts. No construction for supporting floors is better than solid walls under the girders, though solid walls take up considerable space in the basement. When brick piers are used to support girders they are usually 12″ by 12″; concrete piers can be 8″ by 8″ to 12″ by 12″; stone piers are customarily 16″ by 16″, because it is difficult to lay stonework in piers of less size.

Cement-filled wrought iron columns are excellent to support

basement girders. Such are, in fact, of ordinary wrought iron pipe, filled with cement to increase their stability. They can be bought, ready-made, with cast iron caps and bases, and they come in a great many different lengths. The sizes most used for houses are 3-inch and 4-inch columns.

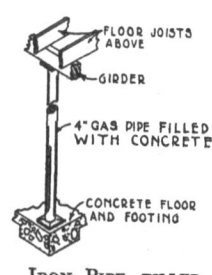

IRON PIPE FILLED WITH CONCRETE.

Footings of liberal size made of stone or concrete should be used under all basement piers. In most cases footings 18" by 18" up to 24" by 24" will be found of sufficient size to maintain the load put upon them. Wooden posts are frequently used in the basement. Cedar posts (or locust) are best for this purpose, and posts 6 or 8 inches in diameter are about the right size. Ordinary timber, 6" by 6" or 8" by 8", is also frequently used for basement posts.

Piers of hollow tile are strong and light, and for this reason are widely used in houses of all sizes.

Area walls around outside basement steps or windows are usually 12 inches thick, for they, also, act as retaining walls. Such walls should be capped with stone flagging or concrete coping to prevent moisture from penetrating and disintegrating the wall. All walls should be started deep enough to be well below frost.

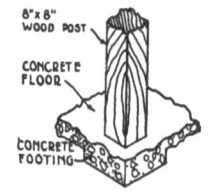

ORDINARY WOODEN POST FOR FLOOR SUPPORT.

Architects, before working drawings are made, usually visit the building site and determine with the owner the height of foundation walls required above ground, to allow cellar windows of the correct size to light the basement properly. If the house stands on the side of a hill, the foundation wall may be higher on one side than on another. With extra large cellar windows placed on the highest side it may not be necessary to put cellar windows on the low side. All these details are shown on the working drawings, and the owner should study them carefully to make sure he understands them.

In best built houses it is customary to dig the basement carefully to just the right depth for the cellar floor. This prevents the necessity of filling up later for the cement floor. Filling is bad under any floor, for it is liable to cause a settlement, cracking the cement. Most basements are 7 feet high in the clear. That is to say, at the lowest point under a girder the head room is 7 feet from finished cement floor to underside of girder. This gives ample space over one's head for steam or water pipes to extend. You should remember, however, that heating mains in the basement are sloped to allow them to drain back to the boiler, so an extra allowance of height may be necessary in large houses where pipe lines are long, in order to secure head room under them. On the other hand, in small houses, 7 feet is frequently decreased to 6 feet or 6 feet 6 inches in the clear, under girders. Do not make the mistake of getting basement head room too low, however, for it is a great annoyance to walk about the cellar in constant danger of bumping one's head on a girder or pipe. Furnace pipes require a greater depth of cellar than hot water and steam pipes.

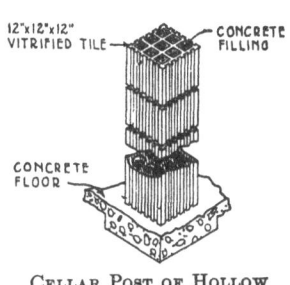

CELLAR POST OF HOLLOW TILE.

Cellar windows should be ample in height and width. The tendency in modern houses is to place the first floor as close to the ground as possible, in order to diminish the number of steps between grade and first floor. This is excellent in effect, as will be noticed in so many of the charming little houses which, placed close to the ground, seem to fit the landscape so much better than houses standing boldly up in the air. Each cellar window can be made as small as 12 inches in height, if plenty of them are used. Short windows can be made wider, or they can be placed in groups of two or three, with the result that there is the same total area of glass as with fewer windows, extra large. For a house of ordinary size, cellar windows are most frequently about 16 or 18 inches high, which admits of glass about 12 to 14 inches high. Windows can be placed directly under floor joists, as the weight of the floor above can be kept off them by using headers. It is best to keep the first floor as near the grade as is practical.

After the cellar is dug and before the foundations are started, some problem of drainage may be necessary to solve. If the ground is clay and water runs into the excavation, it may be necessary to make some provision for permanently draining the subsoil in order to keep the finished cellar dry. In best practice it is customary to lay a line of agricultural tile or broken stone, cinders, or gravel around outside the cellar wall. The idea is that water on the surface of the ground strikes the outside of the cellar wall and runs down to the bottom. Any little crevices in the wall permit this moisture to penetrate the wall, making the cellar damp. With a well-built wall, water is not apt to work its way through, but it often runs down outside the wall until it strikes the projecting footing, where it seeps through into the joint immediately above the footing course, or it runs under the wall and seeps up through the cellar floor.

To catch outside surface water before it can get through the wall, lay a line of 3-inch or 4-inch agricultural tile just above the footing course, outside the wall. These should be graded to slope slightly to a low point, from which they lead into the sewer or into a pit filled with broken stone (called "dry well"). Thus, during a heavy rain, water outside the foundations runs down until it reaches the open joints of the tile conduit, which it penetrates, draining to the low point and thence into the sewer or dry well. Another good way to provide subsoil drainage is to dig the trenches for the foundations about 8 inches deeper than required for the footings, filling the bottom with broken stone. These trenches can be graded to a low point, from which the water is led away to the sewer or dry well. Cinders or broken stone filled in outside foundations for a thickness of 4 to 8 inches often proves sufficient to carry away surface water, preventing it from entering the cellar. Where soil is composed of sand or gravel (or a porous mixture of clay and sand capable of draining water away quickly) often it is not necessary to provide for subsoil drainage. Water outside the foundation walls in such a case usually drains quickly away before it can enter the cellar.

One should remember that ordinary cement cellar floors are not waterproof, and water or moisture which gets under the footings is apt to rise up through the cellar floor. In a wet location it is sometimes necessary to waterproof the basement wall and cellar floor by using a waterproofing compound in the cement (when the foundations are of concrete), or by a tarred felt lining, mopped to the masonry like a composition roof. If compound is used, select a brand that is manufactured by a reliable firm, as many waterproofing compounds are not desirable. The best compounds are mixed with the cement when the concrete is mixed.

The most successful waterproofing of all is composed of good, thick, tarred felt similar to that used in composition roofs. After the footing course is built a thickness of this felt is laid below the level of the future finished basement floor. This strip of felt is left projecting temporarily on both sides for attaching the felt which is to cover the outside of the wall to that which lies under the basement floor. Later, when the basement floor is laid, a groundwork of cement concrete about 3 inches thick is placed over the entire cellar bottom. On top of this a water-tight sheet of tar felt mopped with pitch like a composition roof is attached to the strip left sticking in the footings. Then the layer of tarred felt applied to the outside walls is attached, thus producing a waterproof skin, covering foundation walls and cellar floor, making, in fact, a great water-

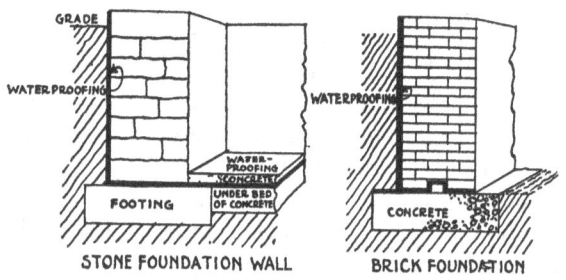

Two Practical Methods of Waterproofing the Basement.

proof bowl. On top of the waterproofing, a finished cement floor is laid two or three inches thick.

Concrete foundations are excellent when the cement concrete is properly made. Contrary to popular opinion, concrete is not cheaper than stone, however, except in localities where the latter is difficult to obtain. The greatest cost in concrete foundations is the wooden forms. Cost of lumber and price of labor in most communities usually brings the cost of concrete foundations up to the price of stone. Concrete is the best material for footings (the undermost part of the foundations, made slightly wider than the main wall) because it fills compactly the slight variations of surface apt to exist at the bottom of the trenches. In addition, concrete footings (being in one mass) spread the weight of a building better than footings composed of many units like stone footings.

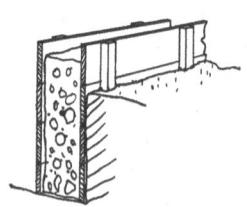

Best Concrete Foundation; Wood Form Both Sides.

For that portion of the foundation walls which extends above the footings, concrete is no better than good, sound stone. Concrete is more porous than stone and water, or dampness is more liable to penetrate in the former than in the latter. In fact, it is rarely safe to build concrete foundation walls unless waterproofing is resorted to.

Concrete for foundation walls should be mixed quite wet so that the material, flowing readily to all parts of the forms, can be spaded or rammed into place. When too little water is used a wall becomes spongy, as all the voids are not properly filled with material; a spongy wall is easily penetrated by dampness. Use small-sized crushed stone or gravel in your concrete foundations, and after the forms are removed plaster both sides of the wall with cement mortar, applied firmly with a trowel and smoothed sufficiently to close the grain of the cement and sand. Concrete should be put into the forms in layers not more than 12 inches thick, for it is impossible to pack material down tightly when it is too thick.

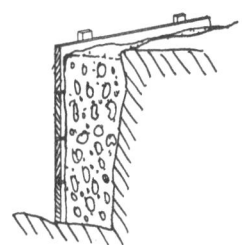

CHEAP CONCRETE FOUNDATION; FORM ON ONE SIDE, ONLY.

There is no better material for foundations than good, sound stone, and it will be found as cheap in most localities as any other material. Stone is so dense that when joints are properly cemented the wall is quite waterproof. Except when soil is unusually wet it will not be necessary to waterproof the outside of such a wall, but tile or broken stone subsoil drains can be used to prevent the excess of water from rising up through the basement floor. Hard stone makes the best foundations, and all stonework should be pointed both sides with cement mortar. For this purpose excavations are always made at least 8 inches larger than the cellar, so that workmen can get down into the trenches and point up all the joints. Walls should be as smooth outside as they are inside, for irregular, jagged projections on the exterior catch against the bank, leading water into the cellar. Besides this, projecting stones are heaved by the frost, causing a building to move slightly, cracking the plastering.

Stone should be trimmed so there are no thin edges; good stone masons knock off all weak angles, leaving the blocks fairly square, and these blocks are laid in the wall with cement mortar thick enough so that the material flows into all the irregularities of the stone, filling up the cavities. Of course all blocks of stone are not the same size, but a large proportion should be "through stones," that is, extending entirely through the wall from front to back. Smaller stones, when they are sound, can be used to fill in between the large blocks, but chips should be used very sparingly and then only when slushed up solidly with mortar. In a poor job of stonework the tendency is to use a few large blocks set loosely, and filled in between with small stones and chips. A little mortar troweled over the top of these filled spaces covers up the voids and then another larger block is laid on top. Such a wall, containing, as it does, a number of hollow spaces, is liable to settle or give way after it is built.

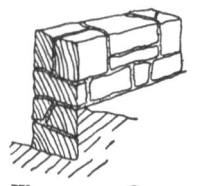

WELL-BUILT STONE FOUNDATION.

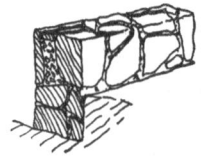

POORLY BUILT STONEWORK.

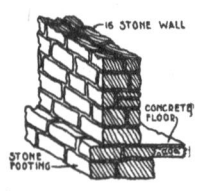

STONE FOUNDATION ON STONE FOOTINGS.

A well-built wall is solidly built with stonework. Prodding the joints of such a wall with a stiff piece of wire, one finds it impossible to penetrate very far. In a poor job a wire will sometimes penetrate through the entire wall. It is poor policy to skimp on foundations of a building. Spend enough money here, at least, to get a first-class job, even if it is necessary to curtail elsewhere.

That portion of foundation walls extending below ground should always be laid in cement mortar, consisting of 1 part of good Portland cement to 3 parts of clean, coarse sand. Above ground lime mortar can be used, but a small portion of Portland cement should be added to the mortar to make it stiffer, — 1 part cement, 1 part lime, and 3 parts of sand make a good mixture.

All lime used for mortar should be fresh, and it must be kept in a dry place to prevent air-slaking. Cement should also be fresh, carefully stored away, free from danger of any possible dampness. Sand should be sharp and clean (no loam or clay mixed with it). Sand dug from a hillside is usually best, for lake or river sand, though clean, is apt to be too smooth; rough, coarse sand is preferable, as it offers the best bond with cement or lime. Sand from the sea is not suitable for mortar.

In mixing lime mortar, the proper way is to spread a bed of sand in the mortar box, on which is then laid evenly a layer of lime (carefully measured out). Water is then poured on, after which the lime is covered with a layer of sand, to retain the vapor which quickly begins to rise from the moistened lime. The proportion of sand to lime is usually 1 to 3, or 1 to 4. Lime is customarily slaked in this way in large quantities, as it takes several days for it to cool sufficiently to be used.

In mixing cement mortar, 1 part of cement to 3 or 4 parts of sand are used, thoroughly mixed dry. Then sufficient water is added to make a thick paste, after which the cement mortar is ready. Unlike lime mortar, cement mortar does not require to stand; indeed, cement mortar more than one day old should never be used. In using lime mortar to which cement is to be added, the ready-mixed lime mortar is simply "tempered" with a small proportion of cement. Mortar can be colored by mixing mineral pigment, dry or in paste form. Lime mortar should be slaked at least 24 hours before color is added, and one should remember that mortar color dries a lighter shade than the natural color, therefore a shade darker than the desired tint should be used.

176   SUCCESSFUL HOUSES AND HOW TO BUILD THEM

After completion of the foundations, joints on the outside should be gone over again and pointed up with cement mortar, for during the building of the wall it is customary to merely bed the stones in mortar without pointing the joints. All joints should be completely filled with mortar, pushed in with a pointing tool, and joints should have a tendency to dip downward so that moisture will drip off instead of being carried down into the stone. Walls built carefully in this fashion are not cheap, to be sure, but they are solid and durable. As a matter of fact, the cost of good work over and above poor work is not great and the difference in price is usually worth while.

Brick is not an ideal material for foundations below ground, for the reason that bricks (made of clay) are inclined to grow soft in a wet soil after a few years. This doesn't necessarily mean that a house is insecurely supported when on brick foundations, for brick, even when slightly soft, would probably carry the load. But soft brickwork is easily penetrated by dampness, and after a few years brick walls are apt to let moisture into the cellar.

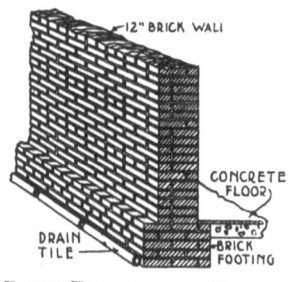

BRICK FOOTINGS AND FOUNDATION; AGRICULTURAL TILE, OUTSIDE.

In some sections of the country, however, brick is cheap, stone or concrete being high, so the former is naturally used. It will prove a practical material if used understandingly. Get the hardest brick, only, selecting those which come from points in the brick kiln nearest the fire. These are easily recognized, as they are usually much darker than ordinary brick. Such brick laid up in good cement mortar can be depended upon. If the soil is wet, it is well to waterproof brick foundations on the outside. Concrete footings can be used, or brick footings, composed of several courses of brick on edge.

Hollow tile is a good material to use for fountain walls, providing it is vitrified or salt glazed. Ordinary tile may prove too soft. Hollow concrete blocks can be used with safety, providing they are made of the best of materials, properly cured, — a very difficult grade to get, by the way, as a large number of concrete blocks are poorly made, some of them being so porous they soak water like a sponge. Concrete blocks, clay bricks, and hollow tile can be readily tested for density by sprinkling them with water. If water soaks rapidly into the material one may know that it is not sufficiently dense to make good foundation walls.

Modern Frame House in Colonial Style

CHAPTER X

ADVANTAGES OF A FRAME HOUSE

MORE frame houses are built than any other kind, and it isn't strange when one reflects that America is really a lumber country. Though lumber is fast disappearing to give way to more permanent materials, timber is still the cheapest, most easily worked material for building houses, and it continues to be used for that purpose in enormous quantities in spite of the introduction of the more ideal fireproof construction. Properly built frame structures are economical, strong, and reasonably weather-resisting. Though not so durable as stone, brick, or other masonry materials frame houses wear fairly well and are easily kept in repair when properly constructed in the first place.

The evolution of framework for houses is interesting, showing as it does man's inventive genius and his mastery over problems of all sorts. Every section of the country has its own type of frame construction, worked out especially to take care of the conditions of labor and material in that particular section. This has given rise to many ingenious types of construction.

Reviewing briefly the history of timber as used along the Atlantic coast where early settlers first established their homes, it is interesting to note the evolution of house construction from early log houses, built hastily but thoroughly from rough-hewn logs laid horizontally, to the admirably built frame houses of the present day. There was no need of conservation of timber in the early days, or at least early settlers did not see the need of it, so they felled trees lavishly, using for their houses twice or thrice as much timber as was necessary or even desirable.

First using roughly hewn logs, it quickly became the custom to hew logs smooth in order to secure a better fit. Some early settlers, it is said, lost their scalps by wild animals reaching their muzzles through open chinks while the family slept. Finally logs were fitted closer and better until the house evolved into a strongly constructed building that would withstand the ravages of the weather and siege of a hostile foe.

But naturally, as settlers prospered and had more time to devote to planning and building houses, they began to build more in the manner of the countries oversea where they had formerly lived. Settlers hailing from England began to build somewhat along English lines, — Dutch settlers built houses showing Dutch influence, and settlers from France copied as nearly as they could the pretty types with which they were most familiar.

Forms of construction in America are not the less American, however, nor were they so from the start, for settlers found conditions in this country very different from conditions in the mother countries, where skilled labor had developed types of construction not practical for new America. For this reason, though American houses somewhat resembled in exterior appearance their European prototypes, they were really quite different in structure. Brick was used largely in European houses; — either brick alone or brick in combination with heavy timbers. But brick was rarely used in the earliest houses of New England, Pennsylvania, and the South, timber throughout being the typical construction.

Early timber houses in this country were built with heavy frames consisting of large, square-hewn timbers at the corners, 8 by 8 inches or larger, frequently of oak or similar hard wood.

Sills were equally heavy and roofs were framed with heavy purlins (much as churches are framed nowadays) supporting rafters of large size. The framework of timbers was securely braced by diagonal pieces, all being thoroughly tied together by mortise and tenon joints pinned with wooden pins. Such frames were marvels of strength and durability, and it is no wonder that so many of the old houses are still standing as sound as when first built.

It was the cheapness and convenience of timber that caused these early American houses to be so heavily built. Forests were plentiful, — near at hand in most cases, — and there was no need to economize in the use of material. Steel and iron nails had not come into the market, and large timbers were necessary in a construction requiring wooden pins. All these conditions made for somewhat wasteful use of timber.

After timber became more scarce and consequently rose in price, builders began to make the framework of their houses smaller. Timbers of large size were too costly to be used so lavishly and constructors began to conserve material, working out a system of construction more practical than in earlier houses. Modern methods of sawing timber instead of hewing it made it possible to get more sticks from each log. Timbers for inside partitions were reduced to 4 inches thick, and 4 by 8-inch corner posts were substituted for those of larger size. Finally, when it came to the roof, it was discovered that timbers could be thin and deep, — instead of square, — so rafters were made 2 by 6 inches and 2 by 8 inches, extending across wider spans and leaving out the heavy purlins.

Present-day frame construction in Eastern States is the result of this evolution, and methods of framing are excellent. A sill, usually 4×6 inches or 4×8 inches, is laid on top of the underpinning, its corners halved together and pinned with wooden pins or spiked with heavy spikes. At each corner of the building a 4×8-inch post is set up, extending in one piece to the plate.

182 SUCCESSFUL HOUSES AND HOW TO BUILD THEM

These corner posts are mortised into sill and plate. At frequent intervals along the sides of the building similar 4 × 8-inch posts are set up to strengthen the wall, and between these posts ordinary 2 × 4-inch studs are spiked in place, supporting the girt to which the second-floor joists are secured. These girts (which are really girders) extend horizontally around the walls of the building just under the second-floor joists which they support. They are framed into the corner posts with mortise and tenon joints, pinned with wooden pins or spiked. To further brace the frame, wind braces (as they are called) are cut in diagonally from sill to post and from girt to post, and framed into each. The result is a skeleton framework of utmost strength, though each timber is comparatively light. Floor joists are cut out to rest on the sills, the heels of the joists resting on the underpinning and the toes on the sill, to which they are strongly spiked. In addition, it is customary to have as many joists as possible applied directly at the sides of studs, to which they are spiked. It would be hard to imagine a stronger frame for a house than is provided by this excellent method of framing, and houses built in this way are undoubtedly as strong as old-time houses, in which frequently the amount of timber used exceeded by 30% the amount used to-day.

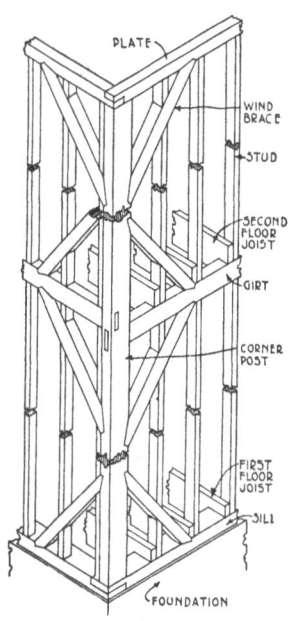

THE STURDY NEW ENGLAND FRAME.

The following table shows stock sizes of lumber used in house construction : —

STOCK SIZES OF LUMBER

Size in Inches	Length in Feet							
2 × 4	12	14	16	18	20	22	24	26
2 × 6	12	14	16	18	20	22	24	26
2 × 8	12	14	16	18	20	22	24	26
2 × 10	12	14	16	18	20	22	24	26
2 × 12	12	14	16	18	20	22	24	26
3 × 4	12	14	16	18	20	22	24	26
3 × 6	12	14	16	18	20	22	24.	26
3 × 8	12	14	16	18	20	22	24	26
3 × 10	12	14	16	18	20	22	24	26
3 × 12	12	14	16	18	20	22	24	26
4 × 4	12	14	16	18	20	22	24	26
4 × 6	12	14	16	18	20	22	24	26
4 × 8	12	14	16	18	20	22	24	26
4 × 10	12	14	16	18	20	22	24	26
4 × 12	12	14	16	18	20	22	24	26
6 × 6	12	14	16	18	20	22	24	26
6 × 8	12	14	16	18	20	22	24	26
6 × 10	12	14	16	18	20	22	24	26
6 × 12	12	14	16	18	20	22	24	26

Able designers of house construction to-day are as eager to save in the amount of material used as they are to excel in durability and safety of construction. No house can be considered good in design unless it is economical as well as sound. High cost of labor and material makes it necessary to conserve materials, and skillful designing produces this result without damaging the construction.

In the West, another type of house construction is used, cutting down the amount of labor and material required even beyond results obtained in Eastern States. This type is called "balloon frame" construction, and it is claimed by western

184   SUCCESSFUL HOUSES AND HOW TO BUILD THEM

builders to be as strong as "pinned and framed" construction. These are the two leading types of house construction, — the eastern "framed" type and the western "balloon frame" type. Of course there are various modifications of each used in different sections of the country.

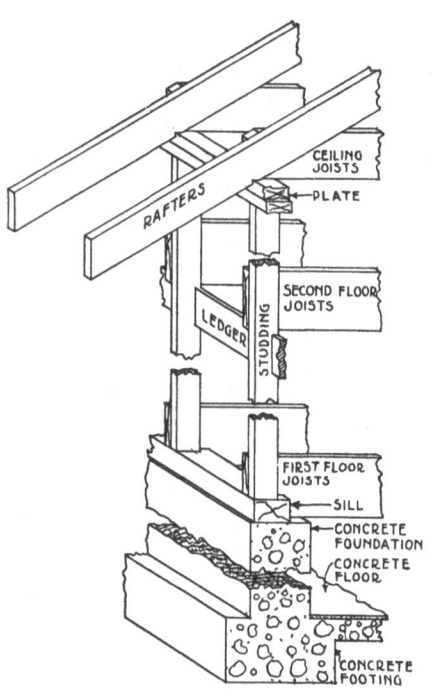

WESTERN "BALLOON" FRAME ON CONCRETE FOUNDATION.

Notwithstanding claims made by western builders, it is doubtful if "balloon frame" construction is as strong as "frame" construction. The former when properly built is sound and durable, but a house built in that way vibrates more in the wind, as it is not so securely braced. A further disadvantage of the former method is that the strength of the skeleton depends largely upon the holding power of the spikes, as all timbers are secured with spikes instead of being mortised and tenoned. Nevertheless, balloon frames are perfectly practical, and there need be no hesitancy in using them.

Balloon framing of the better class consists of a sill, usually a single 4 × 6-inch piece (though frequently two 2 × 6-inch pieces are spiked together) set on top of the underpinning. Ordinary 2 × 4-inch studs are set upon the sill and spiked to it.

These studs usually extend in one piece to the plate and they are notched out just below the level of the second floor to receive a 1 × 4-inch ledger, which supports the second-floor joists. At the corners of the building two 2 × 4-inch studs are spiked together, making a substitute for a 4 × 4-inch post. On many houses with "balloon frame" not a timber is used thicker than 2 inches. Thus, the 4 × 6-inch sill consists of two 2 × 6-inch pieces spiked together; a 4 × 4-inch post is built up from two 2 × 4-inch pieces, and so on. Girders for supporting the first-floor joists are made up from three 2 × 8-inch pieces, making in effect a 6 × 8-inch girder. Theoretically, timbers built of several pieces are as strong as a solid timber, providing they are so strongly put together as to make in effect a single solid stick of timber. Actually, however, it is almost impossible (with ordinary care) to build a large timber out of smaller pieces which will be as strong as a single large piece; spikes may give slightly, with the result that the built-up girder is not quite so efficient as a single large piece.

The balloon frame is usually strong enough for most houses, and there is no objection to using this type when it is properly built; that is, when the pieces are thoroughly spiked together in the most workmanlike way. If a ledger is used to support the second-floor joists, it is necessary that the joists be applied to strike the sides of studs so that they may be spiked together. Joists are also frequently notched on to the ledger, — a further precaution to prevent them from pulling away. First-floor joists rest on the sill, with heels on the underpinning, as in ordinary frame construction.

A new type of frame house has come into vogue in the Middle West, in which the underpinning is practically eliminated. In houses like this the foundation wall extends just above ground and is surmounted with a concrete, stone, or brick base. The wooden sill is laid on top of this base, the studs extending from it up to the plate. Thus, the first-floor joists are supported on a ledger precisely like second-floor joists; cellar window frames are set in the wooden wall of the building like first and second-story window frames. The idea is to eliminate the underpinning, not only for the slight saving in cost which it involves but also to obtain a pleasingly simple effect. With a house built in this way, however, care should be taken to have the inside of the wooden outside wall in the cellar plastered, in order to make the cellar warm. An ordinary masonry underpinning 12 inches or more thick makes a sufficiently warm cellar, but when for this masonry wall there is substituted a wooden wall only 4" thick, it is necessary to line the latter with plaster to make it warm. This plaster should extend between the joists up to the under-side of the flooring at the first-floor level.

One of the chief requisites in good house construction is freedom from lumber shrinkage; or more correctly, freedom from *excessive* shrinkage of lumber, for no matter how dry it is, lumber is bound to shrink somewhat. Timbers do not shrink lengthwise so much as they shrink crosswise. In other words, after the house is built, every timber in it shrinks slightly as, month after month, the lumber dries out and its fibers contract. Beginning at the sill and first-floor girders, which carry the greatest weight (as they are the bottommost timbers), sills and girders contract slightly, allowing the building to settle, though it may be ever so little. Every floor joist also contracts slightly; ledgers or girts shrink a bit, allowing further settling of the building, and plates supporting rafters, as well as the rafters themselves, shrink slightly, adding to the general contraction and consequent settling of the upright walls of the building. The result is that the sum of all this shrinkage of timber may equal as much as an inch or two, — sometimes more. When this occurs, the plaster on inside and outside walls begins to crack, for plaster is not elastic enough to stand even slight displacement without cracking.

It is apparent that as every horizontal timber shrinks (for

vertical timbers alter so slightly that their shrinkage may be considered negligible), the less amount of horizontal timbers there are the less will be the shrinkage. Clever constructors have taken advantage of this well-known fact to design framework for buildings with a minimum amount of horizontal timber. For example, instead of using girders in the basement with the first-floor joists laid on top of them, first-floor joists are framed into girders, flush, so that (assuming a girder is 10 inches deep and the floor joists also 10 inches deep) the total timber for shrinkage is only 10 inches. In the ordinary method of construction when floor joists are merely placed on top of girders, there would be 20 inches of timber for shrinkage, that is, 10 inches for girder and 10 inches for joists. To cause less shrinkage of timber many skillful builders use only one plate for inside partitions instead of (as is so frequently the custom) using two, thus saving 2 inches of shrinkable timber.

There are many modifications of flush joist and girder construction. One method frequently used is to cut out the joists sufficiently to allow them to extend as little as possible above the girders, spiking a 2 × 4-inch strip to the sides of the girders below the heel of the joists for their further support. This allows several inches less shrinkage than by the method of having the entire depth of joists above the girders, and it will be found a practical substitute for the more expensive flush framing. Aside from the expense of flush framing by reason of the additional thickness of girder required (to admit of so much being cut away in framing without impairing its strength), an additional disadvantage in flush framing is that it is frequently inconvenient to extend plumbing and heating pipes horizontally

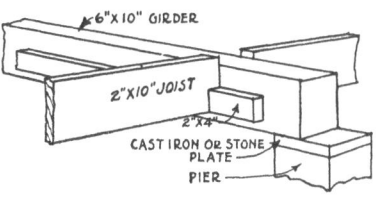

FLOOR JOISTS FRAMED FOR MINIMUM SHRINKAGE.

across the basement ceiling. Such pipes usually extend between the joists, but every time a flush-framed girder is to be passed it is necessary to cut holes to permit pipes to pass through, greatly weakening the girder. When joists extend slightly above girders, pipes can be easily extended through the space thus left between flooring and girder, — a great saving of labor. In flush framing, therefore, careful consideration should be given to the running of pipes; frequently they can be extended entirely under the basement ceiling, or else, with a little care, they can be run mostly on the wall, where they will not interfere in any way with girders.

When beamed ceilings are desired in various rooms, it is a good idea to frame timbers in the floor to take care of the beams. In other words, real beams are better than imitation beams (such as thin shells planted on the ceiling after the floors are laid). Beamed ceilings are often considered as merely decorations, like a paneled wainscott on the wall, but it is in much better taste to consider beams as structural, — as they were, indeed, in houses built in times gone by, in which beamed ceilings originated.

Methods for building inside partitions vary in different communities, though good construction is always founded on the same principles. There are in general two ways to build inside partitions. In one method the first-floor joists are laid over the entire floor which is then boarded over with flooring. On top of this flooring is placed a partition base for each partition consisting of a 2 × 4-inch strip, laid flatwise. On each base or sill is erected the upright studs. The objection to this method is that the weight of the partitions comes upon the joists themselves so that when they shrink (as they are bound to do) the inside partitions go down with them, causing cracks in the plastering. A better way is to build inside partitions directly on the more solid basement girders, by resting them on the girders instead of on top of the flooring. Where a partition extends

ADVANTAGES OF A FRAME HOUSE

over a girder this is easy to do. When a partition extends at right angles to a girder, two joists are spiked together, forming a stout beam on which the partition rests.

All these little points about framing are more important than they seem, and the house-owner who wishes to have best possible construction should carefully consider them. Even slight carelessness in building the framework of a house almost always causes trouble later on, cracks appearing in the plaster walls, sags in floors, or slight deviations from the level in cornices and door casings.

Most walls, both inside and outside, are built of 2×4-inch studding, though frequently outside walls which are to be plastered on the exterior are built of 2×6-inch studding. The latter are excellent to use as they are stiffer than the more ordinary 2×4-inch studs. Bathroom partitions should be of 2×6-inch studs in order to provide sufficient room for the soil pipe without making a jog in the room.

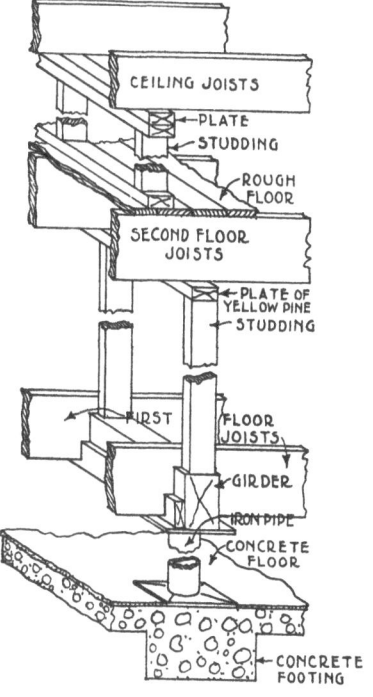

GOOD METHOD OF BUILDING INTERIOR PARTITIONS.

To avoid cutting into girders when flush framing of floor joists is used, many architects and builders install steel hangers for supporting joists and holding them next to the girders.

Where one girder comes against another at right angles to it, the same kind of hangers can be used to good advantage; the point of intersection should always come directly above (or very nearly) a supporting basement post. Framing is largely a matter of common sense. Once a houseowner knows the best general types of construction it is comparatively easy to apply his knowledge in checking up the work in his own house. The general results to be sought after are: first, minimum of lumber shrinkage; second, maximum of lumber size to prevent sagging.

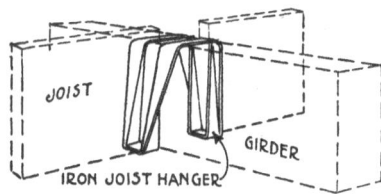

FLOOR JOISTS HUNG ON IRON HANGERS.

Across wide spans, such as where a bedroom partition comes over a large room below, it is necessary to truss the beam which supports the bedroom partition. This can be easily done by spiking two of the joists together, with two V-shaped boards between. The tendency in such a beam is for weight to compress the V-shaped boards, and the resistance these offer to compression helps to carry the weight. Another way to take some of the weight of a bedroom partition off the floor below is to truss the partition by putting diagonal timbers at the ends

The framework of a house is often materially helped by the outside boarding, which contributes to the stability of the structure when it is good material well applied. Tongued and grooved boarding applied diagonally is excellent, as diagonal boarding tends to hold the structural members of the framework more rigidly than horizontal boarding. Horizontal boarding, however, is most often used, for it is a little easier to put on and answers very well when thoroughly nailed to a well-built frame. In many sections of the country ship-lap laid horizontally or diagonally is used in place of tongued and grooved boarding. It has the advantage of requiring less labor to apply it.

The best method for laying underfloors is to use tongued and grooved boards laid diagonally. In this way the diagonal boards help to tie the structural timbers together (like diagonal boarding on the side walls), and it is very convenient to lay finished flooring on top of diagonal underflooring. The finished floor boards are always laid across the underfloor, *not parallel to it*. Thus, with diagonal underflooring the finished floor boards may be laid in any direction, either lengthwise of the room or crosswise, and in every case the boards will extend crosswise (or nearly so) of the underfloor. This will be found a great convenience when a house is being finished, as one can then have the finished floor extend in any direction, uninfluenced by the direction of the underfloor. Finished flooring usually extends lengthwise of a room, for it is considered that it looks best that way.

An excellent floor construction consists of $\frac{7}{8} \times$ 2-inch strips on the underfloor, nailing the finished floor to them. The idea is to provide an air space between underfloor and finished floor, which is good insulation against cold and sound. Always lay heavy building paper between the two floors, whether strips are used or not, as this layer of felt keeps out cold and acts as a sound deadener. Another advantage of a stripped floor is that it provides an excellent place between the two floors for running gas pipes or electric conduits.

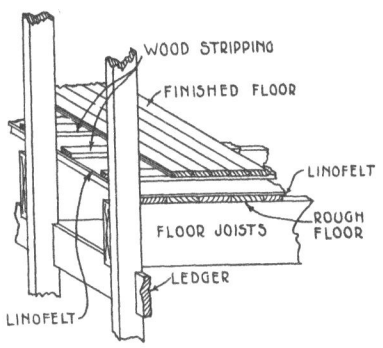

STRIPS BETWEEN ROUGH AND FINISHED FLOORS.

Insulation is a very important part of house construction.

192   SUCCESSFUL HOUSES AND HOW TO BUILD THEM

Cold houses are annoying, and the additional cost of some good system of insulation is well worth while. Various kinds of insulating materials are excellent for the purposes for which they are sold. Hair felt, linofelt, sea-weed quilt, and other like products, consisting of insulating material pressed between two layers of heavy building paper, can be used with good effect, and they will be found to make any house warmer and

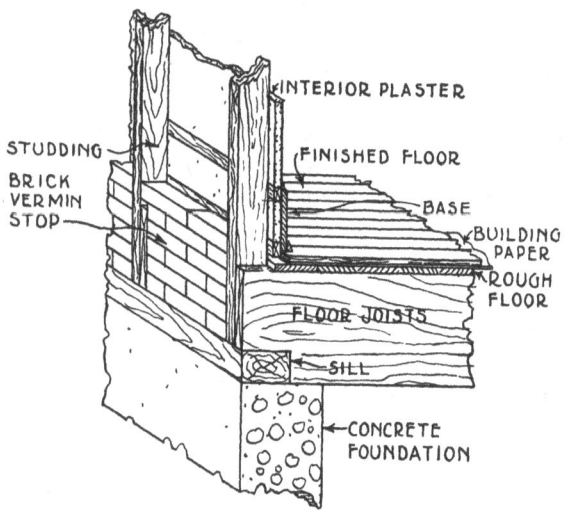

BEST KIND OF VERMIN STOP.

drier. Insulating felts and papers are used on outside walls and between floors. Another good method of insulation (suitable for outside walls only) is back plastering, in which rough plaster is cast against the inside boarding of a house before the finished lath and plaster is applied.

Timber not used for inside finish but ordinarily used for other buildng purposes is most often of the "Evergreen" class. In this class are white pine, Carolina pine (quite free from pitch), Georgia pine (containing much pitch), spruce, Norway spruce,

ADVANTAGES OF A FRAME HOUSE

hemlock, white cedar (used for shingles), red cedar, cypress (used also for inside trim), and redwood (California giant trees resembling pine in texture). One of the chief troubles with frame houses to-day is the constant deterioration of lumber. A few years ago spruce and pine were used almost exclusively for the framework of houses. This was very good material to stand the strains to which it was subjected in house construction, but pine and spruce are now practically out of the market, and hemlock, Norway pine, tamarack, and Southern pine have been substituted; all inferior to white pine and spruce. In some sections of the country it is very hard to get lumber properly seasoned, as timber owners have been unable to cut their lumber fast enough to supply the heavy demand for building.

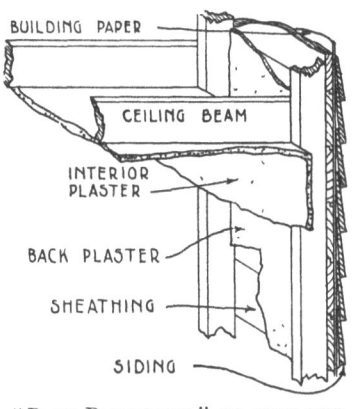

"Back Plastering" to keep out cold.

As a consequence, dealers do not have time to hold lumber long enough after cutting to dry it out properly, and it is frequently sent to buildings quite green. Dry, well-seasoned lumber should be demanded at all hazards, as green lumber is bound to shrink after it has been used in a house, causing cracks in the plastering and settlements in the building itself. Hemlock is particularly susceptible to shrinkage. Sometimes a bonus offered to the lumber dealer will cause him to send material that is properly seasoned, and the additional cost is usually well worth while. Seasoned lumber is lumber which has been stacked in open sheds for at least six months; year-old lumber is even better. Framing lumber is never kiln-dried like inside finish.

o

Present grades of hemlock, Norway pine, tamarack, and Southern pine do very well for house construction when thoroughly seasoned, if free from "shaky" places and excessive or loose knots. In other words, hemlock, Norway pine, or Southern pine is fit to use when it is of the best quality. The following table of lumber grades may be found helpful: —

GRADING OF PINE OR HEMLOCK TIMBER

No. 1.

Must be good and sound.
Defects not impairing strength are permitted.
Wane on one edge, $\frac{1}{2}''$ deep for half the length, is permitted.
Wane on two edges, of a proportionate amount for shorter distance, is permitted.
Shall present good nailing surface on at least one side and two edges.
A few wormholes are permitted.
Stained sap is permitted.
20% of No. 1 tamarack is permitted.

No. 2.

Large, coarse knots are permitted (not necessarily sound).
Considerable wane is permitted.
Shake, wormholes, and red streaks are permitted.
Crooked or other defective pieces, not fit for No. 1, are permitted.
Any amount of No. 2 tamarack is permitted.

No. 3.

All imperfections in Nos. 1 and 2, but to a greater degree, are permitted.
Considerable rot is permitted.
Any amount of No. 3 tamarack is permitted.

Southern pine timber is used principally for heavy timbers, such as girders or joists which are to be placed over extra wide spans. North Carolina Southern pine is better for house construction than Georgia pine, as the former is a softer wood to work and is sufficiently strong. Georgia pine is used mostly for factories and mills, where loads are excessive. It is a very hard, tough wood to work and therefore not desirable for house construction.

After lumber of first-class grade is obtained, care must be taken to have it piled in the right way on the building site, for many a load of good lumber has been injured by improper stacking. Lumber should be dry and well seasoned, first of all. Then when it is delivered from the yard it should be piled up in straight piles and covered with boards to protect it from the weather. If lumber is carelessly piled, — helter skelter, — it is apt to warp and twist. Every stick of it should be perfectly straight and true when it is put into the building, so in order to keep the lumber in good shape before it is used, pile it carefully and protect it from the weather.

Suburban House of Cement Plaster with Wood Trimmings

CHAPTER XI

EXTERIOR FINISH

AFTER the framework of the house is constructed, — that skeleton on which so much depends (which must be so carefully wrought if the house is to stand for the long lifetime one ought to expect), — comes the outside boarding, and after the outside boarding comes the exterior finish. Unlike the framer

NARROW SIDING WITH CORNER BOARDS.

work this exterior covering is visible. Thus it is really part of the design and produces a good or bad effect according to the taste with which it is chosen.

The most common covering for frame houses is what is termed "siding," consisting of ordinary sawed and lapped clapboards, ship-lap or other siding material. Clapboards come in several widths, varying somewhat in different sections of the country. In the West, narrow siding is largely used and the effect when laid is quite different from the wide siding of the East.

In old-fashioned houses siding was quite wide. Facilities for sawing boards were inadequate, and boards of considerable

SIDING WITH MITERED CORNERS.
Claude F. Bragdon, Architect.

width were used to reduce the number required for the exterior of a house. The effect of these wide pieces is very quaint when mitered at the corners (no corner boards), though in old houses corner boards were used almost entirely.

In addition to clapboards (thicker at the bottom than at the top), there are various other patterns of boarding, narrow and wide. Ship-lap is much used for siding, with excellent effect. It can be applied either with or without corner boards.

When corner boards are omitted and siding is "mitered" it is better to butt one board against another at corners, planing off the rough edges. The effect is the same as with a mitered joint, but this method is much more durable.

Some houses are covered with smooth, matched boards, and the effect is very pleasing. This is done successfully with

Lionel Moses, II, Architect.

narrow, matched sheathing $\frac{5}{8}$ or $\frac{7}{8}$ inch thick and not more than 4 inches wide. The joints should be painted as each board is laid with white lead mixed with boiled linseed oil, so that when all is completed there will be no danger of future decay from moisture entering the joints. Sheathing like this should be thoroughly "blind" nailed to hold it securely and prevent buckling after it is laid. That is, nails should be driven diagonally through the groove of each board before the tongue of the next board is placed in the groove. A diagonal slant is given to the nails so they will drive one board tightly against the next one. Nails applied in this way bury themselves in the grooves and are not visible.

Boards and battens, either horizontal or vertical, are often tastefully used for the exterior covering of a house. In the

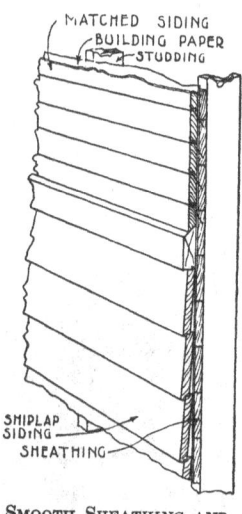

SMOOTH SHEATHING AND SHIP-LAP.

BOARDS AND BATTENS; VERTICAL AND HORIZONTAL.

best work of this kind, battens are specially made with tongues to fit tightly to grooves formed in the boards. Vertical boards and battens are more durable than horizontal, as it is less possible for moisture to enter the joints and cause decay. Horizontal boards and battens, however, make the best appearance and they will be found to be quite durable when battens are grooved into the boards, the former projecting slightly over the latter to cause rain to drip off instead of penetrating the joints. All such joints should be painted with white lead and oil before the boards are applied.

Shingles are excellent for covering the outside walls of a building and they will doubtless continue to be used more or less, regardless of changing fashions. The ordinary way to

THE CHARM OF SHINGLES.
Claude F. Bragdon, Architect.

apply shingles on wall surfaces is to lap them so that the distance from the butt of one shingle to the butt of the next is about 4½ to 6 inches. This is called laying them "4½ inches to the weather," or 6 inches. Shingles should be coursed before they are laid by spacing them out equally so the rows will line up properly with window and door frames.

When shingles are used, corner boards can be applied at the corners, or mitered corners can be used (no corner boards).

202 SUCCESSFUL HOUSES AND HOW TO BUILD THEM

In the latter method one shingle is brought up against another at the corner and trimmed off. Thus one shingle really laps against another instead of being mitered to it, though the effect is "mitered."

There is something cottage-like about shingles, and they are quite durable for siding if the best grade of red or white cedar or

SHINGLES APPLIED WITH ALTERNATE WIDE AND NARROW COURSES.
Tallmadge and Watson, Architects.

California redwood is used. White pine shingles such as were in the market twenty years ago are excellent, but they are practically out of the market now. Another good material for shingles is cypress, — a very enduring wood and one which takes stain artistically. Some of the best of the cypress shingles are hand made. That is, they are split out by hand instead of being sawed by machine and are thicker than machine-made shingles, with pleasing irregularities on the butts. Hand-made cypress shingles are said to be everlasting and they require neither stain nor paint, as the natural color of the cypress takes on a pretty tint with age.

The exterior covering of the house must not only protect a building from the weather, making it warm within, but it also has a strong effect on the design. For this reason, the designer should carefully consider what material he will use, that it may not merely wear well, but look well also. The underboarding of a house should be entirely covered with good, stout sheathing paper before the outside finish is put on. It is this layer of paper which adds greatly to the warmth of the building, for no matter how carefully siding is applied, if the paper underneath is not tight, cold winds blow through, making the house cold. Sheathing paper should be carefully fitted around all windows and door frames, and one sheet should lap over another at least two or three inches.

Brick-veneered houses are really frame houses, covered with a thin, outside skin of brick, so this method of house building will be treated in this chapter. Just as outside siding covers the boarded framework of a house, protecting it from the weather and improving the design, so brick veneer keeps out the cold and contributes to the finished appearance of the building. Houses which are brick veneered are built precisely like any other frame houses. The skeleton is erected, boarded on the outside, and papered, after which it is ready for the exterior surface of brick. Brickwork, a single thickness (4 inches), is laid against the underboarding, and the appearance when completed is precisely like an ordinary solid brick house, except that there are no headers in the wall, all bricks being laid the 8-inch way ("stretchers").

Brick veneer will not support itself, so the brickwork is secured to the wooden framework of the house by driving spikes into the boarding every few courses of brick. Masons lay up a few courses; then they drive a row of spikes into the frame of the house just touching the brick, after which they go on and lay up a few more courses and then drive more spikes.

Mortar slushed on the rows containing the spikes soon hardens around them, binding the brickwork fast to the frame. To take the place of spikes one can use metal anchors specially designed to attach brick veneering to the frame. Some of these are flat bands of galvanized iron spiked to the boarding and built into the brickwork. Others are similar, but sharpened at one end to be driven into the framework.

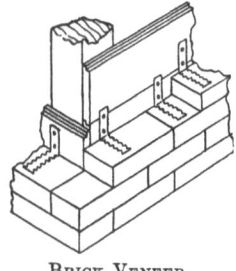

BRICK VENEER.

Brick veneer is not as damp-proof as wooden siding, for the latter, painted after completion, absorbs no water. For this reason brick-veneered houses should be covered with waterproof felt applied underneath the brick. This does not mean that brick veneer is not desirable. On the contrary, brick veneer is an excellent way to build; it is warmer than solid brick walls and, when damp-proof felt is used underneath, it makes a drier building.

Contrary to popular opinion, brick veneer is not much cheaper than solid brick walls. In both cases the price is about the same, with possibly a slight advantage in favor of brick veneer. Joints in a brick-veneered wall should be slushed full of mortar, carefully pointed up in pure cement mortar after completion. The fact that the brickwork is only 4 inches thick makes this doubly necessary, for poor mortar soon drops out of the joints, allowing bricks to come loose.

Cement plaster is one of the most important materials now used for the exterior covering of houses. Within a few years it has forged to the front until its use is well-nigh universal, and we can do no better than devote the remaining pages of

EXTERIOR FINISH 205

this chapter to a description of some of the characteristics of cement.

Most cement-plastered houses are frame houses with lath and plaster on the exterior. Thus they usually come in the frame-house class. Framework used for plaster houses is built

HOUSE OF CEMENT PLASTER
Perkins and Hamilton, Architects.

precisely like any other framework, but after the underboarding is applied, the construction is somewhat different. In the first place waterproof felt must be used next to the underboarding, for ordinary cement plaster is not waterproof. Even when "waterproofed," some dampness is apt to penetrate the outside plaster and go through the wall in spots.

In good cement plaster construction vertical cleats are

applied on top of the waterproof felt about 12 inches apart. To these the outside wood or metal lathing is secured. Such cleats (called "furring strips") may be ½ inch thick and 2 inches wide, or they may be as thick as ⅞ inch. Experts dis-

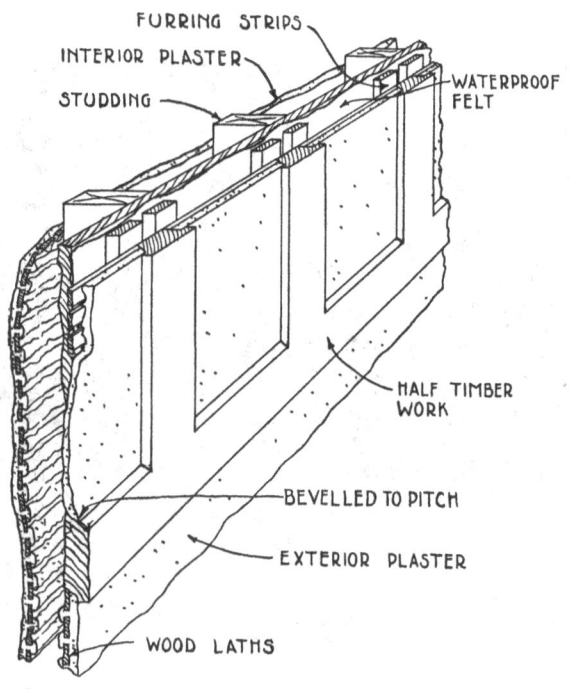

Cement Plaster on Wood Laths with Trimmings of "Half Timber."

agree as to which is best — thin furring or thick furring — exponents of thick furring claiming that thick cleats are stronger, and exponents of thin furring claiming that with ½-inch strips, mortar, as it is pushed through between the laths, strikes the boarding underneath, flowing sidewise around the laths, burying each in mortar and providing a better "key." More thick furring is used than thin furring, however, though there are plenty of good jobs in each class.

The various advantages and disadvantages of wood laths and metal lathing are taken up in another chapter. Both methods are good when lathing is properly applied, neither affecting the finished appearance of the plastering. Details of applying exterior plaster will also be found in another chapter.

In considering cement plaster for the exterior covering of a house, one should remember that cement is prettiest when combined with some other material. Cement borrows — borrows heavily — from other materials, as even the stanchest friends of cement are ready to acknowledge. Taken entirely by itself, cement is rarely successful when used for the exteriors of houses. To reach its point of highest usefulness from the standpoint of design, it must be combined with other materials, and this fact should be understood by all designers and builders of cement houses.

In England, where designers use cement extensively, houses are frequently constructed of brick, plastered on the outside with cement plaster. Nestling down in some beautiful garden spot, each building composes well with the landscape, — the neutral gray of the cement acting as a foil to brilliant flowers and foliage. Our English cousins know how to take advantage of every characteristic of this material to bring out its charms, adding just the right touch of harmony to the composition. English landscape gardeners are the best in the world, and cement is the medium which comes most naturally to hand. Cement steps, terraces, walls, and pools extend down many a vista, opening up avenues hedged in by lofty elms or gnarled oaks, with here and there gleams of high light where the cement is fascinatingly flashed by sunlight.

Cement plaster has no color. It is toneless and lifeless like a gravel roadway or the palest gray sky over the western plains unflicked by clouds. A desert has color in the gold of its sand;

the dreariest prairie abounds in green, brown, and yellow, but a surface of natural cement is entirely colorless. No other building material is quite so dull and uninteresting.

Another drawback to cement plaster is lack of texture, — that other requisite of all useful materials. Stone may be had in any texture, — rough-sawed, smooth-rubbed, rock-faced, ledge-grained, — it comes in every variety of form and surface. Blocks can be used just as they are, rough-hewed from the quarry with undulations of grain and seam laid to the outside, or they can be tooled to any degree of smoothness. Brick also can be of any degree of texture, rough or smooth, — but this quality, so necessary to the artistic architectural expression of every building, is almost lacking in cement. To be sure, cement may be troweled rough or smooth, or all the varying degrees between, but it is, nevertheless, merely plaster, and that is why cement texture is less interesting than stone texture or brick texture. There are no joints to show the pleasing irregularities of the units as in a stone or brick wall. Cement plaster, whether applied with trowel or cast (as in "rough cast"), is a flowing material, jointless and consequently shadowless. Taken by itself it is monotonous, — yes, even dreary in appearance.

If this is the case, — if cement is neither pleasing in color nor interesting in texture, how can one account for the thousands of attractive cement houses scattered over the entire country?

Analyze the charm of cement houses and you will find that it is the *combining of cement with other materials* which makes the designs most effective. Gray cement makes an excellent background for painted window frames and sash. Like the plain setting for a jewel, cement serves as a foil to bring out the beauties of more decorative materials. And this is the true field for cement. Used in this way, the result is good from an architectural standpoint as well as structurally.

To get best results, cement should always be trimmed with some materials having more color and texture values. Never paint your cement house cement color. Paint it instead some contrasting tint that will give life to the design and bring out the pretty points of the composition. For this reason, white trimmings, contrasting very little with plaster, are rarely effective unless there are green blinds or window shades of some warm, cheerful color. White trimmings on a cement house with no color on the roof give a disagreeably cold, bare effect, which can be easily counteracted by hanging green blinds at the windows. Immediately, the entire composition takes on new interest. The monotonous gray is changed into a warm, sunny, delightful tone.

These are the subtle points which make or mar cement houses. Understood and properly used, cement is ideal, but used unintelligently the effect is far from satisfactory. An entire street may easily be harmed by one ugly cement house, while a succession of poor designs will do more toward depreciating the æsthetic value of the entire town than anything that could be done, perhaps. Cement plaster makes a house so conspicuous, even when weathered by years of wear, that ugly designs are bound to assert themselves and create a bad impression.

Rough-cast cement plaster trimmed with material of pleasing color is perhaps the most practical method, for the texture is a little more pleasing than with smooth plaster, and it wears better. Broken stone used in rough cast gives a strong wearing surface to the plaster, not unlike stone itself. Each piece of stone embedded in hard cement contributes to what is really a veneer of crushed stone, most useful in protecting a building from the elements.

Another interesting characteristic of cement and one which should be recognized when using it for building is that cement reflects the color of materials combined with it. If a cement house is trimmed with green blinds, curiously enough, the cement seems to be slightly green in tone. When the trimmings of a house are brown, the plaster takes on a brownish hue. Designers

P

take advantage of this fact to produce many beautiful effects in their cement designs.

Brick veneer and cement are two materials which will stand the closest possible relations. When combined, the architectural effect is most pleasing. Brick, brown in tone, laid with very wide mortar joints to produce a wall of rough texture, are usually particularly engaging.

Cement plaster rightly used is a most desirable addition to the building family. Cement may be colored, of course, but treated thus it is rarely so satisfactory as when used in its natural state, with dependence upon the color of surroundings to give it a pleasing tone. Cement can be given a pleasing texture of varying degrees of roughness, but this alone will not ordinarily produce an effect equal to that obtained by the discriminating use of other material for the purpose. Cement plaster is best when used merely as a foil to reflect shadows. Do not expect too much of it. Borrow elsewhere those qualities which cement does not possess and your house will be an architectural success.

There are other materials to be used for exterior siding besides wooden siding, brick veneer, and cement plaster. Of these, a form of heavy prepared felt roofing covered with gravel has been used quite successfully on houses where it is desired to get the effect of cement plaster at less cost. This roofing, coming in rolls ready to lay, consists of several layers of felt, asphalted or tarred, with an outside coating of fine crushed stone or gravel. The latter is stuck to the felt by means of plastic composition. When used for siding, this material is usually applied horizontally, but as it is only about 30 inches to 32 inches wide, cleats or battens of wood must be nailed over each joint. Thus a house sided with gravel roofing takes on, somewhat, the appearance of a plaster-covered exterior marked off into squares by outside casings of wood. Upon close inspection, siding of this sort does not look exactly like a plastered exterior; however, it makes quite an attractive appearance and will be found durable when properly applied. The way in which felt gravel-covered siding is most frequently used is as a frieze up under the eaves of a house, with some other material below. Felt siding must be well secured to the boarding, as it is apt to dry out in the sun, in which case its elasticity is impaired and it stretches and falls slightly away from the building. Plenty of wooden cleats or battens will usually prevent this.

CHICAGO HOUSE BUILT OF ROUGH BRICK
J. K. Cady, Architect.

CHAPTER XII

HOUSES OF MASONRY

HOUSES of masonry have a much longer life than even the best frame houses of most careful construction. Materials of wood are not so enduring as materials of stone, clay, or concrete, and it is largely for this reason that so many masonry houses are built. Add to this increased efficiency and durability of masonry materials their increased attractiveness, and you have multiplied the desirability of building a house of masonry.

In some places, of course, where stone, brick, or cement is not easily obtained at fair prices, no one would consider it practical to build anything but a frame house. In other sections, where lumber is not close at hand or where masonry materials are particularly cheap, one should use the latter by all means.

In spite of much that has been said in favor of masonry houses, it is not generally true that they cost no more than fráme houses. Except in certain sections where lumber is rare, and stone, brick, or cement is plentiful, houses built of masonry cost more than houses built of frame. These sections should not be taken as typical. Conditions vary, of course, but America is typically a lumber country. In spite of high price of lumber, it is still the cheapest material for buildings and promises to be so for many years to come.

Masonry houses usually pay, however, — pay in increased durability and attractiveness. For what could be more durable than well-made brick laid up carefully in cement mortar; what could be more attractive than good, sound stone; what more substantial than thoroughly mixed concrete?

214 SUCCESSFUL HOUSES AND HOW TO BUILD THEM

Well-designed houses of masonry are always good looking and they remain so as years roll on. Brick, stone, and cement are materials particularly susceptible to soft, pretty tones produced by wind and weather. Another advantage the masonry house has over a frame house is lack of paint. Frame

HOUSE BUILT OF BROWN BRICK.
Spencer and Powers, Architects.

houses must be painted outside at least once in three years if they are to be kept in good condition; the masonry house escapes this requirement. Window frames, cornices, and doors must be painted, of course, but that is a small item compared with the wooden sides of a frame house, in which the cost of painting (averaging from $150 to $300 or $400) would in a short time pay for the additional cost of masonry construction.

HOUSES OF MASONRY

Brick houses are variously built in different sections of the country. In this chapter we will consider several of the best systems for building brick walls (not including brick veneer, which is treated of in another chapter).

Most two-story brick houses are built with solid walls, 12 inches thick on the first story and 8 inches thick on the second. Face brick are used for the outside of the wall, with common brick inside, except in Eastern States where clay burns to a pretty shade of red, and the same kind of brick are frequently used inside as well as outside. In this case it is customary to select from the piles the best looking brick for outside; that is, the straightest, most perfect brick, most dense in texture.

The following table indicates the kinds of brick which come from the kilns, graded according to their desirableness: —

GRADES OF BRICK

(Grades according to layers, the outside being No. 1.)

(1) Outside brick, farthest from the fire, are not desirable as they are too soft.

(2) Next layer, called "pale" or "salmon" brick, are also underburned and consequently soft.

(3) Third layer, produces "hard-burned" brick, which are the most suitable for general building purposes.

(4) The inner layer, just over the flues, are overburnt and consequently very hard and brittle. They are usually distorted and cracked, but as they are practically vitrified, owing to the great heat to which they have been subjected, they make good paving brick.

Merchantable brick are divided into two classes: common brick (used chiefly for the back of the wall), and pressed brick or "face" brick (used for the outside of the wall). Common brick are divided into three grades, — "arch" or "hard" brick (suitable for paving brick), "well burned" (the most desirable), and "soft" or "salmon" brick (not suitable for building purposes).

Face brick may be "dry-pressed" or "re-pressed," according

MOLDED BRICK ARCH OVER AN ENTRANCE.

to the process employed in their manufacture. In either case they should be very hard and smooth, with sharp angles and true sides. Face brick cost from two to five times as much as common brick.

Special or molded brick are often used for house trimmings, such as moldings, architraves, and the like. For arches over windows, brick are frequently ground with oblique sides to fit the radius of the arch. On the corners of bay windows it is well to use "hexagon" bricks. These transfer the vertical joints from the corners, thus making them stronger and more attractive, a very much better practice than clipping bricks at the angles, using a long, vertical joint liable to disintegrate after a time. Over window and door openings arches may be turned with ordinary bricks, or when flat arches are used it may be necessary to have bricks of the arch ground to fit the radius. In many of the most attractive brick houses 4-inch angle irons are laid across openings to support the face brick, which are then laid across on top of the angle precisely as they are laid elsewhere in the wall.

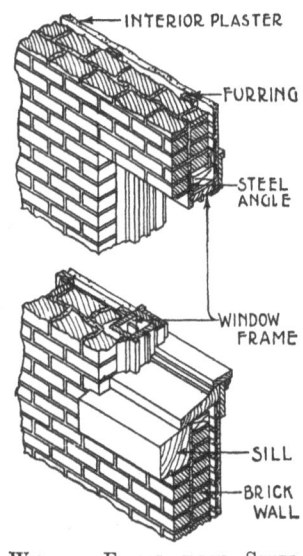

WINDOW FRAME WITH STEEL ANGLE TO SUPPORT BRICKWORK.

HOUSES OF MASONRY 217

Paving bricks are becoming popular for the exterior walls of houses and they make an excellent wall, — sound, waterproof, and enduring. In cost, paving bricks are economical, as they are usually less expensive than face brick, though they cost more than common brick.

HOUSE FACED WITH PAVING BRICK.
Frank Lloyd Wright, Architect.

Contrary to popular opinion, brick are not, as a rule, dampproof. Clay, even after it is baked in a kiln, is not usually sufficiently dense to be entirely nonabsorbent. To be sure, some varieties of brick of the natural chemical consistency to burn into an unusually dense clinker-like material are practically waterproof, — comparatively nonabsorbent, but most brick take up an amount of dampness, however slight. For this reason it is customary to fur and lath the inside of a brick house instead of plastering directly upon the inside of the brick walls. Plaster would adhere very well to the inside of a brick wall, but dampness, almost certain to come through, would stain wall paper or tint on the inside. Furring a brick wall inside with $\frac{7}{8} \times$ 2-inch cleats attached to strips built into the brickwork (afterwards lathed and plastered like ordinary wooden studs) produces a small air space between the brickwork and inside plaster which effectually prevents dampness from reaching the interior of rooms. It is excellent practice to waterproof the inside of a brick wall by painting it with one of the chemical preparations made for this purpose. Waterproofing, however, is not strictly necessary if ordinary, first-class, hard-burned brick are used, laid up in a good grade of mortar.

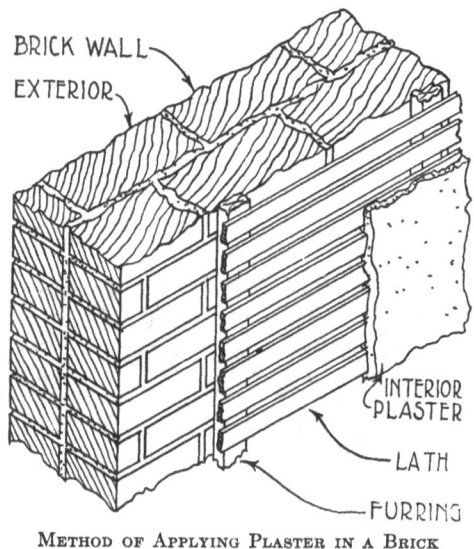

METHOD OF APPLYING PLASTER IN A BRICK HOUSE.

When waterproofing is applied to the inside of a brick wall, it is possible to plaster directly on the brickwork. This is doubtful practice, however, as wooden furring strips cost but little and they will be found very convenient for nailing up casings, base, and other inside trim. When walls are to be plastered directly on the brickwork, wood strips should be built into the wall, carefully choosing the places where inside trim is to be nailed.

In the West and in many other parts of the country, common brick are yellow in tone, as the clay burns yellow instead of red. These yellow brick can sometimes be used effectively even in the face of the wall by picking out the best looking ones for the outside and laying them up in colored mortar, — notably, brown. After the building is completed if the wall is

GRAY BRICK IS ATTRACTIVE WHEN WHITE TRIMMINGS ARE USED.

washed down with acid or cleaned with a wire brush, it looks quite attractive, especially when the window frames and other wood trimmings of the building are painted some pretty color (like brown or green) to give life to the design. As a rule, however, yellow brick are undesirable for the outside of a house, as they make a somewhat depressing appearance. On the contrary, brick in shades of red and brown are always

220 SUCCESSFUL HOUSES AND HOW TO BUILD THEM

attractive, — the older they get the better they look, and this is one reason why brownish and reddish brick are so frequently used.

Of course, no general rules concerning color can be laid down, some yellow brick being attractive and others not, depending upon the shade. It is usually safe to use reddish or brownish brick, however, so when in doubt it is a good idea to select brick of these shades. Brick of purple tones are frequently pretty when quite dark. Gray brick are apt to be depressing, as gray is a depressing color, though it is sometimes skillfully combined with pleasing color applied to the outside trim and cornices to make the design an attractive one. Color is entirely a matter of taste. Artists get good effects using almost any color of brick, by means of colored mortar or painted trimmings. Amateurs frequently spoil brick of a pretty tone, by poor taste used in the color of the trim.

WHEN ATTRACTIVE ROUGH BRICK ARE USED.

Modern tendency in brickwork is to use face brick of a rough texture instead of brick of a smooth texture, and this tendency is not a mere fad but is the result of years of experimenting in textures and colors. Rough brick should be used in preference to smooth brick, in most cases, — first, because they are less expensive, and second, because they usually produce more artistic effects. Smooth-faced brick, to be perfect in outline and of even color, must be composed of materials most carefully mixed (sometimes artificially colored). After they have been cut into shape they must be re-pressed in molds to make them smooth on all faces. This makes them expensive, frequently costing from $10 to $25 per thousand more than the rougher brick. As a matter of fact, this additional care only makes such brick less attractive, for a perfectly smooth brick wall formed of bricks every one the same shade is not usually pleasing. The very effort to make smooth brick more attractive only defeats the purpose of the makers, as a wall built of rough-faced brick is infinitely more beautiful than a smooth wall. Brickwork to be effective must have a play of light and shade, one brick being darker than another.

The joints of brickwork need not be absolutely level and plumb, a variation ("texture," it is called) being more delightful. Such a wall is not so perfect that it looks artificial, — resembling painted bricks, as it were.

Rough brick are made by running a stream of well-mixed clay through a machine which cuts them off the right size and shape with a piece of wire, — much as a grocer cuts butter by drawing a piece of wire through the cone. Wire drawn through clay does not cut smoothly as it does in butter, however. It tears its way through, making brick slightly rough on the surface.

Some of the most modern brick are purposely made even rougher by tearing them more than ordinary brick. These, when baked in a kiln, take on beautiful tones difficult to get in any other form of brick, making a most attractive wall when laid. The history of one of these brands of brick is interesting. A brick with very rough surface which now comes in many pleasing shades of reddish tones was originally made in one shade only. Quite by accident the manufacturer discovered that the clay would burn with pleasing variations in color. The bricks were brought to the attention of architects and they are now used extensively in houses of all grades, inexpensive as well as costly.

222 SUCCESSFUL HOUSES AND HOW TO BUILD THEM

"Tapestry" brick are among the most beautiful of the rough-faced brick, and very attractive effects can be obtained with them. They are cheap in price, their durability is unquestioned and the effects obtained can be got in no other way. These brick come in many shades of red, brown, gray, and yellow. Even yellow and gray shades, unpleasant in almost every other kind of face brick, are pleasing in tapestry brick.

TAPESTRY BRICK LAID WITH WIDE, DEEP MORTAR JOINTS.

Of smooth, re-pressed brick, the best are those which are mottled in color. Though practically yellow in tone, they have a brownish appearance caused by iron mixed in the clay, which burns with brown spots on the surface.

Enameled brick are used with good effect inside a house in kitchen or bathrooms, but they are not usually effective on the exterior. Outside brick should be soft in color, — not hard and individually conspicuous. One must use the same good taste in selecting colors that is used in selecting tints in interior decorating, — that is, choose quiet tones that will harmonize with surroundings, — not clash with them.

In laying up face brick, there are many ways for forming joints. Ordinary bond consists of several rows of brick stretching lengthwise (usually six or seven rows) called stretchers, and then a row of brick laid with ends toward the outside, called headers. As most walls are thicker than one brick in width, the face bricks on the outside of the wall must be tied (bonded, it is called) to the bricks in the back of the wall by this row of headers, laid across from face brick to back brick. Thus, in ordinary bond, the six rows of stretchers are not really bonded

HOUSES OF MASONRY

with the bricks behind, though the joint between is slushed up with mortar. But each row of headers ties the face and back of the wall together, and a wall is considered to be well built when it is thus tied every six or seven courses.

In England, where houses are more carefully constructed than in America, often a course of headers is laid on top of every course of stretchers. Thus, every course of stretchers alternating with a course of headers, the front and back of the wall are securely bonded every other course. This makes the strongest possible work.

BRICKWORK LAID IN ENGLISH BOND.

In ordinary American house building, however, such extreme care is hardly possible, for price of labor and material is about twice what it is in England. Ordinary bond well done, when plenty of good mortar is slushed into joints (filling them completely) will be found quite good enough for any house.

FLEMISH BOND WITH DARK HEADERS.

Flemish bond is frequently used on account of its pleasing appearance as well as structural durability. It consists of a stretcher, followed by a header, laid side by side in the same course. When brick are laid Flemish fashion, it is frequently the custom to use headers of darker shade so that the pattern of the bond, pleasingly regular as it is, becomes apparent in the wall. Double Flemish bond is a pleasing variation of ordinary Flemish bond. It consists of two stretchers and one header laid side by side in the same course, bringing the headers directly over the vertical joints of the stretchers.

DOUBLE FLEMISH BOND.

Sometimes the face of a wall consists entirely of stretchers, these being secured to the common brick backing by metal wall ties laid into the joints of the brickwork every five or six courses. This method is somewhat saving in labor, as it is easier to lay up a wall composed entirely of stretchers. Some wall ties are of wire, with loops formed on the ends to bed into the mortar and become fast in the wall; others are flat strips of corrugated, galvanized iron or steel.

Brick comes in a variety of sizes and shapes though, broadly speaking, there are only three or four general shapes. First, there are ordinary brick approximately 8 inches long, 4 inches wide, and 2 inches thick. These are called "standard" shape, though the size varies somewhat in different sections. Clay shrinks slightly in the burning and this shrinkage varies according to the consistency of the clay used, therefore some "standard" brick are $7\frac{1}{2}$ inches long, $3\frac{3}{4}$ inches wide, and $1\frac{7}{8}$ inches thick; others are slightly smaller or larger, according to the size they are originally cut and the amount of shrinkage in the kiln.

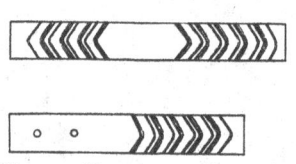
METAL TIES FOR SECURING FACE BRICK TO BACK OF WALL.

Long, thin brick called "Roman" brick are frequently used, this designation referring to the shape, — not to the brand. "Roman length, standard thick-

HOUSES OF MASONRY 225

ness" are long, thick brick, combining the length of "Roman" brick with the thickness of standard. Brick called "half standard" are of standard length, but half the standard thickness.

Such are, briefly, the most used sizes and shapes to be found in the market. Slight variations occur in every section of the country, but sizes and shapes are now generally standard.

THE DIGNITY OF ROMAN BRICK WITH LIMESTONE TRIMMINGS.

The following table shows the stock sizes of common and face brick holding in most sections of the country: —

STOCK SIZES OF COMMON BRICK

		SIZE OF WALL (INCHES)			
New England States	$7\frac{3}{4}'' \times 3\frac{3}{4}'' \times 2\frac{1}{4}''$	8	12	16	20
New York and New Jersey	$8'' \times 4'' \times 2\frac{1}{2}''$	8	12	16	20
Western States	$8\frac{1}{2}'' \times 4\frac{1}{8}'' \times 2\frac{1}{2}''$	9	13	18	22

226 *SUCCESSFUL HOUSES AND HOW TO BUILD THEM*

STOCK SIZES OF FACE BRICK

Standard, practically throughout country, $8\frac{1}{4}'' \times 4\frac{1}{8}'' \times 2\frac{3}{8}''$
Roman, $12'' \times 4'' \times 1\frac{1}{4}''$

The exact size and pattern of brick to use in the face of a wall is largely a matter of taste. Some designs look best carried out in "Roman" brick, others are more attractive in "standard." Standard sizes are less expensive than Roman and are therefor used more often. Rough brick look quite as well in standard sizes as they do in Roman, but smooth brick usually look best in Roman sizes.

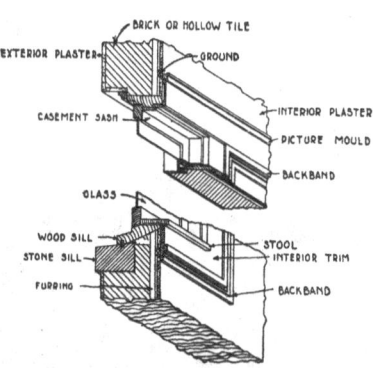

EIGHT-INCH MASONRY WALL WITH EXTERIOR CEMENT PLASTER.

Mortar joints in brickwork have as much effect in the appearance of the wall as anything else and are frequently made a means of greatly improving the result. There are the ordinary mortar joints about ¼ inch in thickness in which mortar is used without color, and there are the wide mortar joints sometimes as large as ⅝ inch or even ¾ inch, using natural, uncolored mortar, or sometimes mortar slightly whitened by the addition of marble dust. The effect of wide joints is quite striking, but this method should be employed judiciously, preferably by an expert.

Rough, ordinary red brick are frequently attractive laid with wide joints, whereas smooth, slick brickwork is usually disappointing laid that way. In the latter case, bricks closely resemble a painted wall, presenting an artificial appearance quite unattractive.

Mortar joints are frequently colored brown or black. When

rough-faced brick are used, mortar joints can be colored about the same shade as the brick with good effect, but it should be remembered that mortar color fades, so it must be mixed darker than desired, as it invariably dries out lighter in tone. Mineral colors are usually employed for coloring mortar. These can be bought, ready to mix with the mortar, and are known as "mortar colors" or "mortar stains."

In addition to the color in mortar joints, brickwork can be helped or marred by the way in which the joints are formed. Tight joints, that is, joints which are as narrow as $\frac{1}{4}$ inch (about the smallest joint possible) are usually struck flush with the outside of the wall. After a few minutes, when they have "set" sufficiently hard, the joints are "pointed" by means of a piece of telephone wire or with a tool having a wire-like edge. Pointing forces mortar tightly into the joint and at the same time gives a smooth, finished appearance, slightly concave. Wide joints are frequently raked out so that the mortar is incised $\frac{1}{4}$ inch or more, allowing the upper and lower edges of each brick to show, giving a rugged appearance to the wall which is quite attractive. When bricks are not too rough, this is a good joint to use, but if very rough brick are used, they are apt to have such uneven edges that they do not look well with wide joints. When joints are to be raked out, bricks are laid in a full bed of mortar, then the loose part that squeezes out when each brick is bedded can be struck off with a trowel flush with the face of the wall. Afterwards, a hook-like tool is used to rake out the mortar to the depth desired. After raking, it is the usual custom to use another pointing tool in the joints to put a hard, firm finish on the outside of the mortar. Pointing in this way makes joints much more weatherproof than ordinary struck joints, as the pores of the mortar are closed. Struck joints are joints in which the excess of mortar is merely chopped or struck off with the trowel. After striking, joints are pointed by drawing the point of the trowel over them.

Your brick wall is only as strong as the mortar joints, no matter how firm the bricks themselves may be. For this reason it is necessary to have mortar properly mixed, using only the best grade of lime, cement, and sand, and pointing joints carefully to make them hard and weather resisting. Sometimes mortar for brickwork is mixed entirely of Portland cement and sand, using equal amounts, but more frequently a good, stiff mortar composed of well-slaked lime and sand is used, slightly tempered or stiffened, with the addition of a small amount of Portland cement. Mortar composed entirely of Portland cement and sand, with no lime, sets so quickly it is very difficult to use it in laying brick, for it is very apt to harden slightly before it can be carried from the mortar tray to the wall, making it very difficult for masons to spread it properly. On the contrary, lime mortar sets quite slowly so that it is easily worked with the trowel, and when stiffened slightly with Portland cement it makes very good mortar.

Most brick houses are built with a 12-inch wall on the first story and 8-inch on the second story. When an 8-inch wall is used, the brick must be carefully laid, or the wall will not be sufficiently strong to withstand the thrust of the rafters at the roof. Mortar acts in a triple capacity, — to unite the brick units into one homogeneous mass, to fill all interstices and keep out moisture, and to form a cushion under each course of brick, filling all irregularities and distributing pressure evenly. The first object is accomplished by thoroughly flushing the joints with mortar, the second depends upon the strength of the mortar, and the third is affected chiefly by the thickness of the joints, which vary slightly, according to the varying thickness of each brick.

The proper way to lay brickwork is to set the outside and inside courses, then prepare a full bed of mortar for the bricks which come between, placing each in position with a firm "shove" into place. After this is done, all joints not entirely

HOUSES OF MASONRY

filled with mortar should be slushed with a trowel until they are full. Another method is to lay the bricks dry, after which joints are slushed or "grouted" with thin mortar; but the former method is most generally used. In order to get straight joints, a straightedge should be frequently applied to the wall.

A good piece of brickwork is always perfectly plumb at the corners and level on every course. The front of the wall is thoroughly bonded to the back, one vertical joint being directly over another.

In hot weather, brick should be thoroughly wet before laying, using the hose on them as fast as they dry out. If this is not done, brick, which are more or less absorptive, suck all the moisture out of the mortar as they are laid, leaving it dry, lifeless, and crumbling.

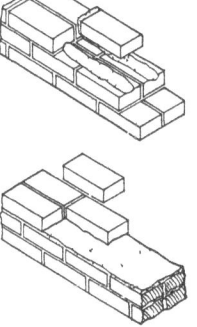

UPPER: WESTERN METHOD OF LAYING BRICK.
LOWER. EASTERN METHOD.

The following table indicates the ordinary tests as applied to common brick: —

BRICK TESTS

Strength. — Should be free from cracks or flaws, holes or humps.

Size. — Should be very nearly uniform in size.

Compactness. — Should be well burned. Upon striking two together, the bricks should ring true.

Absorption. — Should not absorb more than $\frac{1}{10}$ their weight in water after soaking 24 hours.

Shape. — Slight twists and distortions are acceptable, but excessively misshapen brick should be rejected.

Most bricks are made of clay, hard burned in a kiln, but there are other types made in other ways. Sand-lime bricks are made by combining lime and sand. When properly made, they are excellent, but the chief objection to them is in point of color, for in their natural state they are dead and lifeless, making them unfit for the face of a wall, though they do very well for backing. In most sections, however, sand-lime bricks are as costly, or more costly, than clay bricks, so there is no inducement to use them, as they are no better than first-class clay bricks. Cement bricks are satisfactory when properly made, though not every brand is fit to use. Here, again, color is against them. The natural color of cement is monotonous, and when bricks are artificially colored they do not make as pleasing an appearance as clay, for each brick being exactly the same shade, the wall has an artificial, painted appearance. One of the chief beauties of clay bricks is their variable color, one being lighter and another darker. This effect is lost when cement bricks, artificially colored, are used. Sand-lime and cement bricks are at best only substitutes for clay bricks. Except in sections of the country where clay is rare and sand-lime or cement bricks are cheaper, it is not advisable to use them.

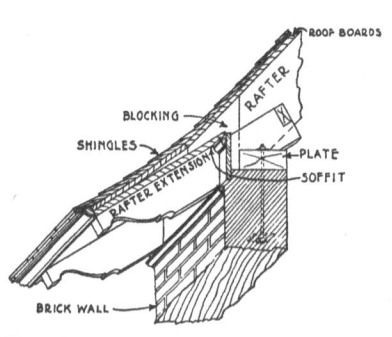

GOOD WAY TO SECURE PLATE TO BRICK WALL.

Through the inside of a masonry house, partitions are built as they are in a frame house,—that is, girders resting on brick piers, cast iron or wooden posts in the basement, support partitions consisting of 2×4 or 2×6-inch studding. At the wall end of the joists it is customary to bevel the timbers. When building, the masonry walls are laid up to the level required for the joists. Then carpenters place the girders and set the joists on top with the beveled ends resting on the wall. After this, masons build the walls around the ends of the joists.

To tie the walls of the building securely it is a good plan to build in anchors, consisting of wrought-iron rods, sharpened at one end and driven into about every sixth joist, with the other end built into the masonry. Thus the floors and walls are securely united, contributing much to the stability of the building. The plate supporting the rafters is secured to the masonry by bolts built into the walls.

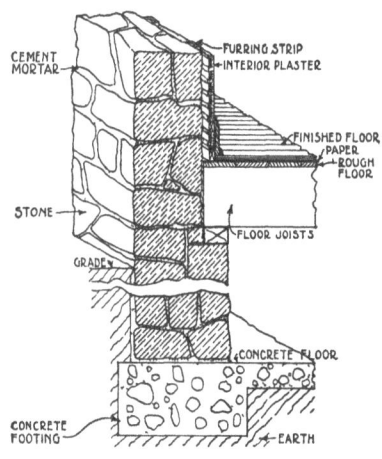

STONE WALL FURRED ON INSIDE.

The underflooring on a masonry house is laid diagonally or not, just as it is in a frame house. The underflooring should never be fitted too tightly to a masonry wall, however, for in course of construction it is almost sure to become damp, when it is liable to swell, pushing against the walls and often causing them to lean slightly from the perpendicular.

A green wall, that is, a wall freshly built, in which the mortar has not completely set, is very easy to disturb, a comparatively slight pressure sometimes producing a deviation from the perpendicular. For this reason it is a good plan to brace green walls longer than twenty-five or thirty feet with timbers set securely against them, which can be removed after the mortar has set. This is not usually required, however, as floor joists are most often laid soon after a section of wall is built, and these, tied as they are to the wall by means of anchors, hold it sufficiently.

Stone houses are not infrequently built, and stone is an excellent material to use when the walls are furred on the inside. Otherwise a stone house would not prove a dry house. Local ledge stone can be obtained in most localities and its cost is frequently no more than brick, though labor on a stone house is usually higher than on a brick house, as so much cutting and fitting is necessary.

The following tests for stone will be found useful: —

TESTS FOR STONE

Compactness. — When dense and strong, stone rings with a clear metallic sound if struck a blow with a hammer.

Absorption. — A sample cube of stone, after being immersed in water for 24 hours, should not increase in weight more than 5%.

Solubility. — Crush a sample and place the pieces in a glass of water for $\frac{1}{2}$ hour. If of good building consistency, the water will remain clear. If the stone contains much earthy matter, the water will become muddy.

Stone used for houses can be finished in a variety of ways. The following being frequently employed: —

FINISH FOR STONE

Rock-faced or "pitch-faced" is stone left in the rough but with the edges pitched off to a line. Hard limestone and granite is often finished in this way and a wall built of it is rough looking and artistic.

Margined finish, is rock-face with a straight draft line tooled around the edges.

Broached Work. — Continuous grooves all over the surface. Usually with draft lines at the edges.

Pointed Work. — Rough faces pointed down all over. May be either rough or fine-pointed.

Tooth Chiseled. — One of the cheapest methods. Resembles pointed work, but is not quite so smooth.

HOUSES OF MASONRY

Tooled Work. — A chisel 3 to $4\frac{1}{2}$ inches wide is used to make continuous lines across the width of the stone. Especially suitable for sandstone or limestone.

Crandalled Work. — Tooled lines run diagonally across the stone, one way or both ways. Good finish for sandstone.

Rubbed Work. — Rubbed by hand or machine with soft stone, water, and sand until smooth. Suitable for sandstone or limestone.

Bush-hammered. — Surface full of fine points. Good for hard sandstone or limestone, but not suitable for soft stone.

Patent-hammered. — Stone is first pointed, then finished with a patent hammer, leaving the stone with a coarse or fine finish, according to the number of blades used in the tool. The finish most frequently used is 8 to 10 cuts to the inch. This is a good finish for hard limestone or granite.

Houses are frequently built of what is known as "rubblework," or sometimes of "ashlar." Rubble is the ordinary rough work where local stone is used, and it proves satisfactory when the work is properly done. In good rubblework there is a bond stone (large stone extending through the wall) at least every 4 or 5 feet of wall in length; the largest and soundest stones are placed at the bottom of the wall, and every angle in it is formed with alternate headers and stretchers. Weak edges on each stone should be broken off before the stone is laid. While a few spawls (small chips) are permissible on the inside of the wall, they should be carefully slushed up with cement mortar.

Field stones are frequently used in rubblework, as the effect is picturesque and pleasing. Small boulders and field stones from old stone walls in the country are excellent for this purpose, especially those which are weather beaten (often covered with beautiful green moss). Rubble stone is sometimes coursed, in which case it is called "coursed rubble." In this type of

234 *SUCCESSFUL HOUSES AND HOW TO BUILD THEM*

Various Types of Stonework.

work every stone is trimmed and squared up, though each is of different size.

Ashlar is cut stone on the face of a wall, backed up with common stone or brick. Usually the ashlar is from 4 to 8 inches thick, and when of brick the backing is most often 8 inches thick. In every 10 square feet of wall surface (at least) one of the facing stones should go through the wall for bonding purposes. When marble or limestone ashlar is used, it may be as thin as 2 to 4 inches, bonded to the rough backing with iron clamps (at least one clamp to each piece). When metal clamps are used, they should be dipped in asphalt before applying, to prevent rusting.

Cut stone quoins are often used at the corners of a stone house, as well as at jambs of window and door openings. Cut stone sills and copings are used, and sometimes stone cornices and moldings. Cut stone pieces should be thoroughly secured to the wall by means of metal clamps wherever necessary.

In pointing stonework, the pointing material should be composed of equal parts of cement and sand, extending into the wall from $\frac{1}{2}$ to 1 inch. This work should be done in moderate weather (to prevent freezing), and the joints should be cleaned and moistened before the cement is applied. After stonework is completed, it should be cleaned down by vigorous brushing, using weak acid and water. Although a stiff, wire brush can be used safely on hard stone, a brush with bristles is preferable for soft stone, which might be injured by wire bristles.

When inspecting a piece of stonework, examine all parts carefully in search of weak, cracked stones which should never be permitted to remain in the wall. Before the stones are laid it is easy to test them by sounding with a hammer, — a dull sound indicating a hidden crack. In sandstone, every piece which contains holes should be rejected, and all stones should be of uniform color.

Patching (where a broken stone is mended by inserting a patch) should never be permitted in any stonework, for no matter how skillfully it is done, it is almost certain to become displaced later. In molded work one must be careful to see that all the cuts in each section of stone match perfectly, otherwise, when the moldings are completed they will appear wavy in outline.

Concrete blocks have been quite extensively used for houses throughout the country, and walls made of good, sound concrete blocks are very enduring. It cannot be said that they are attractive in appearance, however, for there is a deadly monotony to concrete block houses, owing to the exact similarity of each block in color and shape. In stone houses, one stone is not precisely like another; color varies, and this makes a pleasing irregularity in the appearance of the wall. When concrete blocks are used, however, walls are artificially regular in appearance, which detracts from their sightliness. Concrete blocks, as a general thing, are most useful when covered with some other material, like cement plaster. Rock-faced concrete blocks made in imitation of rock-faced stone are unattractive.

HOUSES IN A FIREPROOF COMMUNITY NEAR NEW YORK
Mann and MacNeille, Architects.

CHAPTER XIII

HOW TO BUILD A FIREPROOF HOUSE

FIREPROOF houses are of masonry, but they are so different in construction from ordinary masonry houses that they are

AN ATTRACTIVE FIREPROOF HOUSE.
Mann and MacNeille, Architects.

described here in a separate chapter. No development in house design and construction more ideal than modern fireproof houses could be conceived, and no method of building could be more practical or more useful to mankind.

238 SUCCESSFUL HOUSES AND HOW TO BUILD THEM

An era of sensible building is rapidly evolving. Thousands believe in it, and are planning to take advantage of the opportunity offered by new methods of fireproof construction.

Fireproof construction of the better class is permanent. Walls do not crack nor do floors sag, and the owner is protected from excessive repairs on his property because there is nothing

FIREPROOF HOUSES IN A NEW YORK SUBURB.

to wear out. Window frames and doors are made of wood, but in addition to the trim, these are the only parts of a fireproof house now built out of wood.

As a matter of fact, even furniture, trim, and doors can be made fireproof. Steel is already used for this purpose in office buildings, but it will be a long time before it will replace wood in house construction. Wood, as years go on and lumber becomes more scarce, will be conserved and used merely for trim, frames, and doors.

Two powerful forces are always at work improving house building. One is the tendency to build less expensively — to economize — and the other is to improve construction and build better. Every manufacturer who brings out a piece of machinery and puts it upon the market strives to make it as perfect as possible. Even after the most correct model he can devise has been put on sale, he continues to study it in the light of the added experience which comes to him when he has marketed his product, in order to bring it to a higher state of perfection.

Housebuilding is precisely the same; the house is a manufactured article built to order. Every reputable architect and contractor is earnestly and loyally trying to improve his work and bring out better finished product. They carefully watch new methods advocated, keeping in touch with the results of experiments constantly carried on by building material experts, so that they may incorporate the ideas in their own work as soon as they are assured successes.

These two tendencies — economy in first cost and improvement in quality — are evolving better buildings. Brilliant minds have produced brilliant results, and houses of the class worth considering at all — the honest class — are built better than ever before. There is hardly a person in the smallest village who has not some expert knowledge of good building. Construction is tolerably familiar to every man or woman who has ever seen a new house go up in the neighborhood, and this great public eye, keenly observing, always watchful, helps along the good work of better building.

Fireproof construction is not really fireproof, paradox as this statement may seem. That is, houses said to be "fireproof" (as the term is usually employed) are not strictly unburnable. Some inflammable material is to be found in the ordinary house of fireproof construction; doors, door frames, windows, and cornices are of wood and (on most fireproof houses) the roof is of wood, though frequently covered with non-inflammable material, such as slate or tile. Thus the term "fireproof" is really a misnomer. Such houses are not entirely fireproof, and in a severe conflagration they might be greatly injured, if not entirely destroyed. But the term "fireproof" has come to mean a type of construction which, while not strictly fireproof in the sense that it is unburnable, is truly fire-resisting. Very few houses with fireproof walls and floors will ever burn by reason of the wooden doors, windows, and cornices. Fireproof to a large extent, they are practically *entirely fireproof*, and a town or city with residence districts built in this way would undoubtedly be found practically fireproof. With roofs covered with non-inflammable material (slate or tile) and exterior walls of fireproof material it is quite likely that houses attacked by fire on the outside would resist successfully. Fire on the inside of such a house could hardly get sufficient headway to destroy the building, if floors and walls were fireproof.

To make houses completely fireproof it would be necessary to build them like fireproof office buildings, — that is, using fireproof walls and floors, with wire glass windows and metal doors. This would hardly be practical for houses, and it is doubtful if such construction will ever be generally adopted. Houses with fireproof walls and floors are considered sufficiently fireproof for all practical purposes, this method making ideal, fire-resisting, weather-resisting, wear-and-tear-resisting construction adaptable to all houses. This is undoubtedly the type of construction toward which all house building is slowly but surely trending.

Strange to say, it isn't the fireproof quality that appeals first to the builder of a fireproof house. It is permanency of construction evident in a fireproof type that makes so many owners turn from lumber to fireproof construction. Lumber shrinks, twists, turns, swells, and cracks; fireproof construction is enduring. That means freedom from repairs, — permanency in construction.

HOW TO BUILD A FIREPROOF HOUSE

In making designs for a fireproof house one should not merely take the plans of a frame house and try to adjust them to the requirements of fireproof design. Lumber may be sawed off at any length. It can be planed and trimmed to fit; you can bend it and split it. Materials in a fireproof house, however, are not so elastic. To build such a house economically, you must be familiar with the various types of fireproof construction. This does not mean that fireproof methods are difficult. On the contrary, they require no more skill in building than frame construction.

Stone, brick, concrete blocks, and terra cotta hollow tile are all good materials for fireproof houses, but of these four, terra cotta hollow tile is by far the most practical, as up to the present time it is the only material which has been particularly developed for fireproof houses and put upon the market in large quantities. Cement tiles suitable for fireproof houses have been made, but up to the present time they have not been manufactured to large extent.

Terra cotta hollow tile and Portland cement are the great materials which have opened up new possibilities in ideal construction.

HOLLOW TILE STACKED READY FOR USE IN A FIREPROOF HOUSE.

The ideal suburban community, the dream-city of the future, will be largely composed of these two fundamental materials, both coming right from the earth where all good things come from. Clay is present somewhere in almost every square mile of the habitable parts of the earth, and minerals which form

Portland cement are as readily found. For this reason there is no limit to the growth of these materials, which are supplanting more perishable wood.

Mud, molded into hollow blocks and baked hard in the fire, is what terra cotta hollow tile really is. If every houseowner had a clay bank in his back yard, he might make his own hollow tile, though probably he could not produce it as cheaply or of such good quality as the manufacturers.

After a terra cotta hollow tile structure is built, Portland cement comes into play in the shape of plaster for outside and inside, applied directly to the hollow tile. No lathing need be used. To perfect this rapidly increasing class of houses (plaster exteriors on terra cotta hollow tile) manufacturers now make tile especially for house use. This is "deep-scored" tile, — that is, on all four sides of each tile deep grooves are cast in the tile. When plaster is applied, it flows into the grooves, sets hard, and sticks. Plastering well done on a good brand of terra cotta hollow tile virtually becomes part of the wall. It is more like a plating than a coating, and will endure as long as the wall.

FIREPROOF PARTITIONS OF HOLLOW TILE.

Terra cotta hollow tile blocks come in several sizes, that most frequently used for outside walls being 8 inches thick (from outside to inside), 12 inches high (from top to bottom), and 12 inches wide. Thus a single block fills a square foot of wall, 8 inches thick. When fireproof houses first began to be built it was the custom to have a 12-inch wall on the first story (using blocks 12 inches thick) with an 8-inch wall on the second story, but it has since been found more convenient to build outside walls 8 inches thick throughout. Inside partitions are usually built 3 or 4 inches thick, using blocks $3'' \times 12'' \times 12''$ instead of $8'' \times 12'' \times 12''$, as is customary for outside walls.

The following table, prepared by the National Fire Proofing Company, shows load-carrying capacity for tile used in exterior and interior partitions: —

LOAD-CARRYING CAPACITY OF DENSE HARD-BURNED NATCO HOLLOW TILE

Size of Tile	Width of Wall 1 Tile Thick	Ultimate Load per Lineal Foot of Wall in Pounds	Width of Wall 2 Tiles Thick	Ultimate Load per Lineal Foot of Wall in Pounds
$4'' \times 12'' \times 12''$	$4''$	114,201	$8''$	228,402
$6'' \times 12'' \times 12''$	$6''$	142,862	$12''$	285,724
$8'' \times 12'' \times 12''$	$8''$	202,131	$16''$	404,262
$10'' \times 12'' \times 12''$	$10''$	228,226	$20''$	456,452
$12'' \times 12'' \times 12''$	$12''$	259,300	$24''$	518,600

In another type of hollow tile construction special interlocking blocks are provided, laid horizontally instead of vertically. It is claimed for them that they produce a stronger wall; however, it is doubtful if horizontal blocks will ever take the place of vertical blocks, as the latter are more universally employed.

A more expensive type of vertical block construction consists of special terra cotta hollow tiles set on edge with reënforced concrete placed between each tile, forming a vertical strut from base to roof. This is excellent construction, though it will hardly be widely adopted for houses, owing to its greater complications over ordinary hollow

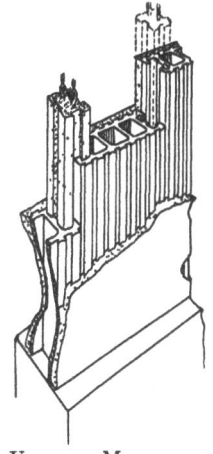

UNUSUAL METHOD OF FIREPROOF CONSTRUCTION.

244 SUCCESSFUL HOUSES AND HOW TO BUILD THEM

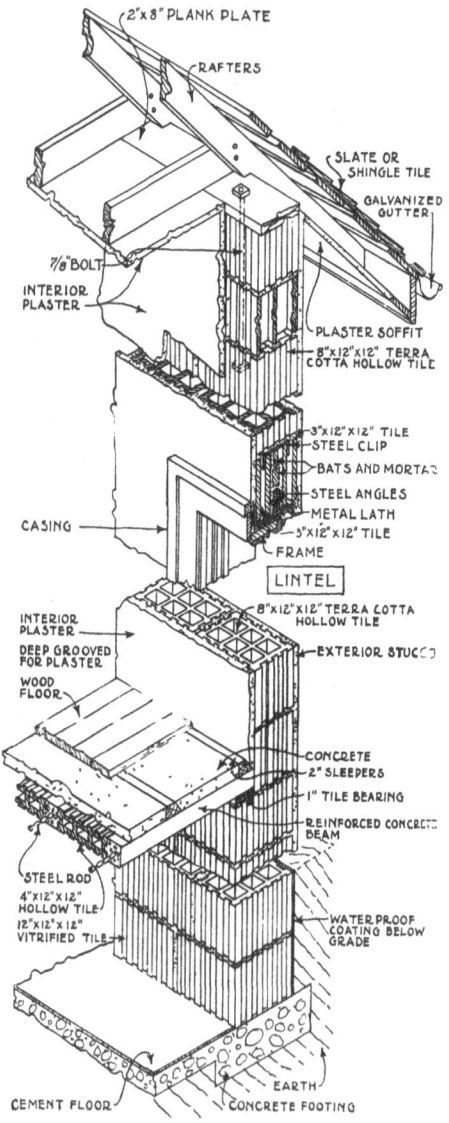

GOOD SYSTEM OF FIREPROOF HOUSE CONSTRUCTION.

tile construction, — greater cost and longer time required in building.

Below ground, concrete or stone foundation walls can be laid as in ordinary construction, or one may use vitrified hollow tile. The regular grooved $8'' \times 12'' \times 12''$ tile start at the grade and continue up to the plate which supports the rafters precisely as in a brick house. When the wall is up to the proper height for the fireproof floor a flat tile is laid on the floor-supporting shelf. Then a wooden scaffold is built to hold the floor temporarily.

For a practical and economical fireproof floor lay rows of $4'' \times 12'' \times 12''$ tile about $4''$ apart, and after laying steel reënforcing rods in the channels between the rows of tile, fill them with cement concrete. The result is a succession of reënforced concrete beams with hollow tile fillers between, temporarily supported by the wooden scaffolding. No expensive forms to mold the different parts of the floor construction are required, — a great saving of expense over most fireproof floors.

FIREPROOF HOUSE WITH CEMENT-PLASTERED EXTERIOR.

The precise thickness of a fireproof floor for houses is easily determined when the span and load are known, by referring to construction tables furnished by manufacturers of terra cotta hollow tile. The thickness varies from 4 inches to 6 or 15 inches according to load and span.

The following table, prepared by the National Fire Proofing Company, shows safe live loads for a fireproof floor composed of hollow tile and reënforced concrete, with concrete finish at top 2 inches thick: —

SIZE OF TILE

Span	4 in.	5 in	6 in.	7 in.	8 in.	9 in.	10 in.	12 in.	15 in.
5'-0"	665	—	—	—	—	—	—	—	—
6'-0"	446	660	—	—	—	—	—	—	—
7'-0"	314	470	655	—	—	—	—	—	—
8'-0"	229	347	487	650	—	—	—	—	—
9'-0"	170	263	372	490	645	—	—	—	—
10'-0"	128	202	290	392	509	640	—	—	—
11'-0"	97	157	229	313	408	515	635	—	—
12'-0"	74	123	183	252	332	421	521	—	—
13'-0"	55	97	147	205	272	348	432	625	—
14'-0"	41	76	118	168	225	289	361	526	—
15'-0"	29	59	95	138	187	242	304	447	—
16'-0"	—	45	77	113	156	204	258	381	610
17'-0"	—	34	60	93	130	172	220	328	527
18'-0"	—	—	48	76	108	145	187	283	459
19'-0"	—	—	37	61	90	123	159	245	402
20'-0"	—	—	—	49	74	103	136	212	352
21'-0"	—	—	—	38	61	86	116	184	310
22'-0"	—	—	—	—	49	72	98	159	272
23'-0"	—	—	—	—	39	60	83	138	240
24'-0"	—	—	—	—	30	49	70	119	212
Reenforced Steel	$\frac{5}{8}''$ sq	$\frac{11}{16}''$ sq	$\frac{3}{4}''$ sq	$\frac{13}{16}''$ sq	$\frac{7}{8}''$ sq	$1\frac{3}{16}''$ sq.	$1\frac{1}{8}''$ sq.	$1\frac{1}{16}''$ sq.	$1\frac{3}{8}''$ sq.
Wt. of Floor Per Square Foot	50 lb.	55 lb	60 lb	65 lb.	70 lb.	75 lb.	80 lb.	90 lb.	105 lb.

Above table is figured for continuous span with the following stresses which are very conservative:—

500 lb. per square inch, extreme fiber composition in concrete.

16,000 lb. per square inch, tension in steel (to be medium open hearth).

The end sheave and longitudinal sheave should be investigated, and sheave reenforcement provided when necessary.

NOTE. — Designs made in accordance with the above table of loads will conform with the building laws of most large cities. However, a more economical design may often be obtained where building laws permit higher stresses.

Safe live loads for a similar floor, but with the top coating of concrete omitted, are indicated in the following table: —

SIZE OF TILE

Span	4″	5″	6″	7″	8″	9″	10″	12″	15″
5′–0″	82	162	262	388	540	—	—	—	—
6′–0″	49	103	170	257	360	482	—	—	—
7′–0″	29	68	115	177	252	340	438	—	—
8′–0″	—	45	79	125	181	248	322	499	—
9′–0″	—	29	54	90	133	185	242	380	—
10′–0″	—	—	37	65	99	140	185	295	506
11′–0″	—	—	24	46	73	106	143	232	404
12′–0″	—	—	—	32	54	81	110	184	326
13′–0″	—	—	—	—	39	61	86	146	266
14′–0″	—	—	—	—	27	46	66	117	218
15′–0″	—	—	—	—	—	33	50	93	179
16′–0″	—	—	—	—	—	—	37	74	148
17′–0″	—	—	—	—	—	—	26	57	121
18′–0″	—	—	—	—	—	—	—	44	99
19′–0″	—	—	—	—	—	—	—	32	81
20′–0″	—	—	—	—	—	—	—	22	65
Reenforced Steel in Each Rib	$\frac{3}{8}''$ sq	$\frac{3}{8}''$ sq.	$\frac{7}{16}''$ sq.	$\frac{1}{2}''$ sq	$\frac{1}{2}''$ sq.	$\frac{9}{16}''$ sq.	$\frac{9}{16}''$ sq.	$\frac{5}{8}''$ sq.	$\frac{3}{4}''$ sq.
Wt. of Floor Per Square Foot	26 lb.	30 lb.	38 lb.	43 lb.	48 lb	52 lb.	58 lb.	68 lb.	82 lb.

Above tables are figured for continuous spans with the following stresses, which are very conservative: —

500 lb. per square inch extreme fiber composition in concrete.

16,000 lb. per square inch tension in steel (to be medium open hearth).

248 SUCCESSFUL HOUSES AND HOW TO BUILD THEM

On top of the tile work composing a fireproof floor, gas and water pipes and electric wires are laid. Then these pipes are covered in by a coating 2 inches thick of concrete, spread over the area of the floor. Embedded in the concrete are beveled strips to which the wooden, finished floor boards are nailed.

AN ATTRACTIVE COTTAGE OF FIREPROOF CONSTRUCTION.
Squires and Wynkoop, Architects.

The under side of a fireproof floor is plastered directly on the materials, no lathing or furring being used. There is no vibration in a fireproof floor of correct thickness. Such a floor is as solid as a wall, — as indestructible as the very foundations, and equally fireproof. There are no sags to crack the plaster nor spaces for vermin. In addition, hollow tile floors and partitions are soundproof.

When the first floor is laid, you may proceed with the exterior walls up to the level of the second floor, which is laid precisely like the first floor. A scaffolding is built temporarily of 2" × 4" uprights with common boards on top, on which the rows of tile are laid out, the channels being filled with concrete, reënforced by steel rods. Over the tops of windows, lintels are made of reënforced concrete slabs, or a number of hollow tile units can be laid in a row, stuffed with concrete reënforced by steel rods, and lifted up into place over a window. Wide interior doorways are covered the same way, though narrow doorways, where the load above is not too heavy, do not require a special lintel.

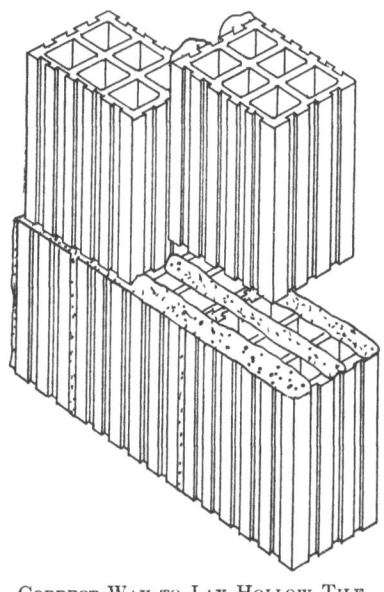

CORRECT WAY TO LAY HOLLOW TILE.

Terra cotta hollow tile may be cut to fit, like brick or stone. If a course is being laid and an aperture is left too small to be filled by an entire tile the mason scores a tile with his chisel, a sharp blow of his hammer breaking it off.

Hollow tile blocks are made of clay, molded with interior hollow spaces called "cells," and they look like little boxes with cavities inside. Partitions forming the tile "webs" are about 1 inch thick. Tile are strongest when set on edge, and this is

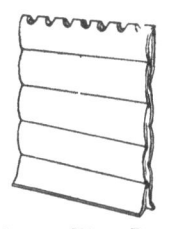

METAL WALL PLUG TO WHICH TRIM IS NAILED.

the proper way to build walls for a house, though when laid on their side tiles are amply strong for all ordinary loads as found in most houses. It is very much better to set them on edge, however, for the vertical bond is better this way and the cells being vertical, slots for pipes and electric wires can be readily cut in the wall by breaking through the rear webs of the tiles.

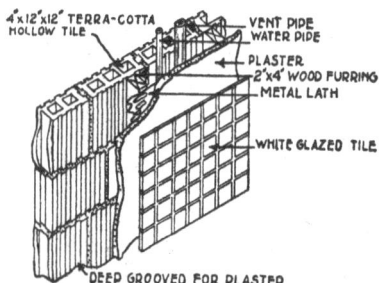

METHOD OF RUNNING BATHROOM PIPES.

Terra cotta hollow tile are laid much the same way as brick. That is, a block is picked up by the mason and "buttered" on the edges with mortar. Then the tile is shoved down on the wall and the excess of mortar flowing out on the edges is "struck" off with the trowel. Although there is only a thin filament of mortar between each tile owing to the fact that tile are hollow instead of solid, this has been found sufficient to make a strong, durable wall, ideal for house construction. Clay (terra cotta) blocks might be made solid like bricks, but blocks of large size warp, twist, and crack so in the kilns when burned, they are not practical. Besides, the cellular construction of hollow tile provides excellent insulation against heat and cold, keeping out the warm air of summer and cold air of winter.

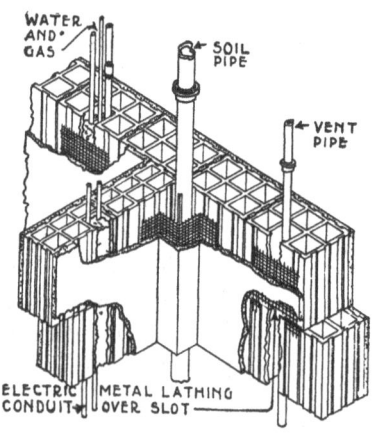

VERTICAL PIPES IN A HOLLOW TILE WALL.

HOW TO BUILD A FIREPROOF HOUSE 251

The air space is the best known means of insulation. Many refrigerators are built on the air-space method, providing several layers of dead-air space, interposed between the outside and inside. Vacuum water bottles are notable examples of the efficiency of air-space insulation, the little hollow walls sealed into the bottles being the only method of insulation. It is the same with a hollow tile wall, which when entirely built contains an air space about 6 inches wide from top to bottom.

Another advantage of hollow wall construction is freedom from dampness. Few materials except pitch or paint are entirely waterproof. The hardest brick or stone, unless artificially damp-proofed, will not keep out moisture.

TILE HOUSE IN PROCESS OF CONSTRUCTION.

Hard-burned hollow tile are as damp-proof as any material can be, and when moisture of even the most infinitesimal amount enters the outer wall (as it might do in a long, hard rain) the interior air space conducts the moisture to the bottom of the wall instead of allowing it to penetrate through to the inside of the rooms. Brick and stone walls have to be furred inside with wood, or else they are painted inside with waterproof paint in order to keep out moisture, but a hollow tile wall can be depended upon to prove damp-proof when the tile are hard burned as they ought to be.

The best hollow tile blocks are vitrified. They are even more dense and hard than the glazed sewer pipe with which we are all so familiar. This does not mean that they are glazed on the outside like sewer pipe, for they do not have the appearance of being glazed, but when a small quantity of water is poured on the outside of a piece of hollow tile it will not soak in, proving that the material is exceedingly dense. Hard-burned hollow tile are not necessarily red nor do they look burned on the out-

STEEL FRAMEWORK FOR FIREPROOF HOUSE.

side. Made in many sections of the country from clays of different chemical composition, they are sometimes red and often yellow, depending upon the location of the factory where the tile is made. Red tile are no harder burned than yellow tile. Owing to the difference in clay in different sections, the exterior appearance of hollow tile blocks is also quite different. In Ohio, and some parts of the East, tile comes out slick and

HOW TO BUILD A FIREPROOF HOUSE 253

smooth, each groove being as perfect as though modeled by hand. In Illinois, tile blocks are rougher and the grooves are slightly warped. In other parts of the country, tile vary in smoothness according to the consistency of the local clay and the consequent mechanical difficulties to overcome in manufacture. The degree of roughness or smoothness has nothing

STEEL FRAME HOUSE COMPLETED.

to do with the durability of tile. Rough, slightly twisted pieces are quite as good as straight, slick tile, the only requisite being that they shall be hard burned and dense. When picked up in the hand and rapped sharply with a hammer, each block should ring true like a bell. A dull, soggy sound means that the tile are soft, and such should be rejected.

Hollow tile go into the wall more rapidly than brick because one tile, filling a space a foot square, is more quickly laid than the several brick necessary to fill a space of like size. For this reason brick fireproof houses are frequently built with face brick backed up by hollow tile, instead of building a solid wall of brick. The former method is better than a solid wall, owing to the celular construction of the hollow tile backing, which is more waterproof than a solid brick wall. When face brick are backed with hollow tile in this way the former are usually anchored to the backing by metal wall ties; or sometimes a row of brick headers every few courses is laid back into the tile wall.

Very few blocks of special shape are required in hollow tile house construction. The entire building may be built of ordinary blocks, but it has been found convenient to use special jamb blocks at window openings. These have a rabbit (rebate) molded in them to receive the window frame, making an excellent weatherproof joint between wall and frame. Where special jamb blocks are not used a good method is to set the face casing of each frame into a groove in the tiles, thus allowing no gap between frame and wall. When the exterior of the house is to be plastered, this plaster coat is made to stop against the frame, giving additional protection. Any method of building window frames can be used. Ordinary tiles may be simply plastered up under sills with smooth cement to form a wash, or stone or cast cement sills can be used as in any brick building. Sometimes wooden sills on window frames are made extra wide to extend out over the tile wall, in which case no other sills are required.

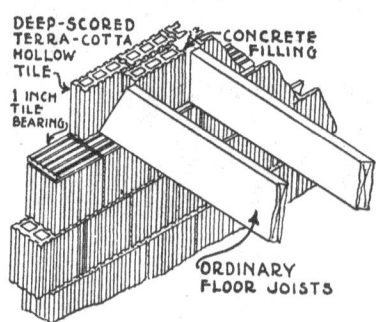

HOLLOW TILE WALLS, WOODEN FLOOR.

How can flooring and trim be applied in a hollow tile house

HOW TO BUILD A FIREPROOF HOUSE

when there is no wooden framework to nail to? As has already been explained, the wooden finished flooring is nailed to wood cleats embedded in concrete, and this provides a space underneath for the horizontal gas, water, and heating pipes. On the walls, corrugated metal wall plugs are driven into the joints of the tile at points where trim is to be afterwards applied. Just before the building is ready for plastering, wooden grounds are nailed to these wall plugs by driving nails through until they are gripped by the corrugations of the metal. Then the building is plastered up to the grounds, and trim is afterwards nailed through to them. Another good way is to build laths into the wall every few courses precisely as is done in a brick house. To these laths wooden grounds for trim are secured.

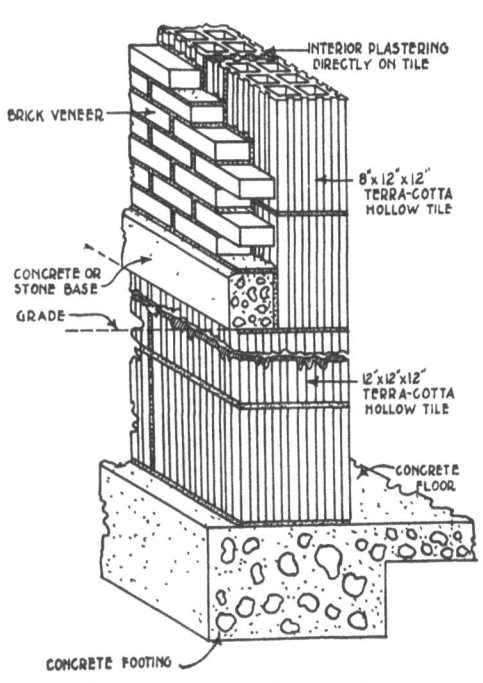

BRICK VENEER ON HOLLOW TILE.

One of the first questions asked a fireproof expert is "how do you run bathroom pipes in a hollow tile partition?" The easiest way is to fur out the wall inside, with ordinary $2'' \times 4''$ studs nailed to the tile partition. In this space you can run all the horizontal and vertical pipes necessary for bathroom fixtures.

In a tiled bathroom apply the tile to this furred-out partition. On the floor, apply the tile directly to the concrete.

The best roofing materials for a fireproof house are tile or slate, though of course shingles can be used when desired.

A new method of construction for fireproof houses has recently been put upon the market consisting of a skeleton framework of concrete-filled steel pipe (ordinary 3 or 4-inch pipe, usually). Vertical struts from 6 to 10 feet apart are formed by the vertical pipes, and these are tied horizontally by horizontal pipes. A like pipe skeleton forms the structure for floors. Webs of wire are used for walls and floor slabs, covered with metal lathing. Thus, outside walls as well as floors are of reënforced concrete.

Many houses are built with hollow tile exterior walls and ordinary frame inside walls and floor joists. Though not so ideal as fireproof house construction this is an excellent way to build, as hollow tile exterior walls are easily arranged to carry the wooden joists. Houses are built in this way precisely like brick or stone houses, the joists resting on the walls and tile being built around the ends.

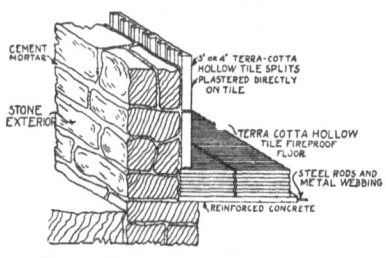

STONE HOUSE LINED WITH TILE.

As an indication regarding the cost of standard hollow tile construction as compared with other methods of construction, consult the following table (courtesy of the National Fire Proofing Company):

HOUSE CONSTRUCTION

COMPARATIVE TABLE OF COSTS

Comparative building costs of different systems of building, based upon an average frame dwelling costing $10,000, complete, located in the vicinity of New York:—

(a) $10,000 Frame.
(b) $11,000 Brick outside walls, wooden inside.
(c) $10,800 Brick outside walls, backed up with hollow tile.
(d) $10,250 Stucco on expanded metal, wooden inside.
(e) $10,500 Hollow tile, stuccoed, wooden inside.
(f) $12,000 Hollow tile stuccoed, — fireproof throughout except roof.
(g) $14,000 Hollow tile walls faced with brick, fireproof floors and roof.
(h) $15,000 Brick walls — fireproof floors and roof.

The above figures are based on an average taken from two architects and two builders, who have had experience with the methods of construction designated.

Fireproof House of Concrete.

Cabinet Work in the Dining Room of a New England House

CHAPTER XIV

CARPENTRY AND CABINET WORK

ONE of the most important branches of work in connection with the building of a house is carpentry, for whether the building is of masonry or frame construction, carpenter work is bound to be more or less extensive, consisting of floors, roof, inside trim, outside and inside millwork in the former, and the entire framework of the building (including its finish) in the latter.

Different methods of building the framework of the house are described in another chapter. During construction the owner should watch the work carefully, for his house will only prove as strong as the framework. Errors in the latter are hard to correct after the building is completed.

It is part of the carpenter's job to temporarily inclose a building during its construction with doors and barricades. As soon as the roof is on, window openings should be barricaded and stout temporary doors should be hung, permitting the building to be locked up at night.

Mechanics who are proficient in building the rough framework of a building are rarely good men to employ on inside finish. For this reason most carpenter contractors employ two kinds of men, — one kind for rough framing and another kind for inside finishing. It is always a good plan for the owner and his architect to keep an eye on each man employed on the inside finish, for frequently a new workman gets on the job, — a man who is not inclined to do high-grade work. If his deficiencies are discovered in time, the contractor (who is usually just as anxious to do a good job as the owner is to have him) can be informed, and the man may be set at less important work.

260 SUCCESSFUL HOUSES AND HOW TO BUILD THEM

Window frames and door frames are usually made at the mill, using either stock patterns or patterns designed by the architect. In frame houses covered with siding, exterior door and window casings are frequently 4 or 5 inches wide, molded or plain. In cement-plastered houses wide casings can be used,

NARROW WINDOW CASINGS AND CASEMENT WINDOWS.
Lawrence Buck, Architect.

or narrow casings, — not over $2\frac{1}{4}$ to $3\frac{1}{2}$ inches wide. Frames for masonry buildings usually have narrow casings, as the frames are set into the masonry.

Door and window frames arrive at the building ready to put in place. In a frame building after the framework is erected and boarded over, the frames are set, after which the exterior siding is applied. In masonry buildings, window and door frames are sent to the job in advance of the mason work; masons build the walls up to the height of the window sills, whereupon the frames are set up and braced by carpenters, after which the masons proceed to build them in. Cleats or anchors are provided for anchoring the frames properly to the masonry walls.

The woods most used for frames and cornices (all exterior finish, in fact) are white pine and cypress. In the far West, redwood is also used for exterior finish. For inside finish there are many woods to choose from; white oak, red oak, ash, walnut, cherry, birch, basswood, North Carolina pine, maple, and mahogany are what might be termed hardwoods; white pine, cypress, redwood, and whitewood are soft woods frequently used for interior finish. Gumwood is one of the newer woods, and it is said to give satisfaction, looking well when finished natural or when painted white.

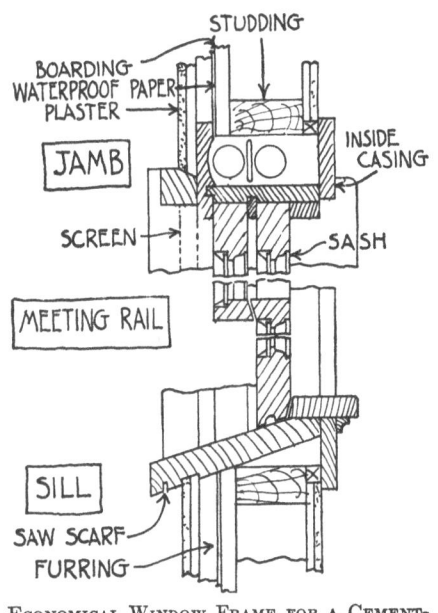

ECONOMICAL WINDOW FRAME FOR A CEMENT-PLASTERED HOUSE.

Before the finished floors are laid all underflooring should be carefully examined for broken or loose boards or holes. These should be carefully repaired. Then the floors are swept clean and covered with building paper, when all is ready for the finished floors. In some houses the finished floors are laid directly on top of the underfloors, using nothing but building paper between

262 SUCCESSFUL HOUSES AND HOW TO BUILD THEM

the two. In other houses, the underfloors are stripped with 1″ × 2″ cleats, and to these the finished floors are laid. Thus a space an inch thick is provided between underfloor and finished floor, and when a good brand of deafening felt is used between the two this air space serves as a deafener. Deafening materials are usually about ½ inch to ⅜ inch thick, being composed of two layers of heavy building paper stuffed between with hair felt, tow, or seaweed. The latter is coarse grass from the sea, such as is cast upon the beach by the waves. The grass is dried and then woven into a heavy fabric, excellent for deafening, and good, also, for insulation.

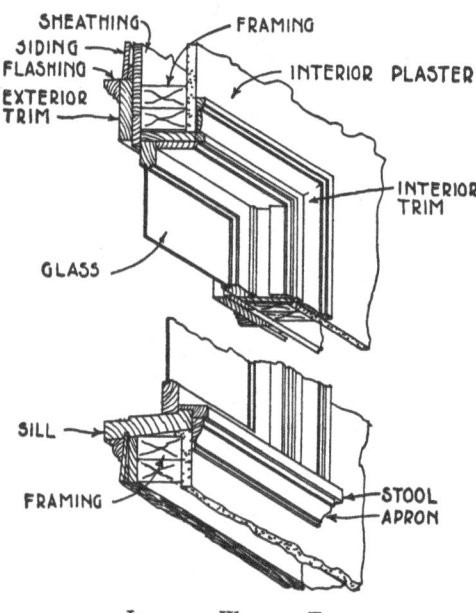

INTERIOR WINDOW TRIM.

Finished flooring comes in several widths and thicknesses, from ⅝ × 1¼ inches up to ⅞ × 3½ inches. A good size to use is ⅞ × 2¼ inches. Oak flooring is most frequently used for all rooms except kitchens and other rooms in the service portion of the house, for it is but little more expensive than cheaper woods and has the advantage of being particularly durable. Thin, ⅝ inch flooring is most often used for remodeling houses, as it can be nailed down over the old floors. Flooring customarily used for ordinary work is ⅞ inch in thickness, tongued and grooved on the ends as well as the edges. Thus, when the joints are driven up right (as they should be) an excellent job is the result. Nails are driven through in the grooves (called "blind nailing") so that they are invisible after the floor is completed. When such a floor is finished it should be scraped carefully over its entire surface, using machine or hand scrapers.

The grades of flooring are so variable and they change so much from season to season, it is impossible to give specific information concerning them. Good flooring is not difficult to procure if you insist upon getting the best. As a general thing, the description "best, prime, clear, selected," will procure the best grade of flooring.

Maple flooring is usually preferred for kitchens and servants' quarters, as it is a more dense wood than oak and will stand more wear. Southern pine flooring is also frequently used in servants' quarters. It is the cheapest flooring on the market, but will not stand as hard usage as oak or maple.

Flooring comes straight-sawed or quarter-sawed, the latter costing more than straight-sawed flooring and is the best for wear. All flooring for inside use should be strictly kiln-dried, and it must be stored in a dry place. A better way is not to allow finished flooring to be delivered until the building has been plastered and is thoroughly dried out. Fir is an excellent wood for outside porch floors, $1\frac{1}{4} \times 3\frac{1}{2}$ inches being the size most used for this purpose. Such flooring can be tongued and grooved or it may be square-edged; in the latter case the boards should be laid from $\frac{1}{8}$ inch to $\frac{1}{4}$ inch apart. All porch flooring should be painted on the under side and on the joints before laying, as this will greatly prolong its life.

Tile floors are sometimes specified in the carpenter's specifications and sometimes in the mason's specifications. In any event, all tile floors should be mentioned in the carpenter's specifications so that the carpenter will be warned to prepare the underflooring for receiving the tile.

Tile floors are excellent for bathrooms, porches, vestibules, and halls. Tile is also used a great deal for fireplace hearths. The tile can be laid on a wooden floor if a layer of concrete 2 to 3 inches thick is laid on top of the underflooring; tile is then laid on this concrete base, bedded in cement mortar. For porches and vestibules use ordinary red quarry tile, 6 × 6 inches or 9 × 9 inches with wide mortar joints, natural or black. The tile are spaced out on the concrete base first, after which thin cement mortar is poured into the joints.

Floors of rubber tile are excellent for halls and kitchens, — especially for the latter. Rubber tiling is more expensive than ordinary tiling, but it is so soft it wears practically forever. Such tiling is cut with dies, one tile interlocking with another.

Linoleum is the most used material for covering kitchen and pantry floors. After the wooden floor is built and before the quarter-round has been applied linoleum can be laid, after which the quarter-round is applied as usual. Thus, the joint between linoleum and baseboard is covered.

Tile facing for mantels and tile walls in bathrooms are laid by smearing mortar on the walls and sticking the tile thereon. One tile is laid closely to another, and after all are in position, thin cement mortar is brushed into all the joints, after which the walls are washed down, leaving the work complete. On bathroom walls it is necessary to provide metal lathing attached to the studding, to which the mortar groundwork is applied. On mantel facings the mortar groundwork sticks directly to the rough brickwork of the fireplace and chimney breast. Tile fireplace facings are finished on the edge with iron or brass angles, or in some cases, "bullnose" tile can be used in place of metal edges.

Do not permit any inside trim to be delivered at the building until the rooms are entirely dry. More trim is spoiled by applying it in a damp house than in any other way. All trim should be thoroughly kiln-dried. That is, it should be placed in a kiln at a temperature of about 140 degrees F. and kept there for at least 48 hours, permitting air to circulate for the purpose of removing all moisture from the lumber. Kiln-dried lumber is so dry it will soak water like a sponge, and this is why it is necessary to keep it away from any possible dampness, however slight.

In first-class work it is expected that carpenters, when trim is applied, will finish the joints by hand, correcting any irregularities of surface. It may even be necessary to sandpaper the trim all over in order to get a first-class job, but if this grade of work is to be required it should be mentioned in the specifications. Otherwise, on ordinary work it is not customary to scrape or sandpaper trim except at the joints.

There is a difference between ordinary workmanship and "cabinet" workmanship, the latter being expected only on the most expensive houses. Good, thorough work should be expected, of course, but one cannot expect "cabinet work" unless it is so mentioned in the specifications. In ordinary work, joints of the trim are mitered neatly and carefully nailed together. Joints in cabinet work are "splined" (fastened with pegs or metal ties much as a good picture frame is fastened at the joints). Ordinary joints wear very well if the wood is dry and the workmen are skillful. Joints made "cabinet work" fashion are practically indestructible.

Inside door frames are not made at the mill. Thin boards of the right size and shape are sent to the building, and these are sawed up and fitted on the job by the carpenters. Baseboards should be carefully fitted at all angles, and the crack left between floor and baseboard should be concealed by applying "quarter-round" or similar molding. The latter should be nailed to the floor (not to the wall), so that the flooring when it settles slightly away from the baseboard (as most floors do) will carry the quarter-round down with it and not disturb the baseboard; the quarter-round hides the joint. In kitchens it is customary to use a baseboard narrower than that used in other rooms.

At all inside and outside doors the carpenters should nail wooden blocks between the studding and the door frames, in order to strengthen the latter so they will not jar when a door is slammed. Many little points like this should be carefully watched. Carpenters are inclined to do good work as a rule, but one cannot expect them to go out of their way and use extraordinary care of their own volition, so it remains for the owner and his architect to check up little things and see that they are properly done.

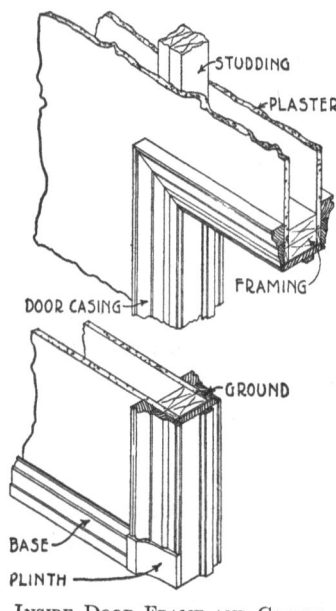

INSIDE DOOR FRAME AND CASING.

The underflooring should be carefully fitted against all outside walls so as to permit no cold air to enter at these points. An excellent way is to run the underflooring tight against the outside boarding of the outside wall, thus stopping that gap into the cellar which so often exists. Another — the best way of all — is to lay two or three courses of brick between the studs on top of the underflooring, forming an effectual fire, cold, and vermin stop from the basement.

Before any inside and outside doors are hung the owner should visit the building and carefully note where each is to swing, making a chalk mark on the side on which he desires it to be placed. This should be done whether the doors are located on the plans or not, as it is much easier to judge of the proper swing of doors at the building, and the owner may desire to change many from the positions shown on the plan. See that all doors are swung high enough from the floor to clear any rugs placed there. In locating the swing of doors be careful to choose positions which will not permit one door to jam another; prevent doors from striking lighting fixtures, radiators, or registers. As a general thing doors swing into the rooms in which they are placed. For instance, kitchen doors open into the kitchen; bedroom doors open into bedrooms (not into the hall); bathroom doors open into the bathroom.

In a bedroom it is good practice when possible to hang the door so that the bed will not be visible when the door is partly open. In a bathroom it is customary to swing the door against a water-closet, so the latter will not be conspicuous when the door stands open. Closet doors should always be swung away from a window so that light will enter the closet when the door is open. Mirrors of full length are frequently applied to bedroom, bathroom, or dressing room doors. When this is done, care should be taken to hang doors in such places that one may back off far enough from the mirror to permit a good view.

Inside and outside trim should be painted on the back before it is put in place. Moldings or horizontal members should never be spliced other than in a corner where the splicing will not be visible. Long, mitered joints should always be reënforced by "splines," or some other method should be used to prevent joints from opening after the job is completed. When trimming the interior of a house in damp weather it is an excellent idea to have a fire in the furnace or boiler, maintaining the same degree of heat that the rooms will be subject to after the house is completed. Thus, any dampness in the wood will show up immediately and can be remedied before the carpenters leave the job. Many houses trimmed when the weather is damp begin to show defects after completion when fires are started.

Stair building is a distinct trade in itself and the carpenter

268   SUCCESSFUL HOUSES AND HOW TO BUILD THEM

contractor usually prefers to sublet his stair work. When the rough hatchway for future finished stairs is framed, it is a good idea to check up the size and see if it will be amply large to contain the stairs. Usually the finished staircase is not built until the building is nearly completed; often, when carpenters come to put in the stairs they find that, through some error,

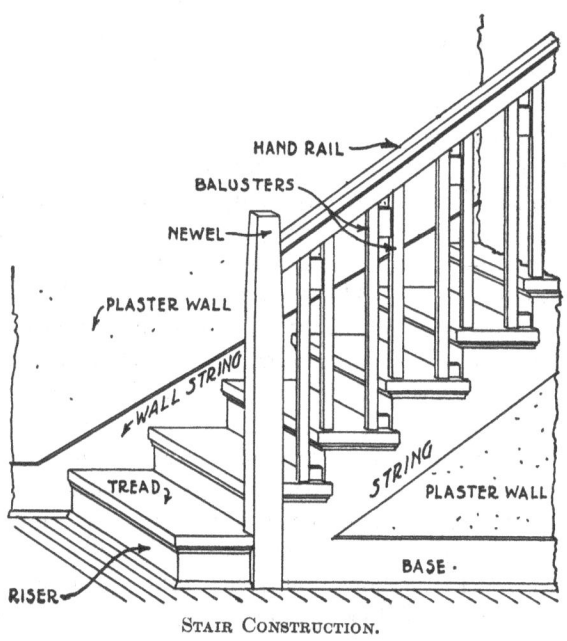

STAIR CONSTRUCTION.

sufficient space has not been left for them, with the result that the staircase has to be squeezed in, — a condition very detrimental to the stairs. Pay especial attention to head room, insisting that the contractor arrange the stairs so there will be plenty. Stairs should be thoroughly wedged underneath and glued, so as to prevent "squeaking." No other part of the house gets so much wear as the stairs, and they should be properly made, to stand the strain. As soon as they are finished, stairs should be carefully covered with heavy paper, held in place with cleats to protect them until the building is completed. The painter should "fill" the woodwork of stairs as soon as they are ready.

Windows (sash, as they are called) are made at the mill, of

GREEN SHUTTERS ON A WHITE HOUSE.

the right size to fit the window frames. Upon arriving at the building these sash are fitted by the carpenters who plane off the edges until they fit the frames properly. Then the painter takes them to his shop where he gives them a heavy coat of oil (taking the place of the priming coat of paint) after which he glazes them and sends them back to the building. When sash are first put in place they frequently stick. Though carefully fitted, a slight swelling often takes place in new sash, making them bind slightly. Owners annoyed by binding sash often order them to be planed off, but this is usually a mistake, for later when the sashes have become seasoned they may shrink, and if they have been fitted too loosely in the first place shrinkage causes them to rattle in their frames. This also applies to new doors, which should not be fitted too loosely.

Outside blinds are used in a large number of houses, and they accomplish two purposes, — making the appearance of the house more attractive, and providing means of shutting out the sun in summer. Blinds are often made with pivoted slats in the lower half, but as these soon work loose it is more practical to use fixed slats throughout. In place of blinds, paneled shutters are frequently employed, and the exterior effect of these is very pleasing. Shutters are useful during periods when the house is not occupied, as they may then be closed, affording some protection to the windows. Inside blinds, called "Venetian blinds," will be found useful in some cases. These are built of wooden slats through which vertical cords extend, allowing the blinds to roll up like a curtain. Old-fashioned inside blinds, hinged at the side, are rarely used now.

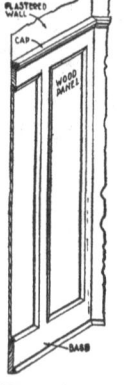

WALL PANELLING.

Beams for ceilings are sometimes built up, being in fact hollow boxes attached to the ceiling. Inside posts are built up of thin stock in the same way. Stair newels are usually hollow, and the stair rail is composed of several moldings skillfully joined. This multiplicity of pieces composing inside millwork is not altogether on account of reducing expense by using lumber of smaller size, but it is chiefly done to make the work more durable, as it has been found that posts or molded work built up of small pieces, are less liable to crack open from shrinkage.

Paneling on walls or ceilings is built up of several layers of wood (3-ply or 5-ply as the case may be). Door panels are made in the same way. Even the stiles and rails of doors and wainscots are now frequently built up of many small pieces of wood, glued together, as such work has been found to stand better than solid wood. Panels in doors or wainscots should be fitted loosely into the stiles and rails so as to permit them to swell and shrink (with the changes of heat and cold to which they are subjected) without causing panels to warp or split.

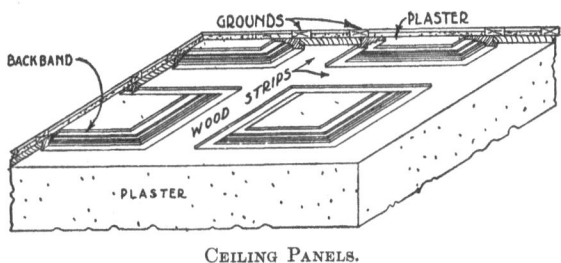

CEILING PANELS.

Occasionally a new door becoming damp in some way, shows signs of twisting or warping. Such a door can be straightened by sending it back to the mill, where it is steamed and pressed out, making it as good as new.

After the house is lathed inside ready for the finished plaster, measurements are taken (usually by a workman from the mill) for all built-in furniture such as sideboards, china closets, kitchen cupboards, and similar pieces. This furniture is then made at the mill, after which it is brought to the building and put in place by the carpenters.

BRICK AND PLASTER HOUSE WITH A SLATE ROOF
Wm. G. Purcell, Architect.

CHAPTER XV

THE IMPORTANCE OF A GOOD ROOF

CARPENTERS lay the shingles for a shingle roof, but slate are laid by the roofing or metalwork contractor. The following table will be useful in determining how many shingles are required for a roof:—

SHINGLE ROOF WITH HANGING METAL GUTTER.

SHINGLES FOR A ROOF. NUMBER REQUIRED PER SQUARE
(100 SQUARE FEET)

Laid 4½ inches to the weather	800
Laid 5 inches to the weather	720
Laid 5½ inches to the weather	655
Laid 6 inches to the weather	600

(Standard method is 4½ inches to the weather.)

274 SUCCESSFUL HOUSES AND HOW TO BUILD THEM

Shingles will last longer if they are laid on an open roof, — that is, a roof on which the roof boards are laid about 2 inches apart to allow air to reach the under side of the shingles, which prevents them from rotting. Wrought-iron cut nails are the most enduring.

Hemlock shingles are fairly durable in dry climates. Red cedar lasts well and is excellent for shingles. White pine is

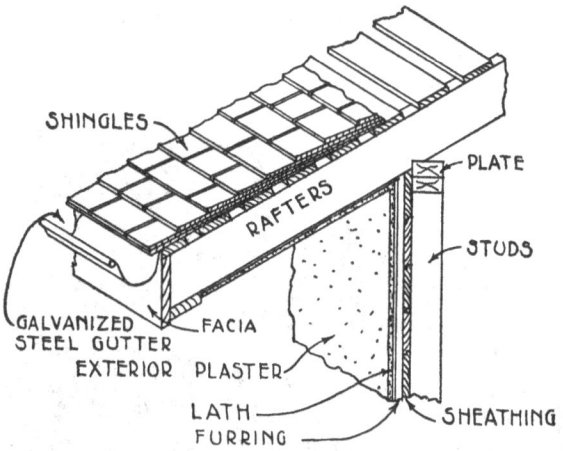

SHINGLES LAID ON AN OPEN ROOF.

very good, but is rarely used on account of its scarcity. Probably the best woods for shingles are cypress and white cedar. Many grades are in the market, — and the owner should remember that it always pays to get the best. In applying shingles it is well to lay the edges loosely, which permits them to dry properly after they are laid, and prevents swelling and curling.

Generally speaking, there are three kinds of slate: ordinary dark blue or black slate, green slate, and brown slate. The former comes largely from Pennsylvania; green slate comes from Vermont, New York, and Pennsylvania; and brown slate comes from New York. Blue or black slate and green slate are the most used, the former being the cheaper.

When slate are used the roof boarding is composed of matched boards, laid tightly with smooth side up, covered with waterproof felt. The three lower courses of slate (next the eaves) should be bedded in slater's cement, which prevents moisture from penetrating when snow backs up from the gutters. Hips and ridges should also be laid in slater's cement.

The following table giving useful information about slate will be found of assistance: —

SIZES OF SLATE, AND NUMBER PER SQUARE REQUIRED (100 SQUARE FEET)

Size in Inches	Number of Pieces Required
6 × 12	535
7 × 12	455
8 × 12	400
9 × 12	358
7 × 14	375
8 × 14	330
9 × 14	295
10 × 14	265
8 × 16	280
9 × 16	250
10 × 16	220
9 × 18	215
10 × 18	195
12 × 18	163

(Larger sizes are in stock, but are rarely used for houses.)

Slate have to be punched or drilled either by hand or machine, with two holes in each slate for the nails. Machine-*drilled* holes are better than machine or hand-*punched* holes, as the latter frequently chip around the holes, weakening the slate. Nails are galvanized, solid copper, or copper-clad. Galvanized nails rust out after a few years. For this reason solid copper or copper-clad are to be recommended. The latter are excellent, for they are as permanent as solid copper, but much stronger and less costly.

Asbestos shingles are made, generally, in three colors, — natural (gray), green, and red. They cost more than wood shingles, being approximately the price of slate. Asbestos shingles are applied on a tightly boarded roof, like slate.

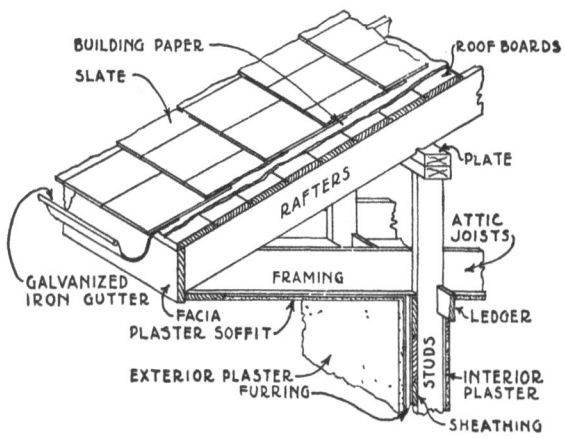

METHOD OF LAYING SLATE.

Tin is frequently used for the flat roofs of a house, such as porch roofs, roofs over dormer windows, and similar places. It is also used for lining gutters at the eaves, and is most frequently used for flashing.

Roofing tin or terne plate is made by applying as a coating an alloy of tin and lead to sheets of iron or steel. The black sheets (or black plate) are rolled from thin, flat bars of soft steel or iron, known as "tin bars" or "sheet bars." This step in the process is known as "hot rolling" and the stands of rolls, the "hot mills."

Coming from the hot rolls the unfinished black plates are sheared to size, and are then pickled in dilute sulphuric acid to remove any scale or dirt, being held loosely in racks or cradles so that the acid in the pickling vats may penetrate between the sheets. The black plates are then washed with water (swilled) in tanks to remove all traces of acid, and are then annealed, being placed in covered iron boxes to exclude the air, heated in a furnace to 1400 degrees to 1600 degrees F. for sixteen to twenty hours.

They are then allowed to cool gradually and are "cold rolled," to produce a perfectly smooth surface. As this makes them somewhat stiff they are then reannealed ("white annealing" or "second annealing") at a temperature higher than before.

The amount of cold rolling, pickling, and annealing depends upon the character of the finished tinplate for which the sheets are intended.

Before tinning the sheets are resquared, again pickled, known as the "white pickling" or second pickling, are thoroughly washed to remove all traces of acid, and kept under water until they are taken out to be run through the tinning process.

The common modern method of coating the sheets is performed in one operation by passing them through a pot of molten metal, between driven rollers arranged in pairs, the last set squeezing off the surplus metal. These mechanical tinning pots are sometimes called "patent stacks." There are several varieties in this country. All are modifications of the early method of tinning, which was done by hand and was more complicated.

Tin for roofing is applied in many different ways. There is the flat-seam method in which the edges of the sheets are turned one-half inch, locked and thoroughly soldered, the sheets being fastened to the roof by means of cleats spaced about 8 inches apart; these cleats are locked in the seams and fastened to the roof with two one-inch barbed wire nails. Then there is the standing-seam method in which sheets are put together in long lengths at the shop, assembled at the building and attached with cleats. Valleys and gutters are usually formed from sheets laid by the flat-seam method.

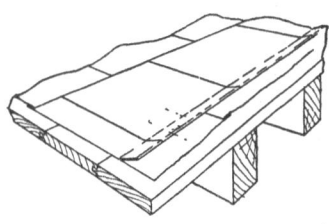

TIN ROOF WITH FLAT SEAMS.

Tin used for any purpose should be of some well-known brand. It pays to use only the best. For roofs of low pitch the flat-seam method is to be preferred, and it is better to use sheets not larger than 14 × 20 inches, so as to have the greatest number of seams and consequently a stiffer, more durable roof. On steep roofs sheets 20 × 8 inches should be used, and the standing seam method should be employed.

The light IC plates are always to be preferred to the heavier IX plates, as the latter suffer more from expansion and contraction. All the best grades of tin are "double dipped" or "extra coated." When sheets are soldered together nothing but resin should be used, as the acid sometimes employed is injurious to tin.

The roof boards under a tin roof should be covered with a good grade of building paper before the tin is laid, and the sheets should be painted on the under side before they are soldered, to prevent moisture of condensation (or injurious fumes rising from rooms below) attacking the tin. After a roof is finished it must be entirely cleaned off, carefully removing excess of resin, and then painted two coats. Tin roofs usually require repainting every 3 to 5 years.

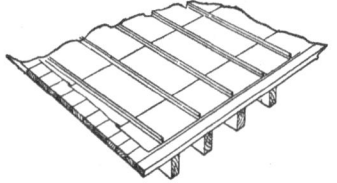

STANDING-SEAM TIN ROOF.

A copper roof is practically indestructible and nothing is

against the use of copper for flat roofs except its cost. Sheet copper is also excellent for flashing and gutters, the 16-ounce weight being the kind most often used. Copper roofs are laid in a similar manner to tin roofs.

Composition or gravel roofs are sometimes used for flat roofs. The standard specifications for a first-class gravel roof are as follows: —

SPECIFICATIONS FOR GRAVEL ROOFING.

First lay five (5) thicknesses of No. 2 wool roofing felt weighing not less than fourteen (14) pounds (single thickness) to the square of one hundred (100) feet. This felt to be smoothly and evenly laid and well cemented together, mopping not less than twenty (20) inches between each layer, with best roofing cement, using not less than one hundred and twenty (120) pounds of roofing cement to the square of one hundred (100) feet. All joinings along the walls and around the openings to be carefully made. Then cover the entire surface with a coating of roofing cement and screened gravel, using not less than one-sixth (1/6) of a cubic yard of gravel to the square of one hundred (100) feet. The gravel to be what will pass through not larger than a 5/8-inch mesh screen and to be free from sand and loam.

This roof shall be guaranteed for a period of five (5) years.

N. B.—Over open board construction and all buildings not plastered, use one (1) thickness of rosin sized sheathing paper.

280 *SUCCESSFUL HOUSES AND HOW TO BUILD THEM*

Tile roofs are used a great deal on houses, as tile has been found to be an excellent material for roofs. Spanish tile (quarter-round, half-round or molded in various forms) and shingle tile (flat, like shingles or slate) are the two principal patterns used. The latter make the best appearance on most houses.

BUILT-IN GUTTERS LINED WITH COPPER.

They are laid precisely like slate, using galvanized, solid copper, or copper-clad nails. Tile ridge rolls and hips are made to fit the slope of any roof. Tile for roofs come in two general colors — red and green. All tile should be hard burned ("vitrified"), as soft tile grow softer upon exposure to the weather. The natural color of tile is red, — green is obtained by glazing.

THE IMPORTANCE OF A GOOD ROOF

The most important work on any roof is the flashing. "Flashing" is accomplished by metal (tin or copper) strips applied where the roof comes in contact with the chimney or other masonry, or where valleys are formed, or ridges.

Metal gutters and conductors (rain-water down-spouts) can be applied in many different ways. Galvanized iron gutters formed in the cornice, or hanging independently below it, are practical when properly made. On wooden cornices made at the mill and built in at the building, copper, lead, zinc, or tin is used for a lining.

A very practical "hanging gutter" consists of a half-round gutter composed of galvanized iron, hung below the wooden cornice by means of metal supports attached to the roof. The chief advantage of such a gutter is that it can be easily renewed without tearing up the roof.

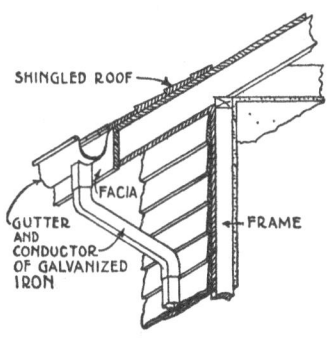

HANGING GUTTER OF GALVANIZED IRON.

Conductors (down-spouts, as they are sometimes called) can be had of galvanized iron or copper, square shape or round. In every case they should be of corrugated metal so that in case they freeze in winter the pressure of ice inside will not destroy the conductors. Being of corrugated metal, they will have elasticity enough to withstand the pressure.

When a gas range is used in the kitchen instead of a coal range, the kitchen chimney is frequently omitted. In this case a metal tube can be inserted in the partition, connected with the gas range and extending up through the roof, to carry away the products of combustion. A line of ordinary 4-inch galvanized iron (or copper) conductor pipe is excellent for this purpose. It should be carefully wrapped with asbestos paper, attached by means of wire. Heat from a gas range is so little there is small danger of fire.

GALVANIZED IRON GUTTER AND CORNICE.

COUNTRY HOUSE OF CEMENT TRIMMED WITH WALL TILE.
Frank Lloyd Wright, Architect.

CHAPTER XVI

PLUMBING THAT IS SANITARY; WATER AND SEWER PIPES

NOTHING about the building is more important than the plumbing system, for a house will be an utter failure if the plumbing is not perfectly sanitary, — a properly arranged, noiseless, convenient system. A modern plumbing system is so different from old-style plumbing there is little comparison between them. Formerly fixtures were cumbersome and inconvenient, in most cases boxed in with wood paneling. To-day more advanced methods prevail and plumbing is exposed as much as possible. The idea in a modern plumbing system is to place the skeleton of pipes and the fixtures in such a way that adjacent space can be kept perfectly clean, and every part of the system can be reached for repairs. This has been made possible to a large extent by nickel-plated piping and modern enameled iron, porcelain, and vitrified fixtures.

Though not himself an expert, any houseowner can easily acquire enough general knowledge about plumbing to enable him to know a good job from a bad one. Let the owner understand in the first place that plumbing should be done only by experts, — mechanics who desire to do a first-class job and are capable of it. Watch particularly when the piping is installed that the plumbers do not cut too deeply into floor and wall timbers. Pipes, of course, are not installed until the framework of the building is up, and frequently timbers must be cut to allow pipes to pass. Some plumbers are not careful about this cutting of timbers, and when they get through, a house is greatly weakened. All cuts in floor joists should be close to the end, so as not to weaken the timber. A little skillful planning of the plumbing system will reduce cutting of timbers to the minimum and any cuts necessary can be made where they will do no harm.

Every system of piping is divided into three parts: pipes for water supply, for sewage, and for ventilation. The former conduct water from the main in the street or from a well to the house and thence to the various fixtures. Pipes for sewage carry off the waste from fixtures, discharging into the sewer in the street, or into a cesspool or septic-tank system. Ventilating pipes admit fresh air to the sewage system; each branch of the work should be built economically and durably. Every length of pipe and every fitting should be air- and water-tight, put together so it can be readily taken apart for cleaning or for repairs, — resulting in a system of plumbing that will carry on the work automatically for years without renewals.

Let us consider, first, the water-supply system usually extending from the water main in the street. It is included in the plumber's contract that he shall dig the ditch out through the street and connect the supply pipe with the water main, running the pipe from that point into the basement of the house. In most towns a fee is charged by the town for the privilege of tapping the water main in the street. Frequently another fee is charged for the privilege of digging up the street, though this fee is ordinarily returned after the street has been restored satisfactorily to its original condition. All such fees should be stipulated in the specifications, "to be paid by the plumbing contractor."

FLEXIBLE CONNECTION TO STREET MAIN.

In most towns and cities a $\frac{3}{4}''$ tap into the street main is the largest that will be allowed by the water company. This is sufficient for a house not too large in size, but where consumption of water is large, a $\frac{3}{4}''$ tap might not be sufficient. To increase the supply of water in such cases, two or more $\frac{3}{4}''$ taps can be made, these branch $\frac{3}{4}''$ pipes finally being gathered into a larger pipe extending to the house. In some towns where streets have been improved and sidewalks laid in advance of building the houses, a supply pipe is often extended to the curb line when the street is improved. In this case the plumbing contractor needs but to connect the water supply with the pipe already extended to the curb.

The water-supply pipe to the house is of lead or galvanized iron, usually $\frac{3}{4}$ inch or 1 inch in size, depending upon the water pressure. Advantages are claimed for both lead and iron pipes. Lead pipe, under ordinary conditions, lasts longer than iron pipe, even when the latter is galvanized, and for that reason lead pipe is used by many architects in spite of its greater cost. Lead pipe for drinking-water supply is not advisable, however, as water of certain chemical consistency will dissolve lead, holding it in suspension in the water. Even so small a fraction as 0.5 part of lead is considered poisonous. When lead pipe is used, it should be "tin-lined," which combines the durability of lead with the purity of tin. In joining one tin-lined length of lead pipe to another, care should be taken to screw the lengths together in such a way as to make a tight joint between tin and tin so that the water will not touch lead at any point in the pipes. Special tin-lined fittings are furnished for this purpose.

While the life of galvanized iron pipe is limited, it continues to be used more than any other kind for water-supply work. Cheap, clean, and quickly laid, it is perfectly practical and can be recommended for all but the most expensive work where funds permit the use of tin-lined lead pipe. Inside the house tin-lined lead pipe, galvanized iron pipe, or white metal pipe can be used for cold water or hot water. Brass tubing is also used for hot-water pipes, plain and nickel-plated. White metal tubing, sometimes called by the trade names "Benedict metal" or "durometal," is made of an alloy of nickel and brass not unlike German silver, and it is excellent for hot or cold-water lines, though this is the most expensive piping made. In exposed work white metal is particularly desirable because its finish never wears off like nickel-plated tubing.

In some places where the town water pressure is excessive it must be reduced by placing a pressure regulator on the water-supply pipe just inside the cellar wall This is necessary in some cases because a house plumbing system will not stand high pressure liable to put too much strain upon it. Water enters the pressure regulator under high pressure and flows out the other end under reduced pressure, the reduction being accomplished by a system of springs and levers inside the regulator. These can be regulated by adjustments to deliver water at any number of pounds pressure, from 40 down to 12 or 14 pounds.

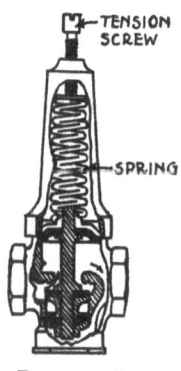

PRESSURE REGULATOR.

When the water-supply pipe has been run to the cellar it is extended on walls or ceiling to the various basement fixtures, then up through floors and partitions to the first and second stories. For the main pipe, ¾ inch is the size generally used, with ½-inch or ⅝-inch branches to the various fixtures (excepting a shower bath, which may need a larger pipe, — usually ¾ inch). The principal result desired in the supply pipe is that it shall be large enough to bring water freely to every fixture at all times, even when several fixtures are in use at the same time. There is not much use in having branch supply pipes larger than ½ inch because the waterways in faucets are rarely larger than this.

Various shut-offs should be arranged in the basement on the different branches of water-supply pipe, so that one branch may be shut down for repairs without disturbing the supply of water to other branches. All pipes must pitch back to these.

One main valve should be provided just inside the cellar wall to shut off the entire supply. It is a good idea to have a shut-off for the laundry tubs, another for the kitchen sink, and a separate one for each bathroom. These valves should be arranged conveniently in the basement, each one tagged with a durable metal tag labeled "bathroom" or "kitchen," so that in emergency one can go to the cellar and quickly shut off any line. After closing a shut-off valve, water contained in the pipe should drain off. This is usually made possible by what is known as a "stop and waste." When the lever handle of the valve is turned, it shuts off the supply of water and at the same time a little valve is automatically opened, allowing all water contained in that pipe line to drain out through a little hole in the side. For this reason it is necessary to place a pail under the valve to contain the water as it drains out, and prevent it from flooding the basement floor.

Where there is danger of frost and consequent freezing, water pipes should always be protected by pipe covering consisting of felt at least ½ inch thick, wrapped securely around the pipe and wired in place. Ordinary sectional pipe covering or asbestos-covered felt or cork is excellent for this purpose. In other places pipes can be boxed in and the space filled with cork shavings, cinders, or other insulating material. Below ground all such insulation must be protected by an outer casing of planks.

The pipe extending from the street should be at least 4 feet deep in the ground, or more in sections where frost goes to a greater depth. In some localities it is customary to have the main water-supply shut-off at the curb line in a "street box," as it is called. The valve, operated by a square-shouldered rod extending up to the sidewalk, is turned by means of a wrench. It is usual for the water company to charge a fee for installing this street box; in fact, the owner will find before his house is completed that many fees are charged for various branches of the work, though fees are usually quite moderate in amount.

290 *SUCCESSFUL HOUSES AND HOW TO BUILD THEM*

Not only does cold water extend to the various fixtures, but hot water must be provided for as well, requiring an independent system of piping. Sometimes a third pipe line is required when hard water and soft water are furnished to fixtures independently. When this is the case, the soft-water line should be valved in the basement so that hard water can be connected if, for some reason, soft water gives out.

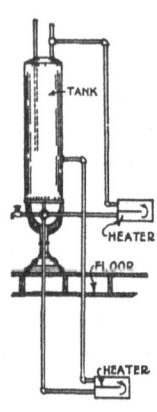

HOT-WATER TANK HEATED BY FURNACE AND KITCHEN RANGE.

A branch from the cold-water supply extends to the hot-water boiler in the basement or kitchen where the water is warmed, flowing to the several fixtures. One cannot think of an ideal plumbing system without hot water supplied plentifully to every fixture. Yet, with all the modern apparatus on the market to warm and circulate hot water to every tap, many are inadequate. After the expenditure of a considerable sum, the owner sometimes finds that after all he hasn't a sufficient supply of hot water, or that it arrives cold at the fixtures. This trouble lies largely in the manner of piping. Hot water can be delivered almost instantly at any fixture, no matter how far away from the range boiler, if what is known as a "circulating system" is employed, consisting of a small pipe returned from the highest part of the hot-water riser back to the boiler. Thus a loop for circulation is established through which warm water circulates constantly from boiler back to boiler, regardless of whether water is drawn at the fixtures or not. The circulating pipe maintains hot water right at the fixtures at all times, but when there is no circulating pipe, water in the pipes quickly cools off when none is being drawn from the fixtures.

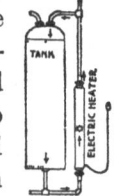

ELECTRICALLY HEATED TANK.

Boilers can be connected up so that water at the top is heated first. This is an advantage when hot water is wanted periodically, and gas is lighted to heat it only as wanted. When piped in this way a small body of water at the top (enough for one bath, let us say) can be warmed, and then the boiler may be shut down. Thus a small amount of hot water can be obtained without warming the entire contents of the tank.

There are many ways for heating water for bathing purposes. The boiler can be connected to the water back in a coal or gas range in the kitchen, or it may be heated by a separate gas or coal heater installed in the basement, — or (in winter) by a coil in the furnace or boiler. One of the best methods is to install a range boiler in the basement, connected to the furnace as well as to a separate coal or gas heater. Piping is arranged so that in the summer, by turning a valve, the furnace can be disconnected and the separate coal or gas heater used for warming the water. In winter the operation is reversed, the water being warmed by a coil in the fire pot of the furnace. Thus independent means for warming water is necessary only in summer, though it should be borne in mind that a larger amount of coal will be burned in the furnace when it contains a water coil. Coils in the furnace for heating are of several different styles, circular and horizontal. Sometimes they consist merely of a coil of 2-inch or 3-inch pipe extending around the fire pot, inside, just above the fuel. Others are hollow iron castings of various shapes, and these are best, as they last longest. Steel from which pipe is made quickly corrodes in furnace gases and must be frequently renewed.

When water is to be warmed by a separate coal heater located in the basement, there are many types to choose from. Heaters containing a small fire pot surrounded by hollow cast-iron sections through which the water flows, are very practical, usually consuming not more than a hod of coal per day to maintain hot water constantly. Many of these have a "magazine feed" which is filled with fuel (usually pea coal) once each day, and that is sufficient for twenty-four hours. Some laundry stoves are made with cast-iron jackets for heating water so that irons may be heated by the same heater that furnishes the supply of warm water for the house. A late development of the water heater is the "garbage burner," which uses garbage as a fuel in addition to coal, and converts it into useful heat for warming water, — a great convenience in any house, and especially desirable from the standpoint of cleanliness.

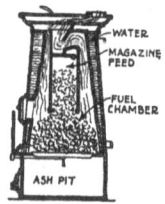

MAGAZINE COAL HOT-WATER HEATER.

Supply of hot water throughout the house is frequently furnished by gas heaters, of which there are many styles, some operated periodically and others maintaining a constant supply of warm water. Various types of gas water-heating apparatus are described in detail in another chapter. There are systems of heating water by injection of live steam from a steam boiler, but these are used chiefly in large apartments and office buildings. Other steam systems warm the water by means of coils in the range boilers supplied with live or exhaust steam, but rarely are such systems used in ordinary housework.

Range boilers are of copper, and plain or galvanized steel, in all sizes from 18 to 200 gallons' capacity. The sizes most frequently used for houses are 30, 40, and 60 gallons, the 30-gallon boiler being sufficient for houses of moderate size and the 60-gallon boiler furnishing sufficient capacity for houses of considerable size. Galvanized boilers are, perhaps, most frequently used, as they cost less than copper. Galvanized boilers should be "extra heavy double riveted, guaranteed tested 250 pounds," as lighter boilers are not safe. Other boilers may be cold-welded (plain, painted, or galvanized), in which case there are no rivets. Boilers of this class should be "extra heavy" or "double extra heavy, cold-weld guaranteed tested 250 to 300 pounds."

Most copper boilers are polished on the outside and tinned on the inside. They are only used where pressure is light, — not more than 20 pounds per square inch. "Safety copper boilers" are the best to use, as they are reënforced on the inside with brass ribs running spirally around the boiler, making them noncollapsible. Such copper boilers should be specified "guaranteed tested 150 pounds" or "guaranteed tested 200 pounds," as the case may be. One slight disadvantage of copper boilers is that they radiate heat more than galvanized boilers (tending to make the kitchen uncomfortable in summer) and require polishing to keep bright.

All range boilers should be piped with a "circulating pipe," and all should be equipped with a mud drum and blow-off cock at the bottom. When the blow-off cock is occasionally opened, sediment collected at the bottom of the boiler can be blown out, thus insuring delivery of pure water at the fixtures.

Range boilers can be set vertically on iron supports, or horizontal tanks may be hung from the ceiling, depending upon location. Vertical tanks are most often used when the boiler stands directly in the kitchen, and horizontal tanks are frequently used for basement boilers. Hot-water pipes are of copper, brass, white metal, or iron. Lead pipe should never be used for hot-water work, as lead will not stand the fluctuations of heat and cold which prevail in a hot-water line. Large pipe should be used for connecting the water back with the boiler (not less than $\frac{3}{4}$ inches), and the best method of connecting up the boiler is to run the vertical hot-water pipe from the water back to the top of the boiler, instead of connecting it at the side. Good circulation is established by this long vertical pipe, whereas a short pipe connected at the

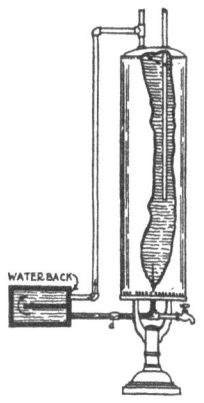

TOP CONNECTION TO HOT-WATER TANK.

294 SUCCESSFUL HOUSES AND HOW TO BUILD THEM

side is a poor circulator. The cold-water supply pipe should extend well down into the boiler.

Branches of pipe extend from the hot-water boiler to the various fixtures, and these lines should never be nearer than six inches to a cold-water pipe, for cold water might greatly lower its temperature. Sometimes on long runs it is well to insulate a hot-water pipe with felt pipe covering to facilitate retaining heat in the water.

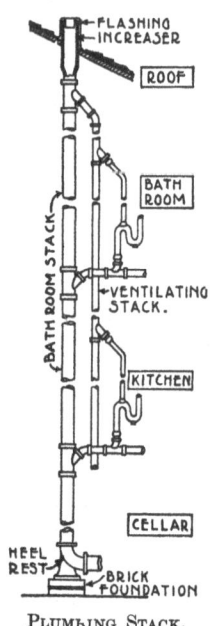

PLUMBING STACK.

The drainage system of a house consists of a complete water- and air-tight system of pipes to carry waste from the various fixtures to the sewer in the street, or to the cesspool or septic tank toward which it pitches. Thus the drainage system is the reverse of a water-supply system, the former running from the street to the house, and the latter extending from the house to the street. From the top of the house, where the cast-iron line of the drainage system ends with a length of pipe extending up through the roof, the stack (called "soil-pipe riser") runs down through the bathroom partition to the cellar, where it connects with a horizontal pipe (also of cast iron) extending across the basement floor or hung to the ceiling. This pipe is extended to a point about a foot beyond the outside face of the cellar wall. From that point a length of tile pipe extends to the sewer in the street, or to the septic tank or cesspool. Thus it will be seen that all pipes of the drainage system inside the house are of heavy cast iron. Each length is from 4' to 8' long, and one length is attached to the next by placing the small end of one section (spigot) into the large end of another (bell) and pouring molten lead into the joint which has been previously prepared by calking in a little oakum. Outside the house, drainpipes are of tile.

At the roof, in order to prevent rain or snow from following down the crack between soil-pipe riser and the roof boards, a sheet of lead is tacked to the roof boarding (under the shingles or slate) and brought up over the top of the soil pipe, turned down inside and soldered, thus making a water-proof apron around the stack. At the bottom of the stack it is well to have a small brick pier to hold up the weight of the pipe without settlement. One of the best ways is to use a "duck's foot ell" or elbow at the base of the stack where the vertical pipe turns to join the horizontal run under the basement floor, supporting this elbow securely on a brick pier or a large flat stone.

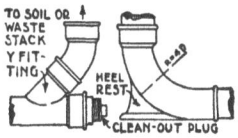

SUPPORTING FITTING FOR STACK.

Any settlement of the soil-pipe riser is apt to dislocate some of the joints between two sections of pipe,—a dangerous condition,—for it must be borne in mind that pipe in a drainage system must be air-tight as well as water-tight to prevent sewer gas from getting into the house. A minute leak allowing water to ooze out in small amounts might not be serious, if water alone was concerned, but sewer gas, invisible and frequently odorless, will flow through the smallest apertures, menacing the health of the occupants of the house.

The soil-pipe riser should be placed in the bathroom as close to the water-closet as possible, to which it is joined by means of a short length of lead pipe of the same diameter as the soil-pipe stack (usually 4 inches), connected by means of a Y fitting. Other fixtures are connected in like manner, but much smaller pipe (not usually larger than 1½ inches) is used for tubs, washbowls, and sinks. All branches attaching to the soil-pipe riser are connected by means of Y fittings instead of sharp, right-angle T fittings, so that sewage will flow as readily as possible through the system. If there is more than one bathroom and they are separated by a distance of more than 8 to 10 feet, a separate riser must be installed for each.

From a point above the highest fixture, beyond the attic bathroom if there is one (or above the second-story bathroom when there is none in the attic), it will be seen that the soil-pipe stack is nothing but a ventilator. So far as drainage is concerned, the riser might be stopped at this point, but it is extended up through the roof to the outside air for ventilating purposes.

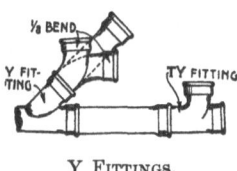

Y FITTINGS.

Thus a constant current of pure, fresh air is maintained inside the riser, and this pipe, combined with branches for ventilating the traps (described later), constitutes the ventilating system.

To prevent sewer gas from entering rooms by means of the soil-pipe riser and branches connecting fixtures, traps are inserted between the branch and the fixture. These traps are frequently little pieces of pipe bent into the form of the letter S or letter P, or sometimes they are of metal cast in the shape of a bottle, containing partitions extending down below the water line. The idea in a trap is to provide a hollow in the pipe to hold water, and this water contained in the trap is an effective seal for the sewer gas on the other side of it. Thus sewer gas permeates the soil-pipe riser until it reaches a washbowl, — we will say; at this point it strikes the crook in the pipe (trap) full of water, which it cannot pass. When the washbowl is emptied, its contents flow down through the trap into the soil pipe, but a portion is retained by the trap, which is, therefore, always full of water. For this reason, in emptying a washbowl one should always allow fresh water from the faucet to follow up the waste water, thus thoroughly washing out the trap. Traps have occasioned much thought, and many ingenious patterns are the result, the most useful of which are described in detail in another chapter.

After the house is "roughed in" (as it is called when the soil-pipe stack and horizontal basement run are installed), the owner should examine the piping, tracing out its arrangement to see that it extends straight from roof to cellar with no unnecessary turns or crooks to stop the sewage. He should make sure that it is properly supported, to prevent settlement.

Never allow a soil-pipe riser to be supported by resting its weight on wooden floor beams, for they are bound to shrink, and settlement (however slight) may be sufficient to break the lead joints between two sections of pipe. Like a chimney, the riser should stand up securely on a firm base. Supports, where the stack runs through a partition, are merely to keep the line vertical, and they should never carry any of the actual weight of the pipe line.

A soil-pipe drainage system is liable to become stopped up even when carried straight and true from beginning to end, and for this reason there should be some way to clean it out without taking the pipes apart. This is accomplished by means of "cleanouts." It is impossible to build a drainage system without some turns in it, but these will do no harm if the turns are not too sharp and a cleanout is placed at every turn. A cleanout consists of a cast-iron fitting not unlike an elbow, containing a cap screwed on at the side. When this cap is unscrewed and taken off, a long, flexible cleaning rod may be pushed through to reach the part of the system immediately adjacent to that particular cleanout. In case of stoppage, "rodding" is the best method of removing obstructions, so the owner will do well to see that every change in direction of the soil pipe is provided with a cleanout so that the cleaning rod can penetrate every inch of pipe. At the bottom of each vertical riser another cleanout should be placed to permit cleaning all vertical runs.

It is the tendency of some plumbers to make the soil pipe too large in diameter, and this is a fault, because a pipe too large in diameter is not flushed clean by the sewage as it passes through. Smaller pipes cause a scouring action in sewage, preventing deposits on the sides of the pipe. In most cases 4-inch pipe is sufficient.

All cast-iron pipe should be what is known as "extra heavy," and every section should be examined to make sure it is free

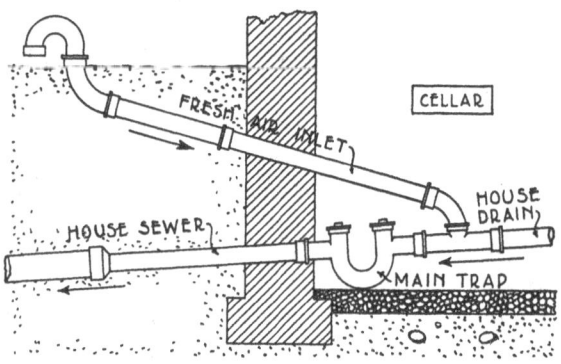

Eastern Method, Running Trap and Fresh Air Inlet.

from splits or sand holes. Any piece of cast-iron pipe can be tested by hitting it a sharp blow with a hammer; it should give out a true, bell-like sound indicating that it is free from flaws. Flaws in tile pipe can be readily seen, and any pieces that are cracked, or sections which are not hard burned and properly glazed, should be rejected. Cast-iron soil pipe coated with asphalt outside and inside makes excellent, smooth pipe, with maximum of cleanliness and durability, though it costs more than plain pipe. All drainpipes hung from walls or ceilings should be supported on first-class hangers made for that purpose; not straps or other makeshifts, which might allow pipes to sag, in time obstructing the flow of sewage.

SANITARY PLUMBING; WATER AND SEWER PIPES 299

The method of connecting tile drains outside the house, with the cast-iron soil-pipe system inside the house, varies in different places. In Eastern cities it is required that there shall be a "running trap" at this point, the function of which is to cut off sewer gas from the main sewer and prevent it from penetrating the soil pipe of the house. When a running trap is used it

PLUMBING STACKS EXTENDING ABOVE ROOF.

should have a vent connected to the side of the pipe line, extending up into an inconspicuous place in the yard (at least 20 feet away from any window), so that fresh air can circulate freely by means of this vent and the open end of the soil pipe at the roof. In most Western cities a running trap is not allowed, the pipe line of each house being required to be left open to the street sewer, in order that the main sewer may be ventilated by fresh air entering from the house lines. Manholes in the street, with perforated covers, assist this ventilation.

"Roughing in" is usually done as soon as the building is roofed and the side walls are boarded. Then the drainpipes stand until the interior of the house is finished and the floors are laid, when the building is ready for the placing of sinks, washbowls, tubs, and water-closets. Immediately after the soil pipe is completed it should be tested to see if every joint is tight, by filling the entire line full of water until it reaches the top of the roof. To do this the plumber plugs the bottom of the line where it extends through the basement wall, inserting caps on all openings left for future connection of the fixtures. Then water is turned on (the plumber having previously connected the pipe with the water supply by means of a pipe or hose) until it reaches the extreme top above the roof. This water is allowed to stand in the pipe for a day or two, and in the meantime every joint should be examined to see if there are any leaks (readily noticeable by the appearance of moisture at the points of leakage). Most leaks appear at a joint between two sections of pipe, caused usually by a split in the seam on account of too violent blows of the hammer in calking. Sometimes leaks are caused by the joints having been imperfectly filled with lead. Occasionally a leak will be found to be a sand hole somewhere in the length of pipe, elsewhere than at a joint. Most leaks are readily discovered, however, by means of the "water test," and such a test should be demanded by the owner.

An old-fashioned way of testing pipe was to pour a two-ounce vial of oil of peppermint into the riser, followed by a gallon of boiling water, after having stopped all apertures. Then the plumber and architect went "smelling around" at every joint, any odors of peppermint apparent along the line indicating a leak. This is a very poor way to test pipe, because even when a leak is detected, it is almost impossible to find the exact location. On the other hand, in the "water test" a stream of water (however small) gives visible evidence of the exact location of the leak, which can then be calked tight until water stops spurting. When testing with water, care must be taken not to fill the pipe in very cold weather, as the water might freeze and burst the pipe. In cold weather some heat should be on in the house when the pipe is tested, — at least sufficient to prevent freezing.

Although the peppermint test is not so good as the water test for testing the soil pipe, it is often employed on extra fine jobs as a *second test*. The water test having been previously applied when the soil pipe was roughed in, the peppermint test is used after all fixtures are connected and the plumbing is completed. Another good test at this stage is the "smoke test," in which a smoke machine (which makes dense black smoke) is connected to the system, and the smoke is pumped through the pipes, quickly indicating any leaks there may be.

On cheap work the horizontal run of pipe under a basement floor is sometimes made of tile pipe instead of the more costly cast iron. This should never be permitted, however, as tile pipe is liable to break, and a broken sewer pipe inside the house, even if only in the basement, is dangerous to health. To be sure, tile sewer pipe *outside the house* is liable to break also, but such breakage is not very serious when it occurs outside. For this reason cast-iron pipe is rarely used outside the building, tile pipe being usually considered quite good enough for that purpose, though cast-iron pipe with leaded joints would be, of course, ideal.

Tile pipe comes in lengths from 2 to 4 feet long. In laying it, the small end (spigot) of one piece is inserted into the large end (bell) of another, just as is done with iron pipe. But cement mortar, instead of molten lead, is used to make the joints tight, though on more expensive work the joints are calked with oakum and filled with asphalt (the best possible practice). Too often the tendency in laying tile drainpipe is to do it carelessly, and workmen should be watched to see that they perform the work properly. In the first place, the ditch should be dug deep enough to bring the bottom below frost; it should be wide enough to allow a man to stand in it with space enough to work. The bottom should be properly sloped so the pipe will pitch from the house to the sewer, septic tank, or cesspool.

When the trench is ready, several lengths of pipe are laid on the bottom of it in a straight line, with spigots thrust into the bells. Just under each bell a slight hollow should be made, to admit of the increased thickness of the pipe at this point, allowing the body of each tile to rest on the firm ground. If this is not done, the bells alone would touch on the bottom of the trench, the remainder of the conical pipe being slightly off ground with no support (liable to break when the trench is refilled with earth).

After a few sections of tile are properly laid, the joints are filled thoroughly with cement mortar, pointed smooth on the outside with a little trowel. Then a scraper, consisting of a rod with a piece of steel on the end, should be inserted at one end of the line, and any little pieces of mortar left inside, scraped out. Otherwise these bits might harden, forming obstructions in the pipe.

A tile drainpipe should be even smoother inside than outside, though some workmen are inclined to be extremely careless on this point unless cautioned. When the trenches are refilled, dirt should be carefully tamped around the tile to hold each section firmly in place.

Water from the roof drainage should always be connected with the sewer instead of discharging on the ground, except when a soft-water cistern is provided to contain the roof water. To carry off this water from the down-spouts, tile drains are

SANITARY PLUMBING; WATER AND SEWER PIPES 303

connected with tile branches outside the building, extending underground to a point under each down-spout, turning up and extending just above the ground ready to receive the spout. At the bottom of each of these branches, place a trap to prevent sewer gas from entering the line above that point.

In many locations where a building site is on low ground and the surroundings are liable to be wet in spring and fall (seasons when there is always an unusual amount of moisture in the ground), the sewer in the street might fill up to a point higher than usual. In fact, the main sewer sometimes overflows and backs up into the house drain as far as the basement. Thus, when there is a basement water-closet, the contents of the sewer might overflow through the basement closet. To prevent such an accident, a "backwater" trap should be placed where the tile pipe joins the cast-iron pipe, just outside the cellar wall. Such a trap allows sewage to pass through from the house, but closes before sewage can back up the other way. There are many patterns, but among the best is a trap containing a ball which rests over the inlet. Sewage passing from the house causes the ball to be displaced sufficiently to allow sewage to pass, but sewage backing up from the street wedges the ball more tightly over the inlet, forming an effective gate against it. Even the best of these backwater traps get out of order occasionally, and for that reason none should be used unless absolutely necessary. To admit of ready repairs it is a good idea to locate such a trap in a brick or concrete box with an iron cover, so that it may be easily uncovered when occasion arises. It should always be vented, and a gate valve should be placed in the line to shut off the entire system.

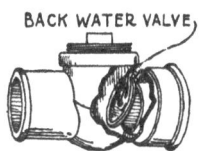

PREVENTS SEWAGE FROM ENTERING CELLAR.

Unlike a bathroom lavatory, the waste from kitchen sink,

pantry, and laundry tubs contains extremely soapy water, and this excess of grease, soluble while the waste water is hot, attaches to the cold sides of the drainpipe when it has cooled off. Successive accumulations of grease deposited inside the pipe grow larger and larger, until, frequently, the pipe is stopped up. There are two ways to prevent this, — one, by placing a grease trap at each of these fixtures, and the other, by discharging waste from kitchen and pantry sinks and laundry tubs into a separate catch basin outside the house, this basin finally overflowing into the drainage system. Grease traps are described in another chapter.

A catch basin is usually made of brick or concrete (in the former case plastered with cement mortar on the inside) about 3 feet in diameter and 3 feet 6 inches deep below where the drainpipe from the fixtures enters it. The catch basin discharges through its own trap into the main drainpipe, and it is located usually just outside the house, near the kitchen. An iron cover is provided at the top. There is no odor from it, though the waste water deposits its grease against the sides of the basin, the clearer waste passing off into the main drainpipe. This is the best method of taking care of grease, for it is done automatically, requiring no care. When grease traps are used, they must be periodically cleaned out, while the catch basin is so large it will last for years without cleaning.

In localities where the town or city water supply is taken from artesian wells, water is usually too hard for bathing and laundry purposes, and it may be necessary to install a soft-water cistern. Such cisterns are constructed, usually, by excavating a square or circular hole in the yard at the rear of the house, lining it with a concrete or brick wall. Brick cisterns must be lined inside with cement plaster to make them watertight.

A wooden cistern may be used instead of brick or concrete, — one built of staves like a huge tub, and tarred on the outside to prevent it from rotting in the ground. Tile pipes from the down-spouts supply the cisterns with rain water and an overflow empties into the sewer. Down-spouts should have a valve at the ends to divert water from the cistern when the latter is full. Pumps, such as are customarily used in connection with cisterns, are described in another chapter.

ATTRACTIVE APPEARANCE OF WHITE PAINT AND RED BRICK
Aymar Embury, II, Architect.

CHAPTER XVII

LATEST TYPES OF PLUMBING FIXTURES

WE will now imagine that your plumbing system is ready for the fixtures. That is, the cast-iron soil pipe has been installed from roof down to cellar floor, and across the bottom of the basement to the outside wall, where it connects with the tile pipe extending to the street, — and this pipe has been tested by means of the water test, and all leaks have been stopped tight. Besides this, the plumber has laid in the lead or iron branches from the soil pipe to the location of the various fixtures in bathrooms, kitchen, and basement, the open ends of these pipes having been temporarily stopped with plugs to prevent dirt, chips, or small scraps of plaster from getting inside the pipe during occupation of the building by other mechanics.

These waste pipes from the soil pipe to the various fixtures, and water pipes from the water-supply system, should be accurately placed so that after the building is completed the sinks, washbowls, tubs, and water-closets will fit.

The selection of fixtures for the house is largely a matter of size and price. Inexpensive fixtures are quite as sanitary as expensive ones when they are made by a reliable manufacturer. All the best lines of fixtures are now practically standard. That is, every first-class concern makes much the same patterns, except in a few instances where some dealers specialize with special patterns.

Five general materials are used for modern plumbing fixtures, — porcelain, enameled iron, vitreous ware, marble, and soapstone. Porcelain is the most expensive and is suitable for all plumbing fixtures. Enameled iron comes next in cost and can be had also for all fixtures. Vitreous ware is used for lavatories, water-closets, sinks, and laundry tubs, but it is not possible to use it for pieces so large as a bathtub. Marble and soapstone are now used only for sinks and laundry tubs.

Porcelain is an excellent material for plumbing fixtures, and it is much used on fine jobs where expensive work is the rule. Porcelain is a hard, impervious material of attractive appearance, and porcelain fixtures come in three grades, — A, B, and C. The grade required should be carefully specified. Fixtures of A grade are as perfect as any clay material can be, — no small imperfections of glaze or color. B grade fixtures (the grade most used for houses) may have slight imperfections in the glaze such as pinholes or very slight discolorations not sufficient to hurt the durability of the fixture or impair its attractiveness. Fixtures with more imperfections than will be admitted in the B grade are placed in grade C, such as crazings and warped or twisted edges. This grade is used chiefly for hospital and school work. The expense of porcelain fixtures is according to the grade, — A costing most, and C the least.

Enameled iron fixtures are made of cast iron, enameled on one or both sides. This ware is sometimes called by the trade name "porcelain enamel," but house owners should understand that it is really enameled iron, not porcelain. Enameled iron has come to be used more than any other material for plumbing fixtures, as it is durable, attractive, and of lower cost than porcelain. Many excellent designs are made by manufacturers, and one will have no difficulty in choosing from such a large variety of excellent patterns. There were formerly two grades in enameled iron ware, but the best manufactures now provide only one grade, — the best — preferring to discard all inferior fixtures. "Firstgrade" enameled iron does not mean fixtures absolutely perfect, free from flaws of every kind. On the contrary, there may be slight imperfections such as slightly warped edges or surfaces. Manufacturers, however, now guarantee their enameled ware to be first class, and one may usually expect good, merchantable fixtures.

Vitreous ware is not unlike porcelain, though it is more on the "crockery" order. Water-closets have been made of this ware for many years. Sometimes it goes under the name of "vitreous earthenware" or "monument ware." It is a coarser material than porcelain and of a slightly whiter tint and many think it prettier, claiming that it wears without crazing (something that porcelain often will not do). By "crazing" is meant the tiny hair lines that may finally appear in enameled iron and porcelain, though frequently crazing never happens. Vitreous ware for lavatories is a newer material than porcelain and enameled iron. It is about the same price as B grade porcelain and is an excellent material for all fixtures except bathtubs, which as yet, owing to difficulties in manufacture, have not been made in vitreous ware. Vitreous ware comes only in one grade.

Marble was formerly used in fine residences for kitchen and pantry sinks and bathroom lavatories, but now this material has been largely crowded out by others. Soapstone is still used in some cases for kitchen sinks (though not so much as formerly). It is a good material for wear and is now used chiefly for laundry tubs. As all fixtures built of soapstone are made of slabs cemented together, only the best grade should be used. Inferior tubs, poorly constructed, are very liable to leak at the seams.

The greatest assurance a houseowner can have on his plumbing fixtures is the name of the manufacturer. For that reason he should buy only standard makes, insisting that the manufacturer's name be attached to every piece on a label showing the grade. Then, in case of error, he will always be able to get satisfaction from the manufacturer, who is bound to maintain the standard of his goods. In selecting from a plumbing catalog, the owner should remember that list prices are always very much more than net prices, — in some places almost twice as much. While a plumbing catalog is very helpful and should be studied carefully by the owner, he should understand that it is much easier to select fixtures after inspection of the actual pieces by visiting the stock rooms of the nearest dealer.

Kitchen sinks of enameled iron are most commonly used and the best ones are cast "integral," with back and sink in one piece. Others are cast with separate back which is secured in place after the sink is set. The latter are not so desirable as the former, owing to the joint between sink and back, which is bound to allow more or less moisture from splashing faucets to pass through to the wall behind. Although a sink with a back is preferred by most housekeepers, there is really no need of the back in a kitchen where the walls are tiled. Several very good patterns of kitchen sink consist of sink and back cast in one piece, with a roll rim in front and an enameled drip board at one end or both ends. Other excellent designs have the drip board at one end, with a back behind it as well as behind the sink. Some patterns are hung from the wall on strong brackets and others have enameled iron legs. All sinks should be provided with strainers to prevent bits of food from entering the waste pipe. When enameled iron drip boards are used, rubber mats should be provided to stand the dishes on, otherwise they are liable to break when set hastily on the enameled surface. Wooden drain boards require no rubber mats.

A sink can be placed on an outside wall under the window if supply and waste pipes are placed inside the room instead of outside in the partition. This is an excellent location, but many owners think pipes in an outside wall will freeze. Placing them inside the room obviates this danger. Windows over a sink should be placed high enough to allow the sink back to extend up below the window sill. Most sink backs are 12″ high, so windows must be placed at least this distance higher than usual. As a matter of fact, high windows in a kitchen are ideal.

Sinks for special locations may be found in great variety. Corner sinks have a returned enameled end to go against the wall. Sinks placed in a niche have returns on both ends, but the standard sink is one which goes up against the wall with space at both ends, and this will be found the most convenient in most cases. One very clever sink combination has a little revolving seat attached, on which one may sit comfortably while washing the dishes.

Porcelain sinks are used in expensive work and many patterns of sinks can be found in Italian marble, soapstone, and vitreous ware. Old-fashioned iron sinks are still made and sometimes used on cheap work but as the cost of an enameled sink is not much greater than one of ordinary iron, the former is well worth while. Sinks enameled inside but not on the outside are quite inexpensive, though they must be painted outside in order to look neat. Three or four coats, the last two of enamel paint, are sufficient to make an attractive and durable fixture. The standard height for setting a sink is 30 inches from the floor. This is too low for all but short people, however, so in many places a sink should be placed 32 to 34 inches from the floor. Adjustable legs are furnished with some patterns, so that the sink can be set high or low, to suit the owner. Of course,

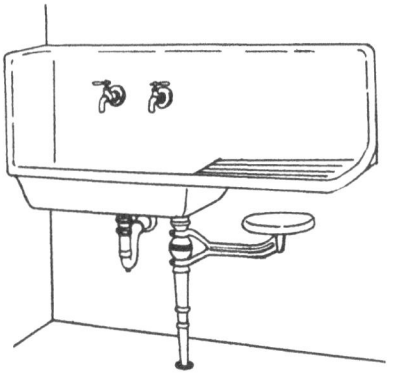

ENAMELED IRON KITCHEN SINK WITH STOOL.

once the faucets are attached, it is impossible to change its height.

The size of sink most often used is 20 × 30 inches, though there are many others in stock, larger and smaller. A very practical size is 20 × 36 inches when there is sufficient space in the kitchen, as it gives 6 inches greater length than the 30-inch sink, — an additional space which will be found very convenient.

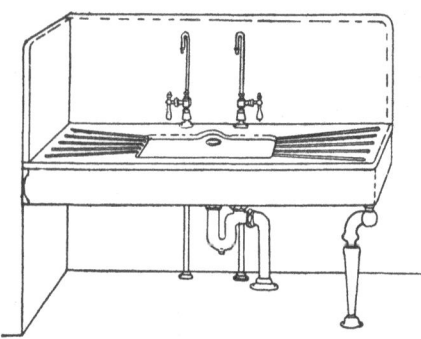

METAL-COVERED PANTRY SINK AND DRIP BOARDS.

Pantry sinks are quite different from kitchen sinks because they answer a quite different purpose. The pantry sink in most cases is really a large dish pan and supposed to be used by placing the dishes directly in it instead of using an ordinary dish pan. For this reason it is most frequently made of metal instead of stone, enameled iron or porcelain. Metal pantry sinks are of copper or German silver and the latter is by far the most practical material, as it does not change color nor require polishing like a copper sink. Drip boards at the side are of wood frequently covered with the same

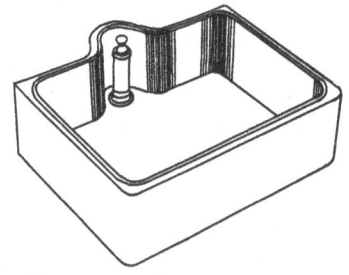

METAL-LINED PANTRY SINK WITH RECESSED OVERFLOW.

metal as the sink. A good size for the pantry sink is 16 × 24 inches, though many come larger and smaller. Square-shaped sinks are more convenient than oval: in the latter, dishes have

LATEST TYPES OF PLUMBING FIXTURES 313

a tendency to slide down in a heap towards the center. Many metal pantry sinks are really wooden boxes lined with metal, and they are perfectly water-tight and durable. Some sinks are divided in the center by a partition, thus being virtually two sinks, — one for washing and the other for rinsing.

Most manufacturers carry, besides metal sinks, porcelain and enameled iron pantry sinks, which are often used in large houses in the same manner as a kitchen sink, a dish pan being placed inside. Most pantry sinks are of metal, however, and the most convenient of the square ones have a recessed overflow so that the standpipe plug (which allows the sink to be filled with water) is out of the way of the dishes.

Other sinks are sometimes used on the first or second floor, particularly a slop sink, usually consisting of a porcelain or enameled iron fixture flushed by a tank like a water-closet or with ordinary faucets. In very large houses a cook's sink is sometimes provided in the kitchen (also known as vegetable sink) for preparing food before it is cooked.

COMBINATION KITCHEN SINK AND WASH TUB OF ENAMELED IRON.

Kitchen sink and washtub combinations are convenient in apartments where clothes must be washed in the kitchen. They are usually of enameled iron or soapstone with a sink at one end and washtub at the other. The wooden cover of the wash tub forms a drip board for the sink. Another combination

314 SUCCESSFUL HOUSES AND HOW TO BUILD THEM

recently brought out for use in small cottages and workingmen's houses is a combination sink, bathtub, washtub. At the bottom is a bathtub, and the sink and washtub are placed at the top, hinged up out of the way when the bathtub is to be used. Of course such an arrangement is not practical for the

A WELL ARRANGED BATH ROOM; WATER CLOSET IN A SEPARATE COMPARTMENT.

ordinary house where the bathtub is placed in a bathroom as it should be.

Lavatories are made in every conceivable size and shape, with oval and round washbowls in every degree of simplicity or luxury. Marble, enameled iron, porcelain, and vitreous ware are the materials employed, and some patterns are supported on brackets or "concealed" wall hangers, others having

LATEST TYPES OF PLUMBING FIXTURES 315

legs or pedestals. A bowl 13 × 17 inches is very convenient, though some of them run as large as 15 × 21 inches (size of the bowl alone). The area of the entire lavatory is from 24 inches wide and 36 inches long down to 21 × 26 inches and even smaller. A good average size of lavatory, complete, is 20 inches wide and 24 inches long, containing an oval bowl 12 × 15 inches.

Pedestal lavatories are among the most attractive patterns. These consist of an enameled iron or porcelain (as the case may be) round, hexagonal, or oval pedestal, supporting an oval or square slab containing the oval washbowl. Usually they come without backs, as most bathrooms have a tiled wainscot, rendering a back unnecessary. These lavatories are usually placed a slight distance from the wall so they may be easily wiped off entirely around the rim with a cloth. Other attractive lavatories have integral back, slab, and front apron (cast in one piece), and are supported on enameled iron legs or brackets. Faucets, traps, and wastes are described elsewhere.

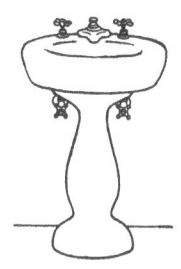

PORCELAIN PEDESTAL LAVATORY.

PEDESTAL LAVATORY OF ENAMELED IRON.

Dental lavatories have recently been introduced in houses. Originally designed for Pullman cars they proved so practical that they are now used as house fixtures also. In the best patterns the smaller, separate dental lavatory is cast integral with the regular lavatory, though it is supplied with separate faucets.

Bathtubs are made in such profusion the owner who does not find what he wants in an enameled iron or porcelain tub is hard to please, indeed. Broadly speaking, tubs are divided into three classes, — tubs with feet (open underneath), tubs with base (closed underneath), and built-in tubs. Ordinary tubs stand on feet of porcelain or enameled iron, which raise the fixture up a few inches, allowing the floor underneath to be washed. Tubs with a base are also set above the floor, but a base fills the gap between floor and tub making it unnecessary to wash under the tub, a very great convenience, and the cost of a base tub is not much more than an ordinary tub. Built-in tubs are built into a niche or set in one corner, and the tub itself in faced with tile, or in some cases an enameled iron slab is furnished to cover the front.

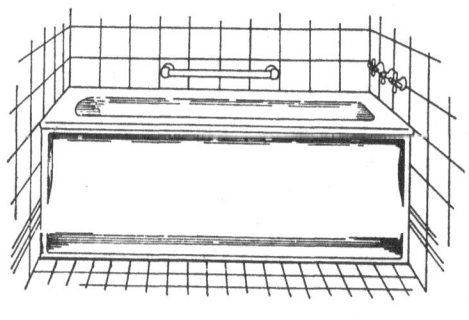

ALCOVE TUB.

Most tubs are made in several styles, sloping on one end and straight at the other (as in ordinary tubs having end supply and waste) or they are "Roman" shape (sloping at both ends) with supply and waste in the center at the back. Tubs with a rather steep slope at the sloping end are more saving of space than others. All enameled iron tubs have roll rims varying in width from $1\frac{1}{2}$ inches to 5 inches, the 3-inch or $3\frac{1}{2}$-inch roll rim being popular shapes, as rims of this width make a very pleasing appearance and do not waste much space. Narrow rims are not so attractive, though they should be used where space is contracted and a saving is necessary. Pretty nearly every style of bathtub comes in lengths 4 feet 6 inches, 5 feet, and 5 feet 6 inches, and most come also in lengths 4 feet, and 6 feet, in each case the length being of the tub itself, outside, not counting piping. For moderate-sized houses tubs 4 feet 6 inches long are most used, though the 5-foot length is always to be preferred when space permits. Difference in price between one length and another is very slight. Tubs only 4 feet are too short for comfort, but where space is limited it is sometimes necessary to use a short tub. The height of a bathtub is usually 23 inches from floor to top of rim. Tubs are in all widths from the narrow 25-inch to the luxuriously wide 36-inch,

ROMAN TUB WITH SHOWER BATH; ENAMELED IRON WATER-CLOSET TANK.

the most-used width being about 30 inches, from outside to outside.

When the bathroom is first considered, each fixture should be sketched out on the plan, drawn to scale at its correct size so as to make sure of a proper arrangement, with the necessary amount of room around each fixture. You must bear in mind that the space for a tub must be larger than the size of the tub itself, to allow room for supply and waste pipes which ordinarily take up at least 3 inches or 4 inches and frequently 6 inches to 8 inches or more, depending upon the pattern used. With niche tubs and with many corner tubs, supply and waste pipes are placed in the wall at one end of the tub, a wood panel being set in the wall to give access to the pipes. To prevent the unsightly appearance of this wood panel (which is visible in the room next to the bathroom) it is a good idea to have a closet, cupboard, or wardrobe at this point, hiding the panel, or a piece of furniture may be placed against it to keep the panel from sight.

Solid porcelain tubs cost about $25 extra when glazed outside, or $15 extra if finished with enamel paint, though the tubs are made of the same material throughout. Enameled iron tubs can be enameled on the inside only. Thus an ordinary enameled iron tub shows the rough cast iron on the outside. If such a tub is built into a niche and the front is covered with tile or with an enameled iron plate no other finish for the front and ends of the tub is necessary, but if the tub is set with outside exposed it is necessary to finish it in some manner. On many small houses the tub, outside, is simply painted three or four coats of paint (enamel preferred) which makes a fairly good job, but the best method is to order in the first place from the dealer what is commonly known as "No. 1 Zinc White Finish." The same finish is used on unglazed porcelain tubs. In making this finish, manufacturers buff off the exterior of tubs until they are perfectly smooth, after which seven coats of enamel paint are applied one at a time, each coat baked on and smoothed off before the next one is put on. The result is a hard, firm, durable white finish almost like glazed enameling. Many owners see these tubs and think they are really enameled both sides. The cost of such finish is usually about $15 over and above the original price of the tub. No. 2 finish, with less coats of paint (consequently a little less perfect looking) costs about $10 extra.

Bathtubs for infants (called "Infants' Baths") are very convenient, being about 20 × 30 inches in size and 12 inches deep set upon legs to bring them to a convenient height from the floor. Other convenient bath fixtures for the bathroom are seat and foot baths. The seat (sometimes called "sitz") bath is a low fixture about 20 × 30 inches, though they come in

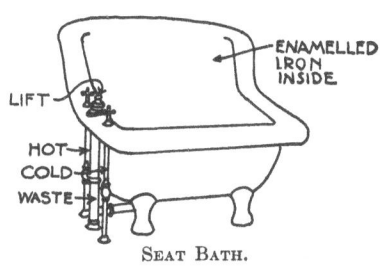

SEAT BATH.

several sizes, furnished with or without the douche supply. The seat bath can be used also as a foot bath, and it makes a very good infants' bath, too, though not at so convenient a height from the floor as the regular infants' bath. Seat baths are distinguishable from special foot baths because the former have high backs, whereas foot baths are boxlike little tubs about 24 × 24 inches, containing a shelf to sit upon (in the best models). The foot bath also makes a convenient bath for infants.

Shower baths are rapidly coming into general use in bathrooms where space permits and where the funds of the owner are sufficient. The least expensive shower bath and the pattern taking up no extra space is the tub bath. Hot- and cold-water supply pipes are connected at the wall above the tub at which point the nickel-plated piping of the shower bath begins. A nickel-plated ring holds the rubber or duck curtain used to keep water from splashing on the floor, the tub taking the place of a shower receptacle. When a tub shower is not used, a separate shower bath can be installed in one corner of the bathroom, or it can

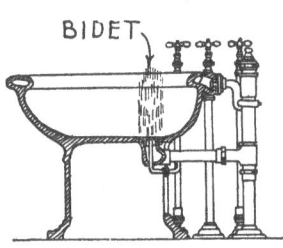

BIDET (DOUCHE) ATTACHED TO A SEAT BATH

be built into the wall. Generally speaking, built-in showers are about 36 × 36 inches (though many are larger), surrounded by marble, tile, or glass partitions, or when a receptacle is used standing out on the bathroom floor, curtains of rubber or duck are supplied, supported by rings. Receptacles or "receptors" (as they are usually called) are basins of porcelain or enameled iron (about 3 feet 6 inches × 3 feet 6 inches) in which the bather stands, surrounded by a framework of nickel-plated pipes at sides and back.

Shower stalls are built of tile, marble, slate, or glass. The latter is one of the best materials for lining a built-in bath. Each partition of the stall consists of one sheet of glass (usually milk-white, something like marble in appearance), one side being united with another by means of clamps and cement to make joints water-tight. Marble and slate slabs put together in the same way are sanitary and attractive, though slate is so dark in color it is seldom used in house work. Built-in shower baths sometimes leak at the joints, so an owner should caution the plumber to make these joints water-proof, and he should require a guarantee from his plumber that they will be tight, testing them carefully as soon as the job is finished. One frequent cause of trouble is the shrinking or sagging of the wooden joists under the bathroom floor, sometimes causing the shower to settle slightly and opening up joints in the shower partitions. For this reason, great care should be taken to provide joists sufficiently large to prevent sagging under the enormous weight of the bathroom floor (by far the heaviest floor load in the entire building), using extra well-seasoned lumber at this point. If joints do open sometime after the house is finished, they can be cemented again and made tight before damage is done, provided the leak is discovered in time. Floor slabs for built-in showers are usually of marble, in one piece, slightly dished out to drain toward the center, at which point is a floor drain. Cast-iron pipe is better for this than lead, as it is stronger. The drain should be extra large (at least 3 inches in diameter) to take the water away quickly. The supply pipe for a shower bath should be of ¾-inch or 1-inch pipe instead of ½-inch (as used for other fixtures), for a shower bath requires plenty of water delivered at good pressure. If an extra large pipe like this is used, it is probable that other fixtures (when the shower is operated) will have a weak pressure, but this is considered but a slight annoyance, as the shower is used only a few minutes at a time.

Pipes for a shower bath (whether tub bath or built-in bath) are ingenious arrangements of nickel-plated loops at sides, top, and back, each spray or stream manipulated separately by a faucet or chain pull, admitting hot water, cold water, or a mixture of both, of any temperature. The owner will do well to consider the various streams and sprays before ordering his fixture, so that he may have an apparatus exactly suited to his needs, bearing in mind that elaborate outfits cost more than simple ones. He can secure a shower-bath outfit containing needle, shower and bidet sprays, liver sprays and shampoo sprays, or he may choose one having a head spray merely, with perforated pipes below at sides and back. It is a good idea to have the head spray operate independently of side and back sprays, as many women like to use the latter without the former. Several clever patterns of tub shower are now made to fold back against the wall when not in use.

In some houses the shower bath has been made to answer every purpose of the bath, a tub being eliminated. It is doubtful whether this is practical for most people, however, as many (especially women) prefer a tub bath; indeed, some constitutions cannot stand the rigors of shower bathing,—a practice which should be resorted to only under the advice of a physician. For those who prefer to take their shower bath sitting, enameled seats are provided, attached to the wall. Portable shower baths consisting of a rubber hose attached to the mixing faucet of a bathtub, with head and side showers, and ring with inexpensive curtain, are fairly good substitutes for the regular tub shower.

Curtains for shower baths are of rubber or duck. The former are of course water-proof, and they look well at first, but, hardening with age like other rubber goods, they soon crack, making it necessary to have new ones. Duck curtains answer every purpose, costing less than rubber, and they wear longer and make quite as good an appearance. An excellent little fixture for the shower bath is a nickel-plated sponge basin attached to the wall, inside. It is also convenient to have a nickel-plated soap dish fastened near at hand.

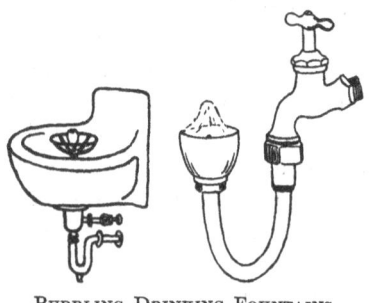

BUBBLING DRINKING FOUNTAINS.

Drinking fountains are not ordinarily considered necessities in the average house-plumbing system, but they are sometimes installed, and usually prove very convenient. For this purpose, an extra jet or faucet for drinking water can be attached to the bathroom lavatory, or a separate fixture for drinking purposes is sometimes located in bathrooms and not infrequently in the dining room, or in a rear or side hall on the first story. The new bubble fountains are by all means the most sanitary, making unnecessary the use of a drinking cup. Pressure on the self-closing valve allows water to escape in a fountain-like bubble from a little pipe with bubble attachment, and one's lips do not touch the fixture. Pedestal bubble fountains are the most convenient, though wall fountains are entirely practical. In old houses, new piping can be put in, converting any fixture into a modern bubble fountain.

When it comes to water-closets, there is opportunity on the part of the owner to exercise more than a little sagacity, for no fixtures in the entire plumbing catalogue are made in more styles, patterns, or shapes. Every one of the models set out on the floor of a plumbing supply display room may look like every other one to the layman, but, be assured, one is very different from another.

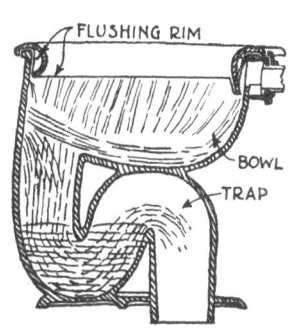

WASHOUT CLOSET.

In the first place, there are three general types of closet,—the washout, the washdown, and the syphon. These are the three general principles upon which water-closets are designed and built,—washout, washdown, syphon,—though there are, of course, many modifications of each style. Taking up consideration of the least sanitary style first, it can be said that a washout closet (now considered old-fashioned and rarely used even on cheap work) is a poor closet in every way, and no owner who desires to have even a moderate amount of convenience and comfort in his home should allow a washout closet to be installed. The emptying of a washout closet depends entirely upon the force of water injected in the bowl, and no closet of this class can keep itself clean, automatically, the body of water contained in the fixture being too shallow.

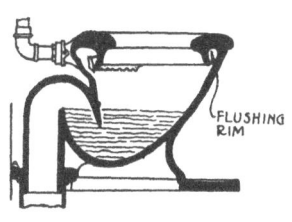

WASHDOWN CLOSET.

The washdown type of closet is an improvement, and many patterns are excellent, except that they are inclined to be noisy in operation. In this pattern a large body of water is contained in the bowl, and its contents are easily discharged into the drain, resulting in a clean fixture. Noise, however, should be eliminated as much as possible and a noiseless closet is much to be preferred. For this and various other reasons the syphon closet is made on a slightly different principle from washdown closet. In the latter all water from city supply enters at the

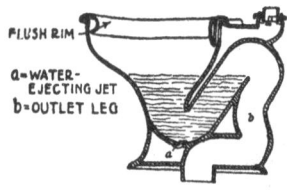

SYPHON JET CLOSET.

FLUSH RIM
a = WATER-EJECTING JET
b = OUTLET LEG

rim above the bowl, and the force of this water (helped by the proper design of waterways) empties the closet. But in a syphon closet the water supply is divided, part entering the rim above the bowl and part entering at the bottom of the bowl in the form of a small, high-pressure jet. The result is, that when a closet is flushed, sudden entrance of a stream of water in the bottom of the bowl (called "syphon jet") starts the closet emptying by syphonic action (suction). Thus, with water pulling below and pushing above, a closet is quickly emptied, the bowl being filled again by the afterwash from tank or flush valve. No closets are absolutely noiseless, but many syphon patterns can be heard only in the room in which they are placed; and this is the standard to demand, — that a closet shall be so quiet in action, no noise can be heard outside the bathroom.

There is another pattern of closet sometimes used, called "Hopper Closet," but it is for cold places, only, where closets containing water in the bowl are liable to freeze. Hopper Closets are dry closets; that is, no supply of water is maintained in the bowl. For this reason they are not sanitary, — requiring frequent cleaning. Such closets are sometimes nec-

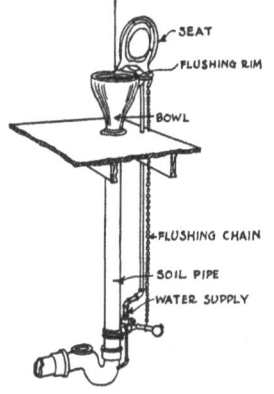

FROST-PROOF DRY HOPPER CLOSET.

essary in the country, however, as they are frost-proof, the trap (which contains water) and water-supply valve being deep in the ground, removed from all danger of freezing. The valve is operated by a long chain pull.

Now that we have considered, briefly, various general types of closet, let us examine in detail some of the characteristics of well-designed patterns, and accessories for no branch of the plumbing is more important. Some models are of enameled iron, others of vitreous earthenware, and both materials are practical and sanitary. The exact shape of a closet varies with each manufacturer, but in a general way all standard fixtures are of similar shape.

Water-closet tanks are now made in two patterns, — high tanks and low. The latter are improvements upon the former, as they are much less noisy on account of a less distance for the water to travel. In houses, high tanks are now used chiefly for cheap installations such as basement and attic, almost every one preferring

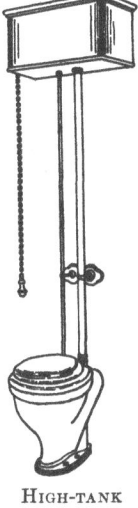

HIGH-TANK CLOSET.

the more compact low-tank type in which the tank is located close to the closet. Water-closet tanks can be had in birch,

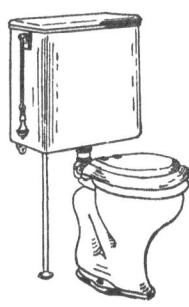

LOW-TANK CLOSET.

solid mahogany, oak, enameled iron, and vitreous ware. The wooden tanks are lined with sheet copper, and in the case of birch tanks the woodwork is usually stained mahogany. Tanks of iron, enameled both sides, are clean and very attractive in appearance, resembling in this way vitreous ware (both ideal materials for water-closet tanks). The valve on a tank is the principal part of the mechanism, and one should be sure to get a valve made by a reliable manufacturer, — one that is mechanically correct and will work noiselessly, wearing well and operating economically without leakage.

Ball cocks for water-closet tanks are made on the compression principle, operated automatically by pressure of the water in the tank exerted on a copper ball float. When the tank is full, the ball floats at the top and closes the valve; when a closet is flushed, the tank automatically empties itself, there being enough water contained inside to properly flush the closet and refill the bowl (forming a water seal). In the meantime, the copper ball drops to the bottom of the tank, at the same time opening the valve admitting water to fill the tank once more. The water contained in the bowls of washdown and syphon closets is what seals the fixture from sewer gas contained in the sewerage system. Sewer gas may fill the pipe as far as the water contained in the closet bowls, but beyond this point it cannot penetrate.

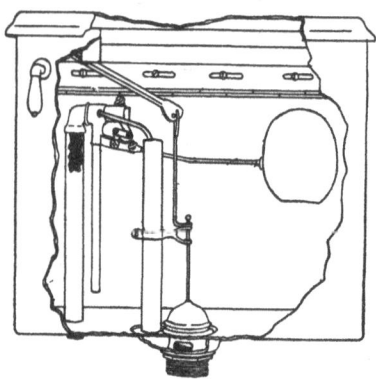

WATER-CLOSET TANK (SIDE REMOVED TO SHOW INTERIOR).

The connection of water-closet to waste pipe is one of the most vital points in a plumbing system, and the houseowner should insist upon best workmanship at this point. The length of pipe connecting the water-closet with the cast-iron soil-pipe stack should always be made up of flexible piping and bends, so that when the building settles, as all buildings are certain to do to a greater or lesser extent, the connecting bends will be flexible enough to stretch slightly without breaking or pulling apart. The flange which connects a closet with the waste pipe should be what is known

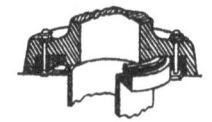

METAL FLANGE FOR CONNECTING WATER-CLOSET TO FLOOR.

LATEST TYPES OF PLUMBING FIXTURES 327

as a "metal-to-metal" floor flange, as this makes a permanent gas- and water-tight connection. Ordinarily, putty joints are made by placing putty or rubber gaskets at the joints of a metal floor flange. Such are not permanent connections, as putty soon loosens and drops out, or rubber gaskets rot away, leaving a crevice for leakage.

In the best patterns of water-closet there are four bolt holes for connecting the fixture at the floor, — two bolts for connecting the metal-to-metal floor flange, and two bolts to screw into the floor itself. Flush pipes should be connected to the closet with flexible rubber or metal slip joints, for sudden jars to which closets are liable may break them when non-flexible joints are used.

One of the latest types of water-closet flushing apparatus is the flush valve or "flushometer," with which no tank is necessary. This is an excellent way, though a flush valve

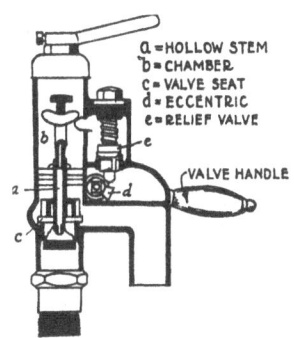

FLUSHING-VALVE FOR TANKLESS WATER-CLOSET.

requires a somewhat different system of piping to secure high pressure, a separate one-inch supply pipe being required for it. Flush valves do away with the tank entirely, which is certainly a step in the right direction, eliminating apparatus and making the plumbing system as simple as possible. The flush valve is operated by pushing a lever which releases a measured flow of water (usually 6 to 12 gallons), discharging it in a few second's time with but little noise. After releasing the lever, the valve automatically closes itself, ready for another flushing.

Water-closet seats have been greatly improved, and are now made so durable they last for years. Wood is chiefly used, either solid mahogany, oak, or birch (stained mahogany in the case of the latter), made up in sections locked together with bolts. Much study has been given to the exact shape of the seat and modern patterns are sanitary and practical. Enameled iron seats have been tried, but are found to be uncomfortable, though, from the standpoint of sanitation, they are, of course, excellent. Wooden seats are also made in white enamel, though they do not wear very well, as white soon turns yellow and the enamel is apt to wear off. Perhaps the best seat is birch, stained mahogany, which makes a good appearance and is very durable. To harmonize with a seat of mahogany one can use a birch-stained mahogany tank, or an enameled or vitreous-ware tank. Oak seats and tanks are used chiefly in attic or basement installations where apparatus is subject to unusually hard usuage.

SEAT OF GOOD MODEL.

Cost of water-closets varies according to the patterns and material used, but generally speaking syphon closets are the most expensive, with washdown closets next and washout and hopper closets least. This does not mean, however, that the best grades of syphonic closets are too expensive for houses of moderate size. On the contrary, syphon closets are quite practical for even small cottages, — practical in cost as well as operation, for many excellent patterns can be bought at moderate prices. Ordinarily, enameled iron or vitreous tanks are more expensive than wooden tanks, solid mahogany costing more than birch or oak, and low tanks costing more than high tanks. It is excellent practice to have a local shut-off valve on the water supply to a water-closet, so that water can be shut off in case of repairs, without stopping the supply of water to any of the other fixtures.

Water-closet ventilation has always been a problem. Some closets are fitted with what is called a "local vent," connecting the space directly under the closet seat with a ventilating flue (sometimes a chimney flue is used). It has been found, however, that local vents are not of much assistance, for rarely do they produce (what is intended) a current of fresh air in the water-closet. A better way is to have a ventilating flue with a register in the bathroom directly back of the water-closet, but such a flue will be of no account unless heat is applied at the bottom to cause a circulation of air. Heat can be applied by burning a gas jet at the bottom, or if the flue is placed next to the furnace flue a circulation could be maintained in that way.

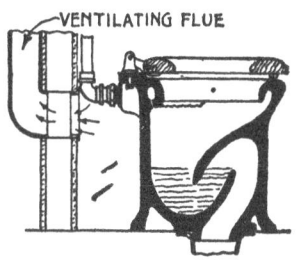

CORRECT VENTILATION FOR WATER-CLOSET.

Most best equipped, modern bathrooms contain, in addition to the various fixtures, articles of furniture such as a dressing table and chair, bath stool, bathtub seat, and a medicine closet. In addition to these are many useful devices for the toilet, — brush and comb holders, tooth-brush holders, soap and sponge containers, and towel racks of every conceivable pattern, and hooks of various kinds for holding the bath robe.

All bathroom fittings which are of metal should be nickle-plated, but many fittings may be obtained in enameled steel, glass, porcelain, and china, and these are always to be recommended in place of nickle-plated metal. Nickle plating soon wears off or grows dull. Of course many articles must of necessity be metallic, but one should choose something else when possible.

When it comes to fixtures for the laundry, one will find the same large number of excellent patterns to choose from as in all other lines of plumbing fixtures. Soapstone is an ideal material for laundry tubs; others are enameled iron and vitreous ware. These are the principal materials used for modern laundry tubs, though many manufacturers use special trade names such as "monument ware," "duroware," and the like.

ENAMELED IRON LAUNDRY TUBS STANDING AGAINST WALL.

No better material than soapstone can be found for laundry tubs. Soapstone is durable and sanitary, besides being moderate in cost. The chief objection to a soapstone tub is that it must be made up in separate slabs, joined together with bolts and cement. For this reason a poorly built soapstone tub is very apt to leak at the joints. However, tubs of the best grade are sound and tight, and, of course, it is assumed that the owner will buy only those made by reliable concerns.

Cement tubs are made in large quantities, and some of them have given satisfaction. As a rule, however, they are not so desirable as soapstone tubs, being frequently rough on the inside and having a tendency to disintegrate around faucets and waste plugs. Besides this, cement tubs are usually quite as expensive as soapstone.

Vitreous-ware tubs are excellent. Made in one piece as they are, there are no joints to leak or become foul, and they are heavy enough to stand the hard knocks usual in every laundry.

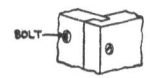

TONGUE AND GROOVED JOINT FOR LAUNDRY TUBS.

Some vitreous ware is white, and other ware is yellow (not unlike a kitchen pudding dish). Soapstone, vitreous ware, enameled iron and cement tubs are mounted on galvanized or painted iron legs.

Enameled iron tubs are not quite so durable as soapstone or vitreous ware, as the hard usuage tubs get in a laundry is apt to chip off the enamel. They are often used, however, especially in combination with a kitchen sink in the kitchens of apartment houses (where there is no laundry). When the best grade is bought, enameled iron usually proves satisfactory. Wooden laundry tubs have been practically done away with. Wood is so absorptive it is not sanitary, and soon wears out.

Whether to have a two-part or three-part laundry tray is largely a matter for the housekeeper to decide. Installations in houses costing downwards from $6000 are usually two-part, while three-part trays are usually installed in larger houses. The third tub is very convenient for blueing or additional rinsing water, and the additional cost is not a large amount.

Vitreous-ware tubs are the most expensive. Less expensive are enameled iron tubs (about the same price as soapstone), and least expensive are cement tubs, though costing very nearly as much as soapstone.

Good Type for Suburban House
Lawrence Buck, Architect.

CHAPTER XVIII

LITTLE DETAILS OF GOOD PLUMBING

Now that we have considered the principal parts of the plumbing system, it will be well to look into some of the details of smaller but not less important apparatus, such as traps, faucets, and wastes. Traps are the little plumbing appliances which prevent sewer gas contained in the drains from entering the house through the fixtures. They are to guard at all times these gateways which admit drainage from the fixtures to the sewage system, but prevent entrance of gas. Sewer gas is often odorless, and much harm might be done by its entrance, undetected, into a home. Consequently traps are very important and should be intelligently selected and efficiently installed, using the right pattern at the right place.

The principle of every trap is that it shall contain a pool of water entirely closing the ingress between drainpipes and house. One of the simplest patterns is the S trap, merely a piece of pipe bent into the form of a letter S (usually placed at or near the fixture), the loop in the pipe retaining water every time the pipe is flushed. Thus, when a faucet is turned (say, at the kitchen sink), water runs down through the grating in the bottom of the sink, through the S trap underneath into the drainpipe. When the faucet is turned off it will be found that the loop in the S trap has retained enough water to form an effectual water seal between drains and house.

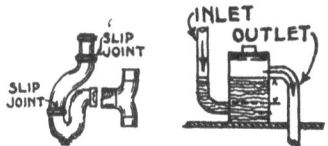

P TRAP AND BOTTLE TRAP.

In a water-closet an S-shaped trap is molded right into the fixture. After a closet is flushed the valve admitting water from the tank or flushometer allows an after amount sufficient to fill the trap with pure water. Of course no connection between fixture and soil pipe can be made *below* any trap. Always the trap must intervene between fixture and soil pipe, though in old-fashioned plumbing one sometimes sees the overflow from a washbowl connected to the waste pipe *below* the trap, thus allowing sewer gas to pass into a room through the overflow passage, though the waste from the bowl is properly trapped.

There are many forms of trap besides the S trap. Traps called "P traps" are used most frequently for lavatories (shaped like the letter P). Bottle traps (much used for bathtubs and kitchen sinks) are bottle-shaped vessels made to hold water and provide a water seal. Laundry tubs and kitchen or pantry sinks, unless they empty into a catch basin separate from the main drainpipes, are often provided with grease traps to catch grease (so prevalent in those fixtures) and not allow it to foul the main drainpipes. Grease traps are large receptacles, with covers for the purpose of removing grease from time to time. As some odor is almost sure to result when a grease trap is opened, all such traps should be placed in the basement.

GREASE TRAP.

Every trap is subject to syphonic action, — that is, the sudden pull as water rushes through is liable to empty the trap, taking the entire contents along to the drains, which leaves the trap dry. Thus, the water seal is lost, and sewer gas has free access to the house. To prevent this, traps are made in two ways, — syphon traps and non-syphon traps, — the latter being used principally in large buildings and the former in houses. Syphon traps must be vented at the top by an air pipe attached at this point and connected to the main soil pipe above where the highest fixture enters. Air admitted to the top of the trap breaks any tendency to syphon, so that the contents of a trap will run through when fixtures are flushed, but leave behind enough liquid to seal the trap. Non-syphon traps are ingeniously constructed to carry such a deep pool of water that the syphonic "pull" will carry only a portion of it away, leaving sufficient behind to seal the trap. They are usually shaped like a bottle trap and they do not require vent pipes like non-syphon traps, thus being especially desirable in office buildings, hotels, and like buildings where there are many fixtures.

Every trap, whatever pattern it may be, should be provided with a clean-out cover, usually screwed in tightly below the water line of the trap so that any leak will be indicated immediately by the leakage of water. Clean-outs above the water line might leak for years with no one the wiser, and the very purpose for which traps are installed (to safeguard the house from sewer gas) would be thwarted.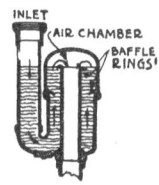

NON-SYPHON TRAP.

Traps are made of many different metals suitable for fixtures with which they are used. Lead is used largely when a trap is concealed in a floor or partition. In cheap work (not necessarily inferior work) lead traps are also used for kitchen sinks, painted two or three coats to make them a little neater in appearance. Brass, nickel-plated, is the material usually preferred for visible traps in kitchen or bathroom. Laundry tubs in the basement can be provided with lead traps, and traps in the basement floor are ordinarily of cast iron.

In connection with the waste pipe for a refrigerator it is not good practice to run a pipe directly to the drain, as any direct connection between refrigerator and sewer pipe is inadvisable, even when the pipe is trapped. The best way is to attach a refrigerator trap on the waste pipe just under the refrigerator, allowing this to drip through a waste pipe discharging over a P trap in the cellar floor. Thus there is no direct connection with the sewer, the P trap sealing the pipe at that point, and the refrigerator trap preventing all basement odors from entering the refrigerator. A refrigerator waste pipe should be kept clean by flushing it out about once a week, pouring hot water down the drainpipe from the ice chamber.

Every faucet in the house is really a machine, — an appliance to hold back the water when not wanted, delivering it as required, efficiently, at right pressure, by a quick turn of the wrist. No part of the plumbing system is more subject to wear than faucets, and they should be chosen with this idea wholly in view, — durability. Brass is the chief metal used for faucets, — nickel-plated in some work and plain brass in others. On most expensive work white metal is used in place of brass, and its chief advantage is that it remains bright, requiring no rubbing.

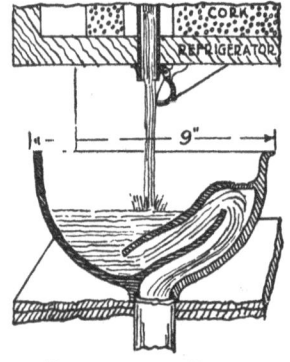

REFRIGERATOR TRAP.

At the kitchen sink solid brass faucets are usually preferred (unless white metal is used), for constant rubbing at these points soon wears off even the heaviest nickel plate, allowing brass to show through. Except in kitchen and laundry, it is good practice to use nickel-plated faucets.

Faucets are of many different patterns, specially devised for all kinds of work. The pattern practical for a kitchen sink is not suitable for a lavatory or bathtub, each pattern being designed for the sort of work it has to do. The simplest form of faucet or cock is the "ground key bibb," in which a lever handle turned one quarter around brings a slot in the plug opposite the waterway in the bibb. The plug (cast in one piece with lever handle) is simply ground to fit tight. This pattern is used in basement work where faucets are not opened frequently.

A similar cock called "stop and waste cock" is used on water-supply pipes for turning the supply off and on. When the lever handle is turned, the supply is cut off and at the same time all water contained in the pipes drains out through a little hole in the side of the cock, thus leaving the pipe line dry and in no danger of freezing.

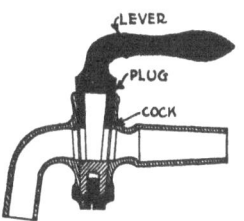

GROUND-KEY BIBB.

The majority of faucets in a house job are "compression" faucets and "Fuller" faucets. These are the two principal patterns and their difference lies in the interior mechanism. Compression faucets include a core (threaded), operated by a handle at one end, containing a composition or metal disk at the other. This disk (closing against the water pressure) is seated against the waterway, shutting off the water. Several turns of the handle are required to do this, so a compression faucet is not what is known as "quick closing." Every well-designed compression cock is fitted with an auxiliary "stuffing box" to reënforce the packing usually placed around the core and prevent water leakage at this point. The disk is removable for renewal when it has become worn.

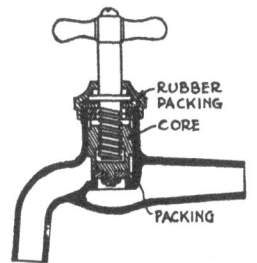

COMPRESSION FAUCET.

Compression cocks are made for every purpose, including kitchen and pantry sinks, laundry tubs, lavatories, and bathtubs, and when properly made of heavy metal and correct pattern they are very satisfactory.

The Fuller cock is an improvement over the compression cock because it is quick opening. The core is connected with a valve stem which opens wide in about a quarter turn, whereas in a compression cock the handle must be turned entirely around one or more times to open the faucet wide. Fuller cocks are not advisable where water pressure is too great, however, for the sudden release of water under high pressure by a quick-opening cock causes "water hammer," and puts too much strain on the pipes. Most houses have water supplies under low pressure, and Fuller faucets can be used with perfect safety, though each faucet must be fitted with an air chamber (an air cushion) to give elasticity to the pipe line. Quick-opening Fuller faucets are usually fitted with lever handles, and slow-opening compression cocks are most frequently supplied with T handles.

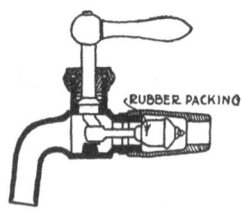

FULLER FAUCET.

In house practice, compression faucets are often used for kitchen and pantry sinks and laundry tubs, Fuller faucets being applied to lavatories and bathtubs. Where the water pressure is high, however, compression work is used throughout, for no matter how carefully air chambers are provided at each faucet, water hammer is liable to result, and nothing is more annoying than the snapping and humming of pipes every time a faucet is opened. Many architects use compression faucets on lavatories instead of Fuller faucets, for this fixture (used so frequently) is more liable to cause water hammer than others.

Another pattern of faucet is the "self-closing" faucet, but this type is rarely used on house work. Self-closing faucets contain a spring which forces the faucet closed when the hand is removed from the handle.

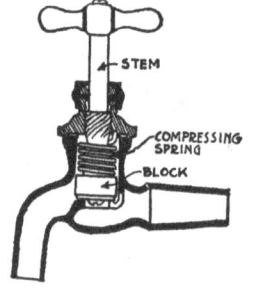

SELF-CLOSING FAUCET.

All faucets, whether compression or Fuller, come in many different patterns. Those for the kitchen sink are usually lever or T-handled, plain bibbs entering through the back of the sink, with or without threading on the end for a filter. In the best patterns, the nozzle is made small to prevent splashing. Pantry cocks extend vertically some distance above the top of the sink, to be out of the way of the hands when washing dishes. Sinks can be supplied with two separate faucets (hot and cold) or with one combination double-mixing faucet (both hot and cold).

Faucets for laundry tubs are similar to those used for a kitchen sink, but shorter, so they will not interfere with free use of the tubs. Some of the best patterns are close to the back of the tub, with very little projection. Lavatory faucets are made in bewildering variety of single and double (mixing) faucets, with T and lever handles. Frequently the handles are tipped with white china, and a jewel-cup is attached for holding rings when using the lavatory. The most practical faucets are those which project but little over the bowl.

Bathtub faucets usually extend through one end or the center of the tub, and they are either single or double, whichever desired. In best patterns the faucets project but little, and china handles are largely used in the best work.

Hose cocks for attaching garden hose at the outside of the house come with wheel handles or loose lever handles. The latter are desirable when there is reason to believe small boys in the neighborhood may play the ancient prank of "turning on the water." Loose keys are a nuisance, however, for they are liable to get misplaced. A stop and waste cock must be placed in every line supplying water to a hose cock, locating it just inside the wall so that water can be shut off from the cock in winter, or when the family is away.

Waste connections for all kinds of fixtures are made in great variety of pattern, from the simple strainer of nickel-plated brass in the bottom of a kitchen sink to the more complex "supply-and-waste" combinations for bathtubs. In a sink, the strainer through which waste water passes may be at one end or in the center. End wastes are considered especially practical for ordinary sinks, as a center waste would be covered by the dish pan and thus might be less convenient. Sink strainers are usually made detachable, — either loose or held in place by two or three screws so they may be removed to clean the drainpipe.

Many pantry sink wastes are placed in the center of the sink like a washbowl, and fitted with a plug and chain. Others have a "standing waste," consisting of a long tube of nickel-plated brass, open on top and set into the waste opening like a plug. Thus, with the standpipe in place a sink can be filled with water up to the top of the pipe, but any excess above this point passes away through the open end of the tube. Standpipes are located at one end of the sink or in a niche at the back ("recessed overflow").

Lavatory wastes may be simple "plug-and-chain" wastes in the center or rear of the bowl, or there are several other patterns that can be used, in which the plug and chain is eliminated, substituting a metal plug operated by a handle or lever. For bathtubs there are plug-and-chain wastes, and combination "supply-and-waste" connections in which one nickel-plated brass-fitting is used containing supply, waste, and overflow.

Cement-plastered Bungalow in the Country

CHAPTER XIX

SEWAGE DISPOSAL IN THE COUNTRY

No branch of sanitation has improved more in the last ten years then plumbing systems for country places. With a sewer in the street, as is the case in cities and towns, the problem of sewage disposal is comparatively simple, merely requiring a connecting line of drainpipe between the house and the trunk line in the street. But in the country districts where there are no sewers, evidently some special method of sewage disposal must be divised in order that dwellers in country houses may have all the conveniences of modern plumbing, as well as city people.

Inside the country house, plumbing pipes are installed precisely the same way they are in the city. Soil-pipe risers extend from cellar to roof, branch lines taking waste from the various fixtures to these vertical lines and carrying it through the cellar wall toward the sewer.

At the end of the drainage line is where a change in the country system occurs, causing the country sewage-disposal system to be different from that employed in town. A cesspool may be built to receive the sewage, or a scientific septic tank may be installed (both taking the place of the city trunk line), but the septic tank is the only scientific and really sanitary way to dispose of sewage.

There are many drawbacks to cesspools. A cesspool built to hold sewage for an indefinite period must be periodically emptied and the contents carted away. In the meantime, seepage from a cesspool leeching through surrounding ground is quite likely to find its way to the well or spring supplying the place, contaminating the drinking-water supply and rendering it unfit for use. Worst of all, this contamination many times is not apparent, and the harm is done and sickness appears before members of the family are aware of the cause. Cesspools have been used for years, — they had to be installed, for formerly there was no other way to handle sewage disposal in the country, — but now there is no excuse for the cesspool, since sanitary engineers have devised septic systems, which are really more sanitary than the trunk-line sewage systems used in towns and cities.

The septic system is not a makeshift designed to reproduce so far as possible the superior sewage-disposal systems of a city. It is, on the contrary, a *step beyond* the city system, — more scientifically correct. A septic system consists, roughly, of a tank or series of tanks for holding sewage temporarily for the purpose of chemically transforming it into harmless elements, — and all through a natural, automatic, chemical process.

With a little expert planning, the septic system may be designed for any number of people from five to fifty. Skilled workmen can be brought from town to do the work or it may be done by amateurs, but at least the design should be made by an expert, for conditions vary in each locality, and the proper working of a septic system depends largely upon local conditions. It is thus a problem requiring wide experience and understanding. Once properly installed, there is nothing about a sewage-disposal plant requiring undue care or knowledge in operating, nearly every part of the system being automatic. When properly designed, nothing is apt to get out of order.

DRAIN TILE LAID WITH OPEN JOINTS.

The principle of modern practical sewage disposal is this: the upper layer of earth contains air, and when dead organic matter is brought into contact with it a transformation takes

SEWAGE DISPOSAL IN THE COUNTRY 345

place. By reason of the oxygen and nitrogen contained there, organic matter is turned into harmless mineral forms. Under proper conditions nitro-organisms multiply and bring about the change.

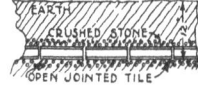

Good Way to Lay Drain Tile in Nitrification Bed.

All that is necessary is to provide a receptacle or flush tank to collect and hold sewage temporarily, afterward discharging the overflow into a subsurface irrigation system of open-joint pipes near the surface of the ground, where natural process of oxidation and nitrification take place. For this purpose use 3-inch agricultural drain tile, laid with open joints, 8 to 12 inches below the surface of the ground. This tile subsurface irrigation system may be placed any distance from the house, each piece laid nearly level, with not more pitch than 2 inches in 100 feet, so that liquids will run very slowly through the tile and discharge into the ground through the open joints. Porous soil is best, or sandy loam,

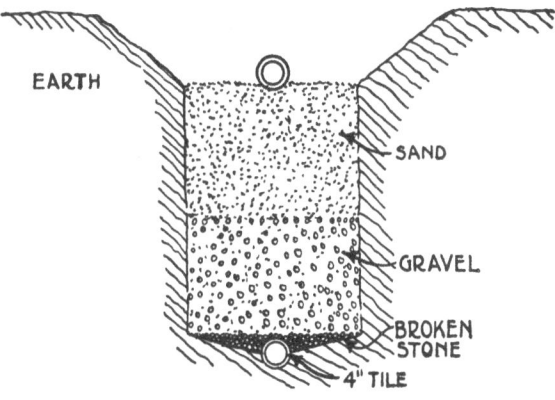

Nitrification Bed in Clay Soil.

and it facilitates the absorptive quality of soil to surround the tile with crushed stone or gravel. In clay soil the bottom of each trench should be drained with 4-inch tile to take away superfluous moisture.

In order not to overload the drains with a constant supply of sewage the subsurface irrigation system is divided into two or three groups of pipes, connected with the main line from the flush tank by a gate valve, allowing sewage to be diverted from any group. By this means any group may be given complete rest for a week, until the soil around it becomes entirely revivified by air in the upper surface of the ground.

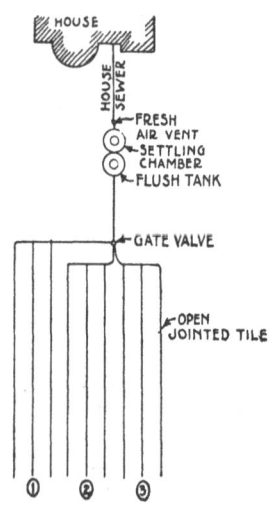

SEPTIC SYSTEM LAID OUT FOR HOUSE OF MODERATE SIZE.

To help the soil in its work of converting liquid sewage into harmless minerals, a flush tank (into which all sewage from the house first discharges) is made to empty into the subsurface irrigation drains — not constantly but periodically. Thus the open-joint drains have an opportunity to recover after each discharge from the flush tank. By means of a syphon the contents of the flush tank are held for about twenty-four hours, until the level of liquid rises to a certain point, when the syphon discharges the entire contents into the drains. The liquid flows through, discharging into the ground by means of

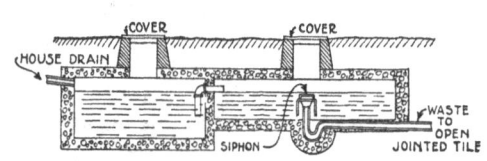

A HOME-MADE CONCRETE SETTLING AND FLUSH TANK.

the open joints of the entire system. In the meantime the flush tank, as soon as it has discharged, begins collecting again, and holds its contents for another twenty-four hours, thus allowing the drains to rest during the interval.

In a subsurface irrigation system laid out for a family of ten, the storage receptacles or flush tanks need not be more than 15 feet from the house, and they are not unpleasant, as nothing is visible but two cast-iron covers.

A simple form of flush tank recommended by the United States Department of Agriculture can be built of stone, brick, or concrete. A tank like this for a family of six should contain

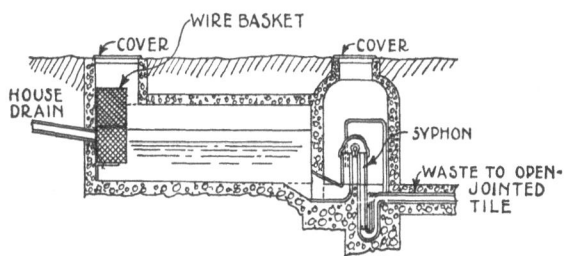

A SMALL SEPTIC TANK OF CONCRETE.

48 cubic feet, and it solves the plumbing problem in a perfectly satisfactory way. When built of concrete, the material costs approximately $23.

Build such a tank at any point in the yard, near the house or at a distance, for there are no odors. Extend the house drain to the tank, discharging about halfway up its height. Over the end of the inlet place a wire basket to interrupt undissolvable material, such as scrap from the kitchen sink or bits of paper.

Tanks with single chambers are effective, but septic tanks with two chambers arranged so that bacterial processes take place are the most scientific and best of all, as they not only retain their contents for periodical discharge, but convert solids into liquids, so that the discharge is practically in liquid form.

In the first chamber of a two-chamber tank, the heavier contents sink to the bottom, while the liquid flows to the second chamber. The solids in the first chamber are broken up, dissolved, and converted into liquids by bacterial action. Thus the septic tank converts solids into liquids in the storage tank, periodically discharging liquids into the subsurface irrigation drains, where they are transformed into harmless minerals by contact with air in the soil.

One of these systems, properly designed, is far more sanitary than town sewers. Compared with ordinary cesspools, so often used on country places, flush-tank systems are ideal beyond

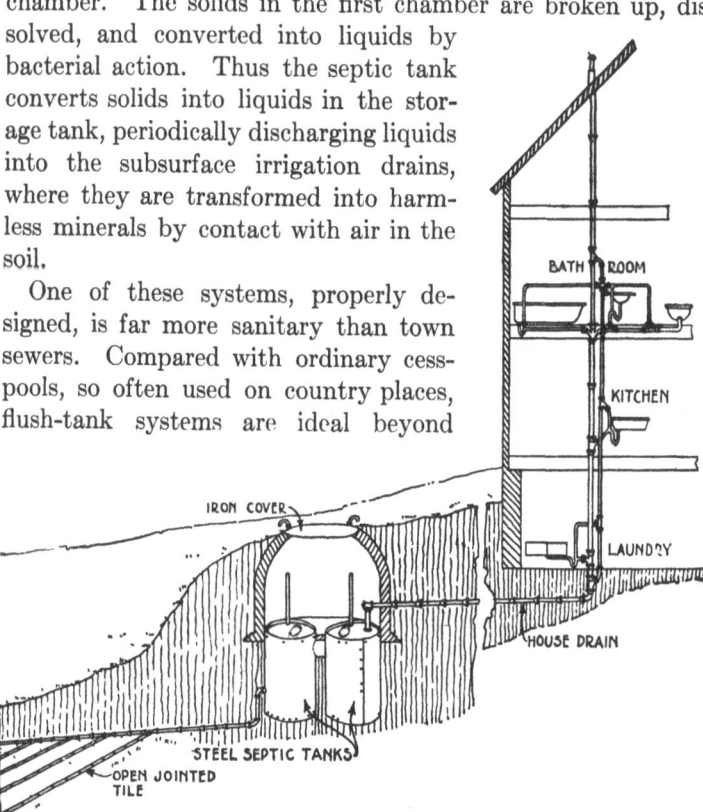

COMPLETE SEPTIC SEWAGE SYSTEM.

belief. Cesspools are dangerous. Nothing more unscientific or unsanitary could be devised for permanent use.

Septic tanks may be bought, ready-made, built of steel plates riveted together like a boiler. The interior of each tank is arranged with settling chambers and syphons of the size and pattern necessary. All that is needed to complete the system is to connect the tanks with open-joint tile drains.

Subsurface irrigation sewage systems should always be designed by experts. The exact size of tank is very important. If a tank is too large, the bacterial process is hampered; and if undersized, tanks cannot adequately handle the material.

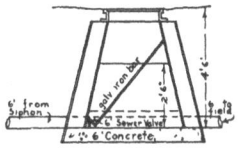

VALVE FOR DIVERTING SEWAGE.

Subsoil characteristics, slope of ground, climate, size of family, and distance of drains from house, all enter into the problem, which requires experience and knowledge for a correct solution. It isn't a problem for an amateur, though the amateur may undoubtedly solve it by study and common sense, for the principles of subsurface irrigation of sewage are so simple that any one can readily understand them. The cost of scientific plants is not excessive.

The interior of a septic tank is very simple; nothing costly enters into its construction, and manufacturers of septic tanks furnish all the data required. As their profit is made on tanks, it is practically the universal custom to make no charge for information.

INTERIOR SHOWING ROUGH-PLASTERED WALLS AND OAK TRIM

CHAPTER XX

EFFICIENT HEATING METHODS

MANY changes in old, established heating customs have occurred in the last quarter century. Some ideas which prevailed years ago are now obsolete. Methods then clung to with persistency have been entirely revolutionized, and present-day heating is quite different from what it was even ten years ago. Probably no country in the world has developed scientific heating to such a degree as America. American heating engineers are known the world over, and American methods are largely followed in England, France, and Germany, though European countries have been slow to adopt any advance upon primitive methods in vogue for years.

It was the invention of cast-iron radiators that gave such an impulse to heating methods. The first radiators were made of ordinary pipe, cut off at the right length and made into coils. Thus, in those days, each radiator was a stack of vertical pipes, screwed to a hollow cast-iron base, — unsightly and inefficient.

With the invention of cast-iron radiators, heating engineers, recognizing their importance, gave attention to developing steam and hot-water heating systems to the highest point of efficiency. To-day, heating apparatus for hot-water and steam systems is largely standard, all manufacturers using similar models. Like plumbing fixtures, most radiators and boilers now made are designed along similar lines, though of course each manufacturer claims points of superiority in patterns of his own manufacture.

In selecting heating apparatus the most important point for the houseowner to remember is that he should deal only with reputable firms, — concerns who stand back of their goods, constantly maintaining them at a high point. After installation of a heating system in his house, the owner wants to be assured that it will do the work properly and wear well, and he wants to feel certain that in the event of apparatus not working well he can fall back on the manufacturer to make it good.

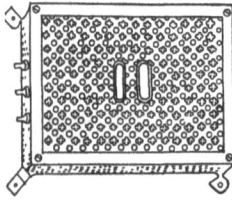

ELECTRIC REGISTER.

A house is usually warmed by one of four different methods: stoves, hot-air furnace, hot-water (gravity), or steam heater. High pressure hot-water systems are rarely used for houses. There are other methods also, such as warming by fireplaces, and by electric and gas radiators, but the former are rarely used as the only means of heating a house, and electric and gas radiators are not yet practical for warming an entire house, though they are excellent as auxiliary heaters.

When hot-water and steam heaters first came into the market in the shape of efficient apparatus it was predicted that the hot-air furnace would be quickly displaced by them. So different has been the result that, as an actual fact, hot-air furnaces are used quite as much as formerly. Manufacturers of hot-air furnaces, driven by sharp competition of hot-water and steam apparatus manufacturers, were obliged to

BRICK-SET HOT-AIR FURNACE.

improve their product. Present-day hot-air furnaces of the best models are excellent for warming, being especially practical for small houses where the cost of hot-water or steam apparatus is prohibitive.

It is not the amount of coal you burn that gives warmth to your living rooms. Tons of coal may only succeed in lining your chimney with soot, and the coal man's pocketbook with your money. A badly arranged heating apparatus eats up coal almost faster than you can shovel it in, and a large part of the heat goes up the chimney.

There are many points in favor of the hot-air furnace, the principal one being that a hot-air system, when fresh, cold air is brought in from outside, circulates pure air and you can give this air, just the right degree of humidity or moisture by keeping the water pan filled with water.

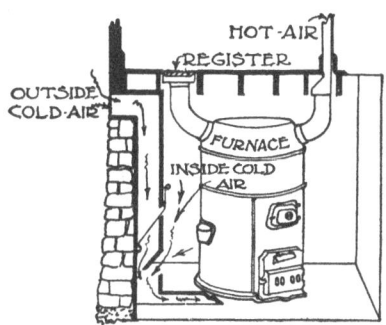

HOT-AIR FURNACE WITH GALVANIZED IRON CASING.

The chief drawback to a hot-air furnace is in windy weather. On the windy side of a house, the warm air is driven back and the circulation impaired. This may be greatly obviated by locating a furnace nearer the side of prevailing winds. In other words, do not put your furnace in the center of the basement, but place it toward the windy side. Select a furnace with an absolutely air-tight casing either of brick or galvanized steel. Then you will not be drawing in foul cellar air and discharging it to rooms above. Arrange the cold-air box so you can get cold air from outdoors in mild weather, and from inside in freezing, windy weather. Keep the water pan filled with clean water.

The owner will not be able to lay out the system of piping himself unless he has made a study of hot-air warming.

2 A

The man he employs, if he is skillful, will have all warm-air pipes as close to the furnace as possible, with no long horizontal runs. For upper rooms it pays to use double-jacketed pipes, for much heat radiating in partitions when single pipes are used, goes to waste.

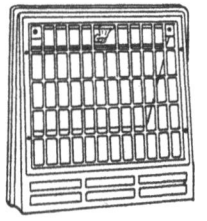

CONVENIENT TYPE OF WALL REGISTER.

In a furnace the best firepots have corrugated sides. This greatly adds to the strength and life of the metal. The best furnaces are made of tight steel sections or drums thoroughly fastened together with air-tight joints, and the whole covered with an air-tight casing of galvanized steel or brick. A large firepot is more economical of fuel consumption than a small one. A furnace larger than actually required is better than one too small, because a slow fire in a large heater is more economical than a forced fire in a small one.

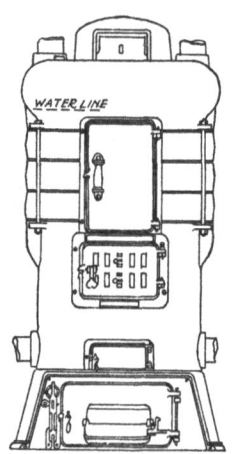

VERTICAL SECTIONAL STEAM BOILER.

All interior parts of the furnace should be large and smooth. Even a slight roughness of surface will catch carbon from the fire and foul the fire ways. On the first story use floor registers of simple pattern; wall registers are best for bedrooms.

Combination hot-air and hot-water heaters are really furnaces containing a hot-water coil in the firepot. The latter is connected with a few radiators on upper floors, the balance of the house being warmed by hot-air pipes.

Hot-water systems of heating are economical because water is so sensitive when heat is applied that a low fire causes a circulation of warm water through the rooms

EFFICIENT HEATING METHODS

and the air is quickly raised in temperature. Then, too, on spring days and cool evenings in the fall, when a fire so low that it scarcely burns at all makes the house comfortable, hot-water heat is particularly desirable.

TABLE SHOWING SIZES OF VERTICAL SECTIONAL BOILERS

STEAM

Height (to top outlet) Inches	Nom Diam Grate Inches	Grate Area Sq Ft	Average Firepot Sq. Ft	Height Water Line Inches	Outlets and Inlets Size Inches	Smoke Pipe Inches	Ratings
45	15	1.21	1.06	$40\frac{1}{2}$	2	7	175
49	15	1.21	1.06	$44\frac{1}{2}$	2	7	200
53	15	1.21	1.06	$48\frac{1}{2}$	2	7	225
$47\frac{1}{2}$	18	1.76	1.53	$43\frac{1}{4}$	$2\frac{1}{2}$	7	275
52	18	1.76	1.53	$47\frac{1}{2}$	$2\frac{1}{2}$	7	300
$56\frac{1}{2}$	18	1.76	1.53	$51\frac{3}{4}$	$2\frac{1}{2}$	7	325
50	21	2.40	2 18	$44\frac{1}{2}$	3	9	400
54	21	2.40	2.18	49	3	9	425
58	21	2.40	2.18	$53\frac{1}{2}$	3	9	450
$62\frac{9}{16}$	21	2 40	2.18	$58\frac{1}{8}$	3	9	475
51	24	3 14	2.82	$45\frac{1}{2}$	$3\frac{1}{2}$	9	525
$55\frac{1}{2}$	24	3.14	2.82	$50\frac{1}{4}$	$3\frac{1}{2}$	9	575
60	24	3.14	2.82	55	$3\frac{1}{2}$	9	625
$64\frac{3}{16}$	24	3.14	2.82	$59\frac{9}{16}$	$3\frac{1}{2}$	9	650
$51\frac{1}{2}$	27	3.90	3 83	$46\frac{3}{8}$	4	10	750
$56\frac{7}{16}$	27	3.90	3.83	$51\frac{5}{16}$	4	10	800
$61\frac{3}{8}$	27	3.90	3.83	$56\frac{1}{4}$	4	10	850
$66\frac{5}{16}$	27	3.90	3.83	$61\frac{3}{16}$	4	10	900

356 SUCCESSFUL HOUSES AND HOW TO BUILD THEM

TABLE SHOWING SIZES OF VERTICAL SECTIONAL BOILERS

Hot Water						
Height (to top outlet) Inches	Nom Diam. Grate Inches	Grate Area Sq. Ft.	Average Firepot Sq Ft	Outlets and Inlets Size Inches	Smoke Pipe Inches	Ratings
40	15	1.21	1.06	2	7	300
44	15	1.21	1.06	2	7	325
48	15	1.21	1.06	2	7	350
$42\frac{1}{2}$	18	1.76	1.53	$2\frac{1}{2}$	7	450
47	18	1.76	1.53	$2\frac{1}{2}$	7	500
$51\frac{1}{2}$	18	1.76	1.53	$2\frac{1}{2}$	7	550
44	21	2.40	2.18	3	9	600
$48\frac{1}{2}$	21	2.40	2 18	3	9	650
53	21	2.40	2.18	3	9	700
$57\frac{5}{16}$	21	2.40	2.18	3	9	750
45	24	3.14	2.82	$3\frac{1}{2}$	9	875
50	24	3.14	2.82	$3\frac{1}{2}$	9	950
55	24	3.14	2.82	$3\frac{1}{2}$	9	1025
$59\frac{5}{16}$	24	3.14	2.82	$3\frac{1}{2}$	9	1075
46	27	3.90	3.83	4	10	1250
$50\frac{3}{8}$	27	3.90	3.83	4	10	1325
$55\frac{7}{8}$	27	3 90	3.83	4	10	1400
$60\frac{3}{8}$	27	3.90	3 83	4	10	1475

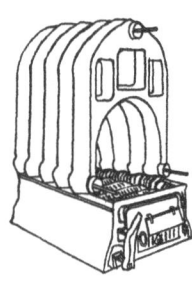

Horizontal Sectional Boiler for Hot-water Heat.

Hot-water boilers can be bought with either vertical or horizontal sections, — that is, with sections piled one on top of the other, or with sections side by side like a radiator. The former are usually best for a house of moderate size. Select a boiler with ample flue ways, easy to keep clean. For soft coal use a boiler with extra large flues. Magazine boilers are labor saving, for they need to be loaded but once a day.

TABLE SHOWING SIZES OF HORIZONTAL SECTIONAL BOILERS

STEAM

Length Total Inches	Grate Area Sq. Ft.	Average Firepot Sq. Ft.	Outlets Inches	Ash Pit (Inside) Inches	Ratings
$40\frac{7}{8}$	1.95	2.47	2–3	$20\frac{15}{16} \times 21\frac{5}{8}$	300
$47\frac{1}{8}$	2.60	3.30	2–3	$20\frac{15}{16} \times 27\frac{13}{16}$	425
$53\frac{3}{8}$	3.25	4.10	2–3	$20\frac{15}{16} \times 34$	550
$52\frac{3}{4}$	3.32	4.00	2–3	$20 \times 29\frac{15}{16}$	600
$58\frac{3}{8}$	4.15	5.00	2–3	$20 \times 36\frac{5}{8}$	750
65	4.98	6.00	3–3	$20 \times 43\frac{5}{16}$	900
$53\frac{1}{4}$	4.08	4.84	2–4	$23\frac{1}{8} \times 31\frac{13}{16}$	800
$60\frac{1}{4}$	5.10	6.05	2–4	$23\frac{1}{8} \times 38\frac{7}{8}$	1000
$67\frac{1}{4}$	6.12	7.26	3–4	$23\frac{1}{8} \times 45\frac{15}{16}$	1200
$59\frac{1}{4}$	5.44	6.48	2–4	$28 \times 35\frac{3}{16}$	1100
$66\frac{7}{8}$	6.80	8.10	2–4	$28 \times 42\frac{7}{8}$	1350
$74\frac{1}{2}$	8.16	9.72	3–4	$28 \times 50\frac{9}{16}$	1600
$82\frac{1}{4}$	9.52	11.34	3–4	$28 \times 58\frac{1}{4}$	1850
60	6.24	7.33	2–4	$30\frac{5}{8} \times 35\frac{1}{2}$	1300
68	7.80	9.16	2–4	$30\frac{5}{8} \times 43\frac{1}{2}$	1625
76	9.36	10.99	3–4	$30\frac{5}{8} \times 51\frac{1}{2}$	1950
84	10.92	12.83	3–4	$30\frac{5}{8} \times 59\frac{1}{2}$	2275
$69\frac{3}{4}$	9.12	10.40	2–5	$38\frac{15}{16} \times 40\frac{3}{4}$	2100
$78\frac{7}{8}$	11.40	13.00	2–5	$38\frac{15}{16} \times 49\frac{7}{8}$	2625
88	13.68	15.60	3–5	$38\frac{15}{16} \times 59$	3150
$97\frac{1}{8}$	15.96	18.20	3–5	$38\frac{15}{16} \times 68\frac{1}{8}$	3675
$106\frac{1}{4}$	18.24	20.80	4–5	$38\frac{15}{16} \times 77\frac{1}{4}$	4200
92	18.00	18.75	2–6	52×55	4750
$102\frac{3}{4}$	21.60	22.50	2–6	52×66	5700
114	25.20	26.25	3–6	52×77	6650
$124\frac{1}{4}$	28.80	30.00	3–6	52×88	7600
135	32.40	33.75	3–6	52×99	8550

358 SUCCESSFUL HOUSES AND HOW TO BUILD THEM

TABLE SHOWING SIZES OF HORIZONTAL SECTIONAL BOILERS

HOT WATER

Length Total Inches	Grate Area Sq. Ft.	Average Firepot Sq. Ft.	Outlets Inches	Ash-Pit (Inside) Inches	Ratings
$40\frac{7}{8}$	1.95	2.47	2–3	$20\frac{15}{16} \times 21\frac{5}{8}$	500
$47\frac{1}{8}$	2.60	3.30	2–3	$20\frac{15}{16} \times 27\frac{13}{16}$	700
$53\frac{3}{8}$	3.25	4.10	2–3	$20\frac{15}{16} \times 34$	900
$52\frac{3}{4}$	3.32	4.00	2–3	$20 \times 29\frac{15}{16}$	1000
$58\frac{3}{8}$	4.15	5.00	2–3	$20 \times 36\frac{5}{8}$	1250
65	4.98	6.00	3–3	$20 \times 43\frac{5}{16}$	1500
$53\frac{1}{4}$	4.08	4.84	2–4	$23\frac{1}{8} \times 31\frac{13}{16}$	1300
$60\frac{1}{4}$	5.10	6.05	2–4	$23\frac{1}{8} \times 38\frac{7}{8}$	1650
$67\frac{1}{4}$	6.12	7.26	3–4	$23\frac{1}{8} \times 45\frac{15}{16}$	2000
$59\frac{1}{4}$	5.44	6.48	2–4	$28 \times 35\frac{3}{16}$	1825
$66\frac{7}{8}$	6.80	8.10	2–4	$28 \times 42\frac{7}{8}$	2225
$74\frac{1}{2}$	8.16	9.72	3–4	$28 \times 50\frac{9}{16}$	2650
$82\frac{1}{4}$	9.52	11.34	3–4	$28 \times 58\frac{1}{4}$	3050
60	6.24	7.33	2–4	$30\frac{5}{8} \times 35\frac{1}{2}$	2150
68	7.80	9.16	2–4	$30\frac{5}{8} \times 43\frac{1}{2}$	2675
76	9.36	10.99	3–4	$30\frac{5}{8} \times 51\frac{1}{2}$	3200
84	10.92	12.83	3–4	$30\frac{5}{8} \times 59\frac{1}{2}$	3725
$69\frac{3}{4}$	9.12	10.40	2–5	$38\frac{1}{8} \times 40\frac{3}{4}$	3450
$78\frac{7}{8}$	11.40	13.00	2–5	$38\frac{1}{8} \times 49\frac{7}{8}$	4325
88	13.68	15.60	3–5	$38\frac{1}{8} \times 59$	5200
$97\frac{1}{8}$	15.96	18.20	3–5	$38\frac{1}{8} \times 68\frac{1}{8}$	6050
$106\frac{1}{4}$	18.24	20.80	4–5	$38\frac{1}{8} \times 77\frac{1}{4}$	6925
92	18.00	18.75	2–6	52×55	7825
$102\frac{3}{4}$	21.60	22.50	2–6	52×66	9400
114	25.20	26.25	3–6	52×77	10975
$124\frac{1}{4}$	28.80	30.00	3–6	52×88	12550
135	32.40	33.75	3–6	52×99	14125

You must buy a boiler at least half as large again as is required by the amount of radiation. If your house requires five hundred feet of radiation get a seven hundred and fifty foot boiler, for a boiler too small will have to be forced in cold weather,

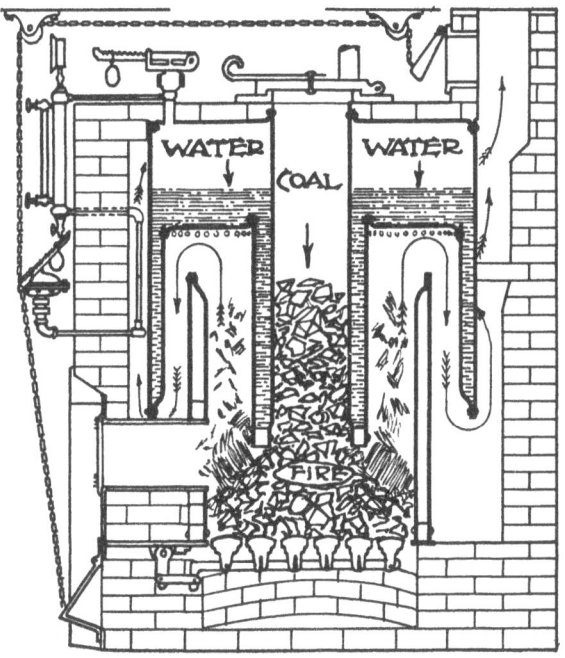

BRICK-SET STEEL BOILER FOR STEAM HEAT.

and that eats up fuel. The following formula can be used to determine the amount of radiation required to properly warm a house: —

FORMULA FOR SIZE OF RADIATORS

Find the cubic feet of air in room. Find the exposed wall surface in square feet less glass. Find the square feet of glass surface. Divide the wall surface by 10, which gives you glass equivalent. Add this quotient to the glass surface, multiply this sum by 75 and add this product to the cubic feet of air in room. Multiply this sum by .0092 for hot water or by .0055 for steam.

After determining amount of radiation required in each room, add the results together to determine amount of radiation required for entire house.

Example: —

Room $30' \times 30' \times 10' = 9000$ cubic feet of air. Exposed on two sides – 480 square feet of wall surface. Four windows, $5' \times 6' = 120$ square feet of glass surface.

480 divided by 10 equals 48.

48 plus 120 equals 168.

168 multiplied by 75 equals 12,600.

12,600 plus 9000 equals 21,600.

21,600 multiplied by .0055 equals 118.8 square feet of radiation necessary to heat said room by steam.

Or 21,600 multiplied by .0092 equals 197.72 square feet, the amount necessary to heat the same room by hot water.

Weather — zero.

Steam 1 lb. pressure.

Water in boiler 165 degrees F.

Your boiler should be equipped with a thermometer to indicate the temperature of the water, and with an altitude gauge to show the height of water in the system. The entire system is filled with water up to the expansion tank in the attic. This latter is open to the atmosphere and acts as a safety valve.

It pays to cover a boiler with asbestos cement or some other insulating material, and it pays to use pipe covering on the basement piping. In this way you prevent much heat from wasting. The owner can buy cement and pipe covering and do the job easily himself if he is so minded.

An automatic circulator is worth while for the hot-water system. This consists of a column of mercury in a tube, connected with the piping system. The mercury causes a pressure in the system which increases the circulation about five times, thus saving considerable coal.

Steam heating is not used much for small houses. Steam is frequently advisable in a country house when the boiler is located in a shed instead of in the basement. If the boiler is in the shed, it must stand in a pit well below the level of the lowest radiator, in order to allow wet, condensed steam to flow back to the boiler after it has done its work in the radiators. The circulation in a heating system is similar to the circulation of blood in the human body, the boiler taking the place of the heart.

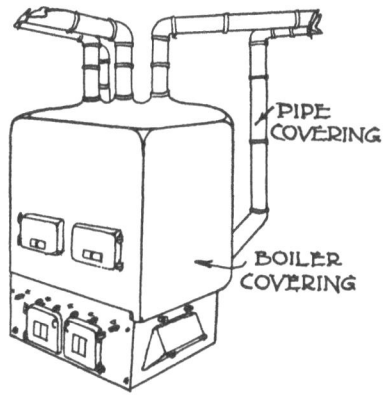

BOILER COVERED WITH ASBESTOS CEMENT.

A steam boiler is similar to a hot-water boiler, but it has in addition a large dome at the top to allow steam to rise from the boiling water and collect. In an ordinary hot-water boiler there is no pressure — or very little — as the water does not need to boil. To make steam, however, water must be boiled, resulting in pressure in a steam system. This requires a safety valve which will pop and relieve the system when the pressure gets too high.

A steam system is a little cheaper than hot water because it requires but one pipe to the radiators, whereas the hot-water system usually requires two; steam radiators are smaller than hot-water radiators, as steam is hotter than hot water.

362 SUCCESSFUL HOUSES AND HOW TO BUILD THEM

A popular objection to steam heating is the snapping and thumping of pipes. This is unnecessary; a steam system may

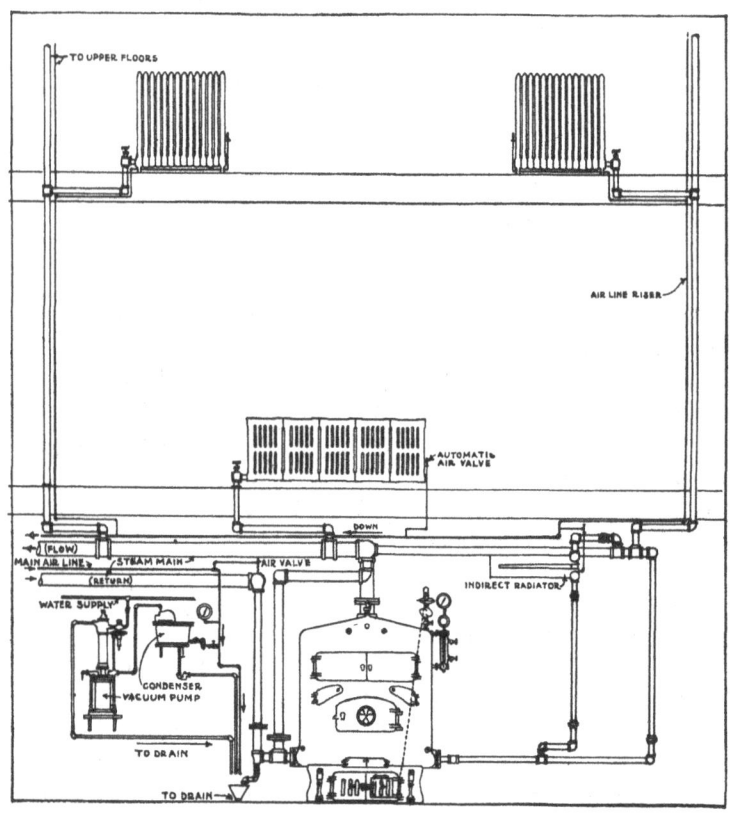

COMPLETE VACUUM STEAM SYSTEM.

be as quiet in operation as any other, if pipes are laid with a slope to drain back to the boiler, and if allowance is made for sufficient expansion of joints to allow pipes to expand and contract when alternately hot or cold.

EFFICIENT HEATING METHODS 363

Vacuum-heating systems are really steam-heating systems, but a vacuum is maintained in the pipes by means of a vacuum pump located in the basement. This form of house heating is now being used quite extensively, though it is more practical for large houses than for small, by reason of its greater first cost. A vacuum system consists of the ordinary single-pipe layout for the house, connecting each radiator with the boiler in the basement, but instead of ordinary air valves special automatic air valves are used. These are connected by means of a small pipe, with a pump and condenser in the basement. The vacuum system operates as follows: when the vacuum pump in the basement is started, air is sucked out of the entire system by means of a small pipe connected with the air valves, thus producing a vacuum in each radiator. Then when steam is turned on it rushes instantly to each radiator. The entire process is automatic, for the vacuum pump is operated by water pressure from the town water supply system or by an electric motor, automatically controlled by the pressure in the system. In connection with the vacuum pump is a condenser into which the moisture-laden air from the radiators is pumped and condensed, thus reaching the vacuum pump in a dry state. It is claimed for vacuum systems that they are more efficient than ordinary steam systems, requiring less fuel and consequently costing less to operate.

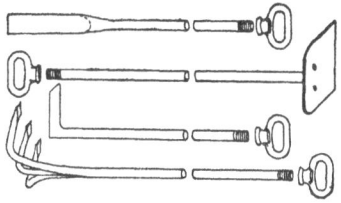

PROPER TOOLS FOR HEATING PLANT.

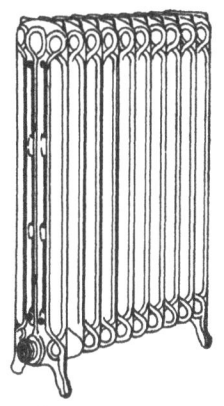

3-COLUMN CAST-IRON RADIATOR.

SINGLE-COLUMN RADIATORS FOR STEAM AND WATER

No of Sections	Length 2½ In. per Sec.	Heating Surface — Square Feet				
		38-in Height 3 Sq. Ft. per Sec.	32-in. Height 2½ Sq Ft per Sec.	26-in. Height 2 Sq. Ft. per Sec.	23-in. Height 1⅔ Sq. Ft. per Sec.	20-in Height 1½ Sq. Ft. per Sec.
2	5	6	5	4	3⅓	3
3	7½	9	7½	6	5	4½
4	10	12	10	8	6⅔	6
5	12½	15	12½	10	8⅓	7½
6	15	18	15	12	10	9
7	17½	21	17½	14	11⅔	10½
8	20	24	20	16	13⅓	12
9	22½	27	22½	18	15	13½
10	25	30	25	20	16⅔	15
11	27½	33	27½	22	18⅓	16½
12	30	36	30	24	20	18
13	32½	39	32½	26	21⅔	19½
14	35	42	35	28	23⅓	21
15	37½	45	37½	30	25	22½
16	40	48	40	32	26⅔	24
17	42½	51	42½	34	28⅓	25½
18	45	54	45	36	30	27
19	47½	57	47½	38	31⅔	28½
20	50	60	50	40	33⅓	30
21	52½	63	52½	42	35	31½
22	55	66	55	44	36⅔	33
23	57½	69	57½	46	38⅓	34½
24	60	72	60	48	40	36
25	62½	75	·62½	50	41⅔	37½
26	65	78	65	52	43⅓	39
27	67½	81	67½	54	45	40½
28	70	84	70	56	46⅔	42
29	72½	87	72½	58	48⅓	43½
30	75	90	75	60	50	45
31	77½	83	77½	62	51⅔	46½
32	80	96	80	64	53⅓	48

TWO-COLUMN RADIATORS FOR STEAM AND WATER

No of Sections	Length 2½ In per Sec	Heating Surface — Square Feet					
		45-in Height 5 Sq Ft per Sec	38-in Height 4 Sq Ft per Sec	32-in Height 3⅓ Sq Ft per Sec	26-in Height 2⅔ Sq Ft per Sec.	23-in Height 2⅓ Sq Ft per Sec	20-in Height 2 Sq Ft per Sec	15-in Height 1½ Sq Ft per Sec
2	5	10	8	6⅔	5⅓	4⅔	4	3
3	7½	15	12	10	8	7	6	4½
4	10	20	16	13⅓	10⅔	9⅓	8	6
5	12½	25	20	16⅔	13⅓	11⅔	10	7½
6	15	30	24	20	16	14	12	9
7	17½	35	28	23⅓	18⅔	16⅓	14	10½
8	20	40	32	26⅔	21⅓	18⅔	16	12
9	22½	45	36	30	24	21	18	13½
10	25	50	40	33⅓	26⅔	23⅓	20	15
11	27½	55	44	36⅔	29⅓	25⅔	22	16½
12	30	60	48	40	32	28	24	18
13	32½	65	52	43⅓	34⅔	30⅓	26	19½
14	35	70	56	46⅔	37⅓	32⅔	28	21
15	37½	75	60	50	40	35	30	22½
16	40	80	64	53⅓	42⅔	37⅓	32	24
17	42½	85	68	56⅔	45⅓	39⅔	34	25½
18	45	90	72	60	48	42	36	27
19	47½	95	76	63⅓	50⅔	44⅓	38	28½
20	50	100	80	66⅔	53⅓	46⅔	40	30
21	52½	105	84	70	56	49	42	31½
22	55	110	88	73⅓	58⅔	51⅓	44	33
23	57½	115	92	76⅔	61⅓	53⅔	46	34½
24	60	120	96	80	64	56	48	36
25	62½	125	100	83⅓	66⅔	58⅓	50	37½
26	65	130	104	86⅔	69⅓	60⅔	52	39
27	67½	135	108	90	72	63	54	40½
28	70	140	112	93⅓	74⅔	65⅓	56	42
29	72½	145	116	96⅔	77⅓	67⅔	58	43½
30	75	150	120	100	80	70	60	45
31	77½	155	124	103⅓	82⅔	72⅓	62	46½
32	80	160	128	106⅔	85⅓	74⅔	64	48

THREE-COLUMN RADIATORS FOR STEAM AND WATER

No of Sec-tions	Length 2½ In per Sec	Heating Surface — Square Feet					
		45-in Height 6 Sq Ft per Sec.	38-in Height 5 Sq Ft per Sec	32-in Height 4½ Sq Ft per Sec	26-in Height 3¾ Sq Ft per Sec	22-in Height 3 Sq Ft per Sec	18-in Height 2¼ Sq Ft per Sec
2	5	12	10	9	7½	6	4½
3	7½	18	15	13½	11¼	9	6¾
4	10	24	20	18	15	12	9
5	12½	30	25	22½	18¾	15	11¼
6	15	36	30	27	22½	18	13½
7	17½	42	35	31½	26¼	21	15¾
8	20	48	40	36	30	24	18
9	22½	54	45	40½	33¾	27	20¼
10	25	60	50	45	37½	30	22½
11	27½	66	55	49½	41¼	33	24¾
12	30	72	60	54	45	36	27
13	32½	78	65	58½	48¾	39	29¼
14	35	84	70	63	52½	42	31½
15	37½	90	75	67½	56¼	45	33¾
16	40	96	80	72	60	48	36
17	42½	102	85	76½	63¾	51	38¼
18	45	108	90	81	67½	54	40½
19	47½	114	95	85½	71¼	57	42¾
20	50	120	100	90	75	60	45
21	52½	126	105	94½	78¾	63	47¼
22	55	132	110	99	82½	66	49½
23	57½	138	115	103½	86¼	69	51¾
24	60	144	120	108	90	72	54
25	62½	150	125	112½	93¾	75	56¼
26	65	156	130	117	97½	78	58½
27	67½	162	135	121½	101¼	81	60¾
28	70	168	140	126	105	84	63
29	72½	174	145	130½	108¾	87	65¼
30	75	180	150	135	112½	90	67½
31	77½	186	155	139½	116¼	93	69¾
32	80	192	160	144	120	96	72

FOUR-COLUMN RADIATORS FOR STEAM OR WATER

No of Sections	Length 3 In per Sec	Heating Surface — Square Feet					
		45-in Height 10 Sq Ft per Sec	38-in Height 8 Sq Ft per Sec	32-in Height 6½ Sq Ft per Sec	26-in Height 5 Sq Ft per Sec	22-in Height 4 Sq Ft per Sec	18-in Height 3 Sq Ft per Sec.
2	6	20	16	13	10	8	6
3	9	30	24	19½	15	12	9
4	12	40	32	26	20	16	12
5	15	50	40	32½	25	20	15
6	18	60	48	39	30	24	18
7	21	70	56	45½	35	28	21
8	24	80	64	52	40	32	24
9	27	90	72	58½	45	36	27
10	30	100	80	65	50	40	30
11	33	110	88	71½	55	44	33
12	36	120	96	78	60	48	36
13	39	130	104	84½	65	52	39
14	42	140	112	91	70	56	42
15	45	150	120	97½	75	60	45
16	48	160	128	104	80	64	48
17	51	170	136	110½	85	68	51
18	54	180	144	117	90	72	54
19	57	190	152	123½	95	76	57
20	60	200	160	130	100	80	60
21	63	210	168	136½	105	84	63
22	66	220	176	143	110	88	66
23	69	230	184	149½	115	92	69
24	72	240	192	156	120	96	72
25	75	250	200	162½	125	100	75
26	78	260	208	169	130	104	78
27	81	270	216	175½	135	108	81
28	84	280	224	182	140	112	84
29	87	290	232	188½	145	116	87
30	90	300	240	195	150	120	90
31	93	310	248	201½	155	124	93
32	96	320	256	208	160	128	96

Hot-water radiators are like steam radiators except that sections are joined together at the top as well as bottom with nipples. In steam radiators the tops of the sections are not connected. Radiators are chiefly of cast iron, though pressed-steel radiators are now to be obtained. Hot-water radiators should always be at least three eighths larger than steam radiators. The preceding tables show sizes of standard radiators.

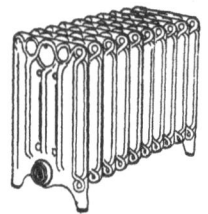

4-Column Cast-iron Window Radiator.

Do not make your radiators conspicuous by painting them with gold or silver paint. If the walls of your rooms are tinted, paint the radiators the same shade. If you are using wall paper, tint the radiators the tone of the prevailing color in the paper. Special radiator paints without oil (oil would never dry out) can be obtained in all shades.

You can find radiators of all kinds, suitable for every purpose. In the pantry use a plate-warming radiator, or you may use for the same purpose a hot closet in the dining-room radiator. If the space where a radiator is to stand is short, use a short, wide, four-column radiator. If the space is long and narrow, a single-column or two-column radiator is best. For very narrow spaces you can get wall radiators which are the thinnest models made. Where space is ample, the pattern of radiator most used is the three-column.

Radiators are least in the way and more efficient under windows. Thus, they do not take up space needed for furniture, and the cold air from the window is warmed as fast

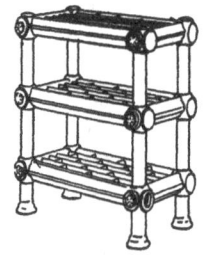

Radiator for Warming Plates.

as it comes in. A ventilating radiator is ideal for freshening the air. By means of a little register cut through the outside wall behind each radiator, fresh air is admitted to the base of

EFFICIENT HEATING METHODS

the radiator, where it is warmed and passed into the room. The amount of cold air may be regulated by a shutter worked from the front of the radiator.

LOW (WINDOW) RADIATORS FOR STEAM OR WATER

No of Sections	Length 3 In per Sec	HEATING SURFACE — SQUARE FOOT				
		20-in Height 6 Sq Ft per Sec	18-in Height 5⅓ Sq Ft. per Sec.	16-in Height 4⅔ Sq Ft per Sec.	14-in Height 4 Sq Ft per Sec	13-in Height 3⅔ Sq Ft per Sec
2	6	12	10⅔	9⅓	8	7⅓
3	9	18	16	14	12	11
4	12	24	21⅓	18⅔	16	14⅔
5	15	30	26⅔	23⅓	20	18⅓
6	18	36	32	28	24	22
7	21	42	37⅓	32⅔	28	25⅔
8	24	48	53⅔	37⅓	32	29⅓
9	27	54	48	42	36	33
10	30	60	53⅓	46⅔	40	36⅔
11	33	66	58⅔	51⅓	44	40⅓
12	36	72	64	56	48	44

Pressed-steel radiators are much smaller and lighter than cast iron, and these are the principal advantages claimed for them. Frequently it is desirable, in small rooms or contracted spaces, to use radiators as small as possible. Pressed-steel radiators are good for that purpose as they furnish the same amount of heat in radiators of smaller sizes. The additional advantage they have in weighing less than cast-iron radiators is frequently desirable where floor loads are required to be lessened.

Indirect radiation by means of hollow pin radiators is another excellent way to heat the house. Such radiators are placed in boxes in the basement, connected by ducts with the outside air. Cool, fresh air after it is warmed is distributed to the rooms by hot-air pipes and registers. This is an expensive way but it gives excellent results.

PRESSED STEEL RADIATOR.

The best radiator valves for steam and hot water are plain quick-opening, nickel-plated valves. For steam, the disk in the valve screws entirely down to shut off the radiator, but for hot water the disk is pierced with a little hole, so that water circulates slightly after the valve is closed. This is necessary to prevent freezing.

A "union L" is used for the outgoing side of a hot-water radiator. This is nickel plated to match the valve and it allows a radiator to be disconnected for repairs. A new combination valve for hot water admits of both pipes being brought to one end of the radiator, which works well with this valve. In some systems an angle valve is used with satisfactory results.

Loose-key air valves are best for hot-water radiators as they prevent accidental opening of the valves, which would allow water to escape and ruin floors and ceilings. It is only necessary to let the air out once each year when the apparatus is first started in the autumn. For steam, use ordinary wheel air valves, or automatic valves. Be sure your automatic valves are of the best pattern, for if a single valve does not work properly, escaping steam may do much damage. Use nickel-plated floor and ceiling plates at the top

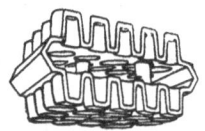

CAST-IRON RADIATOR FOR INDIRECT HEATING.

and bottom of all exposed heating pipes. Where pipes pass through floors and ceilings, holes should be slightly larger than

EFFICIENT HEATING METHODS

the pipes to allow for expansion. Floor and ceiling plates conceal these holes, and metal tubes are frequently placed at such points for the pipes to extend through.

A thermostat is desirable for the hot-air furnace as well as hot-water and steam boilers, as this ingenious little device auto-

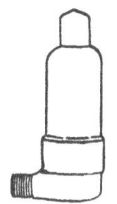
AUTOMATIC AIR VALVE FOR STEAM.

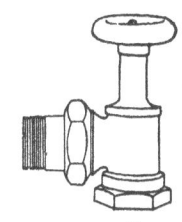
QUICK-OPENING VALVE FOR HOT-WATER RADIATOR.

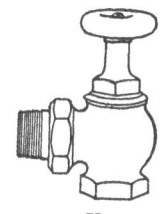
IMPROVED VALVE FOR STEAM RADIATOR.

matically controls the fire in the furnace by opening and closing drafts. The best thermostats consist of a little fixture attached to the wall in the living room or any room in which the average temperature of the house is maintained. In some forms of thermostats the expansion and contraction of a metal blade (caused by varying temperature in the room) makes an electrical connection with a clockwork motor in the basement, operating the direct draft and check draft of the furnace. The apparatus may be set at the exact temperature wanted — say 70

degrees. If the temperature of the room rises slightly above 70 degrees the metal blade expands, touches a metallic point, making an electrical connection which trips the clockwork motor. Then this motor, by means of a lever and chain, closes the direct draft of the furnace and opens the check draft. Of

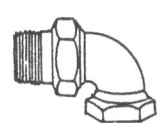
UNION L FOR HOT-WATER RADIATOR.

course the fire immediately slows down and the temperature falls. When the temperature falls below 70 degrees, the process is reversed, the motor opening the direct draft and closing the check draft, thus causing the fire to burn more freely. As an auxiliary to the thermostat a clock may be used, which can be set to cause the draft to be opened at any hour. Thus, one may turn down the thermostat to carry a slow fire upon going to bed at night, setting the clock to operate at six o'clock in the morning, at which hour the thermostat promptly opens the draft, making the house warm by getting-up time. Clockwork motors must be wound about once a week. A battery furnishes the current for operating the electrical part of the apparatus.

VALVE FOR SINGLE PIPE HOT-WATER SYSTEMS.

Other thermostats operate without a clockwork motor, by means of compressed air. The expansion and contraction of the metal sides of a small drum hung on the wall of the living room transmit energy through a tube to the damper regulator at the furnace, no electric current being necessary. Of the newest of these devices is one in which the expansion and contraction of a bellows-like metal compartment transmits energy to the damper regulator by means of a volatile chemical.

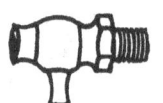

KEY AIR VALVE FOR HOT-WATER RADIATORS.

Thermostats of the best pattern are so sensitive that the opening of a window in a room causes them to operate. They undoubtedly save cost of fuel and are of the greatest convenience. Their cost is so slight compared with the work they do that a thermostat is undoubtedly worth while in any house.

SECTIONAL FLOOR AND CEILING PLATES.

Chains are sometimes connected with the direct draft and check draft of a furnace, extending up to the first floor by means of pulleys. Thus one can operate the drafts from the first floor by pulling the chains. This will be found a great convenience, though not so convenient as a thermostat.

The principles of heating are easily understood if one will give a little thought to them. Remember, heat travels easiest uphill. With a hot-water system your attic rooms may be warmer than those on the first floor, for water circulates more rapidly through the upright attic pipes than through the horizontal first-floor pipes. For this reason, favor the first-floor radiators by having the horizontal pipes as short as possible. Give them a generous slope, with few crooks and bends. Decrease the tendency of attic radiators to draw more than their share of hot water by having attic pipes smaller then first-floor pipes.

The success of the heating system lies largely with the person who runs it. Even the best fuel fails when used unintelligently. On the other hand, by efficient stoking one may get a wonderful lot of heat out of poor fuel. Keep the fire pot clean by punching out clinkers with a clinker bar and not by roughly shaking the grate, which loosens the entire bed of coals, admitting too much air, — burning and wasting fuel and making dust. A mild shaking morning and night will remove loose ashes. The ideal fire from the standpoint of health as well as economy is slow and easy burning.

Chimneys should properly be ranked part of the heating system — quite the most important part, in fact, for no heating apparatus can be expected to work well if the chimney is not properly designed. The following table for determining size of chimney flues will answer in most cases: —

CORRECT SIZES FOR CHIMNEY FLUES (FOR DIRECT RADIATION)

STEAM	SQUARE FLUE (INCHES)	HOT WATER
250	8 × 8	400
600	8 × 12	1000
900	12 × 12	1500
1000	12 × 12	1700
1300	12 × 16	2200

A flue for the heating apparatus should be smooth inside, preferably lined with tile flue lining, though it may be plastered smooth inside, instead. When flue lining is used the last section of tile should extend an inch or more above the top of the chimney to prevent wind from blowing down chimney. The thimble for the furnace, to which the furnace or heater smoke pipe is connected, should not be less than 8 inches in diameter, and the smoke pipe itself should be as short as possible. It is good practice not to extend the chimney flue much below where the smoke pipe enters, as the body of air contained in a flue below where the smoke pipe enters sometimes acts as a check on the draft.

One ring of brick (4 inches) is frequently considered sufficient for a chimney when tile flue lining is used, and the entire chimney should stand free from the framework of the house. It is not good practice to allow any wooden studding or floor beams to stand closer than 1 inch from any chimney. Every chimney should have a cement chimney cap at the top, slightly dished, to cause wind to be deflected instead of blowing down the chimney.

Flues for kitchen stoves are ordinarily 8×8 inches and 8×12 inches; for a fireplace, 12×12 inches. Fireplace flues are frequently made as small as 8×12 inches, but it is better practice to make them larger. The flue for the heating apparatus (size of which can be obtained from the table) should be entirely independent from cellar to roof. The flue for the kitchen range may also receive the smoke pipe from the laundry stove. Each fireplace should have an entirely independent flue.

Chimneys smoke from many causes. In some cases they are not high enough, extending as they do below the highest point of the roof. Other faulty flues are found to have obstructions in them, left through carelessness of masons who did not clean out the flues when the house was completed. Smoke has been known to be caused by a smoke pipe being pushed too far into the flue; other troubles come from the flue being too small, or leaking air through cracks of imperfectly built brick work.

Faults in flues can usually be corrected by masons expert enough to understand them. Frequently a flue is made to work perfectly by merely adding a chimney pot at the top, which often improves the draft.

It is always a good idea to place chimneys near the ridge of the roof. This leaves only the top of the chimney exposed, and the roof, sloping away from the chimney instead of towards it (as it might when the chimney is lower down on the roof), causes water to drain away without danger of leaks. Pay particular attention to the way flashing is applied at chimneys.

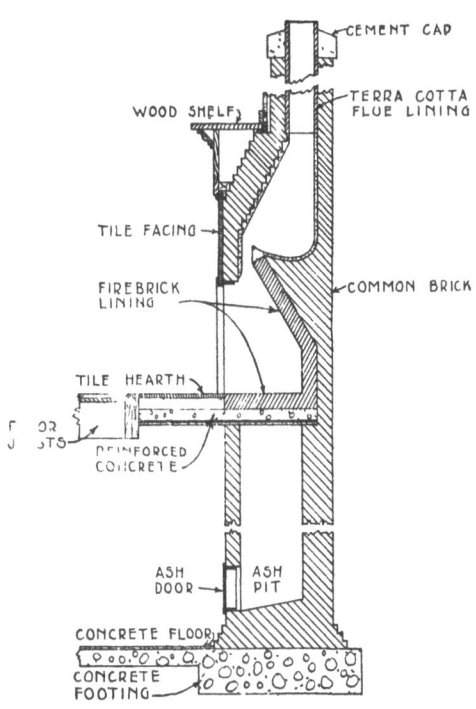

CORRECT DESIGN FOR A SMOKELESS FIREPLACE.

Workmen sometimes flash by merely laying strips of tin on top of the shingles, with one edge turned into the brickwork. This is all right so far as it goes, but another strip of tin should be jointed into the brickwork lapping down over the first tin so as to cause water running down the side of the chimney to drip off. This is called *counter flashing* and it is always demanded in first-class work.

Fireplaces, which may be considered as auxiliary means of warming the house, have caused as much trouble in new houses as almost any other thing. The proportion of fireplaces that smoke is unfortunately large, though every mason claims to have a pattern of fireplace "guaranteed smokeless." It has been the experience of most architects that the average mason knows very little about fireplace design, and most of the developments in smokeless fireplaces have come from the architects, themselves.

Fireplace design is really very simple. In the first place, to secure a smokeless fireplace the throat should be carefully proportioned to the size of the fireplace opening. In other words, since a certain amount of air enters the fireplace opening, the throat must be proportioned to draw this air through as well as the smoke. Narrow throats have been found to draw better than wide throats, and the rule accepted by most fireplace designers is as follows: —

RULE FOR SMOKELESS FIREPLACE

The throat should be $\frac{1}{12}$ the area of the fireplace opening.

Example. — Fireplace opening, $3' \times 2'6'' = 1080$ square inches. $\frac{1}{12}$ of 1080 square inches = 90 square inches (required area of throat), or $3'' \times 30''$.

Next, after the size of the throat is determined, the fireplace should be built with a flat shelf or ledge above the throat instead of the customary sloping wall. With the latter, wind blowing down chimney drives directly into the fireplace, causing the fire to smoke. When a flat ledge is built, wind blowing down chimney is deflected before it can reach the fire. With a fireplace built along these lines there should be no trouble from smoking. Make the smoke chamber above the throat of good size and have the flue as straight as possible. Your fireplace should then be a success.

Rough-cast Cement Plaster

CHAPTER XXI

PLASTERING; INSIDE AND OUTSIDE

PLASTERING is the most difficult operation in the house when it comes to getting a good job. There is no reason why it should be harder to get good plastering than to get a good job of painting or plumbing, but the fact remains that plastering is more often bad than good. Great care should be used in selecting the plastering contractor. Price should not count in this work, for many a house has been spoiled by the poor work done by a plastering contractor who took the job too low, skimping on his work to make up.

It is necessary to watch plasterers in order to get level ceilings and true walls. Workmen should be compelled to use long straight-edges, applied frequently to walls and ceilings to see if the latter are true. Nothing is more discouraging than to find walls uneven and ceilings "wavy" after the house is completed, when it is too late to improve them.

Laths are used to form a firm skeleton to which plaster will cling by flowing into the interstices between laths and then clinching. This clinch is called the "key" and it is the most important part of the work, for when the key is weak plaster soon drops off.

On ceilings, lathing is frequently applied directly to the under side of the ceiling joists and there is no fault in this method, though sometimes when ceiling joists are not uniformly of the same width (one being below another), it is better to cross-fur the ceiling, thus permitting it to be leveled up properly to receive the laths. Cross-furring also prevents trouble when joists warp (which they frequently do).

380 SUCCESSFUL HOUSES AND HOW TO BUILD THEM

Old-fashioned laths were of hard wood. They are now usually of pine, spruce, or hemlock, and the regular size for interior work is ¼ inch thick, 1½ inches wide, and 4 feet long. Studs should be properly spaced so they will come in the right place for nailing the laths. Use only the best laths, with straight grain to prevent warping. They should be well seasoned, free from sap or rot, and they will be found much stronger if free from knots or knot holes. "Live" knots or resinous pockets may cause discoloration of the plaster, so laths should be carefully selected, rejecting those which do not come up to the required standard.

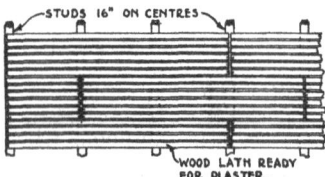

LATHS PROPERLY APPLIED.

In applying laths they should be nailed about ¼ inch apart, the end of one lath coming against the end of another. A continuous panel of laths about 18 inches wide should be formed, after which the joints should be broken to avoid a continuous joint from floor to ceiling (likely to cause a crack). Nails should be large-headed, cut or wire nails 1⅛ inches long, driven well into the studding.

As a substitute for laths a material called "sheathing laths" is sometimes used, consisting of ⅞ × 8-inch boards grooved to receive the plaster. This is claimed to be an advantageous method, as it makes a firmer body than laths, permitting nails to be driven into the wall anywhere, after the plastering is completed, without loosening the plaster. "Plaster board" is also frequently used;

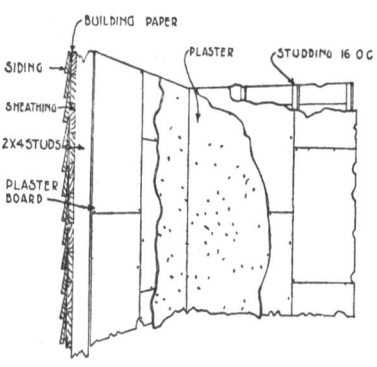

PLASTER BOARD USED IN PLACE OF LATHS.

$\frac{5}{8}$ inch to $\frac{1}{2}$ inch thick, 16 inches wide and 4 feet long, consisting of fiber embedded in plaster of Paris. Both sheathing laths and plaster board are nailed directly to the studding and plaster is applied to them as it is ordinarily applied to laths. Plaster board and sheathing laths can be readily sawed to fit, like ordinary lumber.

Metal lathing is excellent for outside or inside work, as it is considered reasonably fireproof and will not expand nor contract in extremes of heat and cold. Metal lathing should not be applied directly to joists or studs, as the latter, after the plastering is completed, frequently show through in streaks. A better way is to apply furring strips of metal to the studs and on these fasten the metal lathing. More plaster is required for metal lathing than for wood laths, as there is a greater area of laths in the latter (consequently less plaster) than in the former. To be fireproof, metal lathing should be entirely embedded in the mortar (on back as well as front), but it is very difficult to get plasterers to work carefully enough to bring this about.

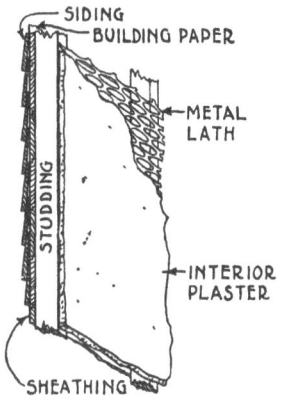

PLASTERING ON METAL LATHING.

Wood laths are satisfactory for exterior plaster if they are "half seasoned" (not too dry) and are not more than one inch wide. They should be laid at least $\frac{3}{4}$ inch apart. Metal lathing should always be of heaviest metal, galvanized or dipped in mineral paint to avoid future rusting. Both metal and wood laths are applied on wood furring strips nailed to the boarding of the house. Waterproof felt must be applied to the boarding underneath the lath and plaster to prevent moisture from entering through the walls, as cement plaster is not in itself waterproof unless made so by some special process.

382 SUCCESSFUL HOUSES AND HOW TO BUILD THEM

"Ingot iron" metal lathing is good for outside work, but as an additional precaution against rusting it is a good thing to have it galvanized or paint-dipped.

Ordinary plaster for inside work is composed of lime, water, sand, hair (or fiber), and plaster of Paris. All lime should be

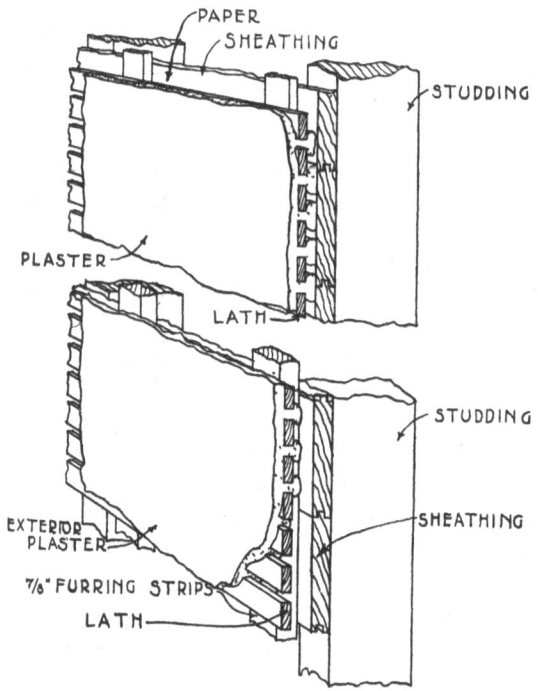

EXTERIOR PLASTERING ON WOOD LATHS.

well slaked, being mixed with water and allowed to stand from 24 hours to one week until it is thoroughly "cold." Blisters which sometimes appear in plastering, weeks after it is finished, are generally caused by lack of slaking, — the lime "popping" after it has been applied to the wall.

Sand used in plaster should be medium fine, clean, and sharp. That is, it should not be too coarse, and it should be free from loam or other foreign matter so that upon rubbing a handful between the hands, no dirt is evident. Sand taken from the bed of a lake or river is sometimes too smooth (not "sharp" enough), thus not offering sufficient bond with the lime. The best sand is screened, washed, and then dried.

To strengthen plaster, cattle hair or Manila fiber is mixed into it, or sometimes asbestos is used. Goat hair is better than cattle hair as it is of greater length.

There are several brands of "patent" plaster on the market, and most of them are excellent when hard walls are required. Keen's cement is used for ornamental plaster moldings and other work which is required to be extremely hard. Once set, it is almost as hard as stone.

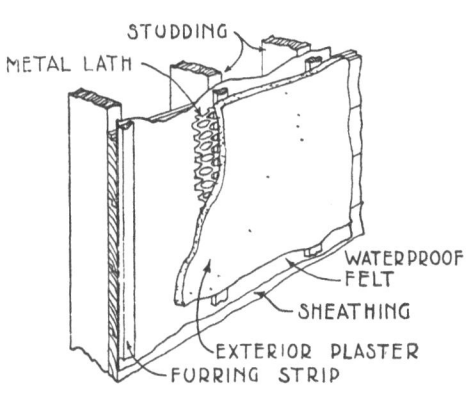

EXTERIOR PLASTERING ON METAL LATHING.

In preparing plaster for inside use about 1 part of lime paste (previously slaked lime) is used to 2 parts of sand. It is customary to mix the hair or fiber with the lime paste, first, — then add sand. The material is stacked up until wanted, after which water is added to each batch as it is needed, and the plaster is applied to walls and ceilings.

Before applying any plaster in the building, walls and ceilings should be examined to see if they are level and true in every particular. Grounds, usually $\frac{7}{8} \times \frac{7}{8}$ inch, are applied around all door and window openings and similar places, and the plastering is brought up to those grounds. Grounds of this size allow for $\frac{5}{8}$ inch of plaster on top of the lathing. Plaster is usually applied in three coats, consisting of the first ("scratch" coat), the second ("brown" coat), and the third ("skim" or "white" coat). The scratch coat consists of ordinary plaster applied to the laths in a layer about $\frac{1}{4}$ inch thick. As this is the coat which clings directly to the laths, the plaster must be firmly pushed against them so that much of it will flow between laths, forming a "key." The scratch coat is roughened or "scratched" with metal combs to provide a good bonding surface for the next coat. It hardens in about 2 to 4 days and should be nearly dry before applying the next. If too dry, the scratch coat should be dampened before the next plaster is applied.

The brown coat is of finer grained material than that used for the first coat. A little hair is sometimes added to it, and it is applied in a layer $\frac{1}{4}$ to $\frac{3}{8}$ inch thick. The exterior surface of this second coat should be floated to a true, even surface in order that it may be smooth enough to receive the final coat. At the time this coat is applied, it is customary to stick up any molded plaster work, all heavy projections of which should be thoroughly reënforced.

The final coat in 3-coat work may consist of smooth, rough sand, or hard finish, — whichever is preferred. Smooth finish is troweled hard to the surface of the brown coat, and it must be kept moist with water during its application. When rough sand finish is desired, the material composing the final coat is mixed with rough sand, and this is floated on the wall by means of a "carpet float" (block covered with a bit of carpet) which has the effect of tearing the surface of the plaster, slightly, giving it a rough sand finish.

When the final coat is to be "hard finish," plaster of Paris is used. It must be used quickly after mixing, as the material hardens very soon after it is applied to the wall.

Patent plaster is used a great deal for kitchens, servants' rooms, halls, and pantries. Most of it is bought ready mixed, including sand and fiber, so that all that is needed is water. It is more in the nature of cement than lime, and must be mixed fresh every hour, as it quickly sets when water is added. Laths should be thoroughly wet before patent plaster is applied. One of the best things about this material is that it is machine-mixed, and for this reason it is always the same, never varying in proportions in any particular. It also makes a much harder and firmer wall than ordinary plaster, and as but little water is used it dries out more quickly.

Plaster for the outside of houses is very different from inside plaster, composed as it is of lime, Portland cement, and sand in varying proportions.

Houses with cement-plastered exteriors though frequently of frame construction are practically masonry houses so far as exterior covering is concerned. Cement plaster hardens on the outside, producing an enduring, plastic outer covering that is wind proof, storm and cold proof; an overcoat that will prove dry, warm, and at the same time pleasing in appearance. With the exception of brick or stone, cement plaster properly applied is the most durable finish for the outside. A cement exterior applied to frame construction or hollow tile makes a warmer, drier house than brick or stone, as cement plaster is more impervious to moisture than both. Cement plaster and stucco have come to mean the same thing, so when one speaks of "stucco," cement plaster is usually meant. There is only one *right* way to cover the outside of a house with cement, and that is by applying cement plaster consisting of Portland cement, sand, hair (or fiber), and frequently on the last coat, crushed stone.

Cement plaster may be finished roughcast, or it can be given a pretty rough sand finish. The former is most durable. Roughcast properly put on hardens into a firm outer covering practically like stone. It is very enduring, and little checks (fine cracks) which may come later from shrinkage of the mortar are not visible in roughcast. Rough sand finish is made of cement and sand. Before the material sets hard it is roughed up slightly by the rotary motion of a "wood float" in the hands of the plasterer. This tears the surface and gives it a pretty, granular appearance. But cracks show quite badly in sand finish, as the grain of the plaster is not rough enough to conceal them. Owners building cement-plastered houses should know in advance that some fine cracks will certainly appear in the plaster after a few weeks. These are caused by the shrinkage of mortar while it dries. Such cracks in a well-plastered house are merely surface cracks. They do not impair the durability of the material, as they extend merely through the outer surface of the plaster skin.

A quite smooth surface is obtained by using stone crushed finer than usual. Coarser stone is used for a coarser surface.

Roughcast is usually applied in three coats. First, a scratch coat of cement, sand, and hair (or fiber). After this is dry a second coat of similar material is put on, and then a last coat of sand, cement, and crushed stone is put on as a finish. This last is "cast" on by throwing the mortar against the plaster previously applied. Many of the best kinds of roughcast come mixed ready for use when water has been added. Ready mixed cement plaster is particularly good because the ingredients are machine-mixed at the factory in careful proportions.

Smooth or sand finish is usually applied also in three coats, the final one being of coarse sand and cement instead of crushed stone.

White Paint and Green Shutters

CHAPTER XXII

FINISHING TOUCHES; PAINTING AND GLAZING

PAINT on the exterior of a house is for two purposes, — protection and appearance. The most successful paint accomplishes both, but often paint only accomplishes one purpose, in

IVORY-WHITE PAINTED TRIMMINGS ON A RED BRICK HOUSE.

many instances affording ample protection to the wood but producing an ugly result. In other cases paint is attractive to the eye, but is poor as a wood preservative.

The best paint for the outside of a house is composed of pure white lead (basic carbonate of lead) and raw, cold-pressed linseed oil. Several new paint combinations have been placed on the market, and some manufacturers have made great claims for their products, composed in many cases of ingredients other than white lead and linseed oil. As yet, however, nothing has

BROWN TRIMMINGS, GRAY PLASTER, WHITE SASH.

been found for exterior use to take the place of old-fashioned paint composed of lead and oil.

White lead is not pure white in color, as it has a slightly yellowish cast. It is better to use lead just as it comes from the keg, however, for all attempts to make paint look more white by mixing Prussian Blue with it are usually detrimental to the paint. Some painters mix zinc white with lead for exterior use,

FINISHING TOUCHES; PAINTING AND GLAZING

but this combination is rarely practical, as zinc white has a tendency to crack unless an unusual amount of linseed oil is used with it and it is applied with extraordinary care, — rather beyond the skill of the average painter.

Outside paint frequently fails for several reasons. First, — pure lead and oil are not used, frequently cheaper substitutes

GREEN STAIN ON SHINGLES AND ROUGH-SAWED TRIM.

being mixed into the paint to save on the cost of material and labor. Second, — the paint is not properly applied, painters slighting the work in order to finish it as quickly as possible. Third, — the woodwork is not dry enough to receive the paint.

The best safeguard in securing the right kind of paint is to use only some well-known brand of white lead, employing a painter who, using the best grade of cold pressed linseed oil, will mix the material faithfully. Many painters do not use enough oil with their paint. From 5 to 7 gallons of oil should be used to every 100 pounds of lead. Lead and oil should be thoroughly mixed, and after mixing, the paint should be allowed to stand for 24 hours, after which it should be strained. A small quantity of drier (Japan) may be used to hasten the drying of the paint, but too much of the latter spoils it; only a slight proportion should be permitted.

In applying paint to the exterior surfaces of a house it should not be laid on too thick. Thick paint soon dries out, when it will begin to scale and crack. Four thin coats are much better than two thick coats, and every coat should be well brushed out into the wood instead of applying it in thick layers. Three coats are usually provided for new houses.

Hard, glossy paint is not durable, for it soon cracks and scales. It is much preferable that paint shall become chalky as it grows old, instead of becoming glossy and brittle, for when new paint is applied to old chalky paint the new permeates the old, going right through it to the wood itself, thus binding new and old into one enduring film of paint. This is the effect desired when painting an old house. When the original paint on the house has become hard and glossy, new paint applied merely forms a plating on the outside of the old paint, and the latter, as it scales or chips off, carries the new paint with it.

Outside paint should be applied in dry weather, only. Even a moderate amount of dampness in woodwork will prevent paint from entering the pores. Undoubtedly the best time is during the pleasant days of early spring when the weather is mildly warm and sunny (before the insects come); or in the fall, after insects have disappeared again. Dust, insects, and rain are three things to contend with.

All outside work on the house should be primed immediately after it is put in place, choosing dry weather in which to do the work. Any knots appearing should be shellaced before the

FINISHING TOUCHES; PAINTING AND GLAZING 393

woodwork is primed, to prevent pitch from staining through the paint, later.

In applying the first (priming) coat of paint to new woodwork, the brush should be drawn parallel to the grain of the wood. On the final coat, paint should be drawn along with the brush from corner to corner or window to window, no spots being allowed to dry until brushed into the next wet paint, so each day's work will be finished at a corner. This is necessary to prevent streaks showing where the paint applied one day has dried before the next section applied on a subsequent day has been painted.

In applying paint the painter should pick out all loose hairs left by his brush as he goes along. Any grains of dust, or insects, should be scraped off with the putty knife.

Mineral paint is considered better for metal work than lead and oil paint. What is known as "red lead" is chiefly used for this purpose (on the first coat only), after which subsequent coats are of lead and oil like that applied to woodwork. On a tin roof the tin should always be painted one coat on the under side before it is applied to the roof. The upper surface of the tin roof should be carefully cleaned of all rosin spots, dirt, etc., and immediately painted. It should be bone-dry when the paint is applied.

The approved paints for tin are metallic brown, Venetian red, red oxide, and red lead mixed with pure linseed oil. Slow-drying paint is desirable, so little or no patent drier or turpentine should be used. All coats of paint should be applied with a hand brush and well rubbed on. Apply the second coat two weeks after the first. The third coat should be applied one year later. The roof can then go for four or five years or more before further painting is necessary. If the roof is steep, so that the surface is washed clean with every rain, painting will be necessary only at long intervals.

All nail holes in exterior woodwork should be puttied after

the priming coat of paint has been applied. Putty applied to bare woodwork quickly dries out and drops off. All sawdust or dirt left on new woodwork should be carefully brushed off by the painters before paint is applied.

Colors for exterior paint are largely a matter of taste. In light, sunny locations darker, heavier colors can be used, and in dark locations colors should be more bright and cheery. The architectural style of a house also frequently influences its color. For instance, Colonial houses are usually white or light yellow, with bronze-green blinds; houses with English timber work are often golden brown or bronze green, — and so on.

Houses with plaster exteriors are not usually painted, — that is, the plaster itself is not painted. Some owners prefer to paint their outside plastering, however, and when this is done ordinary lead and oil paint should not be used, as it does not adhere properly to the cement, soon peeling off.

Paint for outside plaster walls must be of peculiar consistency. It should have enough oil to bind it and make a durable surface, keeping out dampness. At the same time such paint must allow dampness (always present in a plaster wall) to work out from inside. This seems almost an impossibility, but it has been made possible by several brands of paint made specially for plaster houses.

Shingles on side walls or roof may be painted or stained, the latter being the most practical. Stain, applied to rough-sawed surfaces like shingles, soaks into the wood instead of forming a skin on the outside, greatly increasing its life. The best shingle stains come ready-made, and only well-known, reliable brands should be used.

The best shingle stains contain a large amount of preservative, such as creosote or other oil, to which is added the right proportion of finely ground colors, with the proper amount of fixative oil to make the colors durable.

Artistic effects can be obtained by the use of stain, — effects

FINISHING TOUCHES; PAINTING AND GLAZING 395

impossible to get in any other way, for stain permeates the grain of the wood in a way not possible with paint, producing a varying degree of light and shade very attractive. The material is applied with a brush, after the shingles are laid, or shingles can be dipped before they are laid, the latter making the shingles more durable. The following table, showing the amount of stain required, will be found of use: —

AMOUNT OF STAIN REQUIRED (FOR BRUSH COATING SAWED CEDAR SHINGLES)

Number of Coats	Square Feet of Surface	Amount (in Gallons)
1 Brush Coat	150	1
2 Brush Coats	100	1

FOR DIPPING (⅔ Length of each Shingle)

$2\frac{1}{2}$ to 3 gallons of stain required per 1000 shingles.
Add ½ gallon for brush coat applied after dipped shingles are laid.

Frequently the exterior wooden trimmings of a house are stained instead of painted. When this is desired, the trimmings should be rough-sawed instead of smooth, as smooth wood does not take the stain so well as rough wood.

Inside the house, hardwood trim and floors should be filled as soon as the woodwork is in place. Interior work which is to be painted (not stained, shellaced, or varnished) should be primed immediately after it is put up.

Paint for inside woodwork should be composed of pure white lead and linseed oil, but a percentage of zinc white mixed with it gives that agreeable white shade so desirable in white paint. Zinc white is very enduring when used for inside work.

The most practical white paint for inside woodwork is white enamel paint. An inexpensive and fairly good job can be obtained with one coat of white oil paint followed by two more coats of enamel paint. This will leave the wood with a moderate luster. The best enamel jobs require two coats of white oil paint, finished with two to five more coats of enamel. This produces paint almost as hard as tile and quite as durable. Of course each coat should be thoroughly dry, rubbed before the

GOLDEN-BROWN SHINGLE STAIN WITH WHITE TRIMMINGS.

next coat is applied, and only reliable brands should be used If it is desired to have the final coat dull finish instead of glossy "egg-shell" finish should be used.

Hardwood which is to be stained or left "natural" is generally "filled" first, then stained, shellaced, waxed, or varnished. On oak a pretty effect can be obtained by leaving out the filler, using merely a coat of stain followed by wax, shellac, or varnish.

FINISHING TOUCHES; PAINTING AND GLAZING 397

Oak floors, however, should always be filled in order to prevent dirt from entering the pores of the wood.

One coat of stain and two coats of shellac, rubbed between coats, make a very good finish, though an extra coat of shellac will produce a more permanent finish. Instead of shellac, varnish can be used in the same way.

BROWN-FACE BRICK, ORANGE-YELLOW TINTED CEILING, NUT-BROWN OAK WOODWORK.

When varnish is used, get only a well known brand made by a reliable manufacturer; employ only skilled men in applying varnish, for poor work is certain to be the result if inferior varnish is used or if the material is not correctly applied.

Paint used for interior plaster walls is usually what is known as "kalsomine." Many efficient brands of ready prepared paint for plaster work are on the market, and almost any shade can be obtained. Most paints for plaster contain a proportion of glue mixed with the color. Any painter can mix his own kalsomine. Glue should always be used as a binder.

Plaster walls are frequently covered with canvas (a coarse material something like cheesecloth), glued to the wall like wall paper. This makes an excellent surface for the ordinary oil paints used. Three coats are usually required to cover canvas, though plaster, tinted directly, requires but one coat of kalsomine. When kalsomine is used, however, it is a good idea to cover the plaster with a preliminary coat of oil or glue sizing, which fills the pores of the plaster and prevents the kalsomine from sinking into the wall in spots. Walls covered with canvas, painted, are more durable than walls covered merely with kalsomine.

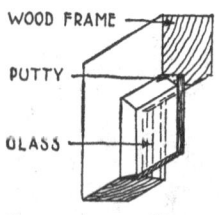

GLASS SET IN PUTTY, FOR SASH.

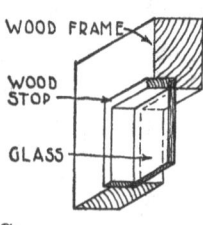

GLASS SET WITH WOODEN STOPS, FOR DOORS.

Color is an important part of the inside painting problem, and great care should be used in selecting the shade for inside trim. Light, fumed finishes are always attractive for oak. This process seems to bring out the grain, and it takes on a beautiful, soft half tone. A deeper shade of brown is attractive, also.

Probably the least pleasing colors of all are dark brown, blackish, and greenish finishes, colors which are apt to appear gloomy, whereas lighter finishes give a cheerful cast to any room.

In a living room or dining room it is better to have each piece of furniture finished alike; when the trim is finished to match the furniture (or *vice versa*) the utmost in beautiful effect is obtained. A living room in which furniture and trim are the same color has a restful, peaceful air, always a delight to every one lucky enough to live there. It is well to note, however, that mahogany furniture is charming with white trim.

Glazing is usually part of the painting contract. The following schedule, showing the various kinds of glass, will be useful: —

SCHEDULE OF GLASS

Sheet Glass. — Ordinary blown glass in which the glass during manufacture is blown out in cylinders, after which the cylinders are cut and flattened out. Such glass breaks easily, and shows imperfections, but it is used for small lights where inexpensive glass is desired.

Double-strength Glass. — Hand-made or machine-made, used for large lights where something cheaper than plate glass is desired. The handmade glass contains a less number of defects, and costs more than machine-made.

"A" Grade Sheet Glass. — Is the grade most used for houses when plate glass is not used. It has, however, many imperfections of a minor nature.

"B" Grade Sheet Glass. — Is an inferior grade used only for factories and greenhouses.

Plate Glass. — May be "cast" or "rolled." Unlike sheet glass, plate glass is poured out on a flat surface when in a molten state, and rolled to a uniform thickness. It is free from defects, and is, consequently, to be preferred, though it is much more expensive than sheet glass.

Polished Plate Glass. — Is plate glass put through a further process by which it is polished to a true surface. This grade is used largely for mirrors.

Cleaning Walls with a Vacuum Cleaner

CHAPTER XXIII

USEFUL APPARATUS AND APPLIANCES

THIS chapter is devoted to special apparatus of all kinds, for making housekeeping easier. The modern house involves a somewhat complex system of processes, and when one considers the many departments to be accommodated it is not surprising to find a large number of details entering into the construction and operation of even the smallest houses. Americans demand every device which makes for more convenient housekeeping, and that is one reason why the various details of plumbing, heating, ventilating, and mechanical cleaning have been developed to such a high state of efficiency. The American idea is to make each house as automatically complete as possible, and that is a very worthy ideal to strive for.

Some of the apparatus described in this chapter is adaptable only for the largest houses where funds permit a more generous expenditure than is usually the case in small houses, though there are many little mechanical devices desirable for the latter as well. The houseowner should remember, however, that it will be well for him to consider carefully, not to say cautiously, his mechanical needs before he invests in, — for instance, an automatic gas water-warming apparatus, — or before he decides to buy an electric soft-water compression tank, — for modern apparatus of efficiency is certainly not cheap. Before he knows it the owner of a house might have a considerable financial load upon his shoulders. Nevertheless, there are many clever devices that are necessities in large houses and by no means mere luxuries in small houses, and the houseowner will do well to inform himself about them.

Compression Tanks. — Of the most necessary apparatus for a country house where there is no city water supply can be mentioned the compression tank, which is largely taking the place of windmill and high tank. The latter continues in use chiefly on farms, though farmers themselves are also installing the more modern compression tank systems.

On the country place or farm the ordinary windmill water-supply installation consists of a wood or steel tower with windmill at the top, erected above a well from which water is pumped into a tank located in the tower or on the top floor of the house or other building. Water flows from the tank by gravity to the various fixtures. Of course, windmills are efficient and cheap means of forcing water into the house, but an objection to them is that the tower is unsightly, and when the tank is located in a tower, water freezes in cold weather.

An improvement over the windmill is the modern compression tank, consisting of a cylindrical tank composed of steel plates riveted together, with a hand or power pump attached. When such a system is used, no tank is required in the attic, as the one compression tank is all that is necessary, water flowing from it under pressure to the various fixtures even to the upper floors. The way this is brought about is as follows: A hand pump or power pump (electric or gas engine) draws water from the well and forces it into the air-tight tank. Continued pumping of water into the tank compresses the air at one end so that considerable pressure is obtained. Pipes extend from the tank to fixtures throughout the house, and opening a faucet releases a stream of water of high pressure (when the tank is well filled) or low pressure when the tank is less full.

With a hand pump the process of pumping water into the compression tank is not, of course, automatic, for some one must pump the tank full periodically to maintain the pressure. This becomes necessary once each day or every two or three days, according to the capacity of the tank and amount of water consumption. Hand pumps are made in patterns which will secure maximum suction at minimum exertion, so the process of filling the tank is not unduly wearying.

With a power pump connected to the pressure tank (by far the wisest procedure in most cases) an installation more or less automatic is secured. When there is electric current to be had an electric pump will be found the most convenient, — automatically controlled by a switch which starts the pump when pressure in the tank falls below a certain point, and stops it when pressure rises above a certain point. This pressure point is fixed at any rate desired. Thus, with an electric pump installation, constant pressure is automatically maintained and water is on tap at all fixtures, as in city houses.

When a gas engine is used for power, the process is not automatic, for no method to automatically start a gas engine has yet been devised. Gas engines are used a great deal in the country for pressure tank installations, however, and they are found to be very convenient. With a large-sized tank it is only necessary to run the engine a few hours every two or three days, — not at all an inconvenience.

Most compression tanks and connecting pumps are installed in the basement of the house, though in the country many are placed in outbuildings. Not too far from the well is the best location, whether in the basement or in a separate building, and it is excellent practice to have the pump so low down (as when in the basement) that water can flow by gravity from well to pump instead of requiring the pump to lift the water up to its level. All compression tanks of the best pattern have an automatic air-intake valve which admits air as well as water, so as to maintain an "air cushion" within the tank and provide sufficient pressure. When water is not drawn from a tank for some days, the compressed air inside is apt to lower in pressure by reason of water taking up some of it, and it is to obviate this trouble that an air-intake valve is installed.

Air Compressor. — Since the compression water tank system was invented, another system has been evolved which does away with the combination air-water tank altogether. In this system an air compressor is located in the basement of the house or in an outbuilding, and the pumping apparatus is located right at the well. Thus water is forced as wanted, directly from the well to fixtures instead of being stored in a compression tank. The air compressor in these systems is usually operated by power (electric or gas engine), air being compressed until high pressure is obtained, and this compressed air being forced through a pipe to the apparatus in the well. At the well is a sort of hydraulic ram or injector which, so long as the air pressure is sufficient, delivers water under satisfactory pressure to the house fixtures. When an electric air compressor is used the entire process is automatic, but when a gas engine is used the process is voluntary, the engine being run for a few hours several times a week, according to the capacity of the outfit and amount of water required.

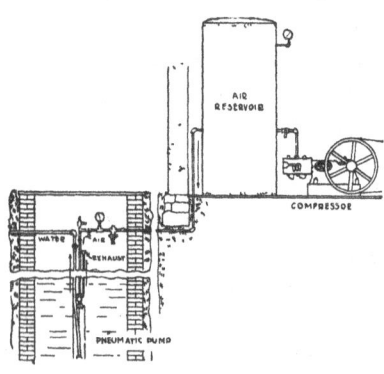

Complete Pneumatic Water-supply System.

Instantaneous Gas Heaters. — Automatic water-warming apparatus for delivering hot water to the various fixtures has recently been developed, and it will be well for us to examine some of the different methods of heating water, voluntarily and automatically. In another chapter the ordinary coal heater used for warming water is described, and all matter pertaining to the range boiler is discussed in detail. In this chapter we will devote a little space to a brief description of water-heating apparatus in which gas is used as fuel.

Of gas water-heating apparatus, the "instantaneous heater" was one of the first devices, and it continues to be used in many houses throughout the country.

In an instantaneous heater cold water flows slowly through a coil of pipe (usually of brass, bronze, copper, or other conductive metal) which comes in contact with a gas flame. After cold water is turned on and the gas burner is lighted, hot water flows almost instantly from the heater. Thus cold water entering one end of the coil, comes out hot at the other end. A very practical place to put the instantaneous heater is in the bathroom against the wall, arranged so that one end of the hot-water flow pipe extends over bathtub and washbowl. To operate this type of heater a pilot light at the side is lighted, and by means of a handle is swung into position over the burner which it ignites. Water is not maintained hot constantly, but is heated only when wanted. When a gas apparatus of this sort is used in the bathroom (or any other room, in fact) a flue should be connected with the combustion chamber to conduct poisonous vapors from the gas flame to the outside air. Persons have been asphyxiated by shutting themselves up in a small room in which an unventilated gas apparatus was burning. Ventilation is easily accomplished by extending a small galvanized iron or nickel-plated tube from the gas combustion chamber to a chimney. If there is no chimney, ordinary galvanized iron spouting such as is used to carry water from the roof to the ground, can extend up through a partition, and project above the roof. There is very little heat from a gas flame after it has been used for heating water in a coil, the only thing necessary being to carry off poisonous gases. However, it is customary to wrap such a ventilating pipe, when it extends

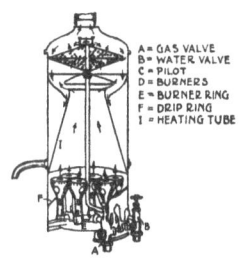

INSTANTANEOUS GAS HOT-WATER HEATER.

through a partition, with asbestos paper, and all joints should be soldered tight.

Ordinary Gas Heaters. — For maintaining hot water constantly or periodically, whichever desired, there are many patterns of gas heaters. Some are designed to be directly connected to the range boiler, in which case the boiler has a hollow chamber, to hold pipe coil and gas burner. Other forms of heater are located in the basement independently of the range boiler. With the latter, a gas flame of moderate size burning all the time will maintain a constant supply of hot water, and where gas rates are not too high it will be found that the cost of fuel is frequently less than the cost of coal in a coal heater. For those who prefer to heat water only as wanted, the same apparatus can be recommended, the flame being lighted only when water is needed. When the boiler is piped as recommended in the chapter describing "range boilers," water is heated at the top of the tank first, and it is not necessary to warm the entire tankful to get water for a bath.

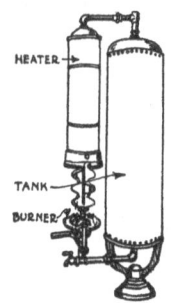

SMALL GAS HEATER ATTACHED TO THE RANGE BOILER.

Automatic Gas Heaters. — Latest types of gas water-warming apparatus are clever, automatic devices for maintaining a constant supply of hot water without burning a full head of gas at all times. They are really a development of the instantaneous heater, with an automatic device added for lighting the burners, so that the mere opening of a faucet at any one of the fixtures turns on gas and heats the water. Automatic gas heaters are usually located in the basement or kitchen. The apparatus consists of a coil of pipe through which water enters cold at one end

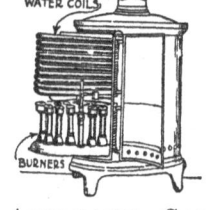

AUTOMATIC GAS HEATER FOR 24-HOUR HOT-WATER SERVICE.

and comes out hot at the other, flowing through pipes to the different fixtures. Under the pipe coil are gas burners, automatically turned off when no hot water is being used. When a faucet — say at the kitchen sink — is opened, however, the release of pressure at that point opens the gas valve, admitting gas to the burners which are ignited by the ever burning pilot light, instantly blazing up to full power, heating water of any amount wanted. When the faucet is closed again, the gas valve automatically shuts off, and only the pilot light is left burning.

Automatic apparatus of this kind is a great convenience, though it will be found expensive to operate, unless reasonable care is exercised in the use of hot water. Before installing one it is well to get some sort of approximate estimate as to the amount of gas consumed per month, by estimating the amount of hot water required. Of course, an automatic gas heater will prove economical when gas rates are not too high, if hot water is not used extravagantly. The tendency, however, is to use hot water lavishly when it is always on tap, so owners who install an automatic heater should caution members of their family against wasteful use of hot water.

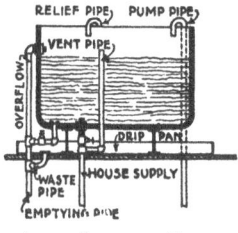

ATTIC STORAGE TANK.

Soft-water System. — In many cities and towns where artesian well water is used for the city water supply instead of river, reservoir, or lake water, it is sometimes necessary to install a separate softwater system for laundry and bath, the artesian water being too hard for these purposes. The ordinary method is to install a steel, galvanized iron, or wooden tank in the attic to which soft water is pumped by a hand or power pump. This necessity for a soft-water supply in the house has occasioned many clever devices, more or less automatic. In the first place, there are the hand pumps used (without the attic tank) when soft water is wanted merely at the laundry tubs in the basement. The most simple of these is the ordinary cast-iron pump at-

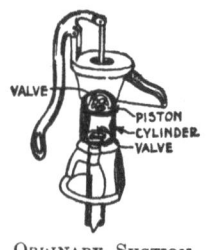

ORDINARY SUCTION PUMP.

tached to the side of one of the tubs, and by means of which soft water can be pumped into the tubs as wanted. An improvement over this ordinary pump is the "double-lift" pump which delivers more water at faster speed than the old-fashioned suction pump. In all hand installations it is a good plan to locate the soft-water cistern (usually in the ground, outside the house) high enough so that water will flow to the suction pipe of the pump by force of gravity, thus eliminating much of the "pull" on the pump.

For elevating soft water from a cistern to fixtures on the upper floors of the house, an ordinary compression tank system can be used, precisely like that used for a main water supply, or if preferred, an attic tank system may be used, in which water is pumped by hand or power up to a tank in the attic, from which it flows by gravity to the different fixtures. When an attic tank is used it should have an overflow piped back into the soft-

water cistern, so that when the tank is too full, excess of water will run back to the cistern. Most pumps used to elevate water to the attic are power pumps, operated by water power from the city mains, or by an electric or gas engine.

Pumps operated by water power have been brought to a high state of efficiency and can be made to operate on almost any pressure, from 20 pounds to 60 pounds or more. Such pumps work

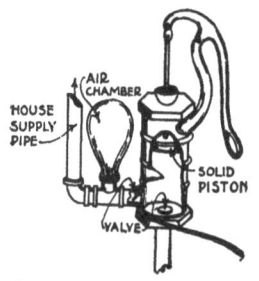

IMPROVED SUCTION AND LIFT PUMP.

automatically; when soft water is drawn from a fixture the release of pressure turns city water into the pump, causing it to operate. Thus a constant supply of soft water is maintained, the attic tank being replenished as fast as water is used.

As an auxiliary to the attic tank some systems use a compression tank, water being forced by the pump into the compression tank, from which it flows to the attic tank. In other systems the attic tank is omitted, a pressure tank being arranged to discharge directly into the supply pipes as in any other compression system, excepting that the pump is operated by the city water supply instead of electricity or a gas engine.

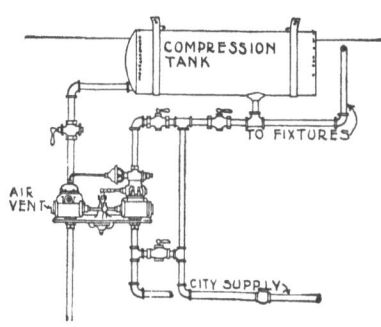

WATER FORCED INTO COMPRESSION TANK BY CITY PRESSURE.

Systems having a pressure tank are usually more economical than systems pumping into an attic tank, for in the former compressed air does some of the work, and less city water is necessary. When one's city supply is "metered," as it is in most cities and towns, water rates are frequently too high to operate a water lift economically, and the compression system, either entire or as auxiliary to an ordinary system, is desirable to decrease expense.

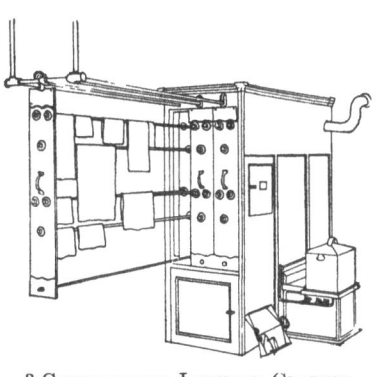

3-COMPARTMENT LAUNDRY CLOTHES DRIER.

Laundry Clothes Drier. — For the laundry there are many desirable devices to reduce labor and turn out work at less cost.

Laundry clothes driers are used in many houses, for housekeepers are coming to see their many advantages. With a laundry drier, one is not dependent upon the weather, for every wash day is sure to be a good "drying day," rain or shine. The drier may be briefly described as a group of narrow galvanized iron compartments (each about 7 feet long and 7 feet high) hung to tracks overhead, so that one compartment may be drawn out independently of any other. Inside these compartments are rods for hanging clothes. When the compartments are all in place a complete, air-tight cabinet is the result. Heat for drying the clothes is furnished by a stove placed beside the drier, from which flues cause hot fresh air to circulate through the drier. Fuel is usually coal, wood, or gas (sometimes electricity is used), and the same stove is used also for heating irons and for other laundry purposes.

Laundry Mangle. — In families where a comparatively large amount of "flat work" is to be ironed, it is a good plan to install a mangle (ironing machine), bearing in mind that it will iron only flat pieces such as tablecloths, sheets, pillowcases, towels, and napkins. Machines cannot be used for any starched articles. Small ironers, using hand or electric power, may be had, and they can be recommended for those families where the best obtainable laundry equipment is desired. The cost is not great, and it is offset by the saving in time and consequent decrease in the amount paid to a laundress.

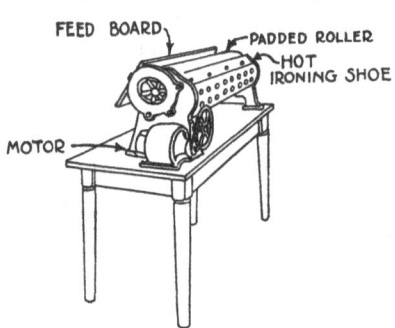

ELECTRIC IRONING MACHINE.

Laundry Washing Machine. — If a washing machine is merely a luxury, why install one in the house? The answer is: a washing machine is no longer considered a luxury where true economy is practiced — economy of wear and tear, time and labor. As a matter of fact, the washing machine, which may cost no more than a sewing machine, is quite as useful. It will minimize labor expenditure and maximize convenience. Some washing machines are hand machines, especially designed to be easily operated and to wash the clothes clean in the shortest time. Hand scrubbing cannot compete with a good pattern of hand machine.

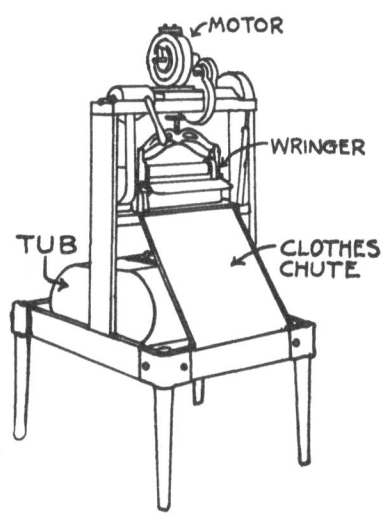

ELECTRIC WASHING AND WRINGING MACHINE.

Power machines are most convenient of all, and they are economical in operation. To run these, some use water power by means of a little water motor attached to the faucet. Others use electric motors. Of electric machines the "oscillating" type is one of the best, in which clothes are washed by the violent rocking, back and forth, of the tub. A wringer is attached to the shaft. Two cents' worth of power is all that is required to do the washing of a family of ten, and the time consumed is just half a day. Everything that can be washed by hand can be washed by machine, with less labor and, quite often, with very much better results.

Vacuum Cleaner. — Vacuum cleaners have done as much to simplify housekeeping as anything ever introduced. Brooms, dusters, mops, and pails seem relics of olden times, for it is really true that vacuum cleaners actually clean, though a glance at the simple machine makes it appear almost impossible.

The vacuum cleaning idea is this: first, it is better to take *all* the dirt out of the rooms than merely to dislodge it from one

Electric Vacuum Cleaner installed in Basement.

place to another; second, once you have got the dirt out of your house it is easier to *keep it out* than it is to allow it to accumulate. Make up your mind it will be hard work the first time the house is cleaned with a vacuum cleaner. If it has never been cleaned this way before, the chances are, no matter how carefully the

USEFUL APPARATUS AND APPLIANCES 413

house has been kept, it has never before been thoroughly cleaned. No amount of sweeping and dusting can do the work of vacuum cleaning, so during this first vacuum crusade you will be gathering up the dust of ages from little corners never noticed before. This takes time, and is no easy job, but once the house is cleaned it can be kept so with a minimum of effort.

Many new houses are now equipped with vacuum cleaners in the basement quite as a matter of course. The apparatus is included in the building contract just as the heater is, — and the laundry wash trays. Even if one does not intend to put a permanent cleaning installation in when the house is first built, it is well to pipe for it. This only costs from ten to fifteen dollars.

It is easier to clean with the tools of a basement-installed cleaner than with a portable vacuum cleaner, for one does not have to drag a machine around from room to room and up over the stairs. You simply connect the hose to the valve on one of two or three locations on each floor, turn the switch, and clean. The apparatus in the basement can be run by electric power or a gasoline engine. Even in a large house you need use the apparatus but once a week; in a small house once in two weeks may do.

Portable vacuum cleaners are remarkably efficient and not too heavy to preclude their successful manipulation. The better designs have handles to carry them by, and long electric cables to be attached to the ordinary light sockets in any room. When buying an electric-driven portable cleaner, one should find out from the local electric company whether the current is alternating or direct, for on the best machines motors are not universal;

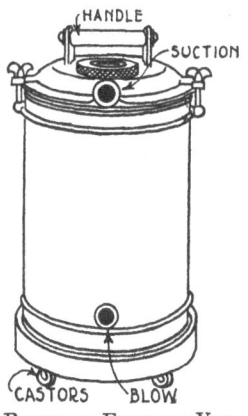

PORTABLE ELECTRIC VACUUM CLEANER.

414 SUCCESSFUL HOUSES AND HOW TO BUILD THEM

an alternating current motor cannot be used on direct current, and *vice versa*.

Some of the successful portable machines consist of a cylindrical metal case about the size of a five-gallon can. The machine is on casters so it may be easily trundled over the floor, or it may be carried by the handles provided for that purpose. In this type of machine the motor and rotary pump is at the bottom of the case, with the dust bag at the top. When a switch is turned the motor operates the pump, which creates a strong suction, and the dirt from your carpet is sucked into the dust bag. After the bag becomes filled with dirt, it is emptied and replaced. Another good model looks like a carpet-sweeper and has a rotary brush in addition to the suction apparatus. All vacuum cleaners are plentifully supplied with tools for every purpose imaginable.

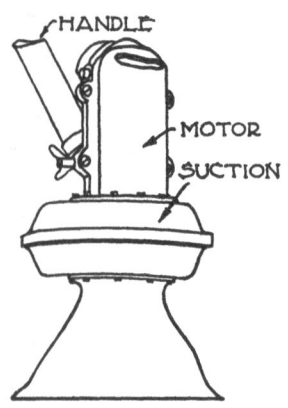

SMALL ELECTRIC CLEANER.

House Electric Plants. — Separate plants for generating electricity for light, heat, and power have now come so prominently into the house equipment field that it will be well to note some of the details of these plants here. Electric lights throughout the house and on the grounds are now possible in any section of the country.

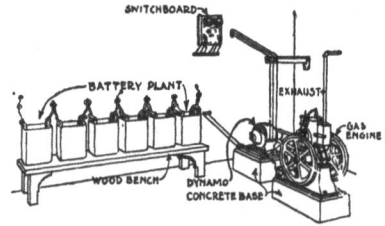

ELECTRIC LIGHT AND POWER PLANT FOR THE HOUSE.

Manufacturers of electrical apparatus have combined the various units of machinery required for simple, easily installed, economically operated country lighting plants.

USEFUL APPARATUS AND APPLIANCES 415

The first cost is not excessive, and the expense of operating one's own electric plant is little. Your house, grounds, and out-buildings may be efficiently lighted whether you live in town or not.

The storage battery has greatly forwarded house-lighting plants. A battery of a few cells, with a small engine, dynamo, and switchboard constitute the entire machinery of the producing plant, and wiring and lamps are located wherever light is wanted. You may place the machinery anywhere, — down cellar, in the barn or garage, or in a separate little building at any convenient distance from the house. A dry place should be chosen, of course, and a window or two must be put in for light and ventilation. All wiring throughout house and grounds can be concealed by running it in conduits, — waterproof for outside work, ordinary for inside work.

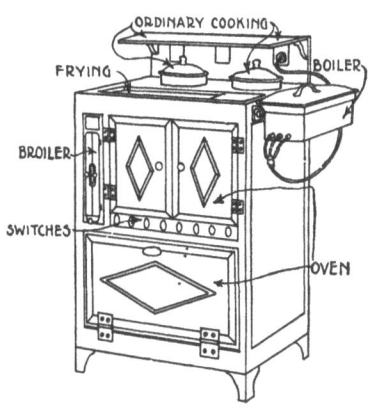

ELECTRIC KITCHEN RANGE.

Three types of engine are used for driving the dynamo, — gasoline, kerosene, and hot-air engines.

Of gasoline engines, you can have an air-cooled engine or one water-cooled. Two cycle and four cycle types are used, varying from 1 to 4 horse power according to the extent of the system. Every automobile owner is familiar with these, and any man will find them easy to operate. With a good system properly installed, troubles are practically eliminated.

Small electric light plants will furnish current for 50 lights, operating day and night if wanted. With gasoline at 16 cents per gallon and a consumption of $1\frac{1}{4}$ pints per horse power hour, cost of a 16-candle-power 20-watt Tungsten lamp is about $\frac{1}{10}$ of a cent an hour. At this rate it costs 5 cents an hour for fifty lights. Of course one would rarely burn more than half or quarter of that number at one time.

House-lighting plants are low voltage plants, and that is the secret of low cost of production. Voltage on a 15-light plant runs only about 13 volts, and a 50-light plant requires not more than 30 volts. Economy is secured because the engine need be operated but part of the time, feeding current from the dynamo into a storage battery which collects and afterwards gives out the energy. Plants are arranged in several ways according to the desire of the houseowner. For instance, you can feed current into the battery and afterwards get light and power entirely from the battery, or you can have light and power from both the battery and the dynamo at the same time. The entire operation is automatic.

Any reliable engine will run the home electric plant, but some are better fitted than others. All dealers in electric apparatus know the best engine to use for any particular place. Your choice of engines should be influenced by cost of fuel in your locality, and desirability of any particular type for the work required.

House Gas Plants. — The gas-lighting system is all very easy to plan when your house is in town where the municipal gas system can be connected, but what of a house built in the country, far away from town conveniences? Country house gas lighting is entirely practical. Small individual plants can be installed on the country place at moderate cost, furnishing gas all over the house, and excellent gas, too, at even lower rates than it costs in town. So there is no reason why the country houseowner and his family should be deprived of this lighting and heating medium any more than the city dweller.

When you first mention gas plants to houseowners, so many

USEFUL APPARATUS AND APPLIANCES 417

of them ask, "Are they safe?" This is a very natural question, for almost every one has heard of at least one instance where an individual gas plant exploded, causing damage to life and property. To any one who will take time to investigate various types of modern gas machines, however, it is apparent that modern apparatus of the best type is convenient, economical, and perfectly safe when operated intelligently. Old-fashioned machines have been wonderfully improved upon. Machines of

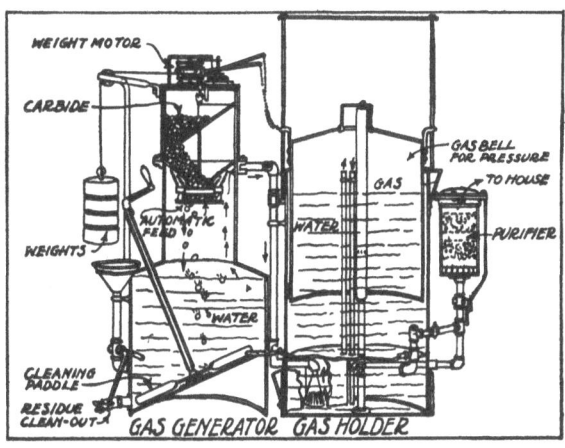

ACETYLENE GAS PLANT.

the latest and best type are heavily built to stand the wear required, and every precaution has been taken to make them safe, — and safe they are when under the care of persons of even ordinary intelligence.

No person not on suicide bent would think of turning on gas in a room tightly closed, allowing it to collect for a number of hours, and then suddenly enter that room with a lighted candle, — but this and similar incidents have happened with a gas machine, and most accidents can be traced back to gross carelessness, ignoring the most simple and explicit rules sent with

2 E

every gas machine. For instance, one man opened up his gas machine and thrust a candle down inside to see how it was working. He found out — but it cost him more than the information was worth. Another man found the water seal of the gas holder frozen and undertook to thaw it out with a red-hot poker. Think of it — a man of intelligence! He might just as well have dropped the poker into a powder barrel.

Generally speaking, there are three systems of gas supply for country places (acetylene gas, gasoline gas, and "bottled" gas), and manufacturers have brought their apparatus up to a high state of efficiency. Acetylene gas machines in many cases consist of a generator and a gas holder, the latter containing gas after it is generated. The generator is a steel tank holding water into which carbide crystals are dropped slowly and automatically, piece by piece. When carbide drops into the water, gas is generated which rises to the top of the gas chamber and then flows through pipes into the gas holder, where it is purified. Every process in the best gas machine is automatic save only that the hopper must be filled with carbide (about once a month) at which time the clockwork mechanism is wound (operating the feeding device) and the residue is cleaned out — an amount of work consuming about a half hour of time. Old-fashioned machines fed carbide regulated by gas pressure, but such methods are dangerous. On latest machines the carbide feed is regulated by a clockwork motor entirely independent of the pressure of the gas. To relieve machines of excessive pressure, a safety blow-off valve allows any excess of gas to escape automatically to the outside air through a blow-off pipe. The gas-making process is entirely automatic, a machine stopping when burners are turned off and starting up again when a jet is lighted, making just enough gas to supply the number of burners in operation. Carbide costing about $4 per hundredweight can be purchased at any agency, of which there are hundreds scattered throughout the United States, and the average lighting cost for a house is

$12 per year. Acetylene gas is excellent for lighting purposes, and by means of an improved burner it is now practical for cooking; the entire acetylene apparatus can be placed in the basement or in a separate outbuilding.

Another gas-making process which has been brought to a high state of efficiency is gasoline gas, — an economical gas, excellent for heating and lighting. Gasoline gas is generated in a carburetor usually placed underground at some distance from the house. The carburetor is a tank containing the gaso-

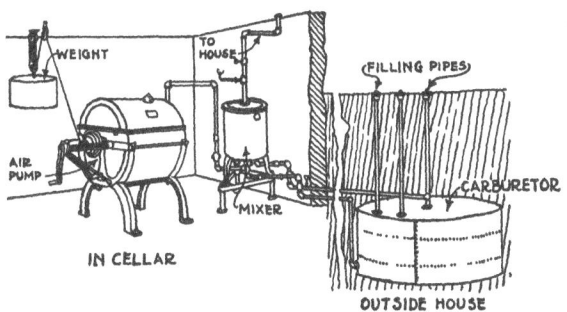

APPARATUS FOR GENERATING GASOLINE GAS.

line supply, and this is the reason why it is located away from the house, as all supplies of gasoline should be. In one of these systems air under pressure (furnished by an air compressor worked by water pressure, windmill, hand pump, or gasoline engine) enters the carburetor where it becomes impregnated with gasoline, thus forming gasoline gas. From the carburetor, gas passes to the governor in the basement of the house, where the pressure is automatically regulated so that gas is made and supplied just sufficient for the number of burners in operation. Operators of this form of gas machine need only occasionally fill the carburetor with gasoline when the supply gets low. Other forms of gasoline gas machines are built on the same principle, but the air pressure is maintained by a revolving drum (a pump, in effect) operated by weights which are wound up about once in 24 hours. Neglect to wind the machine does no harm; simply, the lights gradually grow dimmer, until finally they go out unless the machine is wound up. Of course, once a machine has run down care must be taken that all jets are closed before the machine is started again.

Other types of gasoline gas machines suitable for cottages and small houses require such a small supply of gasoline that the entire apparatus is placed in the cellar or in the kitchen.

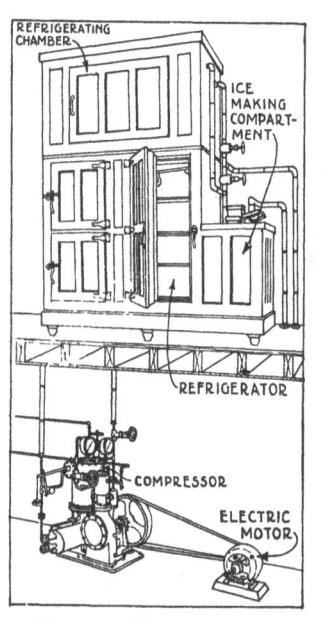

COMPLETE REFRIGERATING PLANT.

With acetylene gas a special gas burner is used, and ordinary gas jets will not do, but with gasoline gas ordinary burners are used with mantles, for illumination. Piping for gasoline as well as acetylene gas is the same as for ordinary gas.

One other kind of gas available for the country house is "blaugas," which is bottled under high pressure at the factory in steel bottles. From the factory it is shipped to any part of the country, a bottle being connected up to the gas system of the house and, when used, a new bottle added. Blaugas will not freeze, so the little steel lockers containing the supply can be placed outdoors at the rear of the house.

House Refrigerating System. — Refrigerating systems for houses have been put on a practical basis. The refrigerating plant will be found to be a great convenience, especially in country houses, and it can be run economically, competing with the

USEFUL APPARATUS AND APPLIANCES 421

cost of ice, if ice has to be shipped in. Of course, when there is a lake or pond near, from which ice may be cut and stored in one's own ice house, ice is cheaper than the cost of maintaining an artificial ice plant.

Plants of small size, suitable for homes, include a refrigerator containing a refrigerating chamber piped for brine. The brine is forced through pipes by a small refrigerating machine contained in a compartment of the refrigerator, or located in the basement. Ammonia brine circulating through the pipes of the refrigerating chamber (much like heating pipes) lowers the temperature. No ice is required, a heavy deposit of frost soon appearing on the outside of the pipes. As artificial ice is needed for table use, however, a small compartment for making ice is frequently attached to the refrigerator. Water contained in metal cans is here converted into ice. The ice machine is run by an electric motor or gas engine, and the entire process is reasonably automatic, requiring less attention, even, than a heating plant. The best refrigerators are lined with glass, porcelain, or tile, or some other material impervious to moisture and odors. A refrigerator ought to be built so it can be as easily inspected as a bathtub, — and it should be kept as spotlessly clean.

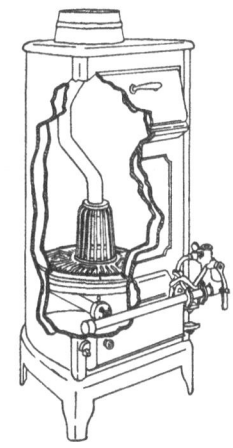

INCINERATOR FOR BURNING GARBAGE.

Rubbish Crematory. — The crematory, for burning garbage and rubbish, may well be considered as indispensable apparatus. A special crematory furnace can be installed, or a crematory can be devised by tapping one of the chimney flues in the basement, placing an iron door a foot or two from the floor, with a few bars of iron built into the flue below, and a damper at the floor level. With the damper open, rubbish thrown on the grate by way of the iron door is quickly consumed.

House Telephone System. — House telephones have been reduced to the extreme of simplicity. They are moderate in cost, and each system requires, in addition to the instruments themselves, nothing more than wire and batteries. The most complete systems are "intercommunicating," with an instrument in every part of the house; usually one in the kitchen, laundry, first-story hall, second-story hall, servants' rooms, and owner's bedroom. The garage or barn is of course connected to the same system.

Modern telephone systems of this class are arranged with any number of instruments, from four to ten or twelve. Each instrument has a button for every room, and when the right button is pressed a bell rings in the corresponding room (but in no other). For convenience in operating, each button has a label holder beside it on which the number or name of the room is lettered.

HOUSE TELEPHONE.

Iron Railing and Brick Piers, with Iron Entrance Lights

CHAPTER XXIV

GAS AND ELECTRIC LIGHTING

WHILE the new house is being built, you will need to give attention to artificial illumination. Remember, lighting fixtures are chiefly for light; for ornament also, of course, but primarily you buy them for reasons of actual utility. Poorly lighted rooms or rooms expensive to light by reason of impracticable methods give poor returns for the money, no matter how well the fixtures look. A living room, dining room, or even a bedroom in which the artificial light is not well distributed is a constant source of annoyance.

Choose fixtures that will give the necessary degree of light at minimum cost; locate them thoughtfully, and see that they are kept in the condition necessary for efficient lighting. Attend to these essentials and your lighting troubles will be little.

Select gas fixtures with care, to do the work required at least expense. That is, a form of burner must be used that will convert the least gas into the most light. All burners should be handy to manipulate and so simple in their parts they may be readily repaired. Of course, they must be made of the most durable materials.

First cost is not the prime consideration in a gas burner, as there are plenty of cheap burners that eat up their saving many times over. On the other hand, some low-priced burners are extremely efficient when of good mechanical design.

The incandescent system of gas lighting has made possible a perfection of illumination never before achieved with gas, though some improvements have been made since the first mantle lights.

The mantle itself has been greatly strengthened by a new method of weaving the threads. Best mantles are double woven, — that is, the fabric composing the mantle is woven with an inner and outer thread. You will know these mantles when you see them by their unusual thickness. Also, the threads of high-grade mantles are larger size, and the weaving is more close. You will also recognize the best by the price. They cost more, but as they wear longer it pays to buy them. Mantles of this sort stand more hard usage; it is the shock caused when a match is first applied, that breaks down the mantle.

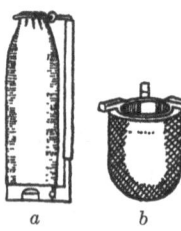

a. ORDINARY GAS MANTLE.
b. MANTLE FOR INVERTED LIGHTS.

For gas lighting use inverted gas lights as much as possible, for they are far ahead of ordinary upright lights, having greater efficiency. A chandelier containing inverted lights looks very much like an electric chandelier. Mantles for inverted lights are small bags of thread, — double woven in the better makes.

In connection with inverted lights or any other it is usually convenient to have a pilot-lighting attachment. Thus, with a pull of the chain you may light any burner without a match. The pilot consists of a very small tube attached to each burner, in which the gas is burning day and night. By means of a chain pull the main supply to the burner is turned on and ignited by the pilot flame. To shut off the light, pull down the chain again, which cuts off the supply from the burner but not from the little pilot tube. This continues to burn with a pinhead flame ready for lighting at any time.

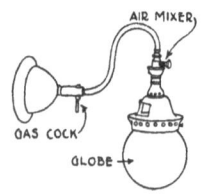

INVERTED GAS FIXTURE.

In other words, the pilot is a burning match, but one extremely cheap to operate, as the cost of a pilot, lighted all the time, is only a few cents a month.

It is customary to have a pilot attachment on one or two burners only, — the lights most often used. A pilot adds to the life of the mantle, as it reduces shocks.

Consider the gas burner, as your duty does not end with the selection of a good mantle. Those gas burners are best which allow correct regulation of the mixture of gas and air, for you must not forget that *air* is as necessary as *gas*.

You can easily test a good burner by lighting it and watching the color of the flame. After adjusting the air supply by manipulation of the key at the side, see that the flame is blue. If it has streaks of red or yellow and you cannot improve it by changing the mixture of air, discard that burner; it will use too much gas and produce light of poor quality, — light that will cost you more money and be less efficient.

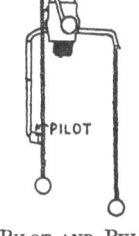

PILOT AND PULL CHAIN.

A gas burner of good design is made in as few pieces as possible, for the less parts, least repairs. It is easy to get practical burners, though it may take a little investigation on the part of the houseowner.

One great advantage incandescent electric lights have over any other form of illumination is that they do not burn oxygen, You will remember that gas lights consume oxygen from the air. but incandescent electric lamps, with the illuminating filament sealed in a glass-bound vacuum, use no air. This is a distinct advantage when we come to consider ventilation.

Another advantage of the electric light is the ease with which it is extended through the rooms of a house. A few feet of well-insulated copper wire with a number of sockets and lamps make a complete lighting system, ideal in every way.

Electric wiring is of vital importance in the house. More

fires are caused every year by imperfect wiring than any other cause, so it is necessary for the owner to get an electrical contractor of known integrity, — one who will do the work right.

Two methods of wiring a house for electric lights are employed, — what is known as "knob and tube" work, — and conduits. The former consists of stringing insulated copper wire through the building in the space occupied by the studding. Where wires pass through timbers a porcelain tube is inserted in the hole, forming a fireproof sleeve through which the wire passes. This is the cheapest method, and it will prove satisfactory in cheap work if the wiring is properly done by an expert. The conduit method is by far the safest and best. Metal tubes are extended throughout the house much like gas pipe, and insulated copper wire is drawn through these tubes (conduit). Thus the wire is protected by its insulation, and in addition it is protected by the metal tube in which all wires are placed, making a perfect safeguard against fire.

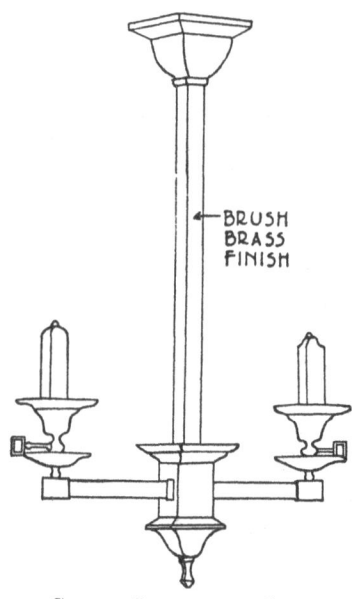

CANDLE FIXTURE FOR GAS.

Slight carelessness in extending wire by the knob and tube method may cause fire at any time. For instance, after wires are extended, if a carpenter or other mechanic happens to saw or cut unknowingly through the insulation on any wire, it may come in contact with timber and start a fire. Another frequent cause of fire is carelessness in soldering the joints. Wire

GAS AND ELECTRIC LIGHTING 429

is not continuous. In many places two pieces must be soldered together to make a complete unit, and if this work is not perfectly done solder may melt at these joints when the current is turned on, with the result that sparking occurs and a fire is started.

After the wiring is completed it should be rigidly inspected before the plastering is started, so that one may be sure the wiring is in good shape before it is covered up. All joints should be, not merely soldered, but wrapped with tape as well, forming a complete, insulated copper-wire system for the current. Do not allow electricians to cover the joints with tape until every joint has been inspected. Examine every inch of the wire to see that porcelain tubes are used wherever wire passes through timber.

DOME LIGHT AT ENTRANCE.

Instead of using conduit, through which insulated wires are drawn after the conduit is installed, it is good practice on some jobs to use flexible metallic cable. This is heavily insulated cable which may be extended through the house like wire of ordinary insulation. It is as safe to use as conduit, and frequently more convenient.

Where wires are applied on masonry walls, conduit or flexible cable should always be used. Knob and tube work at such places is particularly unsafe on account of danger from short-circuiting in damp weather.

Wires from the Electric Light Company's feeder usually

enter at the rear of the house, and just inside the wall a main cut-out box is placed, consisting of a wooden or metal box lined with asbestos (or a slate box). The main "jackknife" switch contained in this box turns current on or off. From the cutout box, wires extend to the different fixtures, arranged in circuits with not over twelve lights on a circuit. Each circuit is "fused." That is, current flowing through each circuit must somewhere in its length pass through a wire fuse which acts like a safety valve,—if too much current is passing (such as might cause copper wire to melt), the piece of fuse wire melts from the heat, thus automatically stopping the current. The most convenient way to arrange fuses is to place them all in a main fuse box, located at some convenient point in the house. With each fuse marked, one can easily renew fuse plugs when they burn out.

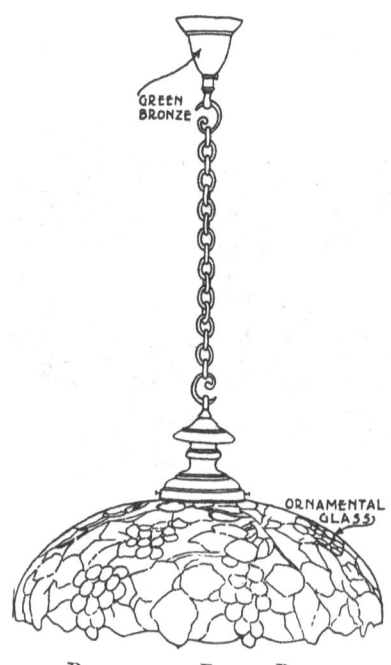

PENDANT FOR DINING ROOM.

Only the best grade of wire should be used in an electric light system. All switches should be of approved quality, and all workmanship should be of the best. Once concealed, the electric system becomes an item of danger when the work is not properly done. The Board of Fire Underwriters has prepared a rigid set of requirements for electric wiring and if an owner will specify for his house, "all wiring to be according to the Code

GAS AND ELECTRIC LIGHTING

of the Board of Fire Underwriters," he will have required the best possible grade of work.

Contrary to popular opinion, electric lighting is not expensive. In most towns the current is moderate in cost.

So many excellent gas and electric light fixtures are manufactured nowadays it is not difficult to select the types most useful and attractive for each room in the house. Of course there is chance to display taste just as in any other decorative part of the house equipment. Fixtures come in all kinds of finishes, solid and plated, and in every variety of design solid fixtures wear better than plated ones. In the dining room a pendant chain supporting a shade or dome of simple pattern is usually best, dropped down over the dining table. Some are in wrought iron with plain ground glass, and others have brass frames and ornamental glass.

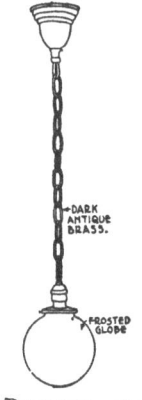

PENDANT FOR HALL OR DINING ROOM.

Modern designers of fixtures for ceiling lights are getting away from the stiff "gas-pipe" pendants which prevailed years ago. One of the prettiest of the new styles is a "shower" of four lights with copper frame and shades.

Indirect electric lighting is accomplished by attractive fixtures made for the purpose, but it must be borne in mind that this method, as attractive as it is, uses more current than is the case with direct lighting. For indirect lighting, ceilings should be painted very light in tone in order to reflect light downward. Indirect lighting is very pleasant for the eyes.

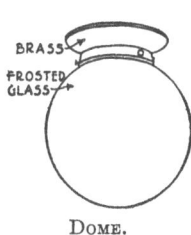

DOME.

Pendant lights and dome lights are good types for a living room. Small fixtures will not give sufficient light if ordinary 16-candle-power lamps are used, but the more efficient Tungsten lamps can be supplied. Wall brackets for living room, dining room, and library, as well as bedrooms, are very practical, whether ceiling lights are added or not. Bracket lights can be used

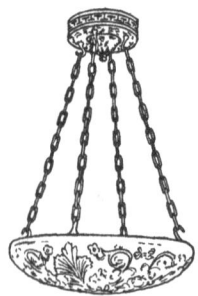

FIXTURE FOR INDI-
RECT LIGHTING.

when the larger ceiling light is not turned on, and they have a very pretty effect at all times. A bracket light is also generally preferred for the front entrance, often in the shape of a lantern made in brass, green finish, with colored glass.

Lamps are important factors in lighting systems. The most practical lamp is the new Tungsten lamp, which gives out three times the light of ordinary incandescent lamps with the same current consumption. In other words, this lamp gives three times the light for the same money. For outdoor lighting, lamps incased in wire frames are particularly useful, as they are not easily broken.

For the house burning gas exclusively, fixtures are made in great variety with ordinary jets or burners and mantles. Of the former, one may use a simple 2-light gas bracket. Chandeliers of the same pattern can be used for ceiling lights. Of the combination gas and electric fixtures simple patterns consisting of two electric lights and one gas light are best, the latter being a "candlelight." For the kitchen ceiling an inverted gas light is very practical, finished in dull black.

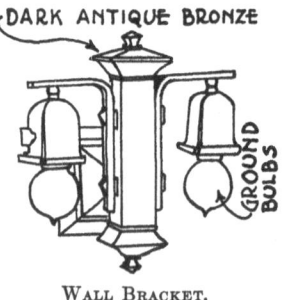

WALL BRACKET.

Both gas and electric fixtures should be made of the best materials. Do not use inferior goods for this purpose, for it doesn't pay. Some fixtures are of cast metal and others spun from thin

GAS AND ELECTRIC LIGHTING

sheets. When of pleasing design and sound construction, the latter are quite as good as the former, and much less expensive.

Like hardware, gas and electric fixtures come in many finishes. Have your lighting fixtures and hardware finished alike. When this is done, the effect is very pleasing.

Light lemon, or brush-brass in the dull finish, dark antique brass or bronze as well as dull black, are equally appropriate for a house. To prevent brass fixtures from tarnishing, have them covered with transparent lacquer before they are delivered at the house. All factories are equipped for this finish which adds but little to the cost and saves work later. Lacquered surfaces must not be polished vigorously when cleaning, however, or the lacquer will peel off.

Globes and shades are made in every form and color. Use judgment and taste in selecting them. Plain patterns are best, especially those made on the lines of Greek vases. Elaborately blown and etched

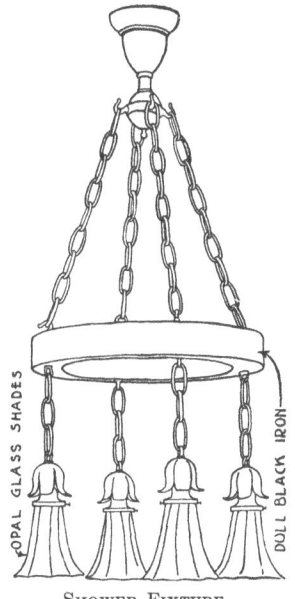

SHOWER FIXTURE.

designs not only reduce the light value of burners, but also stand as monuments to your poor taste.

Prism globes and shades are useful. Ribs or prisms increase the power of the light rays, and (according to the angle and depth of the corrugations) send them just where most wanted. Prism shades are made for lighting up, down, or sidewise in any direction. They are very attractive in appearance.

Kerosene lamps are excellent for reading. The kind known as "students" lamps are very satisfactory. Select a plain model

2 F

finished in antique brass, and you have a durable, attractive lamp, easy to keep clean. Do not entirely fill the reservoir of a lamp; leave a slight air space at the top. A lamp is like a fountain pen in this regard, — it works best when not overfull.

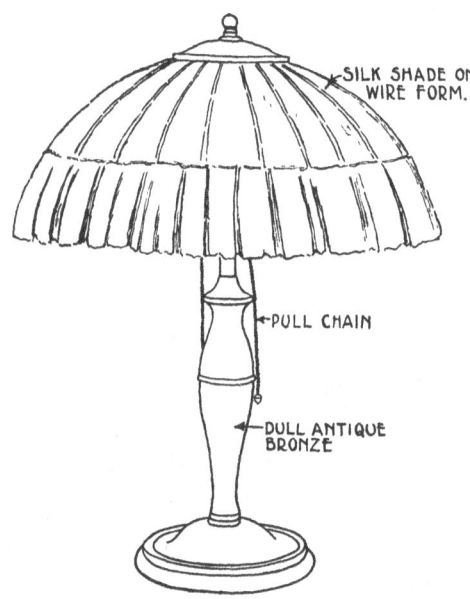

ELECTRIC TABLE LAMP.

Kerosene is the fluid most used for lamps, but alcohol lamps are very satisfactory as well. In these denatured alcohol is converted into gas, and the lamps are really gas lamps. There are kerosene gas lamps, also, and they produce an excellent light.

Ordinary incandescent gas lamps and electric lamps are useful for tables. Select plain designs and use simple silk or paper shades instead of elaborate ornamental glass.

Candlesticks with plain white wax candles are charming on the dining table. They are practical, too, and the cost is trifling. There is something cozy about candlelight. The glow is warm, like sunshine. It gladdens the heart.

House Equipped with Casement Windows, Opening Out.
Spencer and Powers, Architects.

CHAPTER XXV

PRACTICAL HARDWARE FOR THE HOUSE

HARDWARE is the most generally misunderstood material used in the house. "All hardware looks alike" to the average owner, and this is not strange when we realize the almost numberless variations in grades of hardware, — variations which are so slight in some cases that even an expert is puzzled to tell the difference between them.

When the owner selects his hardware he is usually satisfied to make a more or less cursory examination of it, preferring to depend upon the expert knowledge of his architect or the honesty of the hardware merchant to see that he gets the stuff he pays for. It is a good plan, however, for an owner to understand hardware, so that he may make a wise selection. He should give as much attention to this as he does to any other detail of house building.

Price cuts considerable figure with the average owner, who cannot see why one dealer should charge $100 for a bill of hardware when another charges but $75 for the same goods (as the owner thinks). As a matter of fact, prices made and maintained by all hardware manufacturers are now practically standard. Hardware manufacturing has been systemized. In standard styles locks, keys, and knobs are of about the same pattern, and they sell for the same price.

If all hardware is standard, costing about the same price, why is it that prices between dealers fluctuate so much?

Prices do not fluctuate on the *same grade of goods* as much as owners think. When all the retailers bidding on a bill of hardware figure *on the same grade of goods*, prices quoted by them are nearly alike, varying slightly, perhaps, because one dealer might be willing to cut his profit in order to get the job, whereas another charges the regular price. The difference between prices is almost insignificant, for hardware is sold by dealers on a very small margin. Great variation in price is really caused by one dealer, in his zeal to get the job, substituting grades of hardware lower than the standard.

In many instances this substitution is an entirely honest transaction, done with the sanction of the inexperienced owner. For instance, an owner goes to a dealer, makes a selection of high-grade goods, and is quoted a price of $110. He visits another dealer who shows him a slightly inferior line of goods, made perhaps by the same manufacturers (for all manufacturers make several different grades), quoting a price of $85. To the owner both lines of samples look precisely the same. Locks appear alike, — knobs are the same pattern, — escutcheons the same style. But there is considerable variation in price. If the owner asks the last dealer why prices vary, he will in most cases be frankly told that the first line of goods is more expensive, — but "you don't need such heavy escutcheons and knobs as the first man was going to give you," very likely the hardware dealer will explain, "single-tumbler locks for bedrooms are plenty good enough for anybody, and the other dealer is charging you for three-tumbler locks; his cupboard turns are solid brass, — mine are plated. All this is unnecessary expense. It makes his bid higher and does you no good."

An unscrupulous dealer would go beyond this, solemnly affirming to the owner that his goods are precisely like the other dealer's, who being a "high-priced man consequently charges a higher price."

There is, of course, a possibility of buying hardware which is "too good" for the house. In actual practice, however, a large proportion of owners buy hardware which is not good enough.

In their eagerness to save money they frequently buy hardware which is too cheap and which will cause them annoyance later.

In selecting hardware for a house, the owner should proceed much as he does when picking out his plumbing fixtures, dealing only with a concern of known reliability. The owner should insist upon learning all there is to know about the different grades, styles, and patterns before he goes too much into the matter of price. He should examine the interior mechanism of different locks. He should investigate the various weights of plates and knobs. He should familiarize himself with the many finishes for hardware. Then, when he understands the merits of different kinds, he can intelligently decide which is best for his own house.

The lock is the most important piece of hardware. Its principal parts are bolt, key, and key protection (the latter being the obstacle to be removed by the key before it can operate the bolt).

There are many types of key protection, from the simple "wards" (used on cheap locks) to "tumblers" contained in the better grades. In well-known brands each type of lock has been developed to its highest efficiency. Each has its place, and intelligent hardware dealers know where each should be used, though the owner often doesn't. This is the chief reason for buying goods of a reliable concern, — to assure the inexperienced owner that he will be well advised and get the right hardware for the right place.

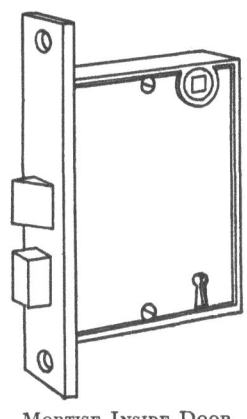

MORTISE INSIDE DOOR LOCK.

Locks with tumblers (called "lever-tumbler" locks) are right for inside doors, and they vary in security and durability according to the number of tumblers, — single-tumbler locks being inferior to three-tumbler locks. The latter are best for first-class work, as they are well built and afford the greatest security possible in a tumbler lock. From 200 to 500 key changes are possible in a good three-tumbler lock, as against 12 to 24 changes in cheap locks, so that the possibility of interchange of keys in the former case is inconsequential.

Tumblers in a lock are levers, which must be moved by the proper key before the key can operate on the bolt. They are, therefore, "key protectors." A single tumbler in a lock is virtually no protection at all.

MORTISE CYLINDER LOCK FOR OUTSIDE DOOR.

Cylinder locks (used for outside doors) are the most perfect of all, affording every protection by means of five pin tumblers (in the best grade of cylinder locks), making possible a large number of key changes.

The mechanism of the lock itself is not the only thing to consider as regards protection. Many locked doors can be opened from without, by means of a thin, steel tool pushed into the crack between door and jamb, making it possible to reach and operate the bolt. To prevent this use a "protected strike" on all outside doors. That is, the plate on the jamb of the door which receives the bolt should be L shaped instead of flat, so that a tool thrust through from outside could not reach the bolt.

Keys are of four general types, — the round key (as commonly used for inside door locks), the barrel key (sometimes used for cupboard locks), the flat key (used for a better grade of cupboard locks), and the cylinder lock key (the highest grade, most perfect key of all).

For cylinder locks there are four types of key, — flat, grooved, corrugated, and paracentric. Of these types the last is the most perfect. Ordinary flat keys are used only on the cheapest cylinder locks. Grooved or corrugated keys, as their name implies, are flat keys wrought with grooves or corrugations on the sides corresponding with grooves at the sides of the keyway. The paracentric key and lock marks a great advance in key and lock design, for the interlocking barriers at the edge of the keyway extend deeper into the key (by reason of the paracentric groove in the latter, which is deeper than an ordinary groove). Thus, the paracentric lock is much more difficult to pick.

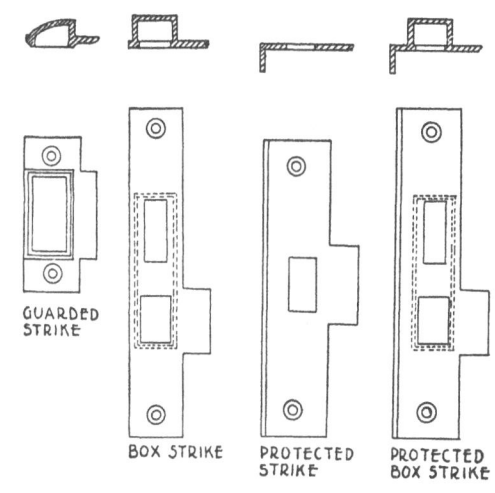

GUARDED STRIKE

BOX STRIKE   PROTECTED STRIKE   PROTECTED BOX STRIKE

FLAT KEYWAY   CORRUGATED KEYWAY   PARACENTRIC KEYWAY

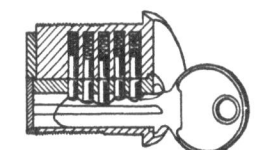

KEYWAYS AND TUMBLERS FOR CYLINDER LOCK.

Incidentally, it ought to be stated that any lock can be picked by an expert equipped with delicate tools for the purpose. The best grade of cylinder locks, however, are practically pick-proof; certainly pick-proof so far as ordinary thieves are concerned.

Pin tumblers in cylinder locks are operated by pins, which are permitted to drop down into the corrugations on the edge of the key when it is inserted in the lock. Thus, cylinder locks have double protection, — that offered by the keyway (which permits only the right key to enter), and that offered by the pins operating the levers (only keys with the right corrugations will allow the pins to drop sufficiently to operate the tumblers). Cylinder locks are used chiefly for outside doors and elsewhere, when it is desired to have more security than is afforded with ordinary lever-tumbler locks.

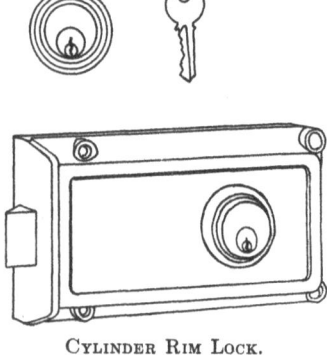
CYLINDER RIM LOCK.

The best locks are made of wrought metal throughout. Cheap locks are made partly of wrought metal and partly of cast metal. Very cheap locks are made entirely of cast metal. Thus, with these different methods there is great variation in cost of manufacture. Take off the cap of two or three ordinary inside door locks, and the case, bolts, and levers may look very much alike, though there will be considerable variation in price, occasioned by inferior material and workmanship in the cheapest — superior material and workmanship in the best.

Wrought metal is vastly superior to cast iron, as the latter is easily broken and less susceptible to a high grade of finish. In a high-grade lock the case and cap (the shell of the lock) should be of cold-rolled steel. The front of the lock (the edge which shows on the edge of the door) should be of wrought steel; the bolt (or bolts) should be ribbed or corrugated to give additional stiffness. Keys for high-grade locks should be of solid steel, cold-forged from open-hearth metal, with the "bit" tapered at the outer edge to give better wearing surface and smoother action on tumblers and bolt.

The mechanical devices by means of which the levers operate

PRACTICAL HARDWARE FOR THE HOUSE

the bolts vary from the crude system employed in cheap locks to the perfect arrangement contained in locks of a better class. Here, again, is chance for a wide diversity of price, and the owner will do well to investigate the interior mechanism of locks, removing the cap and studying the arrangement of levers. An ideal lock has a perfectly "easy-spring" action, caused by a careful arrangement of levers.

Another point to look for in a lock is the system by which the knobs are attached to it. A metal rod called "spindle," long enough to pass through the door and attach the knob at each side, is generally used for this purpose. On cheap locks an ordinary square spindle is used, containing holes at each end to which the knobs are screwed. When this method is used, knobs soon work loose, and the screws by which the knobs are attached to the spindle have to be frequently tightened up. A much better way is to use a spindle consisting of three wedge-shaped pieces of metal, which combined form a square rod. To this, knobs are attached by screws, and when tightened the spindle is wedged in contact with the knobs, holding them securely.

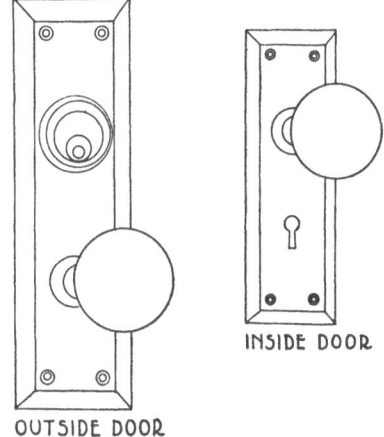

OUTSIDE DOOR

INSIDE DOOR

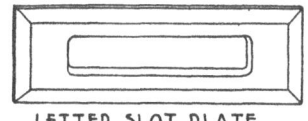

LETTER SLOT PLATE

WROUGHT BRONZE HARDWARE.

On front doors where it is desired to make the outside knob operative or not (independent of the inside knob) the spindle should be of the swivel pattern. Spindles should not be smaller than ⅜ inch, though they frequently come smaller on cheap work.

When it comes to the finish of hardware there are a great many finishes to choose from. The owner should become acquainted with the different metals employed for escutcheons and knobs, and understand the different processes by which they are finished so that he can intelligently consider his hardware estimates. The following are the metals chiefly used: —

METALS SUITABLE FOR HARDWARE

Cast Iron is frequently used, and this metal is particularly suitable for special decorative patterns of escutcheons.

Wrought Iron is used for designs where greater strength is needed than will be possible with cast iron.

CAST BRONZE HARDWARE.

Malleable Iron consists of cast iron treated in a special furnace which converts it into a sort of semi-steel. It is little used for anything but cheap keys.

Wrought Steel is largely used for lock trim. It is the base of all cheap, plated finishes and is a durable metal for inside use, though, of course, finishes plated on a wrought metal base are always inferior to solid goods (unplated).

Copper is never used for lock trim except as an electroplate, it being too soft a metal to employ.

Cast Bronze and Brass are without doubt the best metals for finished hardware.

Wrought Bronze and Brass are of the same material as cast bronze or brass, but made of thinner sheets, stamped out with dies instead of cast (and therefore much cheaper than cast bronze or brass). For inexpensive work of a good grade, wrought bronze or brass is perfectly satisfactory.

After becoming acquainted with the different metals used for finished hardware in the house, the owner will do well to examine the different ways of finishing these metals by means of "electroplating." The following finishes are suitable for hardware: —

FINISHES SUITABLE FOR HARDWARE

Copper Plating is most satisfactory when done on brass, though on cheap work wrought steel is sometimes plated with copper. The owner should remember that wrought steel once it is plated with copper, looks precisely the same as brass, plated with copper, but the latter is by far the most durable, and costs more. Here is a chance for wide variation of price, and the owner should assure himself that his hardware with copper finish has a base of solid brass instead of wrought steel. On the latter, the plating soon wears off, exposing the steel underneath.

Bronze and Brass Plating on iron and steel is suitable for kitchens and attics, but should not be used in the more decorative parts of the house. Bronze-plated steel hinges, however, are suitable for all inside doors, as hinges are not conspicuous, and they are not subject to very great wear.

Nickel Plating on brass is frequently used for bathrooms, though architects are inclining against this practice, as they have found that nickel plate soon grows dull and after a time wears off, showing the brass underneath.

Silver Plating is used on expensive work, and it makes a beautiful appearance, but silver tarnishes and cannot be recommended unless it is to be kept constantly bright.

Gold Plating is often used on high-grade work, and it has a very attractive appearance.

Naturally, on plated work there are some portions of the hardware which are subject to greater wear than others, thus requiring a heavier plating of metal. Single plate should be used only on escutcheons and lock fronts (subject to but little wear). Double plate should be used for articles subject to moderate wear such as bolts, sash fasts, and drawer pulls. Triple plate is used on all high-grade goods for knobs, handles, keys, and other articles liable to much handling. The owner will readily

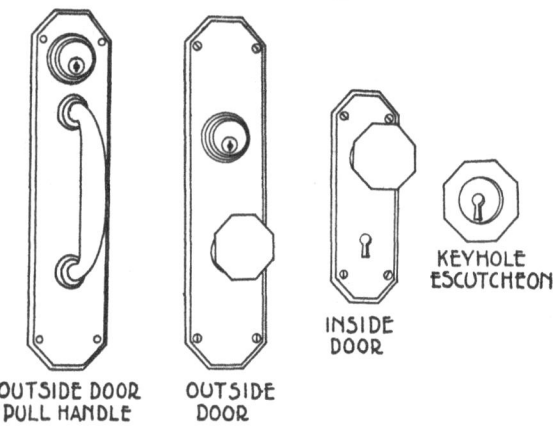

BLACK BOWER-BARFF FINISH.

understand that the amount of plating greatly influences price, so if there is a wide fluctuation in his hardware bids it may be well to find out from the various dealers just what grade of plating is on their goods.

"Bower-Barff" finish is not exactly a plating, since it is a process by which iron or steel is treated in a special furnace until it turns lustrous black in color. This finish is not durable on outdoor work, but inside it makes an attractive, practical finish. In considering dull black for a finish, the owner should ascertain whether he is getting the real Bower-Barff finish or a cheap imitation. Patents on the former have run out, so that any manufacturer can produce this finish, but some do not take sufficient care in the work to produce finish of a good quality.

When it comes to color in finishes, many beautiful tints are obtained by means of the different processes employed. The following are among the colors usually employed for house hardware: —

COLORS FOR HARDWARE

Brass Metal:
Finished natural color, polished or dull.
Plated, "Verde Antique" (shades of green).
Plated, "Lemon Brass" (sometimes called "brush brass").
Plated, "Antique," polished or dull.
Plated with silver, polished or dull.
Plated with gold, polished or dull.

Bronze Metal:
Furnished in several different shades, among others "Statuary Bronze."

Steel or Iron:
Plated in many combinations of copper, bronze, brass, gold, and silver.
Bower-Barff process, dull black.

There are many other types of finish, but these are the standard finishes most frequently used. Many of these look precisely alike, but all are not equally durable, nor are they of the same cost. The owner, therefore, should give considerable attention to the various finishes, inquiring about their cost and the advantages of each. If he deals with a reliable concern, he will have no difficulty in getting the goods he wishes, at the right price.

The most important hardware is, of course, the front door set. In most cases such a set consists of a cylinder lock with fairly large escutcheons and a large knob outside with a smaller knob inside. The best front door locks are arranged so that when the door is locked the outside knob is fixed; when the door is unlocked the outside knob turns and allows the latch to operate. A separate thumb bolt is also frequently included. One pattern of outside door set, called "Unit lock," has the key mechanism and keyhole contained in the knob. The back door should be as securely fastened as the front door, and for this reason a cylinder lock should be used here, also.

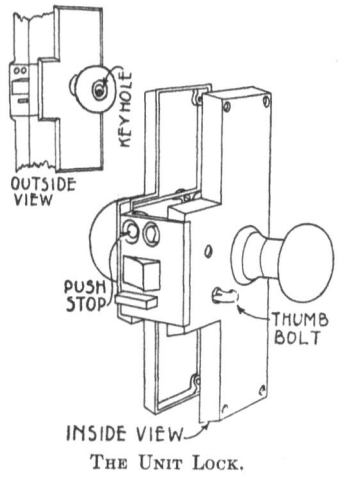

THE UNIT LOCK.

Inside doors are usually provided with a lever-tumbler lock (three-tumbler, preferred), an escutcheon of moderate size, and knobs both sides. Closet doors should also have knobs both sides, though they are sometimes finished blank on the inside. The latter is not the best practice, however, for children might become fastened in a closet, and they could not get out unless an inside knob is on the door.

Inside doors look well when the escutcheon is entirely eliminated and the knob is simply trimmed with a collar ("shank"), and a little rim of metal is provided for the keyhole ("rose").

There are many patterns of knobs suitable for houses, and the owner will have no difficulty in selecting patterns which he likes best, remembering that knobs are subject to the hardest wear. The following are the materials employed for knobs:—

DOOR KNOBS

Pottery Knobs:

    These are of three kinds,—mineral (brown), jet (black), and porcelain (white). They are seldom used now, except on the cheapest work, such as basement or attic.

Wood Knobs:
  Made of various kinds of wood finished in their natural colors. Used chiefly on cheap work, though they are sometimes considered suitable for bedrooms.

Cast-iron Knobs:
  Quite satisfactory when used with "Bower-Barff" finish; otherwise cast-iron knobs are cheap appearing.

Composite Knobs:
  Made of steel or iron underneath, veneered with brass or bronze. When honestly made, composite knobs are durable and attractive, but many of them are imperfectly made, the veneer being too thin to wear well.

Bronze and Brass Knobs:
  All the best grade of metal knobs are of this class. Solid knobs are the best and most expensive. Seamless wrought knobs are quite satisfactory when made of thick metal, properly built. The latter have the appearance of solid knobs, but are really wrought from sheets of metal in two halves, put together and brazed. Cheap wrought knobs are never satisfactory.

Glass Knobs:
  These are very attractive and quite durable. They come in pressed glass (moderate in cost), and cut glass (the latter being quite expensive).

When it comes to hinges, which are called in technical parlance "butts," there are many patterns to choose from, and the owner in considering his hardware bids should inform himself just what kind of butts it is proposed to use in his house. The following are the materials used for butts:—

BUTTS

Cast-iron Butts:
  These are the cheapest kind, and they cannot be recommended for good work. They come plated in many varieties of

450 SUCCESSFUL HOUSES AND HOW TO BUILD THEM

finish, such as brass and bronze. Sometimes owners really get cast-iron bronze-plated butts when they think they are getting solid bronze, as the appearance is the same.

Wrought Steel Butts:

These are excellent for inside work. They come plated with brass or bronze, or can be had finished by the Bower-Barff process.

Cast Brass or Bronze Butts:

These are of the highest grade and should always be used on outside work. On expensive houses they are also used for inside work.

Hinges for inside doors may be plated, but hinges for outside doors should always be of solid brass or bronze, as plated hinges soon rust out when exposed to the weather.

For inside doors, two butts are all that are usually required, though three butts are necessary on glass doors, owing to the weight of the latter. Outside doors should be furnished with three butts.

Inside door butts can be furnished in "loose joint" butts (easily slipped apart for removing the door at any time) or "loose pin" butts. The latter are the most convenient, as they are reversible (can be used either way). The best loose pin butts have five "knuckles" (loops of metal through which the pin passes) in order to provide *two* bearings for the weight of the door. Four knuckles only provide one bearing for the door.

TWO PATTERNS OF INSIDE DOOR BUTTS.

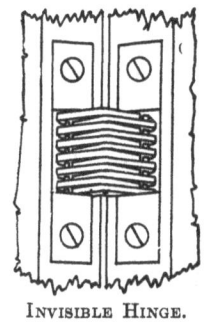

INVISIBLE HINGE.

PRACTICAL HARDWARE FOR THE HOUSE 451

A new hinge sometimes used for inside doors is the "invisible hinge," which is mortised into the edge of the door, where it is concealed from view.

Ordinary bolts, cupboard turns, drawer pulls, sash fasts, sash lifts, and other pieces of hardware used throughout the house are usually well understood by houseowners, but it will be well to mention several forms of casement window hardware, for casement windows sometimes require special treatment.

One pattern of casement "adjuster" suitable for casements opening out (which is the proper way to open them), is installed in the space between the outside window and inside screen, part of the fixture extending down through the sill. By means of a rod grasped in the hand and pushed sidewise, the window opens and closes without the necessity of opening the screen to operate it.

IMPROVED CASEMENT WINDOW ADJUSTER (OBVIATES OPENING SCREEN TO OPEN WINDOWS).

Another pattern is similar in operation, but it is placed directly on the window stool (between screen and window), the bottom rail of the screen being cut out to fit down closely over the swivel. A rod on the room side of the screen opens and closes the window without opening the screen.

There are other types of adjuster suitable for casements opening in or out, but in most cases (with outside-opening

452   SUCCESSFUL HOUSES AND HOW TO BUILD THEM

WITH THIS OUTSIDE-OPENING CASEMENT WINDOW ADJUSTER IT IS NOT NECESSARY TO OPEN SCREEN.

casements) it is necessary to open the screen to operate the window.

Butts for casement windows (when the windows open out) should be of galvanized steel with brass pins, as steel pins soon rust out.

Outside blinds or shutters can be opened from the inside by using one of the forms of shutter hardware operated from inside the room. In the best types the shutter is operated by turning a handle, which communicates motion to the shutter by means of a rod extending through the window casing.

Several forms of hardware are furnished for self-closing doors, such as the double-swing door between dining room and serving room. With the best patterns it is possible to hold the door open when desired, by touching a pin or lever with the foot. "Push plates" should always be screwed to the face of double-swing doors to prevent the door from wearing badly at this point.

One form of sash lock now frequently installed is the

EXCELLENT PATTERN OF CASEMENT WINDOW FASTENER.

PRACTICAL HARDWARE FOR THE HOUSE 453

"burglar sash fast." This is attached at the side of a window, permitting the lower or upper sash to be opened a few inches for ventilation, but making it impossible to open the sash wider. When it is desired to have the windows wide open, a pin at the side is released, permitting the windows to be opened full width.

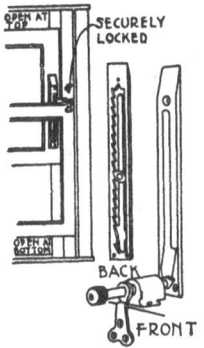

Burglar-proof Ventilating Sash Fastener.

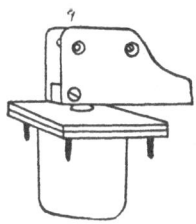

Hinge for Double-acting Dining Room Door.

One of the latest forms of transom lift (when transoms are placed over bedroom doors, for ventilation) is what is known as the "concealed transom lift," in which the mechanism is placed behind the door casing.

Brick and Tile Sun Room

CHAPTER XXVI

HANDY HOUSE DEVICES

THERE are many useful little devices that can be installed in and about the house to make housekeeping easier. Many of these have to do with the furnace or boiler, — handy arrangements for admitting coal and taking out ashes. Others apply to the thousand and one little details of everyday life.

Coal Chute.— A coal window of metal will be found a great convenience, and it is not unsightly, consisting as it does of a metal frame with a swing cover, usually set in the underpinning of a house at the coal bin.

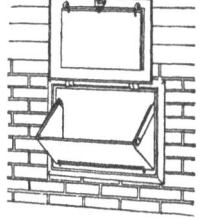

COMBINATION CELLAR-WINDOW COAL CHUTE.

When the cover is opened an inside hopper is pushed forward, thus making a chute through which coal can be discharged into the bin. Frequently the cover is glazed like a window so, even when closed, the chute lets in light like an ordinary cellar window. An ingenious clamp locks the cover firmly, inside.

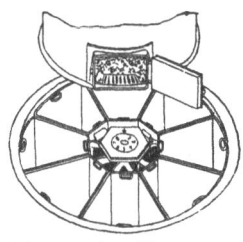

ROTARY ASH RECEIVER.

Ash Receiver.— For storing ashes in the basement after they are removed from the furnace there is the rotary ash receiver, consisting of a group of 6 or 12 galvanized iron cans (holding 8 to 12 weeks' accumulation), wedge-shaped, so they fit within the area of a circle.

To install this contrivance a circular pit is excavated in the cellar bottom in front of and projecting somewhat under the furnace. This receives the steel receptacle which holds the

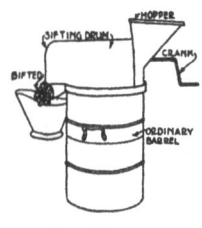

ASH SIFTER.

series of specially constructed galvanized iron cans (of the capacity of the ordinary ash can), arranged to revolve on a central perpendicular shaft by means of a lever, in such a manner as to bring one can at a time directly beneath the ash pit of the furnace. The whole device is covered by stationary top plates on a level with the basement floor, provision being made to receive the ashes through an opening in the floor of the furnace ash pit. One of the floor plates, being removable, permits of the cans being lifted out when filled.

The cans should be filled consecutively, beginning with No. 1. When all of them are filled, the drayman is instructed to remove them as follows: He first lifts the cover plate to one side and, grasping the handles of the can beneath, lifts it out. With the lever he rotates the mechanism sufficiently to bring the next can into position for removal, and so on until the entire lot has been taken out. After being carried out and emptied, the cans and cover plates are replaced in position as before.

Ash Sifter. — When ordinary galvanized iron ash barrels are used for the storage of ashes, it will be found convenient to have one of them fitted with an ash sifter mounted in the cover. One of the best of these

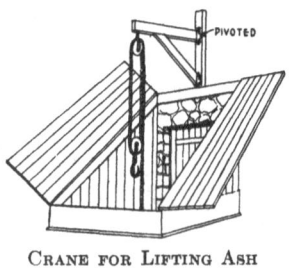

CRANE FOR LIFTING ASH BARRELS.

consists of a tight galvanized iron cover fitted with a hopper and sifting drum, with a crank to turn it. Ashes are poured into the hopper, and a few turns of the crank operating the sifting drum

HANDY HOUSE DEVICES

removes the ashes, discharging the larger lumps of unconsumed coal at the other end.

Ash Barrel Crane. — When ash barrels are stored in the cellar through the winter season, the best way to get them into the yard in the spring is to use a lifting crane. This is nothing but a heavy bracket of timber, bolted to the side of the house above the cellar entrance. It is pivoted to swing a barrel sidewise to the ground, the barrel being supported by an ordinary block and tackle.

Dumb Waiter. — Some houses are planned with the kitchen on the basement level and the dining room above, making a dumb waiter necessary. This arrangement is specially frequent in city houses. Other houses are sometimes equipped with a dumb waiter extending from kitchen to cellar, as it has been found a great convenience, preventing carrying many articles up over the stairs. In country houses where ice is difficult to get, a dumb waiter may be installed extending from the kitchen down into a shaft in the basement, where food supplies can be kept as cold as in a refrigerator.

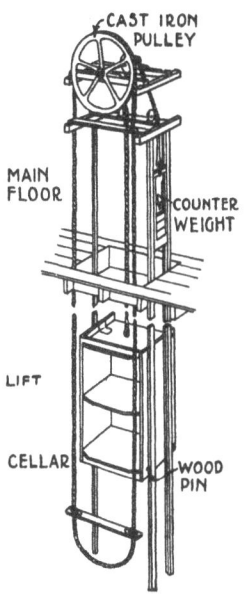

DUMB WAITER FROM KITCHEN TO CELLAR.

Sanitary Garbage Can. — Storage of garbage is quite a problem, and several ingenious devices are made for this purpose. The ordinary method of using a galvanized iron bucket placed near the rear door is not sanitary and should not be resorted to unless a tight cover is provided on the bucket. An improvement on the ordinary garbage pail consists of a galvanized iron

HANDY GARBAGE CAN.

can, set upon four iron legs. The cover is hinged so that it cannot become displaced, and it is opened by pressing the foot on a lever. A better system of garbage disposal consists of a steel receptacle with cover, let into the ground. Inside, the garbage pail is kept. The cover is level with the surface of the ground so it looks like a coal-hole cover. To put garbage in, press the lever with your foot, which raises the small cover. To empty garbage out at the end of the week the large cover is raised and the interior pail is removed and emptied.

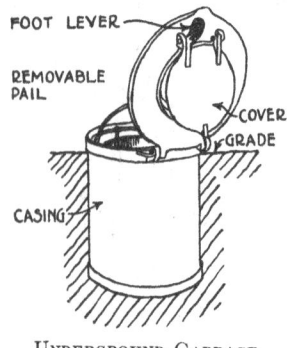

UNDERGROUND GARBAGE RECEIVER.

A garbage receptacle should be tight. If it stands outdoors, it should be painted outside and inside, not merely for appearance, but to preserve it from rust. Galvanizing helps, but it is not sufficient.

Wire Rubbish Burner. — In many houses garbage is burned in a crematory or garbage-burning heater placed in the basement (described in another chapter). The crematory or heater is also used for burning waste paper and rubbish, so much of which accumulates about every house. A cheap substitute for the crematory for burning waste paper consists of a barrel-shaped receptacle made of galvanized iron wire, with a cover. Paper or rubbish placed inside can be burned with no danger that it will blow about the yard.

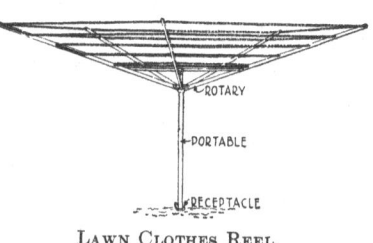

LAWN CLOTHES REEL.

Clothes Posts and Lawn Driers. — Clothes posts in the yard are now often made of concrete. These can frequently be bought ready-made like wooden posts, or they may be cast at the building and set up in place. Many housekeepers prefer rotary lawn clothes driers instead of posts set up in the yard, and lawn driers have the advantage of being taken down when not in use. Lawn driers come ready-made, consisting of a wooden post to which is secured a rotary reel containing arms and clothesline. The yardarms and supporting post are collapsible and may be lifted out of the socket (sunk into the ground) and carried down into the basement. Lawn driers come in several sizes, to hold as many pieces of clothes as the ordinary fixed posts and clothesline system.

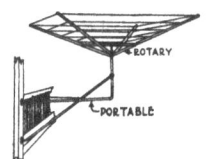

CLOTHES DRIER FOR BALCONY.

With a lawn drier only one path is necessary to maintain in winter (a great saving of snow-shoveling), for one stands in the same spot in hanging or gathering the clothes, and the drier revolves, bringing every article within reach. A little iron cover protects the receptacle when not in use.

A balcony drier is like a lawn drier, but it is attached to the porch. In this way one is not obliged to shovel a path through the snow, as all the articles may be hung and gathered from the porch.

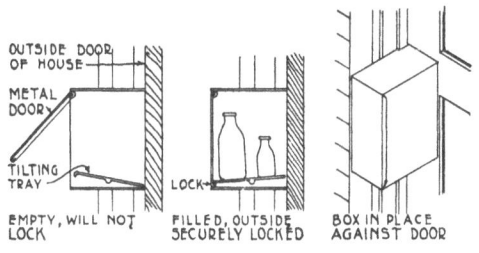

SELF-LOCKING BOX FOR MILK BOTTLES.

Outside Milk Cupboard. — A useful outside cupboard for milk bottles consists of a galvanized iron box, open on one side and closed by a cover on the other. This box is screwed to the door frame of the rear entrance door, with the open side tight against the door. When the milkman makes his rounds early in the morning, he places the full bottles inside the

460 SUCCESSFUL HOUSES AND HOW TO BUILD THEM

box and slams the cover, which locks. To remove bottles you must open the house door. This is a theft-proof, weather-proof device of considerable usefulness. The box ought to be painted to match the door frame, for appearance as well as durability, as galvanized iron will rust when unpainted.

PANTRY WINDOW REFRIGERATOR.

Window Refrigerator. — For winter storage of food a galvanized window refrigerator will be found of great utility. This stands in the pantry window and is large enough to contain food for a family of considerable size. The box has a double metal door, frost-proof and dustless. It should be kept neatly painted. In order to let cold air enter the refrigerator (but not the pantry), have two boards made, one for each side, to fill up the space between the side of the window frame and the refrigerator. Thus when the window is open to cool the refrigerator, these side boards prevent cold air from entering the pantry.

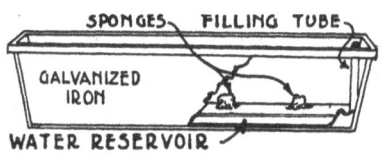

SELF-WATERING FLOWER BOX.

Self-watering Flower Box. — Flowers and flower boxes are now so frequently a part of the house equipment, many clever arrangements have been made for the purpose. Ordinary flower boxes may be built of wood, lined with galvanized iron or copper, or ready-made "self-watering" boxes can be found made of galvanized iron in several sizes. These contain false bottoms, below; water is kept in the compartment under the false bottom by pouring in a supply every few days through the filling tube connected with the compartment. Sponges in the false bottom keep the earth moist at all times.

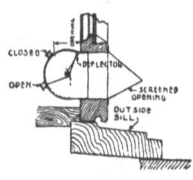

WINDOW VENTILATOR.

Window Ventilators. — Ventilators attached to windows will do much toward keeping a house plentifully supplied with fresh air during the winter months, when windows are frequently tightly closed. One type of window ventilator consists of a perforated metal shelf with a metal plate in front, designed to be used at the sill. By opening the window slightly at the bottom, fresh air enters upward through the perforated shelf, thus causing no draft. The entire device is collapsible and detachable.

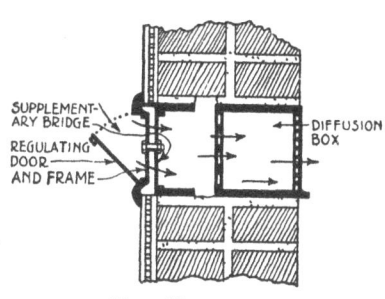

WALL VENTILATOR.

Another type of window ventilator consists of a small metal frame with hinged cover, inserted in a slot cut in the bottom rail of the window. The cover placed on the inside of the window is hinged at the bottom, causing the fresh air to rise, thus preventing drafts.

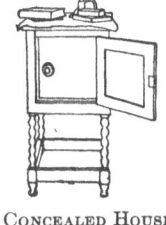

CONCEALED HOUSE SAFE.

A ventilator can be placed directly in the outside wall of any room by cutting a hole of the proper size and fitting it with a metal ventilator. Ventilators of this pattern usually consist of two metal frames, one for the outside of the wall (containing a grating), and one for the inside, with a cover hinged at the bottom.

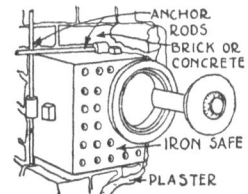

SECRET WALL SAFE FOR JEWELRY.

Silver Safes and Wall Safes. — A fireproof safe is a useful part of the house equipment. Safes come in many different sizes. Most frequently the safe for silver is located in the serving room or pantry, often being concealed behind a movable panel. In other cases a safe is built into a piece of furniture. Smaller safes (called "wall safes") for the storage of jewelry can be placed in the walls of bedrooms. They are little cast-iron boxes about 12 inches long and 8 inches high, with a door closed by a steel disk controlled by a combination lock. It is the usual custom to hang a picture over a wall safe, concealing it from view.

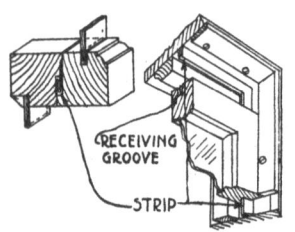

METAL WEATHER STRIPS FOR WINDOWS.

Weather Strips. — Weather strips are frequently used in place of storm windows on all outside doors and windows in the house. Weather strips made of copper are best, as they are practically indestructible. Many patterns are in the market, and it is possible to get weather strips for any size or style of windows, including casement windows.

Window Screens. — Metal-framed insect screens can be used in place of screens with wooden frames. There have been many improvements made in window and door screens in the last few years, modern screens being more durable and convenient than old-fashioned screens. Screens with metal frames are made with a groove into which the screen wire is inserted, and wedged in place with a metal collar. The best patterns of wooden screens are made in somewhat the same way, with a molding of wood to hold the screen wire in place.

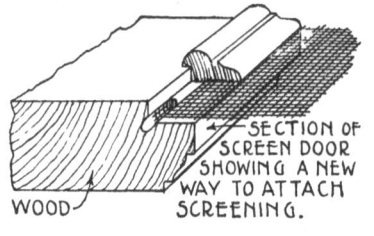

WOOD SCREEN AND METAL SCREEN.

Copper screen wire is the most durable, but galvanized iron wire will be found quite satisfactory when a reliable brand is used. Ordinary black wire is not practical for screens, as it soon rusts through.

OLD HOUSE SLIGHTLY REMODELED
Frank Chouteau Brown, Architect

CHAPTER XXVII

REMODELING; MAKING AN OLD HOUSE NEW

MANY people do not care to build a new house, frequently possessing an old house that has been in the family for many years, and which can be made quite comfortable by modernizing. Others prefer to buy an old house in some good location than to build new; they determine to reconstruct the old building to meet their requirements. For such, this chapter is written, with the hope that it will help some to carry out their purpose of providing new homes from old houses, — homes that will be convenient, practical, and attractive.

Remodeling may be a success financially and artistically, or it may not, depending upon various phases of the problem. Many old houses are not capable of successful remodeling at any price. Constructed along peculiar lines in the first place, the attempt to remodel can only end in failure — or else the building must be entirely wrecked and a new one built all over again. Then, too, some old houses are in such wretched repair that it will not pay to reconstruct them. Money spent modernizing a house is not sensibly spent when the old framework is badly decayed and repairing necessitates such extensive tearing out of walls and partitions that the entire building is practically rebuilt.

On the other hand, many old houses built along simple lines in the first place, and kept in good condition by careful maintenance, are excellent for remodeling. Hardly a city, town, or suburban community exists in which there are not many such fine old places waiting for the hand of some one with taste to make them into modern, well-arranged, attractive houses.

Fortunate is the owner who recognizes the right kind of old house before he buys it for remodeling purposes, and doubly fortunate is the owner who knows what to do with the old place after it has come into his possession, for there are two great factors in remodeling: first, to secure a house with possibil-

PLAIN HOUSE REMODELED.

ities; second, to arrange interior and exterior with accompanying plumbing, heating, and lighting, in an effective way without excessive cost or unnecessary tearing down or destroying. These results are all easy to accomplish after a little study, and every owner who contemplates remodeling should give consideration to the problem *before* he buys a place, in order to begin right by having the right kind of house to start with.

In remodeling, every step should be well planned in advance in order to prevent false steps and save the money lost in experimental building and tearing down again.

Frequently the mere elimination of false ornamental trimmings on an old house will accomplish results quite surprising. Some of the old-time builders who flourished at a later period than the really good designers of Colonial times, were wont to nail ornamental boards and fancy shingles on the gable ends of their houses, producing a result not popular to-day.

NEW PORCH ON AN OLD HOUSE.

What does it cost to remodel? This is usually the first question asked by the average owner, and a very live question it is, — and one very difficult to answer. What does it cost to run an automobile? How much coal will a furnace burn? How many miles from Boston to New York? These are questions to which a like answer may be given, — it depends — depends upon conditions. If you go to Boston from New York by way of the sea, it is one distance, and another if you go by rail. A furnace will burn as much coal as you are willing to shovel into it, — sometimes more, — though scientific stoking greatly cuts down the amount needed to warm a house comfortably. Some men run an automobile on $25 a month, and others hardly squeeze along on $100, depending upon the size and make of car, amount of service, and ability of the man who runs it.

When it comes to remodeling an old house, no two owners

have quite the same experience. One man modernizes in a simple way at a cost of $1000, while another spends $5000, and wishes he had more in order to get what he thinks he wants. But some idea of cost can be obtained of course, and no owner should embark in a remodeling project until he knows somewhere near what the price will be. It is difficult to make a definite estimate on alterations, certainly, but some idea can be gathered by consulting with an expert, one who is familiar with building costs in your neighborhood and therefore qualified to give good advice. But you should remember that the expert can give no information until he knows how extensive the work is to be; so here is where you, Mr. Owner, must give study to the problem, yourself.

In a remodeling project the first thing to do is to examine the old building and determine just what repairs are needed to put the house in good condition, for it is never wise to spend money on remodeling unless the entire building is to be put in good repair at the same time. Rearranged rooms, installation of plumbing, heating, and lighting, and repainting or decorating are thrown away if the balance of the house is not put in just as good condition as the new part. Otherwise, you would be repairing, every year, spots in the house which should have been put in good condition in the first place.

Next, you should draw on a sheet of paper the two floor plans showing the arrangement of rooms as they exist. Make something more than a rough sketch, if possible, for this diagram is to be the groundwork which you or your architect will study for a solution of your problem. On this account the best way is to measure up each room and locate it, carefully drawn to scale (one quarter of an inch to the foot is the most used scale), on your diagram, showing every window, door, and closet. If you have choice pieces of furniture and wish to use them in the remodeled house, show them on your sketch plan so that you may provide space for them in the new scheme.

REMODELING; MAKING AN OLD HOUSE NEW 469

No matter how familiar with the old house you may be, it is difficult to grasp an arrangement of rooms. Walk from room to room as much as you will, trying to determine how to modernize the house, and you will have but a confused idea about the arrangement. But if you make an accurate sketch plan, a plan which can be afterwards examined and studied at leisure, you will have taken

OLD-FASHIONED HOUSE MODERNIZED.

the wisest step possible, and your sketch plan will likely lead to a correct solution of the problem. Take this plan, study it, and determine what is necessary to be done to get the arrangement of rooms desired, bearing in mind, however, that when you remove one partition between two rooms on the first floor for a larger living room, the second-story partition overhead cannot be depended

TWO OLD ROOMS MADE INTO ONE.

upon to hold itself in place. Beams or some such structural members must be built in to support the second story.

470 SUCCESSFUL HOUSES AND HOW TO BUILD THEM

Take care that the new arrangement will not wreck the old building. Modify your desires to suit the character of the old building, instead of arbitrarily demanding that rooms shall be precisely this way or that. The style of the new structure should be determined largely by the style of the old. Plain, old houses are usually more easily remodeled along Colonial lines than any other style.

LITTLE BRICK HOUSE WITH NEW PORCH AND PERGOLA.

When remodeling, a first-class system of heating may be installed in any house without making a shaving on the floor or a scratch on the wall. Careful workmen can put in the system, connect it up, and take away their tools again without annoyance to any one in the house. Hot-water and steam heat are easiest to install in an old house, though furnace heat may be put in with no great inconvenience. Most hot-water and steam pipes are not larger than $1\frac{1}{2}$ inches; rarely do they exceed 2 inches in diameter. That is why they are so easily put in,

REMODELING; MAKING AN OLD HOUSE NEW   471

for upright pipes, or "risers," as they are called, may be slipped from the basement into old partitions.

Modern hot-air furnaces are excellent for old houses, with the advantage that they cost less than hot-water or steam heaters. It is more difficult to get hot-air risers up to the

OLD HOUSE TRANSFORMED INTO A STUDIO.
Frank Chouteau Brown, Architect.

second floor through the old rooms below. However, one can usually find a way by placing them in closets or out-of-the-way corners.

A new plumbing system is almost as easily installed in an old house as in a new. Two vertical stacks are usually required,— one for the kitchen sink and laundry trays, and one for the bathroom. Two bathrooms are always desirable, sometimes three. You can hardly have too many.

Locate the bathrooms as near together as possible so that you may use one vertical stack for both. If they are widely separated, however, you must use a separate stack for each.

CHARMING BEDROOM IN AN OLD NEW ENGLAND HOUSE.

The new vertical plumbing pipes may be placed in a corner, neatly cased up, or you may be able to slip them into an old partition by sawing a narrow slot through the plastering. A break in the plaster is easily patched up again, and wall paper or burlap will hide the patch. In the basement, run new pipes on the cellar wall to prevent breaking into the old cement floor.

Most piping in the new bathroom installation will be under

REMODELING; MAKING AN OLD HOUSE NEW 473

each bathroom floor. Here the horizontal pipes necessary are frequently difficult to build in. Careful planning, however, will usually provide a way of locating fixtures close to the vertical stack so that very little cutting of the old floor timbers is necessary. At the most, a small section of floor can be rebuilt at slight expense.

Kitchen fixtures are easiest of all to install in the old house. One small stack up through the roof connected at the bottom with a line of pipe to the sewer is sufficient. Run the kitchen waste *inside* the room right down through the floor. The ventilating stack above may also be run inside the kitchen, as it can be cased up neatly.

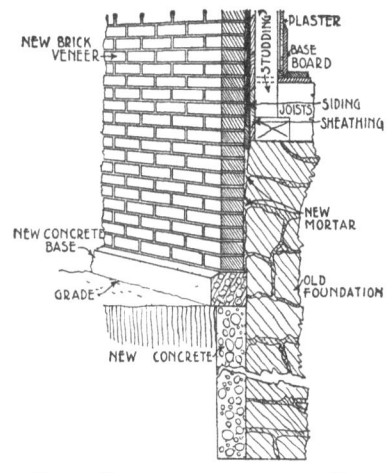

BRICK VENEER APPLIED ON AN OLD FRAME HOUSE.

Before starting any of the work, have plumbing and heating

OLD WINDOWS —

CHANGED INTO NEW CASEMENTS.

contractors make estimates. In a remodeling job, it may not be possible for them to tell you exactly what the work will

474 SUCCESSFUL HOUSES AND HOW TO BUILD THEM

cost, but they should be able to estimate within 10 per cent of the total amount.

The best time to install new heating and plumbing is in warm weather. Consider the problem carefully through the winter months, and begin actual operations during good building weather in the spring. This will give you ample time to complete the work so that another winter will find you and your family enjoying the comforts of modern heating and plumbing.

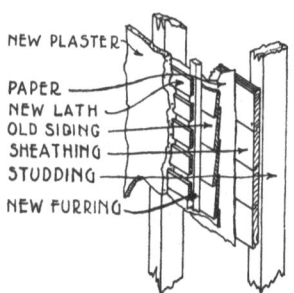

PLASTER EXTERIOR ON WOOD LATHS APPLIED TO OLD HOUSE.

One type of old house frequently successfully remodeled is the farmhouse,—which may be made habitable for summer only, or for all the year.

Old farmhouses are usually well built. A good grade of lumber, thoroughly hard-burned brick, and sound stone are invariably to be found knit into the structure of a farmhouse built years ago before there was depreciation in the quality and quantity of lumber, and before higher prices made builders skimp the work. As a rule, however, old farmhouses do not have good cellars.

When remodeling a farmhouse whether for summer or year-round occupancy, arrange first to put a good cellar and foundation under the entire building, for sound foundations will prevent repairs. Use stone, if stone is plentiful in your neighborhood.

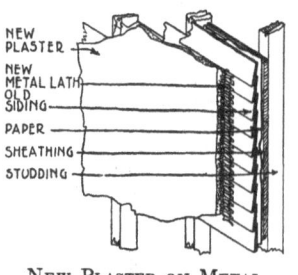

NEW PLASTER ON METAL LATHING.

On many old farms enough stone can be found in an uncleared field or in old stone walls to build the foundations entire.

REMODELING; MAKING AN OLD HOUSE NEW 475

With weather-beaten faces green with old moss and brown or gray from long exposure, old stone makes the most attractive building material for farmhouses. For this reason it is better to save old stone walls for work above ground, using more ordinary ledge stone for below ground. In regions where stone is scarce, concrete foundations will prove cheaper than stone.

OLD HOUSE BEFORE REMODELING.
(See Page 476.)

To put a new foundation under an old building, tear out a small portion of the old wall. Dig new trenches down to the required depth (5 or 6 feet in most cases) and lay in new stone or concrete. After sufficient new wall is built up to underpin the sills of the building above, you may tear out the remaining portions of the old wall and rebuild with new material, bonding it well to the first work.

In building foundations of concrete, trenches are dug down to the required depth (about 12 inches below the cellar bottom). Inside of the wall a "form" of rough boards is built, far enough back from the bank to give the necessary thickness to the wall (10 or 12 inches in most cases). The bottom board of the

As REMODELED.
Frank Chouteau Brown, Architect.
(See Page 475.)

form is left about 6 inches above the cellar bottom, and the trench is made 8 inches wider at this point. Cement concrete, dumped into the space between form and bank, flows out on the bottom, filling the extra-wide trench and forming a broad footing of concrete, as shown. The remainder of the foundation space is then filled with concrete to the under side of the building.

REMODELING; MAKING AN OLD HOUSE NEW 477

Ivory-white is a good color for the outside weather boarding of an old house. Put just enough yellow in with the white to give it an ivory tone. In requesting a painter to mix up ivory-white, however, caution him to get it mostly white. Some painters think "ivory" means deep cream, whereas it is really white, slightly on the ivory shade. With the house painted white, green blinds are almost a necessity.

BEFORE ALTERATIONS
(See Page 478)

On an old shingled house where it is necessary to renew the shingles merely in spots, the fresh patches can be stained to match the old weather-beaten shingles, or, if preferred, the entire building may be stained with shingle stain. To secure with new shingles the pretty weathered effect of old shingles, use "bleaching oil." Ivory-white cornices and green blinds are very attractive against a background of bleached shingles.

Cement plaster is a boon for remodeling, as it quickly makes a decided change in the appearance of an old house. Cement plaster makes a sound, durable, warm overcoat for any house.

478 SUCCESSFUL HOUSES AND HOW TO BUILD THEM

On most buildings it produces a modern effect without more extensive alterations being required.

Select a reliable plasterer to do the work. There is nothing which demands more careful work than plastering. No operation can be so easily slighted, as is explained in another chapter.

For an ordinary house 30 × 40 feet, it costs about $350 to $500 to lath and plaster the exterior, using wood laths. At

AFTER ALTERATIONS.
J. K. Cady, Architect.
(See Page 477.)

these prices one saves the cost of the plaster overcoat in a few years by the lessened cost of painting, alone.

To covercoat a house with plaster on wood laths, nail 1-inch by 2-inch furring strips vertically upon the old siding. These strips should be about 12 inches apart, and wood laths are applied horizontally in the usual way.

Metal lathing costs more than wood laths, but it is economical for an old house, as furring strips are not necessary. You may apply metal lathing directly to the wood siding and save the cost of furring strips. The details of lathing and plastering are described in another chapter.

BRICK AND PLASTER HOUSE IN A SUBURB OF CHICAGO
Charles E. White, Jr., Architect.

CHAPTER XXVIII

SENSIBLE TYPES OF AMERICAN HOUSES

AMERICAN houses are the most scientifically planned of those in any country. In the best American designs, proper consideration is given to the beautiful as well as the practical, but construction is never sacrificed for architectural effect, nor is mere appearance allowed to take the place of actual convenience.

Not a little of the success of well-planned American houses is due to the clear-sightedness of American housekeepers, women skilled in managing the machinery of the house so that it runs easily, smoothly, and with least effort. The shortening of steps, the convenient arrangement of cupboards and closets, the elimination of much that is unnecessary, and the incorporation of everything needful is largely through the efforts of these women. Most architects are glad to acknowledge their indebtedness to their women clients.

Bungalows, many of them ingenious and pretty, others ugly and ill arranged, are built everywhere. The bungalow idea (that is, the house-on-one-floor) is excellent so far as housekeeping convenience is concerned, and bungalows designed by the skillful are very attractive. A bungalow should be something more than a one-story flat building and something less than a palace, though both types are unfortunately very much in evidence. A long, low, "rakish" building is perhaps the best description of what a bungalow should be.

As a rule, bungalows look best perched upon the side of a hill (as they are so frequently in California) with plenty of ground

Bungalow for Two.

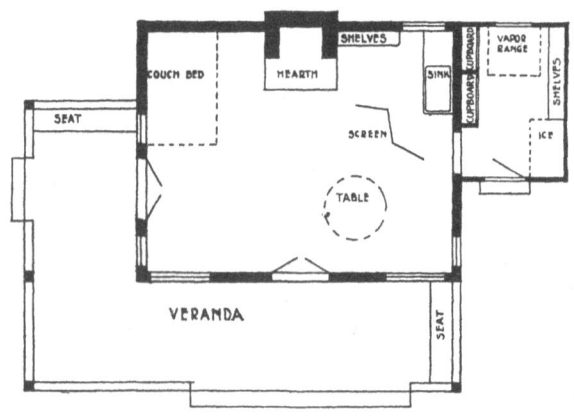

Plan of Bungalow for Two.

A Little Bungalow of Shingles.

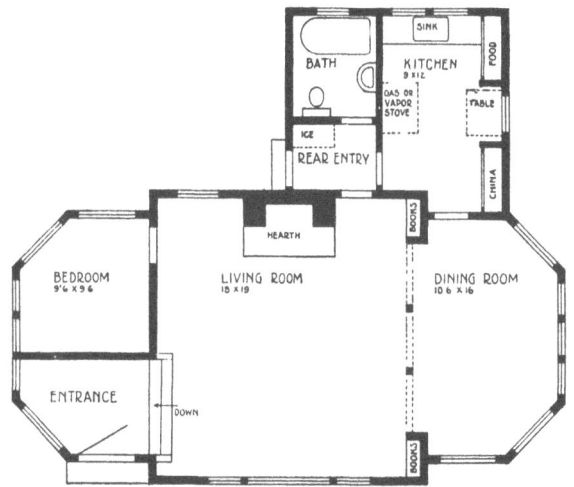

Plan of Shingled Bungalow.

484 *SUCCESSFUL HOUSES AND HOW TO BUILD THEM*

First Floor Plan.   Second Floor Plan.
Cement-plastered Bungalow.

SENSIBLE TYPES OF AMERICAN HOUSES 485

on all sides. On lots of moderate size, tightly squeezed into rows, bungalows are not so attractive.

The bungalow is not cheap. Comparing the amount of space in a bungalow with the same space in a two-story or one-and-one-half story cottage, it will be found that the latter cost less,

SWINGING PARTITION BETWEEN LIVING ROOM AND KITCHEN.
(See floor plan on preceding page.)

owing to the greater amount of cellar and roof in the former, and consequent greater cost.

Next in cost (per cubic foot) to the single-story bungalow is the one-and-one-half story cottage, and next to that comes the two-story cottage in which the second story is of full height (not cut off by the sloping roof). Cottages of the latter type are less expensive than buildings with a steeper roof.

LITTLE SUBURBAN HOUSE.
Spencer and Powers, Architects.

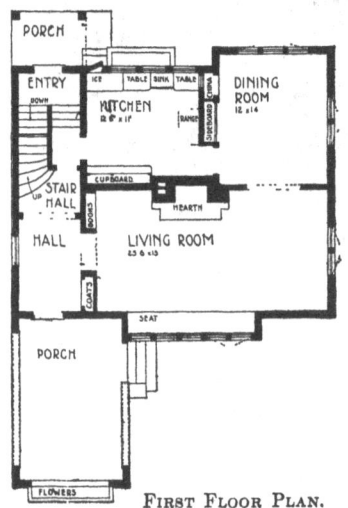

FIRST FLOOR PLAN.

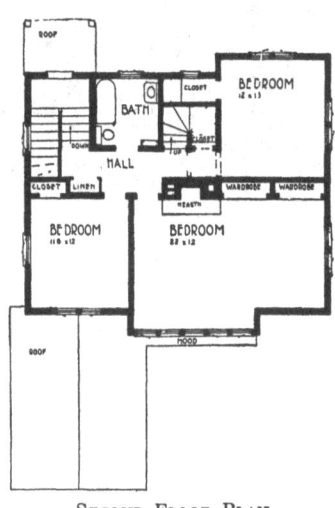

SECOND FLOOR PLAN.

SENSIBLE TYPES OF AMERICAN HOUSES 487

CEMENT-PLASTERED HOUSE OF MODERATE COST.

Charles E. White, Jr., Architect.

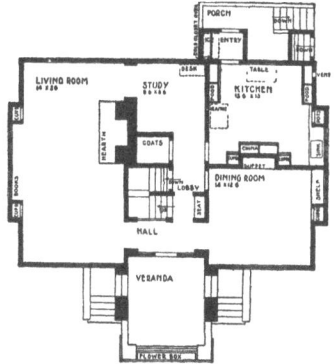

FIRST FLOOR PLAN.

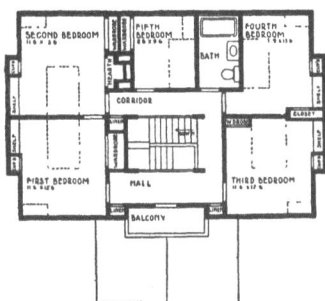

SECOND FLOOR PLAN.

488　*SUCCESSFUL HOUSES AND HOW TO BUILD THEM*

Country House near New York.
Aymar Embury II, Architect.

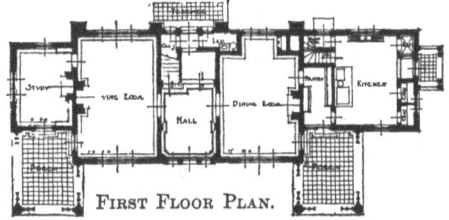

First Floor Plan.

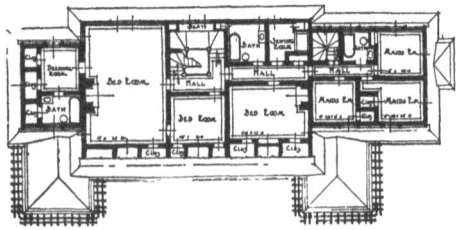

Second Floor Plan

SENSIBLE TYPES OF AMERICAN HOUSES 489

BRICK AND PLASTER HOUSE IN SEATTLE.
Wilson and Loveless, Architects.

FIRST FLOOR PLAN.

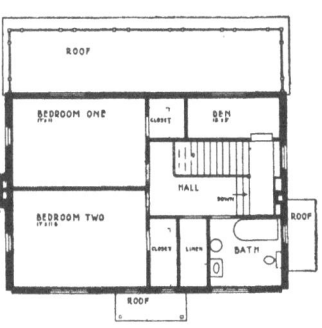

SECOND FLOOR PLAN.

490   SUCCESSFUL HOUSES AND HOW TO BUILD THEM

BRICK HOUSE WITH FRAME KITCHEN WING.
Aymar Embury II, Architect.

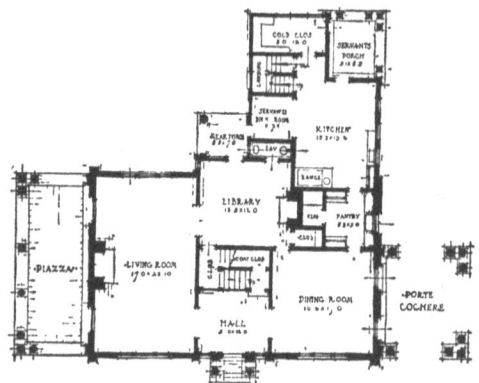

FIRST FLOOR PLAN.

SENSIBLE TYPES OF AMERICAN HOUSES 491

To reduce the cost of a house to the lowest practical point and at the same time have all the necessities, an attic can well be eliminated. Another space saver (consequently, a money saver) is the buffet kitchen, in which food and dishes are kept in kitchen cupboards. Thus, with no food or china pantry, considerable space is saved, and at the same time housekeeping is made easier.

American suburban houses, when there is room to do so, are

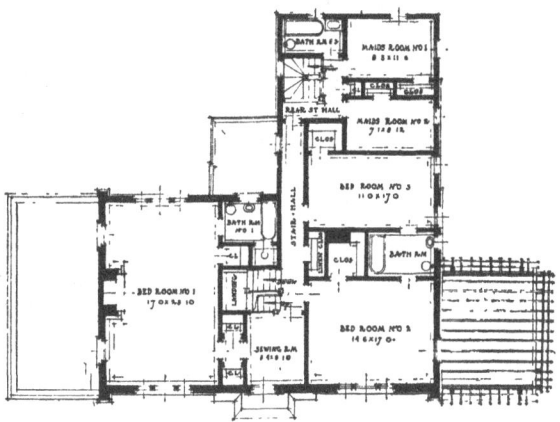

SECOND FLOOR PLAN.

frequently stretched out in a long building, comparatively narrow. This is an excellent type of house when handled with skill, as it makes a charming appearance and is at the same time conveniently arranged. On a smaller building site, however, the house must be smaller and more compact.

The hall-in-the-middle type of so many Eastern houses is always attractive and usually practical. If a vote was to be taken on what is the most popular style of house, undoubtedly this type would win, for Colonial and "Near-Colonial" houses are much admired. Another popular style — and justly so —

492 SUCCESSFUL HOUSES AND HOW TO BUILD THEM

BRICK HOUSE IN CHICAGO SUBURB.
J. K. Cady, Architect.

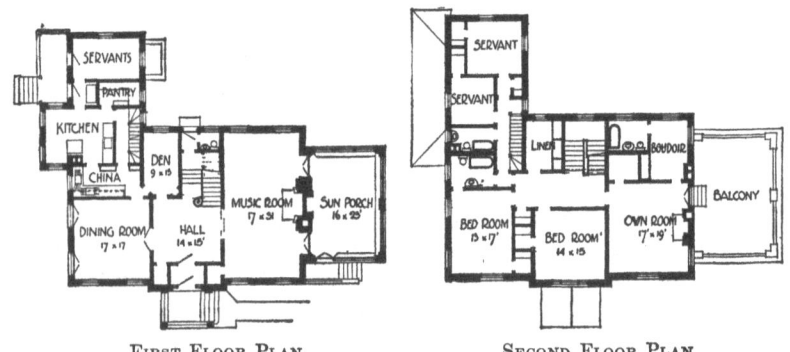

FIRST FLOOR PLAN.   SECOND FLOOR PLAN.

SENSIBLE TYPES OF AMERICAN HOUSES

Brick Country House near Boston.
Frank Chouteau Brown, Architect.

First Floor Plan.

Second Floor Plan.

is the modern English; very much Americanized, of course. The freedom possible in this style is quite remarkable, in many cases the Americanized version of the English style being so different from its prototype as to be hardly recognizable, though something of the spirit of the latter remains, it is to be hoped.

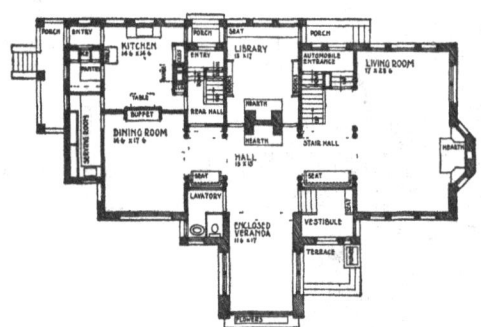

First Floor Plan of House on Page 480.

Second Floor Plan.

A Single-story Garage

CHAPTER XXIX

GARAGES AND GARAGE APPARATUS

KEEPING pace with automobile growth, modern garages are very convenient, and garage apparatus is up to a very high standard of practical utility. There isn't much room left for improvement, though possibly the future will bring out some new ideas. Every conceivable kind of plan and every form of construction has been tried out, so that now garage design is more or less standardized. A man can buy motor cars which cost as much as a house, or he may content himself with a five-hundred-dollar

SMALL GARAGE FOR SUBURBAN HOUSE.

runabout, with the assurance that in any event he can build a garage in keeping with his car and at a cost to fit his pocketbook.

For a small but practical building at lowest cost, one may use a portable garage, built at the factory and shipped in sections. These little buildings come in all sizes and in many designs, with doors and windows arranged to suit any case. It is easy to put the sections together, and most portable garages are quite attractive in appearance, though one must use intelligence in selecting.

For a more pretentious garage it is probably better to build in the ordinary way, using the many good materials for this purpose. Lumber, cement, metal lath, hollow tile, brick, and stone are most frequently used. On large country places a garage is often combined with the stable, for many country dwellers (and city, too, for that matter) keep horses as well as motor cars.

The idea that the garage should be in the same style as the house is most important. Nothing is more unattractive than a place where the house is of one style and garage another. When a garage is combined with the stable, it is necessary to keep the former entirely separate from the latter. Otherwise, ammonia coming from the stable will tarnish the metal work of the cars. The best plan is to have a building in two wings, L-shaped or otherwise, with horses in one wing and cars in another. No doorways should connect the two.

STABLE AND GARAGE COMBINED.

Where no stable is desired in combination with the garage, it is an excellent plan to attach the latter to the house by means

GARAGES AND GARAGE APPARATUS 499

GARAGE ATTACHED TO HOUSE.

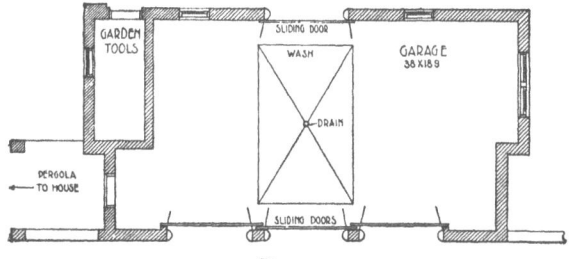

PLAN.

500 SUCCESSFUL HOUSES AND HOW TO BUILD THEM

of a wall, pergola, or fence. The cost of the connecting link, whether wall or fence, is slight, considering the attractive effect obtained in that way. On a corner lot the garage may be built on the side street, attached to the house by a covered pergola. The owner drives into his garage directly from the street, thus making unnecessary a driveway. With two or three doors on

STORY-AND-HALF GARAGE.

the street (one sliding by another), any car may be taken out without disturbing another.

The ideal garages are, of course, fireproof, and many useful methods of building garages at moderate cost have been developed. Cement plaster is an excellent material to use in this way. One of the best systems for building fireproof where cement plaster is used is by means of expanded metal lathing in which is incorporated, every few inches, a steel rib to act as a stiffener. Such a wall requires but few steel uprights to which metal fabric is fixed, so it is exceedingly economical to use on walls and roof. In building such a garage, it is only necessary to provide a concrete floor on cinders directly on the ground, sidewalk fashion. At proper intervals steel angle uprights are set into the concrete floor, and the ribbed metal fabric is fastened to these. Cement plaster is afterwards coated inside and out.

METAL FRAME PLASTERED GARAGE.

So many garages are being built with sliding doors that much study has been given by architects to the proper design for the large doors. Sliding doors are greatly to be preferred to swinging doors in a garage, for swing doors (opening out to save space) cannot be opened when snow becomes banked against them in winter. The great value of sliding doors is that no wall space is required to slide them on. One door slides behind

502 SUCCESSFUL HOUSES AND HOW TO BUILD THEM

METAL FRAMEWORK.

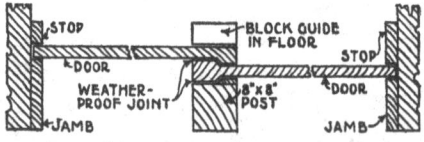

GOOD METHOD FOR SLIDING DOORS.

the other. Of course, both cannot be opened at the same time, but that is rarely necessary.

Much of the new apparatus for garages is very useful, but none more so than a turntable, the installation of which makes it possible to utilize every inch of space in the building, no matter what shape it is. One doorway for cars is all that is necessary when there is a turntable, as each car can be run on to the turntable, turned, and run off in any

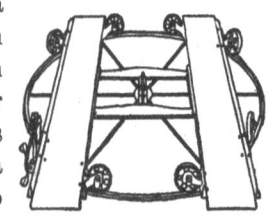

AUTOMOBILE TURNTABLE.

CEMENT TRACKS FOR AUTOMOBILES.

GARAGE IN BASEMENT OF HOUSE.

GARAGE ATTACHED TO HOUSE.

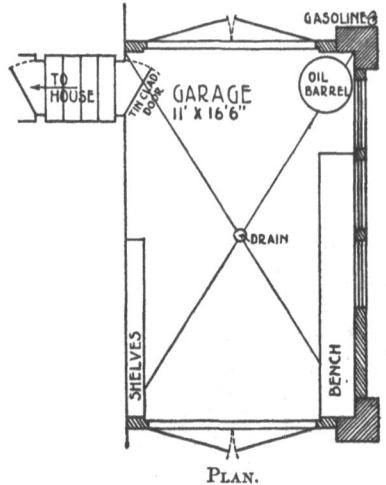

PLAN.

direction to its location on the floor. Some turntables are installed in a little pit built in the concrete floor. Others are bolted on top of the floor, no pit being required.

For access to the garage you may have a cinder driveway, gravel drive, or one of concrete. The latter is most practical, as it requires no repairs, but oftentimes a concrete drive makes an unsightly streak across the grounds. Another objection to it is that the cement surface often becomes greasy from engine drippings. A better method is to build a concrete track with a strip of

GARAGES AND GARAGE APPARATUS 505

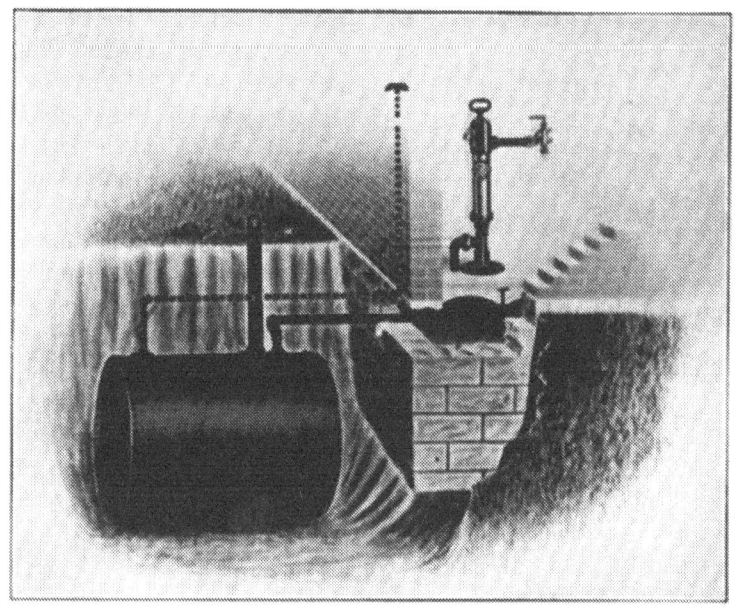

Good Small Outfit for Gasoline Storage.

grass in the center. Grease falls on the grass, where it will not be noticeable.

Cottages or small houses may have a garage built underneath. To prevent the necessity of backing out, a pitless turntable is installed in order that the car may be turned before it comes out. In places like this, a turntable is a special convenience.

Other garages are attached to the house. In attaching a garage in this way, great care must be taken to make

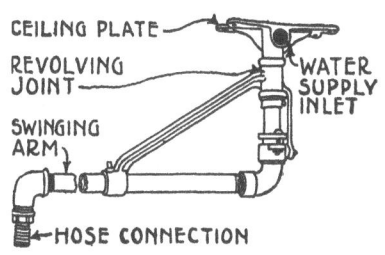

Swinging Ceiling Hose Washer.

LARGE BRICK GARAGE.

a tight entrance between garage and house. Otherwise, gasoline fumes may penetrate the latter much to the annoyance of those who live there, to say nothing of fire risk. A fireproof door is always desirable in such a place. The supply of gasoline should be kept outside, underground. For fireproof construction, terra cotta hollow tile blocks are excellent, producing a safe garage in which one can keep the most expensive cars and apparatus. Cement plaster applied to the outside sinks into the grooves in the tile and clings tenaciously, making a strong, warm, attractive wall. The inside of the wall can be plastered, or it may be simply whitewashed or painted.

Gasoline should always be kept underground. Modern apparatus for gasoline storage is efficient, safe, and clean, the general idea in best apparatus being an

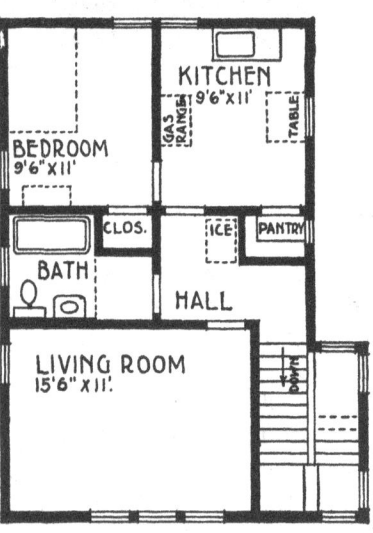

CONVENIENT PLAN FOR CHAUFFEUR'S QUARTERS ON SECOND FLOOR OF A GARAGE.

underground steel storage tank from which gasoline is pumped as wanted. Another useful device rapidly coming into general use is an overhead washing apparatus consisting of a pipe arm swiveled to the supply pipe in the ceiling, for attaching the hose when washing a car. You can thus reach any part of the car without dragging the hose all about the floor.

INDEX

A

agreement — standard form of, 150.
air-compresser, 404.
allowance, hardware, 136.
allowance clauses, 136.
American Institute of Architects, 78
anchors, 231.
architect's duties, 73.
  fees, 78.
  sketches, 80.
area walls, 165.
ash barrel crane, 457.
ash receiver, rotary, 455.
ash sifter, 456.
awnings, 62.

B

balcony, 53.
barricades, 259.
baseboard, kitchen, 265.
basement, depth of, 164.
  height of, 169.
  waterproof, 172.
basement closets, 128.
basement tool room, 128.
basement trunk rack, 128.
basement work shop, 128.
bath, seat douche, 319.
  seat bidet, 319.
bathroom, private, 122.
  size of, 122.
  capacity of, 122.
  location of, 122.
bathroom fittings, 329.
bathroom floors, 123.
bathroom walls, 123.
bathroom windows, 123.
baths, seat, 319.
  sitz, 319.
  foot, 319.
  shower, 319.

bathtubs, 315.
  with feet, 315.
  with base, 315.
  built-in, 315.
  niche, 316.
  Roman, 316.
  sizes of, 316.
  height of, 317.
  width of, 317.
  piping, space for, 318.
  concealed piping, 318.
  porcelain, 318
  enamelled, 318
  zinc white finish, 318.
  finished cost of, 318.
  infants, 319,
    size of, 319.
batter boards, 162.
beam, trussed, 190.
beams, ceiling, 270.
bedroom, owner's, 121.
bedrooms, 99, 120.
  size of, 120.
  windows, 121.
bibbs, ground key, 337.
bids, 86.
  sub-, 87.
billiard room, 120.
  size of, 120.
blind-nailing, 199.
blinds, outside, 270.
  inside, 270.
  Venetian, 270.
boarding, 274.
  diagonal, 190.
  horizontal, 190.
boards and battens, 200.
  matched, 199.
boiler hot water, connecting of, 291
  range, 292.
boiler covering, 360.

boiler insulation, 360.
boilers, vertical sectional, steam (table), 355.
   vertical sectional, hot water, 356.
   soft coal, 356.
   magazine feed, 356.
   horizontal sectional, steam (table), 357.
   horizontal sectional, hot water (table), 358.
   size of, 359.
   equipment for, 360.
bonds, 87.
bookcases, 126
bracing masonry walls, 231.
brick, soft, 176.
   hard, 176.
   grade of (table), 215.
   merchantable, 215.
   common, 215.
   face, 216–222.
   molded, 216.
   hexagon, 216.
   paving, 217.
   yellow, 219.
   red, 220.
   brown, 220.
   purple, 220.
   gray, 220.
   rough texture, 220.
   manufacture of, 221.
   re-pressed, 222.
   tapestry, 222.
   smooth, 222.
   mottled, 222.
   enamelled, 222.
   bonding, 222.
   ordinary bond, 223.
   English bond, 223.
   Flemish bond, 223.
   double Flemish bond, 223.
brick stretchers, 224.
   sizes of, common, 225.
      Roman, 226.
      standard, 226.
   sand lime, 229.
   cement, 230.
brick tests, 229.
brick veneer, 204.
brickwork, 215.
   methods for laying, 229.

building, to own, 3.
   to rent, 3.
   contract, 146.
   inspection, 155.
   paper, 199.
building loans, 4.
building lots, 9.
   skillful buying of, 10.
   details of buying, 13.
   value of schoolhouses and churches 14.
   size, 16.
   inside, 17.
   west frontage, 17.
   corner, 19.
   neighboring houses, 19.
   hillside, 20
   irregular, 21.
   rectangular, 21.
   clear title to, 22.
   abstracts, 22.
   deeds, 22.
   warranty deeds, 22.
bungalows, 481.
   cost of, 485.
butler's pantry, 117.
butts, 449.

C

cabinets, 125.
cabinet work, 259.
cabinet workmanship, 265.
candlesticks, 434.
canvas, 398.
   painting on, 398.
carpentry, 259.
casings, exterior, 260.
catch basin, 304.
ceiling plates, 371.
cement, Keene's, 383.
cesspool, disadvantage of, 343.
   contamination from, 344.
chimney, faulty, 374.
   flashing, 375.
chimney flues, correct sizes of (table), 373.
china cases, 118.
circulating system, 290
circulator, automatic, 361.
cistern, soft water, 304.

INDEX

cistern, brick, 304.
  wood, 304.
clapboards, 198.
closet, coat, 126.
closets, 123.
closets, hat, 125.
  linen, 126.
  preserve, 127.
  basement, 128.
coal bin, 127.
  dust proof, 127.
coal cellar, 127.
coal chute, 455.
coat closet, 126.
coat room, 126.
  size of, 126.
cocks, corporation, 286.
  stop and waste, 289.
  street, 289.
  ball, 326.
  pantry, 339.
  double-mixing, 339.
  hose, 339.
  loose key, 339.
columns, porch, 59.
  Greek, 60.
  Doric, 60.
  Tuscan, 60.
  Ionic, 60.
  Corinthian, 60.
  ugly, 60.
compression tanks, 402.
concrete blocks, 177–235.
conductors, 281.
contract, building, 146.
  uniform, 150.
  signatures, 150.
  compensation, 150.
  seal, 150.
  amendments, 151.
  implied conditions, 151.
  forfeiture price, 151.
  extra work, 152.
  written orders, 152.
  responsibility, 152.
contracts, general, 87.
  employers' liability act, 152.
  insurance, 152.
  architects and owners, 152.
cornices, 57.
  overhanging, 58.

cornices, first-story, 59.
cost of houses, comparative, 77.
  cubic-foot, 77.
cottages, cost of, 485.
crematory, rubbish, 421.
cross-furring, 379.
cupboard, table leaves, 119.
  milk, outside, 459.
cupboards, kitchen, 115.

D

damper chains, 372.
deafening, 262.
den, 110.
design, 25.
  history of building, 26.
dining room, 102.
dining table, 103.
dirt, stacking of, 162.
documents, legal, 145.
door casings, 56.
door frames, 260–265.
doors, entrance, 49.
  inside, 63.
  handles, 64.
  swing of, 266.
  mirror, 267.
doorways, old Colonial, 47.
down-spouts, 281, 302.
drainage system, 294.
drain board mats, 310.
drain boards, 310.
drains, subsoil, 170.
  trenches, 171.
drawings, working, 72–82.
  sketches, 80.
  details, 84.
dressing room, 122.
  size of, 122.
drinking fountains, 322.
  bubbling, 322.
driers, lawn, 458.
  balcony, 459.
dumb waiter, 457.

E

eaves, 58.
  plaster, 58.
  sheathed, 58.

electric conduits, 428.
electric fixtures, 431.
  finishes for, 433.
electric flexible cable, 429.
electric lamps, 432.
electric lighting, indirect, 432.
electric lights, incandescent, 427.
  main, cut-out box for, 430.
  fuses for, 430.
  fuse box for, 430.
electric mangles, 410.
electric plants, house, 414.
  location of, 415.
electric storage battery, house, 414.
electric vacuum cleaners, basement, 413.
  portable, 413.
electric washing machines, 411.
electric wiring, 428.
  inspection of, 429.
engines for lighting plants, 415.
escutcheons, 448.
excavation, 161.
expansion tank, 360.

F

faucets, 336.
  brass, 336.
  white metal, 336.
  nickel plated, 336.
  compression, 337.
  Fuller, 338.
  quick opening, 338.
  self closing, 338.
  for laundry tubs, 339.
  bathtubs, 339.
felt, gravel covered, 210.
fireplaces, 104.
  smokeless (rule for), 376.
fireproof ceilings, plaster on, 248.
fireproof floors, 249.
  safe loads for (table), 246-247.
  pipes in, 248.
fireproof houses, 237.
fireproof lintels, 249.
fireproof materials, 241.
fittings, Y, 295.
flashing, 281.
  tin, 281.
  copper, 281.

floor, cellar, 169.
  cement, 169.
flooring, finished, 191-262.
floor plates, 371.
floors, tile, 113.
  under, 191.
  stripped, 191-262.
  scraping, 263.
  maple, 263.
  Southern pine, 263.
  straight sawed, 263.
  quarter sawed, 263.
  fir, 263.
  painted joints in, 263.
  tile, 264.
  rubber tile, 264.
  linoleum, 264.
flour bin, 116.
flower box, self-watering, 460.
flower boxes, 50-61.
footings, 166.
  concrete, 166.
  brick, 166.
  stone, 166.
foundations, 161.
  concrete, 172.
  stone, 173.
  brick, 176.
  hollow tile, 177.
framing, Eastern method, 182.
  Western method, 183.
  balloon, 184.
  flush, 187.
frontage, 93.
furnace coils, 291.
furnaces, hot air, 352.
furniture, living room, 101.
  dining table, 103.
  sleeping porch beds, 113.
  built-in, measurements for, 271
furring, for brick walls, 218.
furring strips, 206.

G

garage and stable, combination, 500
garage doors, 503.
garage driveways, 506.
garages, 499.
  portable, 500.
  fireproof, 502.

INDEX 513

garages, basement, 507.
  gasoline storage, 508.
  washing apparatus, 509.
garage turntables, 504.
garbage burner, 292.
garbage cans, sanitary, 457.
garbage receiver, underground, 458.
gas, gasoline, 419.
  bottled, 420.
gas burners, 427.
gas fixtures, 432.
gas heaters, instantaneous, 404.
  automatic, 406.
  ordinary, 406.
gas lighting, incandescent, 425.
gas lights, inverted, 426.
  pilot, 426.
gas mantles, 426.
gas plants, house, 416.
  safety of, 417.
  acetylene, 418.
girders, 167.
  flush, 187.
glass, ornamental, 51.
  small panes, 52.
  schedule of (table), 399.
glazing, 399.
globes and shades, 433.
grading, 19.
  finished, 163.
gutters, galvanized iron, 281.
  hanging, 281.

H

hair felt, 192.
hall, 106.
hardware, 437.
  price of, 437.
  selecting, 439.
  metals for, 444.
  finishes for, 445.
  colors for, 447.
  casement window, 451.
  for double-acting doors, 452.
hardware allowance, 136.
hardwood, 261.
hat box, 125.
heaters, combination hot-air and hot-water, 354.
heating, electric, 352.

heating, hot-air furnace, 352.
  hot water, 354.
  steam, 361.
  vacuum, 363.
  plant, tools for, 363.
  principles of, 373.
hinges, invisible, 451.
hoods, 60.
hot-air furnace, 352.
hot-air registers, 354.
hot-water heating, 364.
hot-water system, 290.
houses, square, 93.
  rectangular, 93.
  American, types of, 481.

I

incinerator, garbage, 421.
installments, buying on, 3.
insulation, 192.
  hair felt, 192.
  linofelt, 192.
  seaweed quilt, 192.
  wind-proof paper, 203.
  sheathing paper, 203.

J

joints, leaded, 199.
  mortar, 176, 226.
  colored mortar, 226.
  raked, 227.
  struck, 227.
  pointed, 227.
joist cutting for pipes, 275.
joist hangers, metal, 190.
joists in masonry houses, 230.

K

kalsomine, 397.
Keene's cement, 383.
kitchen, 113.
  old style, 114.
  modern, 114.
  small, 114.
kitchen cupboards, 115.
  size of, 115.
kitchen doors, 115.
kitchen sinks, 310.
  location of, 310.

kitchen sinks, window at, 310.
  painting of, 311.
  height of, 311.
  adjustable legs for, 311.
  sizes of, 312.
kitchen windows, 115.
knobs, 448.

L

lamps, kerosene, 433.
  gas, 434.
lathing, 379.
  sheathing, 380.
  metal, 381.
laths, exterior wood, 207.
  wood, 380.
laundry, 127.
laundry clothes drier, 409.
laundry fixtures, 330.
laundry mangle, 410.
laundry tubs, soapstone, 330.
  enamelled iron, 330.
  vitreous ware, 330.
  cement, 330.
  wood, 331.
laundry washing machines, 410.
lavatories, 314.
  wall, 314.
  marble, 314.
  enamelled iron, 314.
  porcelain, 314.
  vitreous ware, 314.
  pedestal, 315.
  sizes of, 315.
  dental, 315.
lawns, value of, 15.
lead, white, 390.
ledger, 185.
legal documents, 145.
  invitations for proposal, 152.
  standard proposal form, 152.
  proposal, 152.
  bids, 152,
  bonds, 153.
  building permit, 155.
  plumbing permit, 155.
  electric permit, 155.
  waiver of lien, 156.
  architect's certificate, 157.
  insurance form. 158.

legal documents, builder's risk, 158
library, 109
liens, mechanics, 87.
lighting plants, cost per hour, 416
  voltage of, 416.
linen closet, 126.
linofelt, 192.
linoleum, 117, 264.
lintels, window, 216.
living room, 100.
living room furniture, 101.
loam, 163.
loans, building, 4.
locks, 439.
  lever tumbler, 439.
  cylinder, 440.
    pin tumblers for, 441.
  strikes for, 440.
  keys for, 440.
  materials in, 442.
  spindles for, 443.
  unit, 448.
logs, 180.
lot, inside, 16–17.
  size of, 16.
  west frontage, 17.
  corner, 19.
  hillside, 20.
  irregular, 21.
  rectangular, 21.
lumber, 179.
  size of, 183.
  skrinkage of, 186.
  seasoned, 193.
  piling of, 195.
  kiln-dried, 265.

M

masonry, 213.
medicine cupboards, 126.
mortar, cement, 175.
  colored, 175.
  lime, 175.
  mixing, 175.
  sand for, 175.
music room, 109.

O

overflows, recessed, 340.

INDEX

P

paint, exterior, 390–394.
  failure of, 391.
  success of, 391.
  application of, 392.
  priming coat, 393
  final coat, 393.
  mineral, 393,
  for tin work, 393.
  puttying, 393.
  colors, 394.
  for plaster, 394.
  interior, 395
  white enamel, 395.
  for canvas roofs, 398.
painting, color, inside, 398.
paneling, 65, 270
panels, ceiling, 271.
pantry, 116
  butler's, 117.
  serving, 118.
  wastes for, 340.
pantry floors, 117.
pantry sinks, 119, 312.
pantry walls, 117.
paper, building, 191.
partitions, 230.
  inside, 188.
  bathroom, 189.
permit, building, 155.
  plumber's, 155.
  electric, 155.
pianos, size of, 109.
piers, 167.
pipe, water service, 286.
  lead, 287.
  galvanized iron, 287.
  tin-lined lead, 287.
  white metal, 287.
  brass tubing, 287.
  Benedict metal, 287.
  durometal, 287.
  hot water, 287.
  size of, 288.
  tags for, 289.
  water, depth of, 289.
    insulation of, 289.
  soft water, 290
  circulating, 290.
  tile, 294.

pipe, cast iron, 298.
  testing of, 298.
  coated, 298.
  hanging of, 298.
  plumbing, testing of, 300.
pipe covering, 360.
pipe insulation, 360.
pipes, for water supply, 286.
  for sewage, 286.
  for ventilation, 286
piping system, 286
plaster, hard, 114
  cement, 205.
  texture, 208.
  rough coat, 209.
  patent, 385.
  preparation of, inside, 383.
  grounds for, 383.
  scratch coat, 384.
  brown coat, 384.
  finished coat, 384
  smooth finish, 384.
  sand finish, 384.
  hard finish, 384.
  exterior finish, 385.
  rough cast, 386.
  crushed stone for, 386.
plaster board, 380.
plastering, back, 192.
  inside, 382.
  sand for, 383.
  fiber for, 383.
  hair for, 383.
plumbing, rodding, 297
plumbing clean-outs, 297
plumbing fixtures, porcelain, 308.
  enamelled iron, 308.
  vitreous ware, 309.
  marble, 309.
  soapstone, 309.
plumbing stack, 294.
  support of, 297.
pointing, 176.
porch, carriage, 60.
  sleeping, 112.
  double-deck, 112.
porch columns, 59.
porch entrance, 48.
porches, 94–112.
porch trimmings, 59.
post, newel, 64.

posts, 167–168.
  iron, 168.
  wooden, 168.
  hollow tile, 169.
  clothes, 458.
preserve closet, 127.
pressure regulator, 288.
pump, hand, 402.
pumps, electric, 403.
  gas engine, 403.
  hand suction, 408.
    and lift, 408
  water power, 408.

Q

quarter round, 265.
quilt, seaweed, 192.

R

radiation, rule for determining, 359.
radiators, cast iron (tables), 364–368.
  size of (table), 359.
  hot water, 368.
  painting, 368.
  plate warming, 368.
  ventilating, 368.
  indirect, 369.
  pressed-steel, 369.
  window, 369.
  valves, 370.
range boilers, 292.
  copper, 292.
  galvanized, 292.
  size of, 292.
  vertical, 293.
  horizontal, 293.
  connecting of, 293.
reception room, 108.
refrigerating systems, house, 420.
refrigerator, 115.
  window, 460.
refrigerators, house, 421.
registers, hot air, 354.
remodeling, 465.
  cost of, 467.
  plans for, 468.
  style, 470.
  heating, 470.
  plumbing, 471.
  farm houses, 474.

remodeling, foundations, 475.
  painting, 477.
  cement exterior, 477.
renting table, 6.
roofing, tin, process of manufacture 276.
  copper, 278.
  composition, 279.
  gravel, 279.
  tile, 280.
    color of, 280.
    nails for, 280.
    ridge rolls for, 281.
  Spanish tile, 280.
  shingle tile, 280.
roofs, 273.
  shingled, boarding for, 274.
  slate, boarding for, 275.
  tin, 276.
    flat seam, 277.
    boarding for, 278.
    cleaning of, 278
    painting of, 278.
    standing seam, 278.
rubber tile, 264.
rubbish burners, wire, 458.
rugs, 101.

S

safes, silver, 461.
  wall, 462.
sash, 269.
sash fasteners, burglar-proof ventilating, 453.
sash fitting, 270.
savings table, 7.
screens, window, 462.
seats, window, 105.
septic sewage systems, 344.
  drain tile for, 344.
  soil for, 345.
  for houses, 346.
  flush tanks for, 346.
  syphons for, 346
  cost of, 347.
  diverting valves for, 349.
septic tanks, 348.
  concrete, 347.
  steel, 348.
serving room, 118.

INDEX

sewage, pipes for, 286.
sewage systems, septic, 344.
sheathing, 199.
shellac, 397.
shingles, 201
  hand made, 202.
  required number of (table), 273.
  nails for, 274.
  hemlock, 274.
  red cedar, 274.
  white cedar, 274.
  white pine, 274.
  cypress, 274.
  laying, 274.
  asbestos, 276.
shiplap, 198.
shower baths, 319.
  supply pipes for, 319.
  tub, 319.
  built-in, 320.
  sizes of, 320
  receptors for, 320.
  stalls for, 320.
  tile, 320.
  marble, 320.
  slate, 320.
  glass, 320.
  construction of, 320.
  floor slabs for, 320.
  piping for, 321.
  sprays, 321.
  portable, 321.
  curtains for, 322.
sideboard, 105.
siding, 197.
sink and wash tub combinations, 313.
sink backs, 310.
sinks, kitchen, 310.
  corner, 311.
  niche, 311.
  revolving stools for, 311.
  iron, 311.
  pantry, 312.
    tandem, 119.
    metal, 312.
    copper, 312.
    German silver, 312.
    drip boards, 312.
    size of, 312.
    square, 312.
    oval, 312.

sinks, pantry, double, 313.
    recessed overflow for, 313.
    stand pipe for, 313.
  slop, 313.
  cooks', 313.
  vegetable, 313.
sink strainers, 340.
slate, 274.
  blue or black, 274.
  green, 274.
  brown, 274.
  hips, 275.
  ridges, 275.
  required number of (table), 275.
  machine drilled, 275.
  hand punched, 275.
  nails for, 275.
sleeping porch, 112.
  beds for, 113.
sleeping porch doors, 113.
sleeping porch windows, 113.
soft water systems, 407.
soft woods, 261.
soil, 164.
  rock, 165.
  clay, 20, 165.
  gravel, 165.
  sand, 20, 165.
  quicksand, 165.
soil pipe riser, 295.
specifications, 131.
  methods, 132.
  general conditions, 136.
  requirements, 137.
  work and material, 138.
  stored material, 138.
  carting, 138.
  obstructions, cutting and repairs, 139.
  care of building, 139.
  warming building, 139.
  insurance, 139.
  drawings, 140.
  interpretation of, 141.
  property, 142,
  award of contract, 142.
spouts, 281.
stain, shingle, 394.
  amount required (table), 395.
  interior, 396.
stairs, 53–107.
Standard Form of Agreement, 150.

steam heating, 361.
steel framework for houses, 256.
steps, entrance, 48.
   cement, 49.
   brick, 49.
stone, tests for, 232.
   finish for, 233.
   rubble, 233.
   field, 233.
   bowlders, 233.
   coursed rubble, 233.
   ashlar, 234.
   clamps for, 234
stone copings, 234.
stone cornices, 234.
stone houses, 231.
stone inspecting, 235.
stone moldings, 234.
stone patching, 235
stone pointing, 234.
stone quoins, 234.
stone sills, 234.
stonework, good, 174.
   poor, 174
storage tanks, attic, 407.
strips, weather, 462.
stucco, 385.
studding, 189.
style, 27
   old Colonial, 28.
   modern Colonial, 30.
   old English, 32.
   Elizabethan, 32.
   modern English, 33.
   American-English, 34.
   Dutch, 36.
   American-Spanish, 36.
   Mission, 36.
   German, 38.
   French, 39.
   L'art Nouveau, 40.
   American-Japanese, 41.
   Middle Western, 42.
suburban houses, 493.
sun room, 113.
supply and waste connections, 339.

T

Table, renting, 6.
   savings, 7.

tanks, compression, 402.
   attic, storage, 407.
telephone systems, house, 422.
terraces, 112.
tests, plumbing, 300.
   water, 300.
   peppermint, 300.
   smoke, 301.
thermostats, 371.
tile, agricultural, 170.
   cement, 241.
   terra cotta, hollow, 241.
     manufacture of, 249.
   deep-scored, 242.
   hollow, size of, 242.
   for inside partitions, 242.
   safe loads for (table), 243.
   interlocking, 243.
   walls, with vertical struts, 243
     method of laying, 249.
     sills for, 254.
   floors, 249.
   hollow, insulation, 250.
   vitrified, hollow, 251.
   red, 252.
   yellow, 252.
   hollow, backing, 254.
   special blocks, 254.
   jamb blocks, 254.
   flooring and trim for, 254.
   partitions, pipes in, 255.
     quarry, 49.
   hollow, cost of (table), 256.
   mantels, 264.
   bathroom, 264.
   Spanish, roofing, 280.
   shingle, 280.
   ridge rolls, 280.
   hips, 280.
   red, 280.
   green, 280.
tile floors, 114.
tile walls, 114.
timber, history of, 179.
   framing, 192.
   white pine, 192.
   spruce, 192.
   Norway spruce, 192.
   hemlock, 193.
   white cedar, 193.
   red cedar, 193.

timber, cypress, 193.
  redwood, 193.
  tamarack, 193.
  Southern pine, 194.
  North Carolina pine, 194.
  Georgia pine, 194
tin, valleys, 278.
  gutters, 278
  sizes of, 278.
tool room, 128.
transom lift, concealed, 453.
traps, 333.
  running, 299.
  S, 333.
  P, 334.
  bottle, 334.
  grease, 334.
  syphon, 334.
  non-syphon, 335.
  clean-outs for, 335.
  for laundry tubs, 335.
  refrigerator, 336.
trees, value of, 55.
trellises, 50–62.
trim, 134.
trunk rack, 128.
tumblers, lever, 440.

U

underflooring, 231–261.
Uniform Contract, 150.
union L, 370.

V

vacuum cleaners, 41.
vacuum heating, 363.
valves, shut-off, 288
  back water, 303.
  combination, for hot water heating, 370
  air, 370.
varnish, 397.
ventilation, pipes for, 286.
ventilators, smoke, 110.
  window, 461.
  wall, 461
vents, gas range, 281.
verandas, 48, 111, 102.
vermin stop, 266.

W

wainscoting, 65.
walks, brick, 49.
wall plate, 231
wall plugs, metal, 249.
walls, area, 168.
wall ties, metal, 224.
wardrobes, 124.
wash bowls, 314.
waste connections, 339.
wastes, for pantry sinks, 340.
  standing, 340.
  lavatory, 340
water-closets, 323.
  wash out, 323.
  wash down, 323.
  syphon jet, 324.
  frost-proof, 324.
  hopper, 324.
  enamelled iron, 324.
  earthenware, 324.
  tanks, 325.
    high, 325.
    low, 325.
    birch, 325.
    solid mahogany, 325.
    oak, 325.
    enamelled iron, 325.
    vitreous ware, 325.
  water seal for, 326.
  connecting of, 326.
  metal flange for, 326.
  putty joints for, 326.
  flush pipes for, 327.
  flushometers for, 327.
  seats for, 327.
  shut-off valves for, 328.
  ventilation of, 329
water heaters, coal, 291.
  magazine feed, 292
waterproofing, brick walls, 218
water supply, pipes for, 286.
water supply systems, 286.
water table, 59.
wells, dry, 170.
white lead, 390.
windmills, 402.
window frames, 260.
  for masonry, 261.
windows, 51–269.

windows, bay, 53–101.
  corner, 55.
  double hung, 55.
  casement, 56.
  casings, 56.
  cellar, 169.
window seats, 105.
wood, inside finish, 261.
  outside finish, 261.

wood, hard, 261.
  soft, 261.
working drawings, 72–82
workmanship, 134.
workshop, 128.

Z

zinc, white, 390.